KT-394-472

Contents

1	From Kenmare to the Evacuation of Paris, 1908–40	7
2	From Vichy to Berlin, 1940–43	18
3	'Die billige Gesandtschaft': The Cheap Legation, Berlin, 1943–45	59
4	Lisbon, 1945–46	94
5	Interlude Counsellor, 1946–50	112
6	Paris, 1950–54	129
7	Vatican, 1954–56	188
8	London, 1956–58	218
Endnotes		274
Bibliography		322
Index		337

CHAPTER 1

From Kenmare to the Evacuation of Paris, 1908–40

CORNELIUS CREMIN WAS BORN ON 6 December 1908 above the family drapery shop in Kenmare, Co. Kerry. His father, Daniel J. Cremin, was a draper and farmer from Kilgarvan, Co. Kerry and his mother, Ellen Dowling, was a milliner from Bally-glass, Co. Mayo.[1] There were four children, James, the eldest, Con, Francis (Frank) and a sister, Cissy. By the standards of the time the family were relatively comfortable and were only the second family in Kenmare to own an automobile. After the foundation of the state in 1922, the Cremin family would have been known as Cumann na nGaedheal supporters.[2] Nothing is known about the party political leanings, if any, of Con Cremin.[3]

Cremin went to secondary school in St Brendan's College in Killarney and was head prefect in his final year. One of his closest friends was Donald Herlihy, who became the rector of the Irish College in Rome and later, bishop of Ferns; they maintained this friendship throughout their lives.[4] As a boy Cremin was a keen boatman and oarsman. Unusually for the time he played cricket at the local cricket club in Kenmare, which would have prevented him playing any Gaelic games.[5]

The Cremin family were very gifted academically. Both of Con's brothers went to Maynooth to study for the priesthood: the elder, James, subsequently made a different career choice and joined the British Revenue Service; the youngest brother, Frank studied can-on law after ordination and was called to the bar. He spent his life on the staff of the Pontifical University, St Patrick's College, Maynooth. Frank was very different in temperament from his diplomat brother but they had a good relationship and Frank remained a very valuable contact throughout Con's career.[6]

Con Cremin, unlike his two brothers, did not go to Maynooth. He entered University College Cork (UCC) in 1926 where he studied classics and commerce, graduating with a first-class degree in both subjects. In 1929–30 he was awarded the post-graduate college and Honan scholarships and graduated in 1930 with a second first-class degree, this time in economics and accountancy.[7]

The dean of Commerce, Professor John Busteed, urged Cremin to apply for work to the newly formed Electricity Supply Board.[8] Cremin followed his advice, applied and was successful. However, he abandoned the post after a month and instead returned to UCC where he applied for the prestigious travelling studentship in Classics. In order to qualify, he had to write an MA thesis and so he chose as his topic 'Phases of Corcyraean (Corfu) History'. He completed the work in the summer of 1931, received a first-class honours master's degree and won the travelling studentship.[9] He held it for three years. Professor William Holt Porter suggested 'he [did] not do terribly much' during his three years although we do know that he studied in the British School in Athens, excavated at Ithaca, Perachora and Astakos in Greece and at Cush in Co. Limerick, studied German in Munich and received a diploma from Oxford.[10]

During his time abroad, Cremin decided to apply for the position of third secretary in the department of external affairs. The first competition for the post had been held in 1929 and this second entry examination was held at the end of 1934. He passed the written examination in Irish and then went on to interview:[11]

> my impression was that I succeeded in satisfying them. The interview as such was rather general but it involved, I would say, a fair knowledge of current affairs … At that time the successful candidates entered the department under the name of cadets.[12]

Cremin was accepted into the department and began work in 1935; other future diplomats of note who joined at this time were William Warnock and Denis Devlin.[13] Cremin's secretary was Joseph Walshe who, as a former seminarian, was said to run the department as if it was a Jesuit noviciate.[14]

A year later he married Patricia O'Mahony from Killarney, whom he had met at Irish college on Cape Clear in April 1935.[15]

When Cremin joined the department it was relatively small, consisting of about fifteen to twenty people and it was located in the top floor of the department of agriculture in Government Buildings, Merrion Square; it did not acquire Iveagh House until 1940.[16]

According to Dermot Keogh, 'Cremin [became] noted for his calmness and his prodigious appetite for work'. He had 'a memory like a vice'; no detail escaped his attention. He soon gained the respect of his peers and rose rapidly through the ranks of the service'.[17] Early in his career he came into close contact with Éamon de Valera, the Taoiseach and minister for external affairs. De Valera asked Cremin to give him lessons in Ancient Greek and so Cremin would go to de Valera's house a couple of nights a week to teach him.[18] This contact between a relative newcomer to the department and the Taoiseach allowed de Valera to find the measure of the young diplomat. This proved vital later on.

In the fraught international atmosphere of 1936–37, with the Spanish Civil War raging, the Italians invading Abyssinia, the remilitarisation of the Rhineland, German rearmament, and the entire Versailles settlement unravelling, Cremin assisted F.H. Boland who was in charge of the League of Nations' work. This position gave him an early understanding of the workings of multilateral diplomacy.[19] It was also the start of an enduring professional friendship between Boland and Cremin, which lasted throughout their lives.[20]

First Posting Abroad, Paris 1937–40

Paris was Cremin's first posting abroad and it was a challenging one which demonstrated the confidence de Valera and Walshe had in him.

Paris was the epicentre of international politics: 'Ireland's most important listening post in continental Europe'.[21] The political situation in Europe in the late 1930s was governed by the onset of war and the ideological conflict between fascism, communism and democracy. France itself was being governed by the Léon Blum-led Popular Front government, a coalition of socialists and radicals, and was undergoing a time of political instability and financial crisis.[22] In fact, the 'political scene was so divided that some observers thought it close to civil war, and its own elaborate security system in Europe had been almost totally destroyed in a series of shattering blows'.[23]

Cremin was twenty-eight when he set off, as first secretary, to the Irish legation.[24] His wife, Patricia, and their infant daughter, Ann, followed him later.[25]

Cremin and O'Brien

Art O'Brien was Cremin's immediate superior. He had served the First Dáil in London from 8 October 1919 to 19 April 1922 and was one of the first generation of 'revolutionary diplomats'. During the Civil War, while serving in London with the diplomatic service, O'Brien had sided with the anti-treatyites. He was dismissed by the Cumann na nGaedheal government. When Fianna Fáil came to power in 1932, O'Brien was reinstated after it was judged that he had been dismissed for 'political reasons'.[26]

Keogh states that O'Brien's 'style of diplomatic reporting left something to be desired'.[27] During the 1936 Rhineland crisis, when Hitler occupied the demilitarised zone, O'Brien failed to send a report on the crisis for two weeks and only did so having been instructed by Walshe. During the French general election in May 1936 which saw the Popular Front elected 'the relative inexperience of his superior [O'Brien] resulted in Belton [Cremin's predecessor] having to report on the complexities of French political life'.[28] Belton predicted that the primary result of the elections would be a continuation of the government of the prime minister, Albert Sarraut, with some added pressure from the extreme left. Belton was a relatively junior diplomat who had entered the department in 1929. He analysed the developing and highly complica political situation consistently but unfortunately he was quite incorrect in his predictions.[29]

Cremin was, like Belton, among the first of a generation of professional career diplomats who had been recruited through a public competition. He was too young to have played any part in Ireland's revolutionary struggles.[30] When he first arrived in Paris, he was obliged, owing to O'Brien's inexperience, to assume a burden that was much heavier than should have been taken on by a person of his limited diplomatic experience. Together with the normal duties of a first secretary – such as the processing of visa applications, issuing of passports and compilation of reports to be vetted by the minister – Cremin was forced to assume more senior diplomatic duties, including being presented to the British king and queen who came to Paris in 1937, after O'Brien refused.[31]

During the Spanish Civil War O'Brien's personal support for Franco's forces ran 'dangerously close to flouting the official government policy of non-intervention'.[32] An example of this was to be found in the 1938 annual report for the Paris legation. It stated that the legation had extended hospitality to Duquesa de Tetuan (Señorita Blanca O'Donnell), who had supported O'Duffy's Irish Brigade, and a dinner was given in honour of the Infanta Eulalia of Spain.[33] Actions of that kind could have compromised the country's non-interventionist stance.[34]

O'Brien's dislike of the Popular Front government of Léon Blum resulted, in October 1937, in his rejection of the contents of a memorandum prepared by Cremin on the relationship between the French franc and the pound sterling over the following twelve months.[35] O'Brien believed political factors were more important than economic ones and asked that Cremin redraft the memorandum to take this point into account. In the redraft, the Confédération Générale du Travail (CGT) and the Popular Front were together blamed for the instability between the franc and sterling. Divided into two sections – the first part written by O'Brien and the second by Cremin – it is illustrative of the difference in style and formation of the two men. O'Brien stated that:

Any attempt to forecast the probable value of the franc in terms of sterling over the coming year is liable to error in an extreme owing to the fact that the internal political situation overshadows all other considerations and that it is difficult to foretell what developments may take place.[36]

His considered opinion was formed mainly through his contacts with the French Catholic Right.[37] Cremin's section was introduced with the following caveat:

What is said, therefore, in the following paragraphs must be read in light of the foregoing and general statement in realisation that the present political instability leaves no room for a large number of developments any one of which might upset all calculations.[38]

What followed was a very well researched and cogent piece of diplomatic reporting. Cremin, who had received a first in economics, accounting and commerce at UCC, argued that whatever government might take over, they were not going to follow an inflationary line. Cremin stated the net balance-of-payment deficit would be eleven thousand million, and he continued:

It is not impossible that a value for the franc at a point near 150 francs to the pound is that which will be favoured. Some reasons have already been advanced for the contention that the level is a good one – in particular the fact that such a level will tend to redress the balance of trade and that a further fall would be injurious and resisted because of the fact that it would, through imports, increase the level of prices.

Cremin concluded that the franc would be kept at a stable level of 150 francs to the pound sterling in order to ensure British and US financial support.[39]

The report reveals the contrast in diplomatic styles between a 'revolutionary diplomat' and a 'career diplomat' from a new, professional service. The report also revealed the high state of development of Cremin's economic thinking. He had a good analytical mind and was capable of writing in a lucid style, supporting all the time his cogent line of argument with adequate research and documentation.[40] The background to the writing of this report also revealed that Cremin was prepared to fight and argue profession-ally for the inclusion of his ideas in submissions to headquarters. He did not allow himself to be intimidated by his superior into handing in a piece that was unbalanced. O'Brien simply lacked the formation and experience of a career diplomat, similar to the US minister, David Gray, who served in Dublin during the war.[41]

O'Brien was replaced in 1938 and on 7 October presented his letters of recall.[42] Seán Murphy ultimately replaced him.[43] In the meantime Cremin was chargé d'affaires of the legation and in November 1938 attended a reception where he was introduced to Hitler's pre-eminent diplomat foreign minister, Joachim von Rib-bentrop.[44]

Cremin, Murphy and the Build-up to War

Seán Murphy arrived in December 1938.[45] His was 'one of the most important and fortuitous appointments of the period'.[46] He, too, was a member of the first wave of Irish diplomats recruited during the revolutionary period but he had a quite distinctive ap-proach and stood in marked contrast to O'Brien.

The close working relationship between Murphy and Cremin was very different to Cremin's uneasy professional relationship with O'Brien. It may not be a coincidence that Cremin, in his memoirs, does not mention O'Brien or his first few years in the legation in Paris. In his introduction to the unpublished work, he merely stated he was 'present for much of the Paris Exhibition'.[47] His first chapter entitled 'France: Paris and Vichy, 1937–1943' be-gins with the German invasion of France in May 1940.[48]

Even though Cremin feared war was going to break out in 1938, he did not allow his family life to be curtailed. His wife and infant daughter had been with him from the beginning of his diplomatic tour. The Cremin home in Paris received many visi-tors during those pre-war years. In July 1938, a twelve-year-old Dublin boy called Garret FitzGerald, the son of the former minister for external affairs, Desmond FitzGerald, visited him in Paris. FitzGerald, a future leader of Fine Gael and Taoiseach, remembered that Cremin and his family brought him, in July 1938, to the ménagerie to pat elephants.[49] Thirty-six years later, Dr FitzGerald was Cremin's minister and they worked together at the United Nations in 1973 prior to Cremin's retirement.[50]

In the background of Garret FitzGerald's visit, the Sudetenland crisis was building up. The annual report of the legation for 1938 stated that 'Irish nationals were coming to France on holiday in relatively greater numbers exactly during the time when the probability of war seemed greatest'.[51] One of these visitors included Cremin's sister who was on honeymoon. She recalled that 'Con was in an awful state as he thought that war was going to break out and he told us that he could get us into France but he did not know if he could get us out again'.[52]

The Munich agreement ensured the occupation of the Sudetenland in October 1938. The annexation of what remained of the Czech state in March 1939 led to the extension of guarantees to Poland by France and Britain.

By contrast to the storm that was brewing in western Europe, as far as the Irish legation was concerned the storm on the Iberian peninsula was abating and, in September 1938, the number of Irish callers coming from the Spanish Civil War 'was negligible'.[53]

Owing to the probability of war, de Valera wisely replaced O'Brien in Paris and Bewley in Berlin.[54] As a result, Ireland was very fortunate in the diplomats she had in France during the Second World War:

> Neither Murphy nor Cremin was particularly enthusiastic about the French Right. The Irish legation in Paris was also fortunate to have Count Gerald O'Kelly on its staff. Clearly, Murphy, O'Kelly and Cremin were very different personalities, but together they formed a strong diplomatic team.[55]

After the occupation of the rump Czech state in March 1939, Hitler succeeded in isolating Poland diplomatically in central Europe and then secured his eastern front through the Nazi–Soviet non-aggression pact. Unfortunately for Hitler, Britain and France stood by Poland and in 1939 a general European war – which Hitler did not want to fight – began.[56]

September 1939 to the Evacuation of Paris

Paris was Ireland's main listening post on the continent and the legation's reports for 1938–39 'were of the highest standard. Murphy's reporting on the situation in eastern Europe in March 1939 was accurate and kept the department informed about the latest political developments'.[57] On 24 August 1939, the legation accurately warned Dublin that the outbreak of war was likely within the week.[58]

The day after Hitler's invasion of Poland (1 September 1939), de Valera declared neutrality.[59] He had been seen to opt for neutrality as far back as April 1939.[60] The documents that contained the decision to remain neutral were burned on the lawn of Iveagh House during the invasion scare of the summer of 1940 so cannot now be studied.[61] However, T. Ryle Dwyer argues that the antecedents of neutrality go back to the 1920s.[62] Dwyer's assumption is supported by Cremin who was in the department from the 1930s and stated in retirement that: 'Chanak was a precedent that had not been forgotten inside the Irish department of external affairs.'[63] Chanak was the incident where the commonwealth countries refused to send their troops into a conflict without the prior approval of their parliaments. This precedent meant that the dáil could decide whether or not to go to war alongside Britain. It is arguable that Ireland did not have any other choice but to be neutral in that while she was forewarned of the war, she was certainly not forearmed, with a standing army of only 16,000 men and no navy.[64] Walshe, the secretary of the department of external affairs, favoured from the outset a very strict neutrality; de Valera, however, was a foreign policy realist and relied on a form of 'constructive ambiguity' in his form of neutrality, for both internal and external policy reasons.[65] De Valera believed that a policy of neutrality would divide the country least, but at the same time he realised that Britain could not accept a strict interpretation of Irish neutrality.[66]

The historian, T. Desmond Williams, illustrated the duality of de Valera's thinking: 'It was known that de Valera personally favoured the survival of democracy in Europe. It was equally known that he distrusted British and US policies, where neutral Irish interests might be concerned'.[67] This nuanced approach by de Valera was lost on the vast majority of the Irish population. As de Valera also had an innate distrust of his dáil colleagues he would have agreed with A.J.P. Taylor's suggestion that:

> the opinions of the man in the street on foreign affairs (so far as he has any) are by their nature unascertainable; what usually passes for public opinion is the opinion of a small, politically conscious class – leader-writers … members of parliament and the less instructed members of the cabinet.[68]

During the Emergency, all the 'politically conscious class' groups were sidelined and censorship was enacted not only to ensure the appearance of *de jure* neutrality, but also to stifle criticism of Ireland's neutrality policy. De Valera consequently excluded the majority of his cabinet from discussions on foreign policy and Irish neutrality and carried the burden himself. Therefore the role of the professional diplomats in the field reached pre-eminence as their reports were able to influence foreign policy more effectively than the majority of cabinet members.[69]

Throughout April and May 1940 the small European neutrals fell to the Nazis. Denmark and Norway fell in April. Only after Holland, Luxembourg and Belgium fell in May, did de Valera issue a protest to Germany.[70] In June the blitzkrieg brought its devastation on France and precipitated the collapse of the French armies.[71] Cremin recorded in his memoirs:

> The main hint I had that matters might turn out like this (but not of course on such a scale or with such rapidity) was from a conversation at a reception during the spring, with an American military attaché.

He remarked that, while the French army was naturally very good, all French strategy was based solely on the Maginot line mentality.[72]

In May 1940, Cremin succeeded in getting his family on a plane to London through the good offices of a Dubliner in the British embassy, Harry Bradshaw Mack.[73] Murphy and Count Gerald O'Kelly also evacuated their families and the three men opted to live together in the legation.[74] This ensured that the small legation was able to react quickly to events. Owing to the threat of bombing in Paris, the legation was assigned a *point de repli,* or emergency accommodation, in the neighbourhood of Tours in case they had to evacuate. Cremin noted that Seán Murphy 'being of a practical disposition, with a healthy dose of scepticism ... decided we should investigate it'. As it transpired, this was a wise decision, as the building had been rendered uninhabitable by its owner who had demolished all internal walls.[75] The legation later 'hired for the opening months of the war a small villa at a place called Septeil which is about fifty kilometres from Paris, between Mantes and Dreux'.[76] This *point de repli* was never used owing to the rapid collapse of the allied armies and the decision that the entire Irish legation should be evacuated from Paris and its environs.

Under international law any diplomats accredited to France who remained in the occupied territories would not be recognised as accredited diplomats by the French foreign office.[77] The papal nuncio, Valerio Valeri, as doyen of the diplomatic corps, persuaded his fellow diplomats not to contemplate leaving for French north Africa and instead he accompanied the head of the French government, Marshal Pétain, to Vichy.[78] On 10 June 1940, Seán Murphy consulted the US ambassador, Bill Bullitt, on whether or not to evacuate Paris. Cremin recalled that Bullitt believed that Seán Murphy was 'probably the only head of mission not already left'.[79] This reluctance to leave Paris showed the professionalism of the Irish mission; they did not allow the danger of their situation to take precedence over their mission.

CHAPTER 2

From Vichy to Berlin,

1940–43

AFTER THE 10 JUNE 1940 MEETING between Seán Murphy and the US ambassador, Bill Bullitt, 'a good friend of Ireland', it was decided that the Irish legation should evacuate from Paris and go to St Jean de Luz where, through his wife's relations, Count O'Kelly had procured rooms for them in the village of Ascain.[1] Fr Travers, rector of the Irish College in Paris, wrote a vivid record of this evacuation in his memoirs. He recalled:

> I was in constant touch with the Irish legation. The staff, Messrs Cremin and O'Byrne, as well as the minister, Mr Murphy, were very kind to me all through … After the first week in June it was obvious that nothing could halt the Germans. I saw the Irish minister on the 8th or 9th of June and he told me that the legation were preparing to leave Paris as the French government were leaving. He advised me to leave and go back to Ireland, and offered to take me with him in his car. Meantime he gave me an official notice, which I affixed to the door of the Irish College, that the building was Irish property and therefore not to be molested. Then I gave charge of the college to a French servant …
>
> On the evening of the 10th of June he told me to be ready the next morning. I don't think I slept that night. The AA guns were going off and on all through the night.[2]

On 10 June, Cremin and Murphy had 'the doubtful privilege of "closing" two well known restaurants. We were present for the last lunch at Fouquets (well known to James Joyce) and for dinner at the Berkeley'.[3] The well-fed Irish legation departed on the morning of 11 June; the French government and military had left the previous evening.[4] Fr Travers recalled:

> At eight o'clock Mr Cremin called for me in his car. The other members of the legation were travelling in the minister's car. We had also a share of office papers, etc. It was a beautiful sunny morning, but for a thick fog, which was inexplicable.[5]

Cremin for a moment 'thought the Germans might have revived the magic of the Tuatha dé Danan but the explanation was of course more prosaic. Oil reservoirs had been blown up … near Rouen',[6] creating 'a kind of Dante's Inferno background for the pitiful refugees'.[7] Fr Travers continued:

> We joined the stream of refugees and what a sight it was! Bumper to bumper cars and lorries and cattle and wagons of all kinds, transporting all that people could hurriedly get together … As far as the eye could see, before and behind, the stream wound its way slowly, very slowly. Indeed, it was getting on to four o'clock before we reached Chartres. At that point the minister sought permission to take the military road as a diplomat. Permission was given, and from then on our going was much faster. Occasionally we came upon disorganised groups of French soldiers building road blocks, but everything seemed to be in great disorder.[8]

The party encountered danger at this point when:

> Nearing Tours, our objective for the night, we ran into a military party near the aerodrome. They were holding up all the cars for examination. One of the soldiers was prepared to fire on the minister's car, which had not seen the sign to halt, when our second car came up. We showed our papers and were allowed to proceed. It was nine o'clock or so when we arrived in Tours.[9]

The legation party left Fr Travers in Tours where he hoped to get a ship to Britain from St Malo. As it happened, he missed the ship and returned to the Irish College in Paris where he acted as a caretaker for the duration of the war. He even successfully grew vegetables in the Irish College's garden which he distributed to his Parisian neighbours.[10]

Bordeaux to Vichy: Itinerant Diplomats

The legation then went on to Bordeaux, although they had to leave after a couple of nights. While there, on 13 June 1940, the last meeting of the allied supreme council was held in Tours, between the French and British prime ministers.[11] By the evening of 13 June, Marshal Pétain, the hero of Verdun and head of the French state, signalled publicly his intention to request an armistice. The commander-in-chief of the French navy, Admiral Darlan, also wished for an armistice.[12] On 14 June 1940, the Germans entered Paris, which the French had declared an open city to spare it bombardment. Two days later, Churchill proposed the Anglo-French Union which would have enabled France to carry on the war. These proposals were rejected by the peace faction and the premier, Reynaud, resigned in protest.[13]

Meanwhile the Irish legation continued their journey to St Jean de Luz. By 17 June 1940 the legation was installed there awaiting developments.[14] It was here that they heard Pétain state on 18 June: 'I tell you today that it is necessary to stop the fighting.'[15] This announcement brought the collapse of official French resistance. It is unknown if the Irish legation heard de Gaulle's rallying call the same day to the French people to continue resistance. There in St Jean de Luz the legation waited for the outcome of the armistice talks.[16] On 22 June 1940, the armistice was signed and on 29 June the French government abandoned their temporary capital of Bordeaux for Vichy in the Massif Central.[17]

At a meeting of the heads of missions in the Carlton Hotel in Biarritz at the end of June, a suggestion was put forward that the corps should leave for Spain *en masse*. Cremin wrote of Seán Murphy: 'This idea did not commend itself to the Irish minister who, as already stated, took a very calm, cool view of the situation'.[18] This characterised all of Murphy's subsequent reporting from Vichy.

On 4 July, the Irish delegation arrived in the new French capital, Vichy, and after much difficulty found accommodation for the night at the Hotel du Parc. It was the day after 'Operation Catapult' where a large part of the French fleet was destroyed at Mers-el-Kébir/Oran by a British squadron to prevent it falling into German hands.[19] Murphy stated it was possible the 'Oran incident may have far reaching effects in regard to French co-operation with Germany', and quoted the French foreign minister who stated 'It is bound to have [a] profound orientation on foreign policy.'[20] Charles-Roux, secretary general of the foreign office, stated Mers-el-Kébir was a 'dastardly act of aggression' as the French fleet was due to be disarmed by an 'armistice commission'. Charles-Roux stated that the French government wanted the Irish government to know their point of view:

> I [Murphy] made no comment upon this statement. I merely asked what he thought to be the reason for British action. He said he was sure Churchill and the admiralty were chiefly responsible. The latter were enraged at not getting the French fleet which would have been of great assistance to them. He commented very unfavourably on the British army's part in the war and said that even the navy had not done as well as the French navy.

The Irish legation believed the French were belittling British participation in the war 'with a view to ingratiating themselves with the Germans though apparently with little success'.[21] They believed the French defeat 'was a direct product of the prevailing state of French public life and the French philosophical conception of what made life worth while'.[22] Alex St L. Leger, head of the French foreign service, 'believed it had arisen principally from a progressive deterioration in French public life that had become evident some years before'.[23]

Owing to the chaotic conditions which reigned, the legation were asked to temporarily leave Vichy and to travel instead to Bourboule, a fashionable watering place near Vichy.[24] On 9 July 1940, the Irish legation returned to Vichy, the day before the final meet-

ing of the national assembly of the third republic.[25] At this meeting the third republic was abolished; 'it had committed suicide'.[26]
Marshal Pétain was elected head of state in what became known
as the 'revolution of the failures'.[27] The political reports were the
most important function of the legation at this time but looking
after the interests of Irish citizens also took a significant amount
of their energies.

The Irish Colony

Consular support was, as it is now, an important part of the diplomat's work. In 1938, Cremin wrote that some members of the
Irish colony in Paris had their financial difficulties accentuated by
banking strikes and the depressed economic situation, although Fr
O'Grady of St Joseph's Church on Avenue Foch was doing a lot to
alleviate the distress.[28] However, the sudden collapse of the allied
armies in June 1940 caught the entire world by surprise, including
the Irish legation.

One of the several problems the legation had to contend with was
the fact that France was divided into two zones, occupied and unoccupied France. Initially, Cremin wrote during July, 'passage across
the demarcation line was relatively normal and was not thought to
require any special arrangements'.[29] However, the continuation of
two zones caused considerable unemployment and a breakdown in
communication. This also caused great discontent in the occupied
territories as the population felt itself abandoned by its government.[30] In his memoirs, Cremin wrote the following about his time
in Vichy:

> The political aspect of the work was relatively secondary inasmuch
> as Vichy was in the circumstances a kind of international backwater,
> apart of course, from north Africa and the other overseas territories.
> By contrast more mundane but very important questions took on an
> unusually big and quite demanding role: the care generally of Irish
> citizens, including registrations for citizenship under the 1935 Na-
> tionality Act, the issue and renewal of passports and the transmission
> of monthly allowances.[31]

The difficulties of the legation were accentuated by the fact that many of the Irish were travelling on British passports and so were interned. Further problems were caused by the French police's description of Irish passport holders as *sujets britanniques* in their register of aliens.[32]

The work that the legation did during the war increased their standing in the public eye:

> helping Irish citizens stranded in belligerent states altered the public's view of the diplomat, particularly since their services were often rendered under conditions of hardship and physical danger which the Irish public did not share. The diplomat was now seen as a hard working public servant rather than as a pawn in the party struggle. Whereas before the war, references in foreign affairs debates in the dáil to the staff of the department were more likely to be critical than not, during and after the war, it was rare to hear a debate on the department of external affairs in which the dedication of its staff did not receive praise from all sides of the House.[33]

One semi-retired Irish diplomat, Count O'Kelly, was fully reinstated in Paris in 1940.[34] O'Kelly had served in Paris from 1920 and between 1929 and 1935 had been envoy extraordinary and minister plenipotentiary. Cremin described him as being extremely resourceful.[35] In 1935, de Valera had almost retired O'Kelly, but was persuaded to retain him as a special counsellor to the Paris legation.[36] Now, from 11 June 1940, Count O'Kelly began to deal with consular work in Paris – as events would prove, this would be extremely fortuitous.[37] He only officially took up his duties in Paris on 1 August 1940; these duties were in general those of chargé d'affaires in occupied France. His work consisted broadly of helping Irish citizens in distress and the liberation of internees.[38]

On 3 August 1940, the Irish legation, accompanied by the nuncio, Valerio Valeri, attempted to cross into occupied France and were refused; the demarcation line was closed to all without special permission.[39] Cremin recalled that between 17 and 22 August himself and Murphy finally managed to travel to Paris.[40] Murphy reported that they went out to lunch with four Irish priests, O'Grady, Travers, O'Farrell and Griffin. After lunch, the diplomats returned to the Irish College just in time to prevent the attempted requisitioning of the college by the Germans. Murphy explained to the German officer that 'it was the property of the Irish bishops and used by them to lodge ecclesiastical students at present on holiday'.[41] Fr Travers gave an amusing account of the attempted requisition:

> During Mr Murphy's visit word was brought that a German officer was downstairs and wanted to see me, as he was going to requisition the college. Mr Murphy and Mr Cremin came with me to see the officer, who was accompanied by a few soldiers and a French civilian. The officer knew a little French and we knew no German. The Frenchman was trying to convey to the officer that the college was British property. We strenuously maintained that it was Irish property and that Ireland had remained outside the war. I think the officer got tired of the argument. At any rate he went away with the impression that we were expecting our students back in September. That seemed to satisfy him. Never after did the Germans seek to interfere with the college.[42]

What is interesting about this account is the fact that although Cremin was able to speak German, since his time in Munich during his studentship, he did not speak German to the officer.[43] This could indicate either a strategy or a patent dislike of the occupying force and their ideology; more than likely it was both given Cremin's and Murphy's anti-fascist and francophile tendencies.[44]

Although the Irish College was safe, some Irish citizens were in danger of being interned because they were travelling on British passports. Murphy reported to Walshe that such people were unlikely to be interned but all the same he would take their passports and 'issue [Irish] passports valid for one year, renewable gratis'.[45] He concluded his report by saying that most of the Irish colony would soon be destitute owing to the disruption of the French economy and that, owing to the exhaustion of his stock of passports, he was going to print his own.[46] Walshe replied he was glad they had got to Paris, and that he had many inquires that he wanted them to make the next time they went.[47]

From this time on it proved increasingly more difficult to make visits to the occupied zone. In September, when Iveagh House requested that Warnock, chargé d'affaires in Berlin, should make representations to permit Murphy and Cremin to go to Paris, Warnock replied, 'As things stand German authorities do not consider Cremin as having any locus standing in that area'.[48] The German authorities suggested that they apply to the military authorities.[49] This Murphy did on 15 September 1940.[50] He rejected the suggestion from Iveagh House that Cremin be sent back to Paris permanently, as he thought 'changing Cremin's capacity would appear to be a rouse'. In any case O'Kelly was already in Paris and urgent cases could be dealt with by telephone.[51] The department replied that they were not aware that O'Kelly was in Paris, indicating the chaotic conditions within the department at this time.[52]

In November, permission was refused for their visit to Paris and Walshe asked for the 'details of your case and we shall appeal to Berlin again'.[53] In December 1940, Walshe asked Berlin why permission was refused and why Ireland was being discriminated against.[54] The under-secretary of state assured him that there was not any question of discrimination.[55] In December 1940, Warnock applied to the military authorities and suggested that: 'Cremin could go there [Paris] for the time being in that capacity', indicating that very few knew O'Kelly was already in Paris.[56] Cremin did not go however; de Valera and Walshe realised that sending him would have left Murphy alone in Vichy and in any case, O'Kelly was already there.

On 16 February 1941, O'Kelly reported he had just returned from the internment camp at Besançon where he had spent ten days interviewing two hundred interned Irish persons who claimed to be Irish by birth or parentage. Seventy were definitely Irish and he hoped they would all be released shortly. O'Kelly took it upon himself to re-employ the legation's typist, Mademoiselle Marquietout, at the old salary. Murphy wrote to Dublin that: 'She is very efficient and reliable and knows [the] legation'.[57] It is not surprising that the

Irish legation in Paris was being overwhelmed because O'Kelly was now the sole Irish representative for two-thirds of France.[58] Interestingly, O'Kelly did not move into the Irish legation building in Paris but rather preferred to conduct his work from his own wine business offices.[59]

Permission was again granted on 20 April 1942 for Murphy to visit Paris.[60] On 22 June, he reported on the sad condition of the legation building. He stated that all the carpets and furniture had been sealed and stored in the Grand Salon, and that there was a considerable amount of damage done to the electric wiring owing to a roof leak during the winter of 1940–41.

James Joyce, his Collaborator Paul Léon, and Samuel Beckett

The tragic case of Paul Léon demonstrated the powerlessness of the Irish government on matters relating to the 'Jewish question'. Léon, a St Petersburg-born Jew, had fled Russia and arrived in Paris in 1921. In 1928, he met Joyce and became his unpaid secretary, collaborator and closest friend. Having spent the summer of 1940 away correcting misprints in *Finnegans Wake*, Léon returned in September to Paris where he continued to live at great personal risk. He helped save a section of Joyce's library and archive from the family apartment on the Rue des Vignes; the remainder he bought back at an illegal auction which was held by the landlord. They were then handed over to Count O'Kelly. On 20 August 1941, he told Samuel Beckett he was leaving the following day, but he was 'abducted by the Germans in Paris' and imprisoned at Drancy and Compiègne.[61] Through Léon's wife, Beckett sent him his own bread ration and some cigarettes.

The Society of Swiss Writers in Zurich appealed to the Irish government to intervene on behalf of Léon. Dublin informed Warnock: 'in case there is danger that Léon be shot please intervene with foreign office on his behalf.' Warnock replied that actions like that were 'received very badly':

> In my opinion there is danger that intervention on behalf of L. might
> be regarded as interfering in internal German matters where no Irish

citizen is involved and might even have some effect on our good relations.[62]

On 21 November, Joseph Walshe agreed: 'No action possible at
present.' Léon was shot at a camp in Silesia on 4 April 1942. Although unable to help the father, Walshe asked the Irish legation
in Vichy to assist his son, Alexis Léon's, passage from Monaco to
Spain, thus at least ensuring his survival.[63]

As part of his consular functions, Cremin brought money to
James Joyce's family in Saint Gérand, near Vichy.[64] Joyce rejected
the offer of an Irish passport from Seán Murphy which would enable him to avoid internment on the grounds that 'he should not
accept in wartime something which he did not desire in peacetime'.[65] In mid-January 1941, Joyce departed for Zurich; his friend
Beckett stayed in France.

Cremin first came into contact with Samuel Beckett as a consular case when the latter was stabbed in Paris in 1938.[66] When
Beckett returned to Paris after the occupation, Count O'Kelly gave
him a statement of authentication with which he was able to obtain a ration card.[67] Shortly after the arrest of Léon, in August
1941, Beckett joined the resistance cell, Gloria SMH. When the
cell was betrayed in August 1942, he fled from Paris to Vichy: 'At
first they tried contacting the Irish representative in Vichy who,
according to Beckett, was extremely unsympathetic and unhelpful'.[68] Beckett may have been unfortunate in his timing in that
Cremin was temporarily in Berlin so he would not have been in
a position to help him formally without compromising the position of the Irish legation.[69] Beckett went into hiding in 1942 and
thus was out of contact with the legation throughout the rest of
the war. On Beckett's return to Paris in April 1945 Murphy noted
that 'Beckett's Irish passport was still in order, but Beckett had to
explain over and over again where he had been for the past two
years and why he had been out of touch with the Irish legation'.[70]
Beckett later returned to Ireland where he recuperated before returning to St-Malo with the Irish Red Cross.

Life in Vichy

The members of the Irish legation in Vichy had very little communication with their families in Ireland.[71] In Kenmare, few letters arrived and very little information came from the department.[72] They did at least get some news and information through the counsellor of the Canadian embassy to France, Pierre Dupuy; Ireland and Canada were the only commonwealth countries that did not break diplomatic links with Vichy France. Dupuy undertook several missions to Vichy France from London, where he was based.

> Dupuy ... had been many years in France and was a very good friend of the Irish mission. He came back quite often for a few days to Vichy from London and was always a good source of comment on what people in London were thinking of Vichy and events generally.[73]

Dupuy made three excursions to Vichy France in November and December 1940. He met Pétain, and reported that the marshal was still hoping for a British victory. In February and August 1941 and July 1942 he made more visits.[74] While these visits brought news to the Irish legation, Dupuy's 'reports, which continued to be upbeat and hopeful, were increasingly out of touch with the reality of the situation'.[75]

Even with the visits of Canadian friends, the conditions in Vichy continued to be grim. The first three months saw the legation staying at the Hotel des Lilas which they abandoned in October, owing to the lack of heating. They then moved to the Hotel Gallia which was to provide accommodation for them for the next four years.[76] The winter of 1941 was 'what Frenchmen said was the coldest winter in ninety years' and the diplomats accepted visitors while wearing their overcoats.[77] There was continuous overcrowding in Vichy as it was only a small spa town.

Life for the Irish delegation in Vichy was not exciting and as the diplomats were all quite young, they hung out together as a group.[78] The French historian Azéma stated 'the order of the day was austerity, if not virtue' and distractions were few apart from the cinema, a multitude of galas, playing bridge or telling tall stories; Sundays provided an opportunity to make excursions into the countryside to gather food and take the air.[79] Seán Murphy 'sublimated his hostility [to the Vichy regime] by regular rounds of golf' – Cremin admitted that they 'just played golf all the time'.[80] They also held occasional receptions and their hostility to the German presence was manifested by the fact that they were the only delegation in Vichy not to invite Germans.[81]

The Cremin family were finally reunited in March 1941 when Cremin returned to Dublin for debriefing. He stated: 'By the end of 1940 I had come to the conclusion that we had to reckon with a long war and, therefore, that I should bring back my wife and children'.[82] This he did, returning to Vichy via Lisbon. The Hotel Gallia was not suited for family life however and within two or three weeks they found a villa in Cusset, two miles from Vichy.[83] Cremin commuted to work on a small bike for which he was issued diplomatic licence plates.[84]

The unoccupied zone was not self-sufficient in food and in September 1940 Murphy telegraphed to report that:

> Severe food restrictions have come into force at noon today, received by public with resignation. Severity is attributed to requisitioning on a large scale by German authorities and to fact that free zone is poorest in food.[85]

By January the situation had become more serious.[86] For the Cremin family the food situation improved when they found out that:

> the owners of the villa came from farming stock and we were thus able to get a fair quantity of food from the farm. It was of course rather expensive but in the circumstances very well worthwhile.[87]

An indication of the economic situation of unoccupied France was that one of Cremin's official duties was to sit on a committee with some members of the diplomatic corps to decide which other members of the diplomatic corps would be allowed petrol coupons. Cremin related that:

The group met each working day for an hour over several months, in an alcove off the main lounge of the Hotel du Parc and we listened with great sympathy to an extraordinary variety of reasons as to why a 'client' should have a coupon.[88]

After several months the committee was disbanded when the Romanian legation sent a supply of petrol to the diplomatic corps in Vichy.[89] The Irish legation was presented with 7,000 litres of petrol for use by their vehicles.[90]

As the war progressed, the number of legations in Vichy dwindled because when countries went to war on Nazi Germany, the Nazis demanded the removal of their representatives. By December 1942, only eighteen missions remained.[91] In January 1943, the diplomatic missions of Brazil, Peru, Colombia and Ecuador left Vichy under escort by German troops.[92] In February 1943, the Venezuelan, Uruguayan, Paraguayan, Bolivian, Honduran and Chinese missions left as well.[93] By June 1943, all legations were restricted to within fifty kilometres of Vichy by rail or road unless they had special permission.[94] By this stage Ireland was one of only eight remaining missions accredited to Vichy France. The growing number of delegations abandoning Vichy and recognising the Free French as the legitimate government of France placed the Irish legation in an increasingly anomalous position. One of the reasons the Irish had refused to recognise the Free French had its origins at the beginning of the war with the policy conflict between Murphy and the head of the department of external affairs, Joseph Walshe. Walshe was attached to the idea of Pétain's National Revolution, which called for a return to traditional values of work, family and country. Walshe's attachment to this idea continued until 1944.

Policy Conflict

Dublin in the summer of 1940 was, like all non-fascist European capitals, gripped by the terror of how to respond to a '*Deutschland siegt auf allen Fronten*' (Germany victorious on all fronts).[95] Joseph Walshe was the key policy adviser in the department and his role has been much commented on. Keogh stated Walshe 'had reached a point of near breakdown. The policy option as Walshe saw it, was how Ireland should respond to Britain's inevitable defeat'.[96] Lee is critical of Walshe, and has stated that:

> Walshe would have liked to use the German victories in 1940 to have Hitler deliver the north to Dublin. Purporting to be more afraid of Britain than of Germany, he chose to see the Nazi victories partly from the 'England's danger is Ireland's opportunity' perspective, hoping that Hitler's declaration that he had no intention of destroying the British empire 'did not mean the abandonment of Ireland'. The problem was that if the Germans ever came to be in a position to destroy the empire, or to deliver the north, they would be, by definition, in a position to deal as they wished with Dublin. It took no great imagination to deduce who would use whom.[97]

All the Irish legations, with the exception of the Irish legation in France, were predicting a German victory. De Valera, however, rejected the 'temptation to tack tactically closer to Berlin in anticipation of a German victory'.[98] Dr Garret FitzGerald stated that his father, the former minister for external affairs, Desmond Fitz-Gerald, was friendly with Walshe and that they were both anti-communist. Mrs Mabel FitzGerald believed that it was this anti-communism that blinded Walshe to the terrors of Nazism.[99] Keogh has also commented that 'Walshe saw himself as something more than a civil servant. He had a particular ideology and he sought to work for its advancement in the way that one of his political superiors might pursue a party goal'.[100] The most important ideological influence on Walshe was Catholicism, complemented by radical nationalism.[101] Keogh wrote that Joseph Walshe:

> had no time for the left wing politics of the Third Republic. This bias coloured his attitude when France fell in the Spring of 1940 and Marshal Pétain initiated his 'National Revolution'. Walshe remained quite partial to the politics and vision of Vichy and this had a major bearing on the course of Franco-Irish relations during the Second World War.[102]

The reports from the Irish legation in France did not, however, concur with Walshe's vision. Lee argued that de Valera seemed to have kept a cooler head than external affairs officials during May and June but by mid-June 1940 he too 'may have been momentarily gripped by the "panic"'.[103] July 1940 with its rumours of imminent German invasion placed a great strain on de Valera.[104] Walshe's bias in favour of Vichy resulted in one of the greatest Irish wartime policy conflicts between the secretary and his diplomats in the field.

Seán Murphy had great difficulty dealing with Walshe's faith in Marshal Pétain's 'Révolution Nationale' and his reports throughout 1940 reflect the fact that he considered the revolution as only skin deep.[105] Murphy's 'practical disposition, with a healthy dose of scepticism' is revealed in his report that the 'general policy of the government still seems hesitant and undefined'.[106] This provoked Walshe into sending a 'stiff telegram':[107]

> You should keep in close touch with the nuncio who is more likely to know real views of French Right than other diplomats. From all sources of information belief is general, even in countries friendly to England such as America and Portugal, that Britain has lost the war and at the very most can achieve a stalemate which might leave her part of her empire, but it is recognised everywhere that she has no hope of regaining her influence in Europe. We feel the greatest sympathy with France in her difficulties and have so informed French minister. The sympathy of the whole country is with Pétain. It is felt here that our destiny henceforth will be cast with that of the continental Catholic nations … We want to be kept informed exactly as possible of every development. Please always give sources of information.[108]

Murphy did keep in close touch with the nuncio as, a couple of weeks later, Murphy, Cremin and the nuncio were all sitting in the same car under a hot uncomfortable sun on the south bank of the river Allier waiting for German permission to drive to Paris.[109] But that is not to say that he did not consult much more widely. Keogh argued, 'Murphy was very annoyed by the telegram. His professionalism was being impugned', and by association so was Cremin's.[110] Keogh has remarked, 'Walshe had allowed himself to become convinced of the inevitability of a British defeat. Seán Murphy and Con Cremin were two diplomats who shared F.H. Boland's view that Germany would in fact ultimately lose the war'.[111] They also had an ally in the secretary of the department of the Taoiseach, Maurice Moynihan, who recalled 'that he had never accepted the inevitability of a German victory. He felt that the English would somehow muddle through the crisis.'[112] Murphy and Cremin did not wish to see Irish foreign policy develop along pro-Nazi lines.

Correspondence between Walshe and Murphy between late 1940 and early 1941 demonstrates the extent of the policy debate. On 12 November 1940, Walshe telegraphed the legation in Vichy stating that he had had:

> No telegraphic reports from you recently. You should report on situation at least once a week and as frequently as there is anything special to report. Press reports show considerable and very important diplomatic activities in France. Apart from telegraphic reports you should keep whole situation from day to day written up to forward when occasion arises. Families in great form.[113]

Murphy replied that he could not add anything to the radio reports about the meetings between France and Germany because the greatest secrecy was observed:

> The policy of collaboration was received here by public with mixed feelings, and even more so in the occupied territories. Laval [the pro-collaborationist politician] is universally unpopular and distrusted, and public are afraid that he may lead the marshal into an impasse from which he cannot retreat. Laval is avowedly anti-British and pro-German. The marshal is not prepared to follow a policy directed against Britain whereas Laval wants to go 100% in collaboration with Germany.[114]

Murphy reported the 'conversations have had a setback owing to capture of Gabon by de Gaulle and British. The German reaction is that, if France cannot defend her colonies, Germany and Italy must take steps to do so'. Murphy also noted there was a strong press campaign supported by Laval in favour of collaboration and that the Franco-German talks were continuing on the basis of a note that the Germans gave in response to French proposals:

> Apart from this event, there has been nothing important since my last telegraphed report. There are hosts of rumours which everyone hears sooner or later and which have to be sifted carefully to ascertain whether they have any basis of truth. I would have sent telegraphic reports of my impressions of the situation here were it not for the fact that I understood from your telegram 98 that you only wanted reports which could be supported by some authoritative sources and that you were generally better informed on situation here from elsewhere than I could inform you, which is correct. If, however, you desire me to give you my impression of the situation here, I shall do so as often as there is anything of importance to report. [115]

On 25 November 1940, Murphy received a barrage of questions from Walshe:

> It would be interesting to learn nuncio's view of present situation. How is country receiving Catholic and national trend of Pétain government activities? Have they not secured sufficient support to be independent of unpopularity of even important ministers? What are Laval's constructive plans for the future? What classes of people are against him? Is not some future collaboration with Germany accepted as inevitable? What particular political act has made Laval unpopular? What is the view of the ordinary people about de Gaulle? [116]

Murphy's subsequent telegram of 4 December 1940 which emphasised that France was not defeated was said by Keogh to have had a 'significant influence on the development of Irish foreign policy'. [117] In it Murphy gave a perceptive account of the situation in France after making a stout defence of his own professionalism:

I gather … that you have formed a definite opinion on the situation with which the views expressed in my report are not in harmony. I have always endeavoured to give you the facts of the situation as I see it objectively and without prejudice and consequently somewhat disheartened to receive telegrams of the kind to which I have referred, which seem to suggest that I am drawing on my imagination. Whatever may be your sources of information I think my reports are entitled to be taken on their face value until at least they are shown to be incorrect.[118]

Seán Murphy went on to say that 'France has received a knock out blow and has only recently recovered consciousness'; this concurred with the later analysis of Cremin and Robert Murphy. Cremin in his memoirs believed the French people were 'probably deeply stunned for some time'.[119] The US diplomat, Robert Murphy, also agreed with that thesis.[120] At first the French people looked to blame someone other than themselves; eventually they came to realise that they themselves were to blame. Murphy continued:

With the growth of this point of view they became less and less anti-British until now the majority even in this zone are hoping for a British victory … The grant of full powers to Marshal Pétain and the suspension of the parliamentary system was generally accepted for want of a better solution of the existing difficulty.

Murphy stated the granting of full powers to Marshal Pétain while it had support, did not have 'popular support as we understand the term'. Murphy then listed the various measures that the marshal had taken. On the church, Murphy wrote:

The Pétain government has, of course, the support of the Church, not because its policy is Catholic, for it is up to date only incidentally so, but because it is conservative and less anti-clerical than those which preceded it.

Murphy wrote, 'the present regime will last as long as the marshal lasts' and as long as the French hoped they would not have to openly collaborate. On 22 October 1940, Pétain met Hitler at Montoire.[121] The French hoped that the situation would improve following this meeting, but it did not. Murphy reported that the food situation in the occupied zone was very serious and was exacerbated by German food requisitioning.[122]

The subsequent telegram from Walshe on 7 January 1941 'must be read as a form of apology'.[123] In this telegram Walshe stated:

> No criticism intended in our telegrams 98 and 391. You have evidently misunderstood our desire to know Vatican attitude. It is of course of utmost importance for us to know Vatican views at all stages of situation especially owing to the character of the Pétain government. The questions in our telegram 391 were put for purpose of obtaining more detailed information on the matters treated by you and were not in any way intended as criticism of the objectivity of your reports. Questions may often be necessary in order to elucidate special points. The chief thing to keep in mind is that very frequent reports from you are an essential factor in our day to day judgement of a situation which affects the vital interests of our own state.[124]

Murphy's conciliatory reply to this telegram on 13 January 1941 stated that:

> I realise questions may be necessary for various reasons. It was not the fact, it was the way in which the questions were put which led me to misunderstand the position. I am in constant contact with the nuncio. His views regarding the situation here may not necessarily be those of the Vatican. Further views that nuncio expressed to me may not be exactly those he gives to the Vatican. Consider weekly telegraphic reports might often be sheer waste of money for lack of news. Will send reports whenever matters of interest to report.[125]

Dermot Keogh wrote that:

> Con Cremin recalls returning to Dublin [in March 1941] and being interviewed by Walshe and de Valera.[126] He sensed that there

might have been some policy friction and that Murphy's reports were in some way involved. Frederick Boland, in an interview, also confirmed that the Vichy reports were a cause of internal departmental debate.[127]

The Taoiseach's secretary, Moynihan, and F.H. Boland, the assistant secretary in the department of external affairs, were pro-allies. Walshe on the other hand believed it wise to come to an understanding with the Germans. Cremin believed 'he could detect tensions at headquarters while he was home in Ireland for debriefing'.[128] As he was the first Irish diplomat out of continental Europe since the fall of France his role may have been crucial.[129] According to Keogh, Cremin: 'obviously had a lot to tell his minister. Cremin was of the same mind as Murphy and his comments simply reinforced the line of argument advanced by his superior'.[130] After debriefing Cremin was urgently sent back to Vichy with instructions for Murphy.[131] Cremin did not return again to Ireland until 1946. For Murphy and the department, the only sure way that they could speak frankly without risk of being overheard was through that Cremin meeting in March 1941. All other methods of communication risked being breached, with repercussions for Ireland.[132]

In February 1942, Walshe threatened to reopen the conflict with Murphy by suggesting:

Situation at your post is important enough to warrant much more frequent telegraphic reports. We should be kept informed of French relations with other governments especially America and of any modifications in situation leading towards crisis, important social, religious and economic changes and attitude of press toward Ireland. All these matters should form subject of brief telegraphic reports to be followed by written reports in bag.[133]

Murphy replied to Walshe's request by stating that:

There was nothing in my opinion, which warranted telegraphic report. The relations between France and Germany, France and USA, remain confused, though those with latter seem to have deteriorated within the last few days. However, no definite information available to me. I think, however, that the French desire to maintain good relations with the United States is beyond doubt. Food situation still most important issue here. No alarming reports regarding Ireland's attitude.[134]

Vichy was compelled to expel the US embassy after the allied invasion of north Africa. After the invasion Marshal Pétain refused to go to north Africa to join the allies and to lead French resistance and so the US was compelled, reluctantly, to recognise de Gaulle as head of the Free French.[135]

Murphy tried to correct Walshe's distorted view that the majority of the French population were in favour of the Vichy regime. Both men, however, suffered from the conflict. Dr Conor Cruise O'Brien informed me that Walshe was sidelined in the department by the end of the war.[136] Walshe compounded his mistake by being pedantically legalistic in his recognition of the French provisional government which meant that Murphy was ostracised by the French foreign office at the Quai d'Orsay until he left France in 1950.

Spain recognised the Free French on 7 September 1943, the Portuguese on 1 January 1944, the Swiss on 23 October 1944.[137] However Ireland, an island that could not be directly threatened by Germany, dallied:

> Walshe ... communicated on 29 August 1944 to the Free French envoy in Dublin that the Irish government was prepared to give recognition to the de facto French government. This was a source of considerable irritation to the Quai d'Orsay ... [and Murphy] was never allowed to forget in the post-war years that he had served in Vichy.[138]

Murphy served in France until 1950.[139] The pro-Pétainist approach of Walshe could have damaged Ireland's reputation but the state was fortunate in that it had competent diplomats who had not submitted to the belief in 'Britain's inevitable defeat'.[140] To understand the rationale behind their judgement we must examine the political reports that Murphy and Cremin sent back to Dublin.

Political Reports

The political reports of the legation divide into three distinct phases: the first phase was from the fall of France to the invasion of the Soviet Union in June 1941; the second period was from June 1941 until the invasion of north Africa in November 1942; and the final phase was the occupation of Vichy France until Cremin's departure in November 1943. It must be assumed that Cremin, Murphy and later O'Kelly collaborated very closely in gathering information, cultivating different sources and compiling their reports.[141]

One of the first reports that the legation sent related to the condition of the armistice talks between the victorious Nazis and the defeated Third Republic. The Germans were making demands that the French considered unacceptable so it was unlikely that the French government in Vichy would return to Paris in the near future.[142] In July 1940, Murphy paid a courtesy call to Pierre Laval, the new foreign minister, and passed on the sentiments Walshe asked him to express. Laval said he would convey them to the marshal. Laval stated: 'that there were unofficial conversations taking place between England and Germany with a view to a settlement.'[143]

On 26 August 1940, Murphy reported he attended a lunch given by Laval, which Admiral Darlan and Charles Roux also attended. Laval and Darlan were violently anti-British.[144] Admiral Darlan's anti-Britishness must be seen in light of the Mers-el-Kébir incident.[145]

On 26 November 1940, the legation reported that if Bulgaria were to grant right of passage for German troops to Greece, Turkey would declare war and join the British in Greece.[146] Mussolini had invaded Greece on 28 October 1940, and the Germans later invaded Greece from Bulgaria and Yugoslavia. Turkey however remained neutral.[147]

On 21 November 1940 the legation reported that: 'The recent agreement between France and Germany regarding prisoners of war is the first tangible result of a policy of collaboration'.[148] In early December 1940, Murphy reported:

> Had a talk with the nuncio yesterday. He thought public opinion in free zone is hardening against policy of collaboration, for the following reasons. Firstly because of the feeling created by the expulsions from Lorraine, secondly disappointment at lack of results from meeting and thirdly Greek success.[149] He thinks marshal's prestige is very high and that internal policy is gaining ground, but that there is still considerable opposition. The majority in the occupied territory very opposed to collaboration and strongly pro-British. The government can, of course, carry out its policy without popular support, as it is all powerful.[150]

Murphy added that 'All classes of community dislike and distrust Laval'.[151] In addition 'de Gaulle has little personal support: what he represents has considerable support in occupied territory'.[152] The French historian, Lacouture, argued that by the end of 1940 'the inner of France was beginning to stir'.[153]

On 11 December 1940, a report was carried that certain French newspapers were urging France to become an agricultural economy and de-industrialise so that she could not rearm and avenge herself and therefore 'the conditions of peace would be less severe'.[154] Two days later the government announced that Pétain would be installed in Versailles as head of the French state, but 'the seat of government would remain at Vichy'.[155] Marshal Pétain did not return to the Palace of the Sun King at Versailles.

On 16 December they reported on the dismissal and arrest of Laval by Pétain.[156] Laval had been dismissed when it was found that his policy of collaboration extended to 'co-operation on military matters in Africa and [that he] had turned over to the Germans gold held in France for the Belgian government'.[157] The Germans demanded that he be reinstated; Pétain refused.[158] The legation reported that Pétain was going to form a consultative assembly 'fresh on the heels of the dismissal of Laval'.[159] On 18 December, Murphy reported the release of Laval who had fled to Paris and added: 'His reinstatement in government under German pressure is possible.'[160] However Pétain 'accepted the German demand for a directorate presided over by Admiral Darlan'.[161]

In his New Year address Pétain urged the farmers to maximise yields in the coming year.[162] On 10 January, the legation reported on the level of unemployment in the occupied and unoccupied zones, 950,000 and 103,000 respectively; previously the corresponding figures were 734,000 and 90,000. Belin, the minister for industrial employment and labour, stated the 'causes of unemployment in France at present, still remain, viz. lack of raw materials and fuel, difficulties of communication between the two zones and lack of means of transport'.[163]

In January 1941 the legation reported on the reconciliation between Laval and Pétain: 'There is little doubt that Laval's return to favour is due to German pressure … it may mean more practical turn being given to collaboration … following on British successes in north Africa and consequent increased importance in Mediterranean of French fleet'.[164]

On 27 January, they reported on the evolution of Pétain's national council, a purely consultative body which would meet regularly in plenary session. Further to the report 188 members of the senate and chamber of deputies remained suspended as they had been since July 1940.[165] On 3 February 1941, the cession of Bizerta, in French north Africa, was among Hitler's new demands. Murphy also reported that a party called Rassemblement National Populaire had been created in Paris by Déat, a pro-Nazi fascist, and others whose policy was close collaboration with Germany.[166]

In early February 1941, the Irish legation reported that the French government had resigned en bloc the previous night, after being informed that Laval would be appointed to the cabinet.[167] On 6 February 1941, they reported incorrectly that 'Nothing is known for certain except that Laval will be in new government'. Murphy stated: 'What effect next government here may have on political activities … in occupied territory it is not possible to say at present'.[168] Admiral Darlan was appointed vice-president of the new cabinet and heir to Pétain.[169] The legation next reported that the Germans would not insist on the return of Laval until they saw how co-operative Darlan was. Darlan was reported as 'anti-British but is not thought to be pro-German'.[170] Darlan would be vice-president and would hold portfolios for foreign affairs, the marine and the interior.[171]

Murphy and Cremin gave a measured response to the developments in Vichy. They attacked Pétain's concept of the 'Révolution Nationale', which was Pétain's attempt to align Vichy France with the existing authoritarian regimes and reorganise the state on fascist lines. The French Legion of Veterans propagated the cult of Pétain, while attacking bolshevism, Gaullism, judaism and free-masonary.[172] Murphy attributed Laval's decision not to rejoin the government as a strategy by him. Murphy then gave his considered opinion of the Vichy regime:

> The really good Frenchmen – and they are unfortunately not very numerous – are very worried about the present situation. By these I mean those who are prepared to give their services without regard to personal or political gain. They are conscious that the 'Révolution Nationale' does not go very deep. The marshal is very sincere in his intentions and ideas, but unfortunately the application of these ideas is not very widespread. There have been considerable changes in the personnel of the government and municipal administrations, but, with very few exceptions, the faults of the old administration persist. The number of cases of hoarding that have been discovered is considerable, but these represent only a small fraction of the actual cases.[173]

As regards Pétain's personal qualities the legation was not complimentary. They wrote:

> It seems to be certain that Pétain, although universally respected and admired ... is vain, self opinionated, and stubborn. He does not like disagreement with his views, and is apparently a bad judge of persons.

Murphy concluded that the majority of the French public were inclined to wait for a German defeat. They would not commit to any enterprise owing to the uncertain political situation.[174]

In April 1941, the legation reported that the cabinet was once again under strong pressure to return Laval to office.[175] The political situation was uncertain, and there was considerable disaffection in French colonial Syria; 'anti-German feeling in both zones [was] increasing'.[176] In mid-April, the legation reported:

> Cabinet changes under German pressure and return of Laval considered possible in the near future. Strong press campaign in Paris to that effect.[177] Balkans affair has caused much depression here.[178] The food position is very difficult and is main question in internal situation.[179]

The US ambassador, Admiral William D. Leahy, believed the 'Germans were tightening the noose around unoccupied France'.[180]

In May 1941, Pétain made a speech on the negotiations between Admiral Darlan and Hitler, which he said could lead France to 'overcome its defeat and preserve its rank as a European and colonial power'.[181] Murphy reported:

> [the] Americans here seem to feel acceptance by marshal of Darlan's views will involve economic and political, if not military collaboration which can only be harmful to England and therefore meet strong opposition in Washington. The ambassador apparently so informed the marshal on Tuesday.[182]

Admiral Leahy, the US ambassador, stated that May and June 1941 were the darkest days: 'My assurances that Germany would eventually meet with defeat were doubted.' There was also a risk that Vichy would change their policy towards Germany to one of military collaboration.[183] In fact some historians argue that 'Darlan stood on the verge of declaring co-belligerency status with Germany in the middle east' during May–June 1941. Hitler did not entice Darlan into military collaboration however.[184] The allies still had cause to worry though as General Dentz in Syria was ordered by Darlan to collaborate with the Germans 'without reservations' in their attempts to support an anti-British coup in Iraq.[185]

On 24 May 1941, the Irish delegation reported that *Le Temps*, the government newspaper, had referred to collaboration as designed 'to put France in a position which will preclude her fate being put in balance when peace is being made'. This desire to control her own destiny was manifested in an official statement, reported by Murphy to Walshe:

> An official statement this week about succession of colonies said time has arrived for France to regain, particularly in Africa, whole of her empire, and that succession problem is to be settled exclusively between France and dissenters. Interpret this as indicating acceptance of French government to endeavour to recover lost territories by force.[186]

Four days before, Darlan and the German ambassador in Paris, Arbetz, had signed the Paris Protocol which allowed for the Germans to use Syrian and north African territory for military purposes. In return Vichy was authorised to reinforce its own strength to resist British and Gaullist attacks.[187]

On 6 June 1941, the legation reported on Darlan's declaration of 31 May in which he argued a number of points. Firstly, that British policy since 1918 had sought to put France in a weak and subordinate position. Secondly, that British victory was improbable; and thirdly, that it would take so long to effect as to find France in a disastrous condition. Fourthly, the status that France would be accorded following such a victory would be quite secondary and unacceptable to the government. The duty of the government, therefore, was to collaborate with Germany in the construction of the new European order:

> The declaration has all the appearance of having been very deliberately prepared. It is, however, doubtful whether views expressed will have practical consequences which would logically seem to follow, as it is probable marshal does not share fully all Darlan's ideas, and would for example consider entry into war on the side of Germany as incompatible with French honour.[188]

The Second Phase: Operation Barbarossa,
the Opening of the Eastern Front

The Nazi invasion of the Soviet Union, Operation Barbarossa, began on 22 June 1941. The legation reported that:

> German war is likely to have important military and political consequences. [Vichy] seems inclined to believe German military victory fairly certain and argues that Napoleonic campaign not a parallel as distance now much less important factor.[189]

Marshal Pétain warned against communist propaganda resulting from Germany's invasion of the USSR. Following the invasion Vichy broke off diplomatic relations with Moscow.[190]

With the severing of relations with the Soviet Union, the Second World War entered its second phase in becoming a global conflict. The invasion of the Soviet Union ultimately decimated the German army with '80% of German battle casualties' suffered on the eastern front.[191] However the eastern front was not the only front. The north African deserts also saw some bitter fighting with the allies and the Germans fighting epic battles.

In June 1941, the British and Free French forces invaded French Syria. By 11 July 1941, Syria had been captured and 2,120 Vichy French troops were killed. The legation reported that Vichy had expected German aircraft to intervene.[192] On 16 July 1941, the legation reported that the final terms of the Syrian armistice were regarded as honourable. The first set of terms 'involved public abandonment of constant principle that government here is only legal French authority with right of control over overseas French territory and admission that London French have right to speak for French nation'.[193] The continued recognition of Pétain as head of the French state was a blow for de Gaulle, who thought the 'content was far worse than anything I had feared'.[194]

The Catholic Church in France did resist attempts to be amalgamated into Pétain's 'National Revolution' but this did not stop some clergy from offering loyalty to Pétain and decrying Gaullism.[195] The legation said they 'understand from well informed ecclesiastic, back from Paris', that the Germans asked the bishops to deliver sermons 'representing the campaign as [an] anti-Bolshevist crusade' in order to get the moral support of the French in their Soviet war, but the bishops did not adopt the suggestion. The same 'well informed ecclesiastic' stated that Darlan had 'practically no support in occupied territories'.[196]

Admiral Darlan had to contend with German demands for the cession of the French territories of Bizerta, Casablanca and Dakar on the pretext of the Anglo-American threat. The Vichy government refused the demand but the Germans would not let the matter drop.[197] In late August 1941, the legation reported that the Germans were responding to sabotage and attacks in occupied France by taking several thousand hostages and announcing that they would shoot a number of them for every further partisan attack. The historian, Harry Kedward, argues that Vichy's collaboration with these executions was in order to 'salvage the declining status of Vichy'.[198] Meanwhile the Vichy authorities stated they would deal very severely with deserters from the Vichy army.[199]

In October 1941, the legation stated that Franco-German relations were 'more or less stagnant'. The legation wrote: 'The general feeling is that the Germans should do their own dirty work without the assistance or co-operation of the French government'. The legation reported that the National Revolution had not 'taken off' and that Pétain admitted this. They believed eighty per cent of the population in the free zone was anti-German and eighty-five per cent in the occupied zone. In conclusion, the legation stated that the French population held 'great hostility towards the Germans, great discontent with the French government, and great disappointment with regard to the marshal' and that they were 'definitely pro-British'.[200] Nevertheless, Pétain still had to contend with Nazi occupation. Throughout 1941, 'Vichy began to look like a government divorced from the country'.[201] The Vatican too was aware of the growing hostility and rejected proposals for a concordat at the end of 1941 'on the grounds that the regime was a transitory one'.[202]

On 7 December 1941, 'a day which will live in infamy', the

Japanese attacked the United States of America at Pearl Harbour. Although politically and strategically illogical, on 11 December 1941, Hitler committed a 'gratuitous folly' and declared war on the USA.[203] Though the tide was yet to turn against the axis, German defeat was becoming a possibility.[204]

Even though the war had turned global, some Frenchmen were pressurising Pétain to return Laval to government on the basis that Laval would be able to secure more concessions from the Germans than any other group.[205] In order to further ingratiate themselves with the Germans, some Parisian newspapers pushed for the breaking off of diplomatic relations with the United States.[206] On 14 December 1941, Pétain told Leahy, the US ambassador, that he did not know how long they could resist German pressure to return Laval.[207]

The moribund nature of French society at this time was manifested in the Compagnons de France, a form of non-military military service for young men to keep them occupied and employed and out of the hands of the resistance. A speech was delivered by Marshal Pétain who exhorted young men to take long apprenticeships and not to give in to vice.[208]

On 6 March 1942, the legation reported that the allied bombing 'of Paris has provoked deep indignation in government circles and a feeling of certain bewilderment, but no strong feeling among public'.

By 7 March, the legation reported that they understood Franco-German relations had improved.[209] At the end of March, they reported more rumours of Laval's return to government:

> It appears that the Germans want France to declare herself definitely and to show cause by having Laval, Doriot or Déat in government. Darlan is no longer in favour. I am personally inclined to think marshal will not agree to any policy which entails breaking off relations with the United States.[210]

On 30 March 1942 Leahy delivered to Pétain a message from Roosevelt stating 'that the appointment of Laval ... would make it impossible for America to continue its attitude of helpfulness'.[211] However, on 18 April Laval was returned to power as vice-president of the council, minister for external affairs and minister of the interior. The legation wrote that:

> It seems certain that Laval has been imposed on the marshal by the Germans ... His return is due to German reaction to the American statement that such an event would not be regarded as a friendly gesture by them and is designed to show that Germany and not America can call the tune in France.[212]

Pétain announced the formation of a government with Laval as its head. On 21 April, Murphy reported that Admiral Leahy had called on him to let him know he would be leaving for the US. The US had told Pétain that they would regard the appointment of Laval as very serious and would recall Leahy for consultation. Since Laval had now been appointed, Leahy was to leave shortly.[213]

By 7 May 1942, the legation reported that in spite of conciliatory statements by Laval: 'there is a fairly widespread opinion here that diplomatic relations between the French and America are not likely to continue much longer'.[214]

On 10 May 1942, Murphy had an interview with Laval.[215] Laval said he considered the attitude of the United States as intolerable and wondered at how Roosevelt 'assumed the right to tell all countries where their interests lay'. Murphy replied that he thought Roosevelt 'was dignified and calm and that his verbal declaration was very conciliatory in the circumstances'. Laval, who was probably not pleased with Murphy's response, went on to:

> refer to his declaration of policy, and said, with very evident sincerity and conviction, that he firmly believed that policy [of collaboration] was the only policy for France and also for any hope of peace in Europe ... He had always been in favour of understanding with Germany, and now he was more than ever convinced of its necessity.[216]

In June, Nazi-controlled French newspapers were demanding a rupture with the USA.[217] Pétain was not in favour of a break in relations; neither was the USA.[218] This rupture only occurred subsequently when the US landed in north Africa in November.[219] The legation reported that:

> Relations between France and the United States of America have been very strained on the question of French ships in Alexandria. The breaking point I think may depend on results of operations in Libya.[220]

After Murphy visited Paris to inspect the condition of the legation building and look after Irish interests in the city, he sent a report on 22 June 1942. In this he commented on the condition of the occupied city:

> … there seems to be no mixing between the French and the Germans. One thing amongst the French which is very remarkable. They talk much less to one another in the streets than they did and even in caf[é]s conversation is very subdued.

He went on to report the humiliating slights which the occupying forces imposed on the city:

> One hears on every side that the hatred of the Paris population for the occupying authority is beyond belief. It is of course impossible to confirm if that is the true position. One sees notices such as 'forbidden to French cars', 'Reserved for German army', 'Passage forbidden' fairly frequently which gives even a foreigner a funny impression and which must be very galling to a Frenchman.[221]

On 12 May 1942, in an effort to ingratiate himself with the Nazis, Laval offered French workers for work in German factories.[222] On 30 June 1942, the legation reported Laval's statement that French workers going to Germany would allow for the release of French POWs held in Germany.[223] On 10 October 1942, they reported that Laval was confident that he could get more time to organise the deportation of 150,000 skilled workers to Germany.[224] Speer believed the deportation of workers to Germany drove more workers into resistance than any other force.[225] Vichy lost all remaining legitimacy after the Germans occupied all of metropolitan France in November 1942 after the allied invasion of north Africa.

The Third Phase: the Invasion of North Africa
and the De Jure End of the Vichy Regime
The allied invasion of north Africa on 8 November 1942 marked the beginning of the end of the Vichy regime. Pétain refused all entreaties to go to north Africa to lead France from there. He felt it was his duty to remain in mainland France. After the invasion the legation predicted that Vichy France and the United States would shortly break off diplomatic negotiations.[226]

The initial opposition which the allies faced from the Vichy French in some areas quickly came to an end when Admiral Darlan, who was in north Africa at the time, negotiated a separate armistice on behalf of French north Africa, without consulting Pétain. On 13 November 1942, the legation reported on the situation in Vichy:

> … Everything was quiet, but there is, of course, underneath the surface a great sense of uneasiness. It appears certain Germans will require all diplomatic representatives of countries who are at war with, or who have broken diplomatic relations with, Germany and Italy to leave France.[227]

In November the legation reported the arrest of General Weygand, a prominent French general, and noted that Cuba, Guatemala, Mexico and Nicaragua had broken diplomatic relations with Vichy.[228] They further reported that Hitler wanted the demobilisation of the rest of the French army. On the orders of Pétain, the French fleet at Toulon had already been scuttled after the occupation of Vichy France to prevent it falling into the hands of the Germans; the fleet comprised an armada of 'two battleships, two battle-cruisers, four heavy cruisers, two light cruisers, an aircraft carrier, thirty destroyers and sixteen submarines'.[229] Murphy reported that Pétain had now completely broken with Darlan.[230]

On 16 December 1942, Murphy had an interview with Laval during which 'Laval reaffirmed his belief in a German victory' and said he hoped for it, 'not only for his own country, but for the good of Europe in general'. He also reaffirmed 'his distrust in Anglo-Saxon promises'. Murphy wrote:

> he was determined to break without mercy any opposition to his policy now that he has the means. This can only mean German support because he clearly has less material means than ever before ... I am told on all sides, official and otherwise, and this view is confirmed fully by the nuncio, that Laval is fully aware that at least 90% of the French population as a whole is against his policy.

Murphy speculated that Laval's point of view could cost him his life; his personal beliefs were not even endorsed by the civil servants in Vichy.[231] Lagarde, political director at the foreign office, said to Murphy: '*Cher ami, nous sommes dans "un jam" pour employer l'expression anglaise* [Dear friend, we are in "a jam", to use the English expression].' Murphy responded:

> I then said surely Laval must know that 90% of the country are against his policy. He replied without hesitation 'at least that percentage, and he knows it perfectly well, but, according to him, the country does not know the situation and can't possibly judge, therefore it must be led'.

Laval was playing a dangerous game and was leading France towards the path of open collaboration.

With the occupation of all of France by the Germans in November 1942 the legation had been forbidden to send cables in code and this right was not restored until 19 December 1942. Meanwhile, all permits for movement had to be applied for through the Germans.[232]

On 24 December Admiral Darlan was assassinated by a Frenchman in north Africa, leaving de Gaulle the undisputed head of the Free French.[233]

In the legation review of developments during 1942 they summed up the situation in France appropriately:

> Whereas 1941 could be characterised as a year of political 'non-committalism' (*attentisme*), 1942 ended with a French government policy which, officially at any rate, was definitely one of collaboration and the ultimate success of which in the international sphere depended upon a German victory.

The legation were very severe on Pétain in their report, stating:

> The population, with very few exceptions, are now definitely anti-collaborationist and very much more openly anti-German. They feel that the tide has turned and they are only awaiting the moment when the crash, which they have all been waiting for, will come. The marshal's prestige has sunk to zero. Even his past record is forgotten in light of his failure to achieve anything solid for France … The kindest criticism is that he is an old man who should have known that the task was too much for him.

Another issue that concerned all French people at this stage was the worsening food situation:

> The food situation is bad and according to official statements may be even tragic in the months of March, April and May. The Germans and Italians are taking all they can lay their hands on, of any sort or kind. They have requisitioned engines, carriages, trucks and even railway lines in large quantities. Apart from the dislocation of transport services, it makes the task of food distribution almost impossible.[234]

The food situation fuelled resentment towards the Germans and Italians.[235]

In February 1943, only eight legations remained in Vichy. The Irish legation's political reports dried up for the early part of 1943, as Vichy truly became an 'international backwater'.[236]

On 9 July 1943 the allies invaded Sicily. Mussolini was dismissed and arrested on the orders of the Italian King Victor Emmanuel on 25 July. On 2 August, the legation reported it was:

> Impossible to get reliable information here of troop movements in Italian occupied territory [the] particulars of which would indicate German view of Italian government intention. German circles here seem rather hostile to new regime. Some colleagues, including nuncio, seem to think that Italian government is in impasse as incapable of getting rid of German troops.[237]

The legation reported that the French population, both official and non-official, could not conceal their delight at the turn of events in Italy: 'Apart from all other considerations, it makes Italy's territorial claims against France seem less actual.'[238]

On the domestic front in France, the legation reported that the Germans had demanded a further 500,000 French workers for work in Germany. Laval pointed out they had not yet filled a previous quota of 220,000 workers. It was clear to the legation that:

> In the case of 80% at least of the French, they are waiting impatiently for an invasion by the Anglo-Americans. They are quite convinced that Germany is beaten and with typical French shrewdness they think it is a good thing to get in early and well with the opponents. It is the reverse of the coin this time as compared with July, 1940.[239]

In October 1943, the legation reported a massive increase in Gestapo arrests throughout France in an effort to remove all possible sources of revolt: 'It is suggested even the [German] authorities feel themselves menaced.'[240] However, Murphy reported that Laval would not resign in spite of his universal unpopularity and neither would Marshal Pétain. He concluded that 'the only well organised services in France at the moment are the "Black Market" and the "Resistance Movement", red or otherwise'.[241]

At this point, Walshe warned Murphy that if he had to leave

he should go to Lisbon rather than Switzerland 'as we do not want you to be cut off by the war'.[242]

The Jewish Question and the Irish Legation in Vichy
Ever since Cremin's arrival in France, a disproportionate amount of his time had been occupied by the Jewish question and the refugee issue. In the annual report for 1938, Murphy and Cremin wrote:

> Only one new element directly affecting the nature of that work was introduced viz. the decision to impose the visa requirement on holders of Austrian and German passports. Although this regulation only entered into force during the month of May the new conditions in the matter of visa applications resulting from the Anschluss prevailed from the beginning of the period – more than about half of all visa applications received in the period came from refugees of one kind or another from German territory and the number of persons who visited the legation in regard to that matter was relatively quite large owing to the fact that France generally and Paris in particular served as a kind of focus for those compelled to leave.[243]

The refugee crisis led to the convocation of the Évian-les-Bains conference of July 1938 in an effort to resolve the question.[244] F.T. Cremins, the Irish delegate, argued that Ireland was an overpopulated country with not enough land.[245] The question of the Jews did not become a serious one for the Irish legation, and Irish refugee policy in the first years of the war was ungenerous. 'It would, however, be an error to project backwards to 1939 a knowledge of the Holocaust.'[246]

Throughout 1940 and 1941 the legation reported on the infringements being made on the civil rights of the Jews in France. In January 1941, an architectural body was formed whose membership was open to 'persons of French nationality in full enjoyment of civic rights and in possession of a diploma.'[247] This effectively excluded the Jews and was the beginning of a series of laws brought in by Pétain's regime which gradually eroded the rights of the Jews in Vichy France. This was in keeping with the Nuremberg principle which legally ended the rights of Jews as citizens. The Germans thought that the French would benefit materially from the aryanisation of Jewish businesses and positions.[248] In March 1941, a commissariat for Jewish affairs was established by Vichy, with the anti-Semite, Xavier Vallat, as commissar. On 8 July 1942 the first deportation was arranged, made up of 'stateless' Jews from France.[249]

On 21 September 1942, Cremin wrote that de Croux of the Swiss legation believed Laval was anti-Jewish. After a failed Swedish protest about the deportation of Soviet Jews, Laval said 'there is no international law as far as the Jews are concerned'.[250] On 22 September 1942, the legation reported that:

> The measures against the Jews seem to be fairly widely resented both on humanitarian grounds and as going unnecessarily far on German lines. One rumour attributes resignation of minister of agriculture to them.[251]

On 25 September 1942, Cremin reported on the regulations against Jews and stated that they applied only to those Jews who came to France after 1935. The nuncio stated that Laval was anti-Jewish and said he was:

> personally of opinion that M. Laval at least to some extent took the initiative in this matter, i.e. that the regulations in question are not purely the result of German pressure. He then went on to report that Jews have been refused exit visas in spite having entry visas.[252]

On 26 September 1942, Cremin gave a detailed account of the processing of all visa applications. He had spoken to the two relevant officials who stated that all visa applications by French citizens were referred first to the ministry of the interior, secondly to the foreign office and finally, to Laval's office, where he could reverse a previous decision.[253]

Laval's anti-Semitism manifested itself further in September 1942, when the archbishop of Lyon ordered his priests to read

a protest against the deportations from the pulpit. Laval threatened to drag out any Jewish children who had sought sanctuary on
church property and arrested priests who had given sanctuary.[254]
Anti-Jewish sentiment flourished under the Vichy government,
allowing Vichy France to be the only country not directly under
Nazi control to deport Jews.[255] By August 1943, the Germans controlled all of metropolitan France, except the Italian zone, and the
legation reported:

> They have apparently also asked that all Jews naturalised since 1927
> should be handed over to them. All those naturalised since 1933
> have already been handed over and a great deal more who were full
> French citizens by birth. It appears that the marshal regards the re-
> quest about the Jews as outrageous and up to the moment nothing
> has happened.[256]

The deportations did not leave Ireland untouched and members of
the small Irish Jewish community sent requests for information on
relatives in France.

During the deportations of September 1942, a friend of the
Jewish Fianna Fáil TD, Robert Briscoe, was threatened with deportation. Briscoe asked the legation to:

> Please assist secure travel exit permit, Mrs Fay Abusch née Balen,
> Nouvel Hotel, Boulevard Victor Hugo, Nice. American consul at
> Nice already informed all entry visa this end in order and Portuguese
> transit visa. Lady concerned sister very personal friend of mine please
> wire me result.[257]

On 15 September 1942, Cremin wrote to the US consul asking: 'I
would be much obliged if you would be so good as to inform me of
the nature of the passport held by Mrs Abusch and of the nature
of the difficulties in the way of her securing an exit visa'.[258] Fay
Abusch was English by birth and French by marriage, so Murphy
wired Briscoe to state that they could not do anything officially to
help Mrs Abusch but would do everything possible otherwise.[259]

On 23 September 1942, Cremin wrote to Mrs Abusch stating:

> Mr Murphy has now replied to Mr Briscoe to the effect that he re-
> grets that as you are not an Irish citizen, he cannot intervene officially
> in your favour of your being granted a French exit visa. He is prepared,
> however, in view of Mr Briscoe's interest in your case, to assist you in
> this matter in any other way possible.[260]

The next day Fay Abusch thanked Murphy for all his efforts in
seeking to obtain a French exit visa.[261] Initial efforts to recruit US
support were unsuccessful owing to Abusch being a French citizen.[262] Cremin was still hopeful of a favourable outcome and believed that he was successful when the foreign office stated 'they
authorised the visa on 15th October. This authorisation has been
sent to the Prefecture at Nice'.[263] In mid-November, Dublin was
anxious for news of Mrs Abusch.[264] It appeared that she had difficulty obtaining a Portuguese visa. The final correspondence was
in January 1943 when Murphy asked if Mrs Abusch had sufficient
funds for her needs.[265] There the correspondence ended; it is unknown if she survived the war.

On 27 August 1943, Walshe wrote to the legation: 'Asked to
give exit visas so as to enable a number of prominent Jewish personalities to get out of German occupied territory. Our understanding is that there is no prospect of such persons being able to
get German exit permit in those circumstances.'[266] The same day
Murphy replied: 'No prospect whatever.'[267]

Cremin was replaced in Vichy in November by Denis Roland Mac-
Donald who came from the Quirinal in Rome.[268] Before leaving,
Cremin was awarded a Légion d'honneur by Pétain.[269] However
no record for this exists in the National Archives Dublin.[270]

Cremin's first posting had been most trying; however, neither
he nor Murphy, during the heady days of 1940, had allowed their
enthusiasm to get the better of their judgement and both had
avoided the 'panic'. They had displayed a calmness under extreme
circumstances that saved Ireland from a dangerous misadventure

during the panic of 1940, and in the following years had worked well together to keep Dublin informed of the politics of Vichy France, the plight of Irish citizens and the plight of occupied France.

The respect which he had earned from his superiors meant that they considered him one of their best officers to send to one of the most trying and dangerous posts, the dying heart of the Third Reich.

CHAPTER 3

'Die billige Gesandtschaft':[1] *The Cheap Legation, Berlin, 1943–45*

FOR CREMIN, THE ORDER TO RELIEVE WARNOCK in Berlin must have been met with a good deal of trepidation. He knew that Germany was losing the war and that the allied air offensive was gaining momentum. He also knew that diplomats were protected under the Geneva Convention, but in an era of total warfare such guarantees were difficult to enforce.[2] According to T. Desmond Williams, Cremin was in Germany for the fifth and final phase of Irish diplomacy during the war, beginning in January 1943, when the physical threat to Ireland had receded considerably.[3] This did not reduce the importance of the Berlin mission for Dublin though. As Keatinge puts it: 'Ireland's diplomatic relations with the principal belligerents was the lifeline without which Mr de Valera would have been unable to explain or defend his policy of neutrality.'[4]

Cremin was aged thirty-five and Berlin was his first posting as head of mission. Wartime difficulties over accreditation left him with the status of chargé d'affaires, rather than envoy extraordinary and minister plenipotentiary. In September 1939, the department had wanted to send 'Thomas Kiernan, as minister with ambassadorial rank' to Berlin but they decided 'not to risk British apoplexy by requesting the king's consent' as all Ireland was part of the commonwealth.[5] Therefore Warnock, and Cremin after him, both held the rank of chargé d'affaires.

The decision by de Valera and Walshe to send Cremin to Berlin was based on the fact that he was one of the few serving Irish officers with German. His daughter, Dr Aedeen Cremin, recalled that he had 'studied in Munich and was fluent in German'; she also had the 'impression the Irish wanted to keep a lowish profile in Berlin'.[6] If that was a consideration, the Irish government had made a wise decision. 'Cremin certainly had no sympathy for Hitler or national socialism.'[7] Moreover, he had been serving in France since 1937 where he had witnessed at first hand the Nazi occupation and exploitation of that country.[8] His period at Vichy had further reinforced his abhorrence of national socialism.

The Handover of the Mission

Warnock and Cremin had joined the service together in early 1935 and were good friends.[9] Warnock 'reported competently from Berlin but his youthful enthusiasm may sometimes have got the better of him'.[10] This was particularly true in the early stage of the war when Warnock's:

> … 'unquestionable' hostility to Britain could easily be associated with sympathy for national socialism. It remains unclear how far Warnock was acting under general instructions from Dublin, or letting his personal enthusiasm get the better of him, in publicly applauding Hitler's Reichstag speech on 19 July [1940], and in vigorously propounding the view in diplomatic circles that 'Not only the Germans but also other nations could expect the achievement of international justice' following German victories. Warnock's confidence in Hitler's thirst for 'international justice' and in Nazi solicitude for the rights of small states can most charitably be considered a triumph of imagination – whether his own or Walshe's – over evidence.[11]

In applauding the Reichstag speech, Warnock had indeed allowed his enthusiasm to get the better of him. However, so too had many more experienced diplomats and statesmen who felt that Germany would, in the end, be victorious.[12] Warnock's aim may have been 'to say agreeable things without meaning everything that is said'.[13] He was also keeping bad company in the form of Francis Stuart.[14]

Cremin had relieved Warnock once before while the latter recovered from a motor accident in August 1942. Cremin recalled:

> During my first stay in Berlin in the summer of 1942 I met a man who was well known in Ireland, Dr Adolf Mahr, the then director of the National Museum ... He had chosen to return to Germany on the outbreak of the war. He was very doubtful about the prospect of a German victory and I was quite struck by his air of depression.[15]

In 1942, Germany was still advancing in Russia and the deserts of north Africa and her Japanese allies were cutting a swath through the European empires.[16] Adolf Mahr spent the initial war years engaged by the German foreign ministry at Wilhelmstrasse and, on 8 September 1941, set up German radio's daily Irish service.[17] Cremin's report from his first stay contained a perceptive analysis of the situation in Germany, both politically and militarily, especially regarding the allied Dieppe landings, which failed and resulted in the loss of many men and equipment.[18] In spite of this allied setback, Cremin concluded by stating that: 'the majority of the German people thought that the war was already lost.'[19]

Cremin was posted to Berlin to replace Warnock in April 1943, after Warnock asked for home leave.[20] Warnock had not been back to headquarters since 1939 and was largely unsupported except for Eileen Walsh, the legation's typist. Warnock was informed that Cremin would relieve him at the end of May or early June. Warnock would then travel with Eileen Walsh, by air via Stockholm to Dublin.[21] There were delays, however, and on 18 June 1943, Warnock telegraphed: 'I thought Cremin would be here by now.'[22] Walshe replied: 'Cremin coming first week of August.'[23] When he repeated his request for leave, Walshe, who had trained to become a Jesuit and believed in their management philosophy, informed him curtly: 'Regret very much delay in this year's holidays, crisis too grave for even temporary change in Berlin. Please remain at post.'[24] This prompted Warnock to send a very severe letter to headquarters on 12 August 1943. Warnock complained that he was not able to comment accurately on Irish affairs because he was not in touch with the country; erroneously, he believed that the newspapers that did arrive were so out of date as not to be of use to him.[25] He wrote:

Two things have always puzzled the foreign office: 1. That despite the great importance of Berlin and the added interest attached to Ireland since the war, the staff of the legation consists of only one diplomatic officer and one typist. 2. Why, in view of the bad state of communications between Ireland and Germany, I have not once been in Ireland during the past four years to report personally … Occasionally they refer to us as 'Die billige Gesandtschaft' (the Cheap Legation).[26]

Warnock added that this name was usually used in a light-hearted tone. On the situation in Berlin he wrote:

Life out here becomes more dull and gloomy as the weeks go by; Miss Walsh when she arrives will tell you … It is quite possible that you are under the impression that I have been having a fine time during the past four years, with next to nothing to do except to go to dinners and parties and otherwise enjoy myself. To this I would reply that the last traces of social activity vanished in 1941; all the younger men are serving in the armed services … German acquaintances are becoming a nuisance owing to their continual requests for coffee, butter, meat and the use of my car.[27]

The requests Warnock referred to were accentuated by British black (false) propaganda which exaggerated the quantity and quality of diplomatic rations which the British alleged were being given to the leading Nazis.[28] Warnock concluded that owing to the likelihood of the opening of a second front in 1944, he would not get home before 1945 or 1946.[29]

The department took cognisance of his telegram, stating in October that they were awaiting word from Seán Murphy to see if Cremin could go to Berlin.[30] On 2 May 1943 it was decided that Warnock would be appointed first secretary at headquarters in Dublin. Cremin would go to Berlin. D.R. MacDonald, second secretary from the Quirinal, would go to Vichy and P.J. O'Byrne would be promoted to acting second secretary at Lisbon.[31] This was the biggest reorganisation of the Irish diplomats in service during the war.

On 24 November 1943, Warnock was telegraphed to say that Cremin would arrive that evening.[32] However, the task of handing over the legation to another pair of capable hands was severely disrupted by the RAF. Months earlier Warnock had warned that the: 'situation of legation near the main line railways and important anti-aircraft batteries is very dangerous.'[33] The Irish legation was in imminent danger from the allied strategic bombing initiative, which Air Marshal Harris had restarted over Berlin that very month.[34] Cremin arrived in Berlin in the aftermath of the 22-23 November bombing, which killed 1,600 people and destroyed the diplomatic quarter, including the Irish legation.[35] Warnock had:

> … ignored the air raid warning at eight o'clock in the evening and was working on his accounts in an upstairs room when a bomb set fire to the lower floor and walls. Warnock's files and archives were destroyed and he just had time to see the legation's grand piano go up in flames before hurriedly leaving the building as the roof collapsed.[36]

Warnock gave a very detailed account of the fire and the efforts that were made to save the legation. 'I was entitled to go over to the bombproof bunker in the government's guest house across the road, but I felt that it was my duty to remain in the legation'.[37] It is a tribute to all of the Irish diplomats during the war that none of them ever shirked their duty in favour of their personal safety. When Cremin arrived, the legation was a shell. He recalled:

> … walking down the steps, was the messenger, holding in his hand a single jackboot. When I asked him where was Herr Warnock he replied in an ambiguous phrase: 'Herr Warnock ist weg', for 'weg' it could mean either gone away or, in colloquial language, dead. Very fortunately it meant the former.[38]

Cremin learned that Warnock had moved to Schloss Staffelde, sixty kilometres northwest of Berlin, the official German *point de repli*, which was the property of an Irishman, Charlie Mills.[39]

Warnock remained on as chargé d'affaires until he left for

home on 28 February 1944. Cremin wrote that 'Warnock had had a difficult and probably lonely time in Berlin (for he was as yet unmarried) but he had a quite unusual command of German and seemed to have a host of friends. His experience of 22 November must have been for him traumatic'.[40] Cremin's sister believes that: 'Warnock had had a breakdown, caused by nervousness and Con was sent to replace him.'[41] It is likely that the pressure was taking an increased toll on Warnock as he had served as chargé d'affaires since 1939. However, in spite of his own wishes, and poor health, Warnock reported that he felt he must stay and assist Cremin 'owing to total loss of records'.[42] On 3 December 1943, Warnock informed Dublin by telegraph: 'In spite of strenuous efforts everything lost except code and key(s) of Bag 1 typewriter also saved. I have lost much clothing and most of my personal effects but escaped injury except for inflammation of the eyes caused during our fight against the flames'.[43]

In the interests of security the code was considered one of the most important things to save. However, the Irish cipher 'dearg' [red] was obsolete, which some diplomats knew, although it was used up to at least 1954.[44] From mid-1941 cryptanalysts were able to break Irish diplomatic cable traffic from the missions in Europe and the United States.[45] The Germans too were able to read whatever they wished.[46] These telegrams formed part of a wide range of intercepts and according to O'Halpin found their way to Churchill's table.[47] It is likely that Cremin knew the code was obsolete, which made his reporting from Berlin all the more courageous.[48]

Warnock's staying on posed a difficulty for the department of finance whose estimates did not allow for two officers in Berlin. The legation was telegraphed: 'Cremin would get the allowance when you left, can't give allowance to both of you. Have you and Cremin any suggestions on this point.'[49] With great Oliver Twist-like boldness Cremin suggested: 'As regards allowance would suggest that Finance should in the exceptional circumstances be asked to sanction some kind of subsistence allowance at least as long as children elsewhere [Cremin's children had not joined them yet] and in view of very high cost of living in France.'[50] Warnock, emboldened, requested a £200 motorcar allowance, because he was using his car solely for official purposes.[51] The results of their requests are not recorded.

On 13 January 1944, Warnock wrote: 'I must have a rest of some kind and I am in great need of clothing, etc. owing to my losses in connection with the air-raid.' Warnock feared that the opening of the second front would only be a matter of months and that it would destroy all his chances of returning home.[52] He at least got some relief when the Irish minister in Berne, F.T. Cremins, sent a shaving kit to him and rubber stamps to the legation.[53] The latter were vital for bureaucracy in the Third Reich.[54] It was not until 28 February 1944 that Warnock left Berlin for Dublin, via Lisbon.

Life in Berlin

The first issue Cremin had to deal with was that of compensation for the legation.[55] The legation was valued at £4,150.18s.6d.[56] In early January the Irish government requested compensation from the Berlin government, as the building was on their territory.[57] Some progress was achieved by August 1944, when Cremin reported: 'compensation for property is proceeding slowly' but the 'German government has accepted liability'. He pursued the claim until 1 February 1945, when the foreign office official, Steengracht, signed the compensation agreement.[58] This was one of Cremin's last official acts in Berlin as the Soviet armies prepared to strike, but the issue was not finally settled until 1958 when the West German government admitted liability and paid £327,000 compensation for all bomb damage to Irish property during the war.[59]

Cremin's posting to Berlin coincided with the beginning of the heaviest allied bombing raids on Berlin.[60] However, Cremin and his family were fortunate in that they did not have to stay in the city. He tried to complete all his work in Berlin on one day during the week and so in that way conserve petrol and minimise the risk.[61] The only official entertainment was diplomatic lunches given at the Adlon Hotel each Wednesday. Cremin related: 'It was not at all [that] uncommon to see P.G. Wodehouse at that time rambling through the Adlon. He had been picked up in France on the outbreak of the war, but appeared to enjoy a lot of latitude as regards his movements.'[62] These diplomatic lunches sometimes coincided with the weekly visit of the United States army airforce. Cremin was able to give a detailed description of the egg-shaped bunker in the Adlon Hotel, formed, no doubt, during the many anxious hours spent down there.[63] At night of course there was always the danger of being bombed by the RAF. Cremin recorded a lucky escape in Bremen when some bombs landed next to the cellar where they were sheltering.[64]

Life in Berlin was unbearable; residents were often unable to distinguish between day and night, with thousands of incendiary bombs falling every day.[65] Cremin left the following account of the air raid on Berlin on 21 June 1944:

> [it] was manifestly heaviest American raid to date. Some here say that it was as bad as raids on November 22 and November 23. A cloud of smoke and dust over the city all day Wednesday gave impression of continuous twilight. After raid population seemed rather nervous but by 23 June when I was again in Berlin life seemed to be just as usual apart from certain disturbance in transport.[66]

The dangers that Cremin faced were considerable. His daughter Creeda recalled her mother mentioning 'seeing people who had been set alight by phosphorous bombs'.[67]

Cremin's Political Reports

Cremin sent reports back to Dublin on political developments from the perspective of the German government. He related later that 'the diplomatic corps was herded together and treated with contempt'.[68] He did not have any contact with leading Nazis and recounted that the only time he saw Hitler was in July 1932 at a Nazi rally in Munich, where he was within three paces of him. He only once met the Nazi foreign minister, Ribbentrop, in Paris in 1938.[69]

As the diplomat of a small peripheral European state one would expect Cremin's information to be based on minor sources within the Nazi state. This, however, was not the case. One can glean that

Cremin's information came from mid to high-ranking officials within the foreign office, other colleagues within the diplomatic corps and members of the German aristocracy. As a professional diplomat he rarely gave names, unless they were foreign office officials, which was a further indication of his lack of faith in the code.[70]

In March 1944, Cremin initially rejected the suggestion that the Finns were attempting to negotiate an end to the conflict with the Soviets.[71] Several days later he qualified this by stating that Finland might make a separate peace with Russia but:

> Italian precedent implies in the event of a Russo-Finnish peace German troops would resist. The feeling amongst colleagues is that Finland anxious not to close door to negotiations and that Germany powerless to do anything to prevent them.[72]

On 22 March, Cremin reported that the Finns had rejected the peace deal offered by the Soviets.[73] The Finns walked a knife-edge between the Soviets and the Nazis throughout the Continuation War which followed the Winter War of 1939–40, and by September 1944 managed to extricate themselves from the tangled alliance. They managed to retain domestic independence after the war, unlike all of central Europe.[74]

On 27 March 1944, Cremin reported on the Nazi annexation of Hungary: Operation Margarenthe. The German press justified the occupation as eliminating 'anti-German tendencies provoked by Jews and to concentrate all Hungarian force for prosecution of war. *Völkischer Beobachter* says Jews had begun to influence governing circles and were intriguing with hostile Hungarian émigrés'.[75] The Hungarian prime minister, Nicholas Kallay, had been attempting to negotiate a separate peace ever since the armistice granted to Italy in September 1943.[76] Cremin informed Dublin: 'It is quite possible political grounds did play some part in occupation of Hungary, as there had already been criticism of Hungarian government's tolerance in certain respects, e.g. Jews, presence of many Poles and of escaped prisoners of war.'[77] The invasion of Hungary led to the appointment of Dr Veesenmayer as reich minister in Budapest. Veesenmayer was the foreign office official in charge of most Irish matters, including attempting to organise a coup d'état in 1940 in Ireland with the backing of the IRA. Dr Veesenmayer oversaw the deportation of 570,000 of Hungary's 825,000 Jews from March to November 1944.[78] The invasion and occupation of Hungary resulted in the transport and murder of the last bastion of the European Jews.

The landings of the allies on 23 January 1944, north of Rome at Anzio, threatened Rome for the next six months. On 12 March, Pius XII appealed for Rome to be spared, and was closely followed by a similar appeal by de Valera.[79] In April, Cremin acted as a conduit for the 'US note' which stipulated the conditions for the German evacuation of Rome.[80] During April and May 1944, Cremin conveyed the Irish government's concern over Rome and was part of the effort to set up a neutrality commission to spare Rome from their hostilities.[81] In May the commission concept was abandoned and on 3 June 1944 Rome was declared an Open City, as Paris had been in 1940.[82]

The Nazi press reported the fall of Rome on 6 June 1944 as 'being of no military value' and Cremin stated 'general opinion last September was that German main lines of defence are well to the north of Rome'. The Germans had prepared their main defensive line (the Gothic line) along the Arno River through Florence.[83] 'De Valera's initiative to prevent the bombing of Rome had strengthened the "special relationship" between the Holy See and Ireland'.[84]

The second front was opened in Normandy on 6 June 1944. The Germans knew that the opening of the second front would take place in 1944. On 17 April 1944, Cremin reported on the imminence of an invasion of western Europe by the allies, and in early May he stated that in an interview with two foreign office officials both had said that the allied invasion would fail.[85] Cremin reported that a contact in the foreign office thought that the sooner the invasion came the better, because the best German troops were being kept in the west.[86] Cremin prophesised the opening of the second front to a Swiss colleague, much to his own advantage:

I remember at one lunch given by the Countess Dohna there were quite a few diplomats present and the date was the 5 June 1944. In the course of [a] conversation a friend of mine from the Swiss embassy asked me when I thought the invasion would take place. Although I naturally had no information at all I suggested within the next couple of days. In fact as we know it began the following day and my standing with my Swiss colleague soared enormously when the event happened.[87]

The German press reacted to the Normandy invasion with the delusive assertion that a 'decisive phase of the war has now been reached and Germany has within her power attainment of final victory'. The supposedly impregnable Atlantic Wall was reclassified not as an 'impassable barrier but [was] to obstruct landing sufficiently to give time to arrange for counter-measures'.[88] Hitler himself was at the western front trying to boost the morale of his generals.[89] It was, however, too late, and a contact in the foreign office stated to Cremin that the allies had landed twenty-five divisions in Normandy (half of the actual figure).[90] The weight of the allies' industrial might was now being decisively felt.[91]

Two weeks before the July Bomb Plot, Cremin reported that he understood from well-informed colleagues that the government was seriously preoccupied by the military situation and that 'many individual Germans are convinced that all is lost'.[92] Cremin noted that 'The admission publicly by [Hitler] that things are not going well at present is interesting', although German foreign office officials were still optimistic.[93] Cremin's contact ridiculed the idea that political moves were needed in Germany. They still hoped that the British would compromise even at this late stage. Cremin indicated that official policy was that Germany would fight to the end.[94] The allied demand for unconditional surrender was a political miscalculation in that it gave Goebbels a propaganda tool of great value, which explained the obstinacy of the individual German soldier.[95]

The July Bomb Plot, 20 July 1944

The military situation, coupled with a growing abhorrence to Nazism, spurred conspirators to attempt the assassination of Hitler. Led by Baron Claus von Stauffenberg, the July bomb plot of 20 July 1944 was an attempt to wrest power back from the Nazis.[96] On 22 July 1944, Cremin accurately reported the failed assassination attempt against Hitler and correctly argued that the party could still control the country and that there was not any evidence of unrest. He went on to report that: 'the armies abroad are in more independent position. Much seems to depend on how deep the movement has gone among the officers in the field. The most serious defection at home is probably that of Fromm, head of the reserve and as such controlling millions of men. I understand he has been arrested'.[97] The British intercepted this report and it was passed to Winston Churchill, who marked the following section:

> One aspect of the matter is that the Germans are now justified in believing on evidence of presumably competent officers rather than foreign propaganda that the military situation is very serious. This attempt was, I think, a complete surprise to officials. The secretary of state, when he was out here Wednesday night, clearly had no inkling of the plot.[98]

One of the reasons that the British were interested in the Irish diplomat's reports was that as late as 14 July 1944 they did not believe in 'the existence of an anti-Hitler movement'.[99] Cremin's independent report was highly valued by the British.[100]

In Dublin, on 28 July 1944, Warnock added a handwritten note to the file stating Fromm was 'regarded as being very modest and retiring ... I did not get the impression that he was the kind of man who would get mixed up in a revolt'. Warnock warned that: 'If he was actively involved, the conspiracy was more serious than I had thought. It is possible however that he was removed from office as a sort of scapegoat in view of the fact that he had not exercised sufficient supervision.' Soon, Cremin gave a very accurate report for the motivation behind the organisation of the bomb plot:

One explanation I have however, from fairly well-informed non-party source is that plot was organised for purely military reasons by small group of officers in or close to headquarters who blame Hitler for having withdrawn troops too late on several occasions especially in Stalingrad, Crimea and Odessa with a loss of several thousand men.[101]

Major-General F.W. von Mellenthin certainly blamed Hitler for constantly refusing to retreat in time.[102] Cremin telegraphed: 'A party member of the propaganda ministry told me episode is being deliberately used as pretext to introduce various changes, net result of which would be to make party still more identical with the state.' He thought that the bomb plot would not lead to a weakening of German defences. Cremin concluded that Hitler would never negotiate with the Soviets and this might have partly motivated the conspiracy.[103]

On 11 August 1944, Cremin reported to Dublin that:

I think it is quite certain that German government intend neither to capitulate nor to come to terms and failure of recent plot coupled with installation of party men in key army posts is likely to make any organised opposition movement impossible even in army. Hitler said to party leaders 4th August that he is essential to Germany as your government require a man who will under no circumstances capitulate. They have called up youths of 14 years to Helsinki for fortifying eastern frontier.[104]

The only inaccurate report Cremin sent from Berlin was about the concept of 'Southern Redoubt' – the fabled fortified positions in Bavaria from where the Nazis could continue the war, if necessary – which he felt was plausible because the 'government is more than ever based on party rather than nation since June'.[105] This preoccupied British and US strategists towards the end of the war, although it appeared solely in diplomatic and other reports, and it might have led the western allies to a more cautious advance into Germany. Hitler had indeed given orders for this Southern Redoubt to be built, but nothing was ever constructed.[106] This report was also shown to Churchill.[107]

As the autumn approached Cremin reported that the Arnhem battle, the failed attempt by the British under Montgomery to capture the bridges over the Rhine (Operation Market Garden), was being 'saluted as an important victory and the relative spectacle at the present time [on the] western front [seems to me to] prove German ability to [resist] successfully. All official pronouncements are a reiteration of German will not to give in [sic]'.[108] This report was evidently looked at with interest by the British authorities, who continued to consider that Germany was capable of a vigorous resistance.[109]

Within the Nazi state a rumour was circulating that Hitler was suffering severe nerve damage. Cremin reported this along with the belief that Heinrich Himmler had come to the fore. A new law decreed that Nazi party members could remain active even when in the military.[110] This was a serious diminution of the independence of the army. Later that month, Cremin suggested that Himmler might be trying to make peace, but thought it unlikely that Himmler would push Hitler aside.[111] In reality, Hitler had so structured the government that it was virtually impossible for an internal putsch against him.

On 20 December 1944, Cremin reported on the Russo-Franco pact and the beginnings of an ideological civil war in Greece. 'These events cannot fail to nourish pet theory of leaders here that coalition may break up while there is still time for Germany to profit'. He also reported that there was a rumour of an agreement with the Russians.[112] Cremin continued to report the German peace initiative toward Russia until late 1944, when it ultimately collapsed. The fact that Cremin had access to information close to the centre of Nazi decision-making shows the high quality of his sources.

On 24 December 1944, eight days after Hitler launched the Ardennes offensive, also known as the Battle of the Bulge, which saw the German army drive toward Antwerp, Cremin reported that:

Colleague who has many sources of information tells me he has good reason to believe that military aims of offensive are limited and relatively modest, that objective sought is primarily political, and that, should the offensive succeed, Germans might make some kind of peace move.[113]

The Germans' main aim was to capture Antwerp, while the secondary one was to capture a large number of troops. The diplomatic aim was the hope of destroying the US, British and Soviet alliance.[114] Cremin analysed his colleague's deductions as follows:

I think the explanation is, in general, probable: it seems to me this must be objective of all German military operations in the future, as I do not think leaders here, apart from Hitler perhaps, really believe Germany can now impose her terms on her opponents by force of arms and her aim must therefore be to see that they do not impose theirs on her. I think, however, that, even if present offensive succeeds in sense that Germans can reach and maintain their goal, it may not be immediately followed by diplomatic initiative, as situation on Russian front must first, it seems to me, become less unfavourable to Germany either by definite stabilisation of whole front at some point or by German victory, and such an improvement, if possible at all (as some here think it is) will take time.[115]

On 14 January 1945, Cremin reported Hitler's New Year speech, which he stated finally dispelled rumours that Hitler had been pushed aside. On the outcome of the Battle of the Bulge, a foreign office source had confirmed to Cremin that Antwerp had been the objective, but that two million tons of supplies had been lost, including 1,600 planes and 700 tanks.[116] The Battle of the Bulge squandered the last major offensive capability of the German army and after this the political and military reports were essentially secondary to Cremin's main reason for staying in Germany which was to look after the wellbeing of Irish citizens.

The Jewish Question

During his time in Berlin, Cremin worked assiduously to intervene on behalf of some of Europe's Jews. His absence of prejudice
and his professionalism were important in the attempt made by
the Irish legation to protect some European Jews from extermina-
tion. Irish diplomats in Berlin were in an unenviable position in
that they had to appear to be neutral and were unable to be officially critical of the Nazis' Jewish policy. Cremin probably knew
that his actions were futile in the face of the machinery of the
Nazi state but it is also probable that he felt it was important to
place the words and actions of Nazi officials on the record. In all
of his reports from Berlin Cremin rarely uses names except when
it comes to the Jewish question. The frankness of his reports put
paid to the suggestion that Cremin was anyway anti-Semitic: had
he been so these reports would simply not exist.

In early November 1943, Walshe telegraphed Warnock with
the inquiry: 'Have been informed that Jews holding visas from
neutral countries are exempted from deportation and bad treatment. Is this true? I have been asked to give visas to a number of
named Jews from Holland and Belgium as a protection'.[117] Acting
on a telegram sent in mid-December by Isaac Herzog, the former
chief rabbi of Ireland and a personal friend of de Valera, de Valera
instructed Walshe to cable Seán Murphy in Vichy to inquire about
procuring exit visas.

On 28 December 1943, Murphy reported that the German
authorities would not accept French intervention on behalf of foreign Jews in France and suggested that Ireland should contact the
German government directly.[118] In January 1944, Walshe inquired
whether '200 Polish Jewish families … and … 500 Christian children' would be allowed exit visas to come to Ireland.[119] In early
1944, Warnock and Cremin suggested the issues of the Christian
children and Jews should be kept separate: 'You will … appreciate that German authorities are inclined to regard action by other
countries as indirect criticism of their Jewish policy'.[120] In mid-
February 1944, the department suggested that emphasis should
be given to the visas for the Christian children.[121] By March 1944,

Cremin felt able to state: 'Definite reply not yet received but understand from official … unlikely Christian children will be granted visas and more unlikely that Jewish families will.'[122] Cremin confirmed soon after:

Visas for children refused. As regards Jews have been asked by internal affairs section of foreign office why we want them to go to Ireland whether it is intended that they become citizens or only remain there until the end of the war and whether any of them have relatives there. I gather no hope of visas except for such families as have relatives and even then I think little chance. Official concerned inclined to read political implications into our inquiry thinking it had something to do with Anglo-American refugee schemes.[123]

On 24 March 1944, Cremin telegraphed Dublin that the German authorities were anxious to know what would happen to the Jews if they went to Ireland. According to the unidentified official:

If it was intended that these families should become Irish citizens the German authorities would, I was given to understand, '*gladly save us the inconvenience of having so many Jews*' [Cremin's emphasis]; if on the other hand it was proposed that the families return to Europe after the end of the war it could be inferred that a German defeat was presupposed; if it was intended that they should later go to Palestine, the German government could not approve of an arrangement which would have for result to introduce further Jewish elements into an Arab territory.[124]

Having read the subtext of this statement, the department could not be in any doubt that European Jews were being exterminated. Cremin emphasised: 'I have thought it best to give you the above account of this interview so that you may see how enquiries touching on the Jewish question can be made to assume enormous proportions in the minds of certain German officials.'[125] Cremin went on to state that department II in the foreign office had the final word when it came to issuing exit visas for Jews.[126] Having consulted with his Swiss colleagues Cremin said it was the practice of the Swiss not to grant a Swiss entry visa until a German exit visa was already issued.[127]

On 20 April 1944, Cremin received a request from Walshe and de Valera asking if the granting of Irish entry visas would prevent the deportation of Jewish children from the internment camp at Vittel in France.[128] Cremin replied on 22 April that he had already made representations and asked if Walshe had taken cognisance of his 24 March telegram.[129]

In April 1944, Cremin was lied to by a foreign office official who said that 'persons interned [in] Vittel were not to be deported'.[130] Two weeks later Cremin was lied to again when he was informed that the Jews in Vittel had been moved to a deportation camp in France, but was assured that: 'The deportation had been suspended pending [the] decision on our démarche'.[131] On 6 June 1944, Dublin informed Cremin that the Vittel Jews had been transported to the notorious Drancy transit camp, from where over 100,000 Jews were deported during the course of the war.[132] In July Cremin reported to Dublin that: 'the 200 Polish families you have in mind cannot be traced [and] there were 77 individual Polish Jews in Vittel who are now in camp in eastern Europe'.[133] Cremin was told by Eberhard von Thadden, head of department II of the foreign office, that the 'German authorities have been treating application with all possible good will because it comes from Ireland'.[134] On 27 August 1944, Cremin telegraphed:

> Official of Swiss legation dealing with this question has now told me that there were originally 238 such Jews in Vittel; of these 163 removed in April … in May some escaped some committed suicide. He says that the total in Vittel when he was there last month was 14.[135]

On 29 August 1944, Cremin was further able to report that the foreign office had informed him that the Drancy camp was disbanded and that 'the FO doesn't know if they were set at liberty or not'.[136] The camp at Drancy was disbanded on 15 August 1944, when the last wagon left with fifty-one deportees. On 5 October 1944, von Thadden told him that an inquiry had been sent to the authorities of Oswiecim/Auschwitz but no other reply had been received.[137] The authorities at Auschwitz did not get back to Cremin.[138]

In October, Cremin was asked to ascertain the veracity of a 'rumour [which] has reached the Jewish community in Dublin that the Germans plan to exterminate all Jews. Request for assurances from the FO'.[139] Cremin was informed that:

> … rumour of intention to exterminate the Jews being spread by various enemy sources but that as it is pure invention and lacks all foundation the German authorities have no reason to make a statement on the subject. [The official] added that he feels sure that if the camps in question were to be abandoned their inmates would be evacuated and not killed as Germany would have no interest in losing their labour contribution. It is unlikely that we will get any more formal declaration on this subject.[140]

In spite of this statement, Cremin presented an aide-mémoire on the plight of the Hungarian Jews to the foreign office and was informed bluntly that:

> Foreign office in any case could not accept our (nor Swiss) démarche as we have 'no justification for interfering' the persons concerned not being Irish having no Irish connections etc. My Aide-Mémoire was therefore handed back to me.[141]

On 23 December 1944, he reported that Dr Zehnder of the Swiss legation believed that: 'In particular that the USA have been using the Jewish question as a propaganda stick with which to beat the Germans' and that in response 1,300 Hungarian Jews were deposited on the Swiss frontier, by the Germans.[142] On 28 December 1944, while the Battle of the Bulge raged, Cremin reported that the Germans were attempting to exchange with the allies: 'Jews for German nationals and that the German government is currently selling Jews at the rate of $1,000 each'.[143] This is indicative of the

Nazis' desire to get hard capital before the final collapse.

After January 1945 the file ended. It is clear that Cremin did try repeatedly to break through the deception of *Nacht und Nebel* (Night and Fog) that obscured the Holocaust from the outside world, all the time knowing that his reports were being read by the Germans.[144] However unsuccessful his attempts to obtain visas were, he did uphold the honour of the Irish state in constantly confronting the Nazi state about the deportation of Jews and he bore witness to the Holocaust. Not all Irish citizens were as troubled by the inhumanity of the Nazi regime and, indeed, many worked actively to promote their own and Nazi interests, over the interests of the Irish state.

Irish Nationals Collaborating with the Nazis

The three most prominent of these nationals were Francis Stuart, Frank Ryan and Charles Bewley. They were ostensibly 'Irish advisors occasionally referred to by Himmler and Ribbentrop'.[145] Charles Bewley was mainly active in Italy and did not come into contact much with the Berlin legation.

Frank Ryan was a senior IRA activist who had fought in Spain during the Spanish Civil War on the republican side, where he was captured and sentenced to death for presiding over firing squads.[146] The Irish foreign minister in Spain, Leopold Kerney, had been instrumental in Ryan's 'escape' on 25 July 1940. The Germans, interested in him for his republican contacts, took Ryan to Paris and then to Berlin where he met Seán Russell (chief-of-staff of the IRA). In mid-August Veesenmayer, the head of the Irish section of the foreign office, arranged for the two men to go to Ireland by submarine. Seán Russell died at sea, while Ryan chose to return to Germany rather than continue his mission to Ireland.[147] It has been argued that Ryan's sole desire was to return to Ireland; if this was so, why did he not land in Ireland and give himself up to the authorities and possibly be interned? I believe his failure to do so indicates that he did indeed intend to continue working against the interests of the Irish state. In Germany, Ryan lived under the pseudonym of Frank Richard and agreed to participate in making

German broadcasts to Ireland in 1944. However, ill-health prevented him from doing so.

Francis Stuart, a friend of Ryan's, wrote that around December 1943 he went to inform the chargé d'affaires in Berlin of Ryan's illness, in an effort to get him back to Ireland.[148] 'When I called there to put the whole matter before them I found the building bombed and in ruins. The legation had left Berlin and before I could trace it in the growing confusion Frank was too ill for any practical purpose to be served by carrying the matter further.'[149]

The Irish legation's file on Ryan opened on 6 April 1944, when the department of external affairs pressed Cremin to locate Frank Ryan and try to meet him.[150] It was, however, Easter and many government departments were closed.[151] Unbeknownst to Cremin, Ryan died on 10 June 1944; Elizabeth Clissmann, a prominent republican activist, wrote to Leopold Kerney, the Irish minister in Spain, to let him know that Ryan had died but the letter did not arrive until December 1944. Seán Cronin wrote that this was 'on order of an official at the foreign office named Weber who did not want the Irish government informed about Frank's death'.[152] This is unlikely as Weber had taken over the Irish section previously controlled by Dr Veesenmayer and:

> … had no idea that Frank Ryan was the same person as Frank Richard to whom he regularly sent special ration cards and for whom he had finally arranged an ambulance. As a result he told Dr Cremin that he had no information about a man of the name Frank Ryan.[153]

One foreign office official informed Cremin that 'all he knew about Ryan was that he was a communist.'[154] On 20 December 1944, Dublin told Cremin that Frank Ryan had died on 10 June 1944. Walshe displayed his distinct administrative style and anti-communism stating:

> … we know that he was in Germany for most of the time prior to his death. It is better for everybody that we should be able to give details as to illness and death otherwise communists in Britain and America

sure to concoct false story to explain mystery of international brigade going over to the Germans.[155]

By 4 January 1945, Cremin reported that:

Dr Weber ... seemed very sceptical about the allegation that the German Secret Service had something to do with Ryan's escape in Spain and his coming to Germany, and he said he did not understand what interest the Germans could have in a 'communist'. I called his attention to the fact that in 1940 Germany and Russia were on good terms and gave it as my opinion that Ryan might have been of interest to the Germans not qua communist but qua Irish nationalist.[156]

It took until 18 February 1945, when Francis Stuart confirmed that Ryan and Richards were the same person, for Cremin to close the file.[157] Taking this evidence with the testimony of Elizabeth Clissmann, Cremin reported that Ryan's 'death is virtually certain'.[158]

*

Francis Stuart, the novelist, went to Germany in 1939, ostensibly to take up a university post, but also to act as a courier for the IRA. Stuart was employed by the Germans as a scriptwriter for William Joyce, Lord Haw-Haw, but was quickly dropped because of their incompatibility.[159] Stuart soon settled into life in Berlin and in 1940:

... gave a party on St Patrick's Day in a hotel, to which he invited various members of foreign diplomatic corps ... Stuart also particularly asked Warnock, the Irish chargé d'affaires, because he wanted him to notice that he was establishing his own identity, and knew quite well that Warnock would report his activities to Dublin. Warnock had an awkward relationship with Stuart who was closer to his secretary, Eileen Walsh. The three socialised together and later in the summer, swam and played golf, but Eileen Walsh kept Stuart informed about Warnock's thoughts about him.[160] [This early file did not survive the bombing.]

Throughout the war Stuart worked as a broadcaster for Irland-Redaktion, the German radio propaganda service to Ireland. Dan Bryan, director of G2, Irish military intelligence, summarised Stuart's activities thus: 'I am convinced that he was active in the German-IRA conspiracy from at least the outbreak of the war but see no hope of producing any legal evidence to that effect'.[161]

Stuart met Cremin on 27 August 1942, when Cremin informed him of the decision not to renew his passport.[162] Stuart argued that because he was issued a visa to leave Ireland he should have been given a choice to either return home or renew his passport. Cremin replied: 'I explained to Mr Stuart that he had, as a national, no inherent right to receive a passport and that the government is free to act in regard to passports as it sees fit, taking into account of circumstances.'[163] Stuart did not help his own position by going against Fianna Fáil and supporting the opposition because of de Valera's treatment of the IRA.[164]

In late April 1944, Stuart again asked to regain his passport.[165] Walshe informed Cremin: 'For your information only Stuart's passport should not be renewed. For yourself he is regarded as having forfeited any claims to our diplomatic protection by un-neutral and disloyal behaviour'.[166] In September 1944, Stuart and his lover (although in keeping with the conventions of the time Cremin described her as Stuart's secretary) left Berlin in the hope of eventually finding their way out of Germany. They went first to Munich and stayed there until February.[167] On 24 February 1945, Stuart wrote to Cremin from Munich and asked if Cremin would write him a note using the death of Frank Ryan as a pretext to allow him to travel to meet Cremin.[168] Cremin decided to help him, wrote the note and Stuart travelled to Bregenz in Austria.[169]

'Bregenz was a major disappointment, for although they met Cremin of the Irish legation, he only offered a good meal'.[170] On 28 March 1945, Cremin telegraphed Dublin relaying that: 'Francis Stuart has again raised with me the question of the renewal of his passport. Mr Stuart states that he is anxious to return to Ireland and has for this purpose applied for a Swiss transit visa.'[171] However, in light of the instructions given to Cremin on 1 June 1944,

Stuart was officially beyond the Pale of Irish diplomatic protection.[172] Stuart's biographer stated:

> Stuart decided to move closer to the Swiss border in hope of crossing into the neutral country. They travelled by train and foot to Lindau on Lake Constance … It was some time later, after Miss Meissner [Stuart's lover] had found lodgings in Dornbirn, just south of Lake Constance and across the unmarked Austrian frontier, that there was a semblance of stability. She and Stuart were there when Germany surrendered in May 1945.[173]

Dermot Keogh relates that: 'Stuart turned up in Paris in August 1945 and presented himself at the Irish legation. Boland instructed Seán Murphy to give him £15. He was left in no doubt that "his conduct in 1940, at a particularly dangerous moment of our history", had not been forgotten in Dublin.'[174] In early November 1945, Stuart and Meissner were arrested by French troops for questioning and were held until July 1946.[175] Two years after the war, Stuart wrote: 'I came under suspicion not because I was a Nazi, which God knows I never was, but because I was not on any side.' However some might argue 'that being in Berlin and broadcasting on Irland-Redaktion are proof enough of culpability'.[176] There were additional factors, as Dan Bryan wrote:

> I have seen a report from a North of Ireland man who was trained as an agent by the Germans and later met Francis Stuart when they were both employed in Radio Luxembourg. The man told Stuart of his espionage activities and Stuart approved of them. Stuart was still quite anxious that contact should be made with the IRA and gave him information about Russell's and Ryan's abortive attempt to reach Ireland in a submarine. Stuart further indicated to him that if Russell's and Ryan's submarine mission was a success he, Stuart, was later to follow them with a cargo of arms. I am convinced that the gentleman was telling the truth because a good deal of the information he gave was already known to us.[177]

Bryan concluded:

> I would be glad to have a long talk with Stuart if your department is successful in having him returned to this country. Further, an explanation of his activities while abroad should in my opinion be made a condition of any assistance rendered to him.[178]

However, Dan Bryan was forced to admit:

> I was looking into this man's case and find that we have no legal evidence on any point associating him with illegal activities directed against this country. In fact the only point on which there is clear evidence is about his broadcast activities. His history and associations are, however of a very suspicious nature.[179]

Stuart tried to reinvent himself throughout his life, but his German interlude was to mar his career. In 1997, Máire Cruise O'Brien resigned from Aosdána when he was nominated.[180]

Dealings with Irish Nationals

In his memoirs Cremin related: 'Our official concerns [in Berlin] were mainly with trying to ensure proper treatment for Irish nationals and pursuing claims for damage to Irish property'.[181] These activities were important in raising the profile of the department of external affairs at home. They did however entail a huge amount of work for the officials. The 1944 annual report stated there were ninety Irish nationals within the reich and with whom Cremin was in contact.[182] Owing to the large number of cases it is necessary to concentrate on two individual cases which employed a lot of the legation's time, those of Mary Cummins and Robert Vernon.

Irish nationals who fell foul of the German authorities were in a disadvantageous position in that 'the Swiss could get information quickly as they had the right to correspond directly with and see the internees whereas we apparently had not and must pass through the foreign office'.[183] Mary Cummins and Robert Vernon illustrate this point; they had been sentenced to death and the legation worked hard to get them pardoned. In his memoirs, Cremin noted the case of Mary Cummins:

> She had … been condemned to death but we finally succeeded in getting her released. She was released in Chemnitz and one day I went there from Berlin to fetch her. She was not well at the time and stayed with us in Staffelde.[184]

This laconic account belies the intricacies and efforts that Cremin went to in order to help her. The case began on 1 February 1943, when his predecessor in Berlin, Warnock, reported that he was unable to ascertain the particulars of the Mary Cummins trial.[185] By May 1943, he had ascertained that she was in the woman's prison in Amrath.[186] In July 1943, she was moved to Lübeck.[187] After Warnock departed for Ireland, Cremin took up the case and in April 1944, Cremin wrote to the prison to inquire after Mary Cummins.[188] He requested a visit with her but was told that he would have to wait for official authorisation.[189] He subsequently argued with the foreign office official Dr Geheimrat Sethe that the Irish government was not of the view that its nationals should go unpunished but it was of the view that they should know the details. Dr Sethe replied that the German government did not give details of espionage cases. Cremin retorted that the reliability of the Irish government in terms of confidentiality was without question.[190]

In September 1944, the foreign office informed Cremin that 'it was not usual to expect from a belligerent power details of espionage trials which are secret on grounds of security'. Cummins' guilt rested 'largely on her own admission'. She had been moved to Cottbus, seventy-five miles from Berlin, and permission to visit her was now granted.[191] At the end of September 1944, Cremin visited Cummins, but was not allowed to ask questions about the trial.

> She does not look strong to me. She says however her health is generally speaking good but that she does not get enough to eat and is consequently somewhat weak. It is not permitted to send such pris-

oners food or clothing but I propose to raise the question with the foreign office.[192]

In October, Dr Sethe agreed that he would improve Cummins' clothing allowance.[193] By mid-November, he informed Cremin that the Cummins case was being reviewed.[194] By 29 November 1944, Cremin reported that Cummins was to be released.[195] After persistent requests Cremin was informed in mid-January 1945 that:

> the case had been completely neglected by the official in Torgau to whom the file in connection with the release was passed. That official had let the file lie on his desk for several weeks believing that it was just one of the several thousand pardon applications which were before the Kriegsgericht and not realising that this was an exceptional case inspired largely, as Herr von Schonebeck put it, by 'political considerations'.[196]

Finally on 17 January 1945, Cremin reported that Cummins was released and was now staying with the Cremin family.[197]

> Cummins is now much stronger and quite well. She admits being guilty of charge … She says that she belonged to organisation financed from London and working in co-operation with Brit Intel [British Intelligence] Service and French 2nd Bureau and that her motives for so acting were fundamentally charitable and to some extent financial. I intend to take her with us if possible.[198]

Cummins stayed with the Cremin household until the end of the war and was employed doing domestic work.[199] The fact that she was part of Cremin's household made it easier for him to bring her through Switzerland, because she would have been seen as a 'domestic' and not worthy of official scrutiny.[200]

Another case in which the Irish legation were successful in getting the death sentence commuted was that of Robert Vernon. Robert Vernon had been 'imprisoned for an unspecific affair with others apparently awaiting trial by military court'.[201] In October

1943, Warnock was instructed to employ a solicitor on Vernon's behalf.[202] By December 1943, Cremin and Warnock had ascertained that Vernon was condemned to death; 'Vernon's lawyer cannot give details of case without formal sanction'. They suggested to Walshe: 'You might also consider requesting German minister to impress on his government serious view which would be taken of execution of Irish national until at least we are satisfied that evidence justifies sentence.'[203] Vernon's lawyer believed that he had had a fair trial, however, they found that 'Enquiries here show Vernon to be a person of childish mentality virtually case of arrested development. Idea of his being dangerous spy is incredible.'[204] On 11 January 1944, the legation made use of the rescue of German sailors by the Irish coaster, the *Kerlogue:* 'I emphasised the good impression that clemency in this case would have.'[205] On 7 March 1944, the under secretaries replied:

> … while not about to give firm assurance it is probable that sentence will be definitely commuted … He said however there were really serious grounds against Vernon and that if he were German he would have been executed at once.[206]

Cremin's intervention succeeded in having Vernon's case re-examined and he was informed that 'the sentence would not be carried out until re-examination is complete'.[207] A month later the case was still being examined.[208]

In July 1944, Vernon wrote to Cremin that he was in good health and apologised for all the difficulties that he was causing the legation.[209] That September, Cremin was instructed to make an interim payment to Vernon's lawyer to keep him on.[210] Cremin was informed verbally by Dr Weber that: 'German authorities are prepared to exchange Vernon for an equal number of German *"politisch belastet"* [political prisoners]'. Only three Irish nationals could be involved in this exchange: 'Vernon, Cummins and Armstrong'.[211] That December 1944, Cremin admitted to Dr Weber that he had known Vernon slightly, having seen him in Paris on several occasions in 1940:

… that my impression is that if he was guilty of espionage activities it was without any deliberate intention to work against Germany but probably because of the system governing allowances to Irish nationals in France during the war his monthly allowance which may have been sufficient in the first year or so after the armistice and that was inadequate later on to keep him in the lifestyle which he was used to. Vernon's temptation was on financial grounds.[212]

The foreign office must have been convinced by Cremin's case and on 15 January 1945 they suggested that Vernon and Armstrong be exchanged for the ten German agents in Ireland, lest the Irishmen be killed accidentally in the closing months of the war. Cremin passed on the suggestion to the department.[213] At the end of February the foreign office still suggested a swap.[214] The offer must have been rejected in Dublin as it would have brought unwarranted attention to Irish neutrality. Vernon was 'killed during one of the bombardments in Stuttgart'.[215]

In both the Cummins and Vernon cases Cremin succeeded in having their death sentences commuted through assiduous and continued pressure on the German government. He did not stay too much longer in Berlin, having to remove himself from the advancing hostilities for the second time in five years.

The End of the War in Europe and Cremin's 'Strategic Withdrawal' from the Path of the Red Army

As the Third Reich collapsed on all fronts the remnants of the diplomatic community in Germany made arrangements to leave the country. In August 1944, de Valera and Walshe gave Cremin complete discretion on when he thought it necessary to leave Germany.[216] On 28 October 1944, Walshe ordered Cremin to leave for Switzerland.[217] Cremin, however, in defiance of this order, gave his opinion as the diplomat on the ground, stating that he would leave when the situation merited it.[218]

To prevent a reissuing of the order of 28 October, Cremin informed Walshe that the nuncio, Mgr Cesare Orsenigo, was remaining in Berlin as he considered leaving would be tantamount to a split between Germany and the Vatican.[219] This statement would have had a great resonance with Walshe, as Cremin would have known from his personal involvement in the Walshe-Murphy conflict after the fall of France in 1940.[220] However, from the perspective of political reports there was no reason why Cremin should have stayed, as their value was diminishing to Ireland. Yet, in terms of Ireland's policy of neutrality, the maintenance of a presence was of considerable importance.[221] Cremin also stayed on for the Irish citizens who needed his assistance.[222]

In early November, Cremin told Dublin that the Spanish ambassador was considering leaving immediately, as was the Portuguese; both did and were later ordered to return to Berlin.[223] The Swiss minister had arranged visas for all diplomats on safety grounds so that they could travel even if the frontiers were closed. In November, Cremin brought his children to Switzerland as he 'thought it prudent in order to ensure greater mobility'.[224] In Switzerland, they stayed in a privately run children's home.[225] Cremin's daughter, Ann, recalled that when they left:

> Berlin was on fire and filled with smoke and she remembered passing a golden statue that was shimmering in the light of the flames. When they got to the crowded station, they had to get in through the windows of the train because all the doors were locked.[226]

On 23 November 1944, Walshe again authorised, but did not order, Cremin to go to Switzerland.[227] Throughout December Cremin and his wife remained in Schloss Staffelde.

At the beginning of January, the Soviets, under Marshal Zhukov, launched the Vistula-Oder operation which, by the end of the month, brought the Russians to within forty miles of Berlin.[228] By 19 January Cremin stated 'the situation looks very black' for the Germans.[229] Towards the end of January, Walshe again ordered Cremin to leave Berlin. Cremin replied that he had already asked the permission of the foreign office to move out of the line of the Soviet advance.[230] The German head of protocol informed Cremin that he should not go to Switzerland. Cremin retorted that he was going to go to Lake Constance on the border. In the end, Cremin was permitted to go to Salzberg, where the Swiss legation was. Cremin agreed and designated Charlie Mills to stay and represent the legation for the sake of appearance.[231] He then wrote a note to the foreign office 'nominating Charlie Mills as chargé d'affaires and we affixed certificates on various parts of the building to the effect that it housed the Irish legation'.[232] This might have protected the Mills family from the excesses of the Soviet soldiers.[233] In March 1945, Cremin wrote to Liam Mulally, an English language teacher, that 'the final decision to leave Berlin (Staffelde) was taken rather suddenly so it was not possible to advise nationals beforehand of the change of legation's address'.[234] The postal system was so very 'disorganised that it is difficult to get messages through quickly'.

On 7 February 1945, Cremin reported from Salzberg that the city was extensively damaged and that the Swiss had departed.[235] Four days later he reported that the Portuguese minister, Count Tovar, had left.[236] It became obvious 'that Salzberg had one grave disadvantage. Almost every day we had an air alert, which involved taking shelter, which we did by driving out to a wood nearby. But this naturally involved a continual loss of petrol'.[237] The petrol ration of the legation had been steadily cut throughout Cremin's time in Berlin and he knew that he risked immobility through this constant frittering away of petrol. With this in mind, they moved to Bregenz on 19 February, and then to Lake Constance on 23 February.[238]

In March, Dublin was concerned for Cremin's well-being and asked F.T. Cremins, the Irish minister in Berne, for information about him.[239] It was not until 15 March that F.T. Cremins reported to Dublin that Cremin had been in Bregenz, and that if necessary he would go and get him.[240]

Cremin related that in mid-March he was invited to a diplomatic lunch in Berlin, which was to be hosted by the German foreign minister, Joachim von Ribbentrop, himself. Cremin, diplomatically, said he would be delighted to go if they could supply transport for him to Berlin. Unfortunately, as Berlin was in the process of being surrounded by Soviet troops, the foreign office informed him several days later that they would be unable to provide transport.[241]

At the end of the month, as the allies pushed into Germany and the allied air forces continued the devastation of Germany from the air, Cremin said that all methods of communication within Germany were seriously disorganised and that: 'Practically speaking only real function of legation executive officer at this stage is to assist nationals within area of German control.' Politically he believed 'that unless the army takes control the party is still in firm control in the unoccupied areas of Germany'.[242]

On 5 April 1945, Cremin moved to Babenhausen, near Ulm, where they stayed in a castle (schloss) recommended by the Swiss legation with Princess Fugger, part of an old German banking family.[243] One German diplomat staying at the castle was 'very active about looking after our welfare and security. His first action was to arrange to have a big Irish tricolour, which we had with us, hoisted on the highest point of the schloss, where it offered an unusual and visible sight to anyone approaching from the south'.[244] The mayor of Babenhausen who was most 'anxious to ensure that we did not suffer from the approach of the hostilities, proposed that I agree they put up a signpost to the south' saying that the Irish legation was housed in the town. The notice was written in Irish, German, English and French and the mayor reproduced several signs of a 'size which rather startled me [Cremin] when I saw one'.[245]

On 17 April 1945, a telegram was sent to F.T. Cremins in Berne who was told:

> Please tell Cremin he should leave German territory as soon as he thinks no further advantage to be gained by remaining. He should in any case leave before occupation of his area. Since that appears imminent he may think it proper to leave immediately.[246]

One dangerous incident occurred on the night of 24 April 1945, when the sounds of the guns grew a lot closer and the entire schloss retired to the cellars:

We spent the night there and about 5.30 a.m. were startled by the interruption of a German sergeant-major and a few soldiers. The sergeant-major was in a great rage. He had come from the south and found along the Tanksperren the panels serving as signpost. What outraged him most was that they were in languages other than German: this he hotly maintained, constituted a provocative invitation to the invading troops. I explained the genesis of the signposts but was relieved of further explanation by Prince Franz Joseph [grandson of the Kaiser], who got involved in a slightly amusing argument with the sergeant-major who rather threatened to have him shot. However he and his men departed without any untoward incident.[247]

The next day Dublin was informed that Cremin had moved ninety-five kilometres north out of the frontier zone. On 25 April 1945, Cremin reported:

Defeat certain and matter of at most a few weeks ... The entire foreign office has now left Berlin, with the exception of minister for foreign affairs, secretary of state, under secretary of state and some others ... The German government is to come south if, as everyone expects, things go badly in the north. I formed the impression foreign office is in some respects disbanded as many members have remained behind for private reasons and others from north Germany have gone there.

Cremin prophetically reported that the food situation was not critical: 'but it will certainly be worse and there will probably be very serious situation in few months whatever evolution of military operations.'[248] Astutely he reported that:

The belief western powers and Russians will ultimately fall out is widespread: interest encouraging this belief as Germans see on such a development opportunity for Germany to play role in post-war world.[249]

For many the origins of the Cold War date to 1942 when contradictions between the allies failed to be resolved. This was exemplified when Stalin allowed the Warsaw uprising to be crushed by the Nazis.[250]

By 25 April, Dublin was: 'Anxious for news of Cremin', who had been 'liberated' from Babenhausen by a US colonel from Limerick.[251] They did not receive news until 1 May when Seán Murphy received word that 'C is safe in US occupied territory'.[252] On 15 May 1945, Cremin re-established contact with Dublin with the words: 'Report that the town was taken and that in about ten days [we] will proceed to Switzerland'.[253] Cremin, in his analysis of the German people, stated:

> Judging by this region, population, while not completely war-weary, are glad war is ended and that the Americans have got so far. They, of course, hope future attitude of western allies will allow of achievement of some freedom of political development and government. There is no doubt that England and America can profit by the dread of Russia felt by population and so consistently inculcated by government propaganda and practice and that, in the circumstances, they will find no lack of collaboration originally.[254]

On 17 May 1945, Cremin wrote from Berne that he would return to Babenhausen to get the legation records.[255] On 19 May 1945, Walshe wrote to Cremin that he was: 'Glad to hear you have arrived Berne.' Given Walshe's paranoia he posed the rhetorical question: 'Assume you did not leave any secret records in Babenhausen. Please confirm.' Walshe went on to request of Cremin: 'When you have collected records from Germany, we wish you go Lisbon to take charge of legation. As soon as you have settled in, O'Byrne will be sent to Rome to relieve MacWhite who is coming on leave. You could visit France on way to Lisbon'.[256] On 21 May 1945, Cremin replied that he hoped to go to Germany the following day for about three days and to leave for Lisbon a couple of days after that. Rhetorically, he concluded, 'I presume there is no objection to bringing Cummins to France if possible?'[257]

Throughout 1943–45, the reports which Cremin had sent back to Dublin were of the highest standard and accurately kept the

Irish government informed on events within Nazi Germany. The department showed its appreciation of the work that Cremin had done when Walshe wrote to him stating:

> I should like to let you know how very much the minister and all of us here appreciate your excellent work in Germany. We appreciate very fully the trials and difficulties which you and your wife had to overcome during the period of your mission in that country, and we are profoundly grateful that both of you took the whole experience as a great adventure which the department will always remember as a bright and stirring page in the history of its early years of growth. The minister considers that you have given an example of zeal and perseverance in your work deserving of the very highest praise, and he earnestly hopes that the next stage of your adventures at Lisbon will be a period of tranquillity and happiness for you and your family.[258]

On 26 June 1945, Cremin replied:

> I need not say that I am deeply touched by the expression of appreciation on the part of the minister and the department for my work in Germany; and I would ask you to accept my gratitude therefore and to be so good as to convey it to the minister. I will always regard it an honour to have played a small part in the representation of Ireland abroad during such an historic period.[259]

CHAPTER 4

Lisbon, 1945–46

PORTUGAL, TRADITIONALLY AN ALLY OF BRITAIN, was in a precarious position as a neutral country during the Second World War.[1] In order to preserve her neutrality António de Oliveira Salazar (like de Valera) skilfully held the portfolios of prime minister and foreign minister. Although ideologically incompatible with the allies, Salazar, again like de Valera, gave the allies 'certain considerations' and sold them the majority of Portuguese wolfram (a vital component in the production of steel) production.[2] He also granted bases in the Azores to the allies in September 1943.[3] In addition, he was influential in keeping Franco from openly committing himself to the axis camp.[4]

As for the Portuguese, whatever reservations they had about their leader, Kay argues they 'must have known that, in the Second World War, Salazar had done [Portugal] proud'.[5] Small nation states do not have the luxury of independence in foreign policy and Salazar, like de Valera, played the cards he had with skill and discretion.

Maintaining neutrality did not prevent internal dissent and, during the war, a coalition of anti-fascist organisations – including liberals, socialists and communists – came together under the umbrella organisation of MUNAF (Movimento de Unidade Nacional Anti-Fascista).[6] 'From mid-1943 onwards, as the impending defeat of the axis became clear, the Salazar regime began to prepare the ground for survival in a non-fascist Europe.'[7] Salazar aligned Portugal with the British and the Americans. They perceived Salazar as a bedrock of stability in Portugal 'indicating the primacy of anti-communism over democracy.'[8] This perception was reinforced by Salazar who consolidated his position and enabled Portugal to join NATO in 1949. Cremin was to be present throughout this initial post-war reconciliation of the western allies with Salazar, who was rehabilitated more easily than Franco.

The war had stretched Ireland's scarce diplomatic resources to the point of fracture and all of Ireland's ministers were in need of time at home.[9] The decision to send Cremin to Lisbon rather than Rome may have been owing to the fact that Cremin and his family had had such a trying and exhausting time in Germany, and Lisbon was seen as a recuperation post.[10] In reality he should have been recalled to Dublin but the manpower crisis in the department did not allow for that.

This was Cremin's only 'minor' diplomatic posting during his career. Portugal was similar to Ireland in that both countries were next to large neighbours, which dominated their thinking and trade and upon whose stability their own rested. Cremin laconically related that Lisbon 'by contrast with the preceding years … was … quiet and there were few reasons for alarums or anxiety'.[11] Also, the importance of the Irish legation in Lisbon regarding shipping had been radically reduced.[12] Nonetheless Portugal was an important listening post for the Iberian peninsula as the post-war balance of power emerged.

The year immediately after the war was not propitious for Portugal. She met with a series of setbacks, like Ireland: the harvest was disastrous, the balance of payments weakened and Portugal was excluded from the United Nations because she was 'touched … by the fascist smear'.[13] The Portuguese had 'hopefully awaited the collapse of the Salazar regime in the wake of an allied victory'.[14] But that was not to happen, for several decades. During Cremin's term as chargé d'affaires *ad interim* in 1945 and early 1946, he reported extensively on Portugal's prime minister, Salazar's, attempts to consolidate his position. Salazar did this by cloaking his regime with legitimacy through holding elections in late 1945. The outcome of the elections, however, was never in doubt as the Salazar regime engaged in extensive vote rigging and intimidation.

In the immediate aftermath of the war, Cremin recorded the impressions and prophecies of his colleagues. The Spanish ambassador to Portugal, Nicolás Franco (brother of the general), told

Cremin that he had foreseen the defeat of Germany. The Belgian minister, Motte, believed that: 'Europe is finished and he does not believe that, short of war, Russian expansion all over Europe can be limited.' The Finnish chargé d'affaires also held similar views.[15] These views were widespread and reflected the tense atmosphere at the end of the Second World War.[16]

On 2 August 1945, Cremin related that the Labour victory in Britain had been reported with disquiet as the regime felt it might represent the socialisation of Europe.[17] The official newspaper, *A Voz*, condemned the Potsdam conference which finalised the post-war settlement. It stated that the whole of eastern Europe had been given over to be Russified.[18] The *Diario da Manha*, the official government newspaper, suggested that Catholicism could serve as a counterweight to communism, just as it had in 1940 in the wake of the Nazi defeat of France.[19]

Portuguese Elections

A parade of Brazilian and Portuguese troops in September to celebrate the 'discovery' of Brazil 'was probably given a greater importance than would be the case in normal times because of the tendency of the government to emphasise the community of interest with Brazil'.[20] In propaganda terms it was important to emphasise to the rest of Europe that the Portuguese were on the side of the allies. In August 1945, Salazar declared that elections were going to be held in November 1945 and that they would be 'as free as in free England' – a declaration which was greeted with justifiable scepticism in some circles, but was taken by many as an indication that allied pressure was indeed going to impose a return to democracy.[21] Salazar could not avoid going to the people in order to give the pretence of legitimacy to his regime. Unknown to him, the announcement undermined MUNAF's plans for a coup d'état in August 1945.[22] Gallagher stated of the 1945 elections:

> At no time were the candidates given a guarantee that there would be a fair contest. Salazar indignantly refused to allow any neutral international election commission to supervise elections. A recently

published book consisting of official documents reveals in stark form the amount of fraud and impersonation, which went on before and during every poll.[23]

On 7 October 1945, the British *Observer* newspaper had the audacity to state that in Portugal 'elections do not count for much', and was duly confiscated by the censor.[24] The *Diario da Manha* proclaimed that 'each country comes up with the democracy most suited to the idiosyncrasies of its people and that other methods when tried have led to instability and revolution and disorder.'[25] An article in the London *Times* was the subject of much favourable commentary. Cremin commented:

> The main interest of the *Times* article lies in the fact that Portugal is very sensitive to British opinion and that the *Times* is regarded as having official connections … I think the most significant part of the *Times* leading article in the long run is the admission that there is some force in the Opposition request for a postponement of the elections and the judgement that 'Dr Salazar may be led to calculate nicely whether to bid for victory at a later date which, if achieved, might confirm his position the more effectively because gained over fully mobilised adversaries, or to snatch a probably easier but more equivocal success'.[26]

Salazar, like de Valera, had a penchant for snap elections. After Salazar's announcement of free elections a group of intellectuals requested permission to hold a public meeting to discuss the forthcoming elections. This led to the formation of the Movimento de Unidade Democrática (MUD) on 11 October 1945, which incorporated many members of MUNAF.[27]

On 19 October, Cremin related the various discrepancies in the electoral system which the Opposition were alleging. Cremin argued that the number of people who supported the Opposition proved that the government could not have the ninety per cent support it so claimed. The Opposition wanted the liberty to discuss their doctrines and democracy which they were prevented from doing as they were only allowed to hold very restricted meetings.

They also rejected the government's argument that they did not have any experience in government, stating that Salazar had excluded them for thirty years. Cremin believed that:

> [the] Opposition has not yet produced a mature programme but is at present rather concerned with defending and securing the right to exist as a recognised Opposition with the means to express and put through their ideas, of which the immediate predominant one is to re-establish democracy here.

Cremin argued that they had not attacked the government on its foreign policy or the economic situation. Instead they concentrated on the issue of personal liberty. The Opposition were hoping that the elections would be postponed so that a new electoral register could be drawn up.

On the international affairs front, external pressure was placed on Salazar by the US and Britain to force him to introduce reforms. Cremin argued:

> [if] the government is open to the accusation of having stifled the Opposition or, in other words, to practically the same accusation as the British and Americans make against the election systems in Rumania and Bulgaria: this could obviously be an awkward state of affairs among the Big Three, where the Russians could accuse the other two of tolerating in Portugal a state of affairs to which they object so strongly in eastern Europe.

Cremin continued that if Salazar did allow electoral reform then he could be confronted by a strong Opposition in parliament. That Opposition would be 'particularly among the class subject to foreign ideas and influence, and it is probable that the lower classes would provide a big number of recruits'.

In late October the MUD suspended public meetings at the request of some army officers who were planning a coup.[28] The coup never materialised but it was part of the 'almost constant military conspiracy against Salazar from 1943 to 1947'.[29]

The turnout for the Parish local elections, which were over-whelmingly in favour of Salazar's party, was put at sixty per cent. This was a nationwide average however, and in some parishes the figure was as low as twenty-four per cent.[30]

In late October Cremin perceptively reported:

> The Opposition has several underground papers, including a good communist one. The Opposition consisted of 'worthy men but rather idealistic'. The army wants a change but doesn't want a period of disorder, which accompanies a disorderly transfer of power. The 'Opposition' intends to go underground once more if their demand for an adjournment of the elections is not conceded. There is little likelihood that it would be conceded.[31]

On 2 November 1945, Cremin reported on the coup d'état in Brazil: the armed forces had revolted against the politicians who had refused to postpone the elections. Cremin commented: 'While it would be rash to give too much importance to the point, the fact that a bloodless revolution has been carried out by the army in Brazil, which the Portuguese regard as particularly close to them, might have a certain influence here.' He added a note of caution though, in that Salazar's regime gave civil positions to the officers in order to marry them to the regime. When Salazar had become minister for war in 1936, he had also reduced the officer corps by one-third and strengthened ideological and police control over the armed forces.[32]

Still, Cremin added that 'it is apparently also a fact, that the change of ministers of state which took place here last year was directly due to forceful representations on the part of the army', especially the president of Portugal, General António Oscar de Fragoso Carmona, 'so that it would be unsafe to assume that the army is really wedded to Salazar and his nominees'.

The Opposition propaganda was continuing but they had still not nominated candidates for the forthcoming elections. Realpolitik however won the day when Cremin further reported:

there was a theory in some circles here that the elections are the result of direct pressure from England (and possibly also the USA). My contact with members of the British and American Embassies make me doubt whether there is any truth in this opinion. As far as I can gather the official British attitude is that the present regime suits the British interests quite well, as it enables them quietly to transact their business satisfactorily and in the knowledge that an agreement reached today will be observed tomorrow: as far as I can see, too, the claims of the Opposition have not been strongly taken up in England and, at the least, there seems to be no influential persistent propaganda in England against the present government here: I believe that the absence of such propaganda conforms with official wishes. As for the USA ... I think that they are of the view that Portugal is an English preserve and do not feel like taking, at this stage at any rate, any political initiative to change that position.[33]

The British ambassador in Lisbon was Sir Owen O'Malley who, as his name would suggest, had very strong Irish leanings. He was a source of much of Cremin's information. Cremin in retirement recalled:

His wife was the well known author Ann Bridges. On his retirement he settled in the west of Ireland. I remember that when he was on his way to Lisbon to take over his new post he was accustomed to talk a lot about his connections with Ireland – So much so that one might have been pardoned for wondering whether he was coming to Lisbon as ambassador of Ireland or of Britain.[34]

Britain was undoubtedly the closest ally of Portugal; the two had traditionally been allies since the Napoleonic Wars. Arising from that traditional alliance, Britain had deep contacts within Portuguese society. This showed itself during the war when Salazar allowed the British to build a naval and air base in the Azores.[35]

Cremin reported on the Portuguese belief in the expression *para ingles ver*, the historic roots being that the only foreigners worth impressing were the British, and its use in terms of the elections:

The philosophy behind it seems to be that the foreigner would not like the Portuguese or their institutions if he saw them as they really are and should, therefore, be indulged. On the practical side it can mean that the foreigner is somewhat of a simpleton and can easily be taken in and by extension exploited ... As regards the applicability of the phrase on the present occasion, although the director of the *Diario da Manha* has denied having used it in this context, many Portuguese and some foreigners believe that it well expresses the aim of the elections.[36]

The head of the Portugese Catholic Church weighed in behind the government in the run-up to the elections: Cardinal Manual Gonçalves Cerejeira was 'definitely in favour of Salazar'.[37]

Before the election, Cremin reported that although the usual press censorship had been lifted:

The question of public meetings is a different category. Here the Opposition has probably been at a distinct disadvantage from the beginning as it would be quite unlikely, in the nature of things, that say the authorisation for an Opposition meeting should be granted with as much rapidity as for a pro-government meeting.

Cremin reported that although the Opposition was not refused a licence to hold public meetings prior to 19 October, their subsequent decision to boycott the elections meant that the government was logically able to argue that because they were not contesting the election they had no need of electoral meetings.

The Opposition's other grievance was that their petitions were being scrutinised by government officials.[38] Raby has argued this allowed massive intimidation of MUD supporters who feared they might be blacklisted by the Salazar regime.[39]

The Opposition further argued that the elections were unfair as they were not given time to put their case to the country while the government was using all the organs of the state as electoral tools. Government propaganda claimed that the regime had led to political stability and internal peace, and had avoided war in the last six years. The Opposition claimed that the counting organisation for the election had 'been composed in a manner which will ensure a victory for the government list however the votes are cast'; Cremin laconically stated that this fraud was not unknown.[40]

Cremin explained that there was not any formal Opposition programme and the people voting with the Opposition would simply be voting against the government. He argued that rumours of civil disturbances were probably true; 'as the government maintains, there is a strong communist influence among the rank and file of those opposed to the regime and these opponents are not necessarily represented among the present Opposition leaders, who seem to be all professional men of one kind or another.' He considered that it was not unnatural for the people to look to the Soviet Union for leadership since both the UK and USA supported Salazar.[41] The *Diario de Lisboa* proclaimed that the Opposition was prepared to wait for a more opportune time. Most importantly, Cremin observed that the army as a whole remained loyal, especially the three important units, near Lisbon.[42]

Cremin reported that Salazar was hailed as 'the greatest fighter for western Christianity against communism'. He further underlined that this policy was dependent upon a continuation of the anti-communist policy of the state:

> In so far as the regime here is anti-communist the present international conjecture is rather favourable to it. This avowed aspect of the government's policy may, however, constitute a source of weakness if and when better understanding is reached between the Soviet Union and the Anglo-Saxon powers. What might be a recommendation to the latter in a period of discord with Russia might prove an embarrassment to them if they were seeking to appease her.[43]

A couple of days later, the elections took place. Cremin reported that Salazar's party took all of the 120 seats in the assembly:

> One important colleague here gave it as his opinion, when I was speaking to him a few days ago, that the opposition were foolish not to have

put forward candidates – he considers that they were too ambitious in wanting to oust the government at the first stroke and should have contented themselves with showing, at the polls, that they do dispose of a substantial following.[44] He also said that the communist element here can not, he believes, be regarded as a really serious influence.[45]

On 2 February 1946, Cremin reported on a meeting of socialists that was held with prior governmental authorisation and in the presence of the representative of the civil governor. 'A communication read at the meeting from a well known author who offered his allegiance to the cause described the socialists as standing "beyond the radicals but on this side and in Opposition to the communist".' Cremin reported: 'The friendly way in which this meeting has been reported in the *Diario da Manha* and *A Voz*, both pro-government in outlook and quite openly deprecatory of all the "Opposition" activities during the election campaign, is rather curious.' He went on to speculate that this was perhaps because of the perception that the socialists were a legitimate political party. Cremin stated in his annual report that the electoral system had been modified to allow the Opposition to be placed on the ballot. He concluded:

> A new element has, nevertheless, been introduced into Portuguese politics which may have some consequences later on, in the appearance in parliament of an organised Opposition. Superficially, however, the year closed without any suggestion that the internal stability of the government had been impaired.[46]

With the stability of the government assured, Cremin arranged an audience with Salazar.

Audience with Salazar and de Valera's Visit

In his memoirs, Cremin recalled his audience with Salazar in December 1945:

> Given his high reputation and his remarkable performance in the strictly economic and monetary fields – the escudo had become a very

'hard' currency – I was naturally interested in getting to see him and in fact did so through the good offices of a friend in the foreign ministry ... His manner and rather detached, philosophic, approach – he had come from University life (Coimbra) – were impressive.[47]

Cremin stated that their conversation was superficial in nature but he recalled that Salazar believed that de Valera 'had a much more difficult time in maintaining neutrality during the war than he (Salazar) had had'.[48] (Cremin's recollections after forty years are curious in that, although they admire Salazar's economic policies, they do not include an analysis of his corporatism nor his undemocratic behaviour.) In the audience Salazar asked when de Valera would visit Portugal. Cremin gave a diplomatic answer:

I said that I had no information but felt sure the Taoiseach would be very glad to have an opportunity of coming to Portugal both to visit Fatima and also because of the admiration in Ireland for Dr Salazar's achievements as well as for sentimental reasons because of our long standing relations with the country as illustrated correctly by the old Dominican foundation here.

Cremin obviously did not wish to encourage a visit to Portugal which would associate de Valera with the Iberian dictators in world opinion and bring further unwanted attention to Ireland's wartime policy. Salazar stated that de Valera was:

... very much admired here [and] must be a very able man to have succeeded in keeping [Ireland] out of the conflict; that Portugal was, of course, also neutral but that her task in that respect was much less difficult than that of Ireland because of her geographical position and as a member of the commonwealth.[49]

Cremin was not drawn on Salazar's statement on the commonwealth. In response to Salazar's statement that a great number of Irishmen had fought in the British army, Cremin replied that he had not seen official figures, but he 'heard the number put at from

"100,000 to 150,000" [which] seemed to impress him very much'.[50] Cremin stated:

> I do not know what significance he attaches to this fact [of a large number of Irishmen in the British forces], but you are aware that since the war ended the Portuguese government have taken every opportunity to stress their contribution to an allied victory, and considerable publicity has been given here to a few individual cases of Portuguese who served in the British and American forces.[51]

Cremin wrote that the great popular rejoicing at the end of the war 'was probably due in some degree to the pro-allied sentiments of the people'. With the end of the war the Portuguese publicised the amount of aid they had given the allies and cultivated the impression 'that Portugal's neutrality was, and was intended to be, the most effective contribution she could make to the allied cause'. Salazar himself emphasised the 'conditional nature of Portuguese policy', implying that neutrality was 'rather ad hoc than permanently valid'.[52]

Cremin may having been trying to contrast the practical Portuguese policy with the diplomatically disastrous decision by de Valera to extend condolences on the death of Hitler. Cremin might even have obliquely been suggesting that Ireland adopt Portugal's practical policy.

One issue on which Salazar had to be ambiguous was the issue of the restoration of the Spanish monarchy, which affected the internal stability of Portugal.

The Attempted Spanish Restoration

The Spanish monarchist opposition to Franco launched their campaign for a restoration of the Spanish monarchy in March 1945. On 17 July 1945, Franco stated: 'he would be prepared to transform the Spanish state into a monarchy once more'.[53] However,

> ... the Italian, Turkish and Chinese ministers and the Netherlands chargé d'affaires ... expressed the opinion [to Cremin] that it will be

very difficult for the allies within the limits of action set out in the
British foreign secretary's statements in the House of Commons a few
weeks ago (i.e. without direct interference in the country) to bring
about any radical change in the government of Spain.

They all believed that as long as the Spanish army and police remained loyal to Franco, his position as leader would be secure.
Cremin's diplomatic colleagues argued that external economic
pressure by the west was haphazardly applied. This was emphasised
by the persistent rumour that the USA was supplying economic
aid to Spain and was confirmed by the announcement of a French
commercial agreement with Spain.[54]

Cremin argued that the question of a restoration of the Spanish
monarchy organically lent itself to the question of a restoration of
the Portuguese monarchy. Cremin related the opinion of an academic colleague of Salazar who believed that 'at heart Salazar is
a royalist' and would be in favour of a restoration of the monarchy but feared disorder and his party losing power, believing that
'continuity is one of the greatest virtues of any political system'.
Nevertheless, Salazar continued to hold in trust the family property of the Braganca (Portuguese royal family).[55] He had also had
talks with Don Juan, the Spanish prince regent, who had visited
Portugal incognito.[56]

Cremin reported the Spanish ambassador, Nicolás Franco's,
view that Don Juan's visit was purely private and that Nicolás
Franco was unlikely to be ordered to meet him. However, Cremin
could not find any authoritative source to inform him one way or
the other.

The British embassy told Cremin that Don Juan would not arrive on a British plane because Britain did not want to be seen to
be involved in Spain's internal affairs.[57] Mr Caro (a member of
Don Juan's household), told Cremin that:

1. The restoration is inevitable and that it will take place on the king's
terms rather than on Franco's. The main difficulty from the side of
General Franco is that he wants to ensure himself an important posi-

tion under the new regime which the pretender is not prepared to promise.

2. The British are not ill-disposed to a restoration and even prevented a condemnation of it during a meeting at Moscow in December. On the other hand the British didn't think that the time was opportune for Don Juan to visit London.

3. Both Salazar and Carmona are very well disposed towards a restoration of the monarchy in Spain but neither has taken any action whatever in connection with that matter. The Portuguese authorities have been most accommodating all along in the matter of the Prince's visit here.[58]

Caro believed that Britain and the USA had every reason to favour a restoration if they continued to find Franco unacceptable.[59] In February 1946, Cremin learned that the Spanish monarchists were in possession of certain correspondence exchanged between Hitler and Franco, 'which is very compromising for the latter and which they would publish if forced to do so (by General Franco's refusal to hand over power) so as to discredit Franco both at home and abroad'. Based on all this evidence, Cremin drew a number of tentative conclusions:

1. The monarchists in Madrid believe that something decisive will happen in Spain by March;

2. Don Juan's journey here has the agreement of the British and his restoration may well have their support;

3. The monarchists are anxious to have as little as possible to do with the Spanish ambassador here who on his side has been forcing his attentions upon them;

4. The retirement of General Franco this spring is probable;

5. The transition would be made by means of a 'Junta' of generals as representative of all the anti-Franco elements in Spain;

6. The Junta would hold a plebiscite to ascertain whether the country desires a monarchist or republican regime;

7. Moderate elements believe that unless some improvement in the condition of the people comes about very shortly after the change the

results some months later might be very grave;

8. The question of wheat imports following on last year's bad harvest is very important both for General Franco's regime and any regime that might replace it.[60]

He admitted however that another section of informed opinion felt 'there is no immediate likelihood of a change in Spain' and that Franco 'has the country fairly solidly behind him'. Ultimately it was this group that predicted events accurately. Franco was determined to hold on to power.[61] This section of opinion also believed that if the monarchy was reinstated on Franco's terms then the main advantages of ridding Spain of Franco would be lost. Cremin concluded that one of the major difficulties was that Franco would only agree to a restoration where his position as a minister or as head of the army was guaranteed. Cremin stated that some Portuguese with assets in Spain were uneasy with the prospect of a restoration and feared chaos in six months.[62]

In February 1946, Don Juan had audiences with Salazar and the US ambassador, Hermann Baruch. Cremin stated that a contact in the US embassy denied that the US ambassador had an audience with Don Juan. This colleague told him:

> … that the [US] feel that some alternative must be found to the present regime in Spain and that the restoration of the monarchy is the least undesirable alternative; that for that reason [the US] is inclined to be well disposed towards the idea of a restoration and is probably at present better disposed than is Great Britain. He seems to think that the restoration will come about.[63]

In reality, Franco was unwilling to surrender power and was biding his time until the Truman doctrine opened 'the prospect of a polarised international situation which would re-legitimise Franco's anti-communist regime'. Safe from serious international sanctions, Franco was able to pass the Law of Succession, which would recognise Franco 'as the sovereign, constitutional organ of the state'.[64]

While Franco consolidated his position, Salazar was similarly determined that Portugal would not be ostracised by the rest of western Europe and the United States. A statement was expected:

> ... by Great Britain and the United States of America (and France?) making it clear that Portugal was free from any of the condemnations which might be pronounced against the regime in Spain and also of a possible declaration on the Portuguese side on Portuguese/Spanish relations.[65]

A Portuguese official advised Cremin not to leave Lisbon as some interesting declarations were imminent. Salazar's position was strengthened by the US ambassador's statement that: 'this great man of Portugal, Dr Salazar, has given constant proofs of friendships for me and for our country. Salazar has lost no opportunity to demonstrate his good will for America'.[66] Salazar was extremely anxious for international recognition and status and wanted to avoid the western opprobrium heaped on Franco. The Portuguese government placed political significance on the visit by the cardinal archbishop of New York, Francis Spellman, who was perceived as 'the most powerful American prelate'.[67] Cremin indicated that: 'The cardinal's visit here ... is taken as putting Portugal in the right position as far as the USA is concerned'. The comments of the US ambassador were closely followed by the arrival of a British fleet of five destroyers and a battleship. Cremin attended the dinner to celebrate the visit by the British fleet which according to O'Malley, the British ambassador, was primarily: 'to "show the flag" and re-affirm the English position of primacy in Portugal where ... the Americans have been making considerable headway'. Cremin further argued the Portuguese perceived that the visit could,

> ... only serve to strengthen the country's position internationally especially at a time when regimes of the kind in force here are subject to attack from abroad; and such a gesture at this particular juncture is all the more valuable because of the attitude adopted by Britain towards

Spain and the easy tendency to lump the two countries together by reason of the apparent similarity of regime.[68]

In March 1946, Salazar again inquired whether de Valera might visit Lisbon, this time en route to the final meetings of the League of Nations in Geneva. Cremin took the initiative and answered that the lack of speedy transport between Lisbon and Geneva and the 'present unsettled international situation might make a long absence from Ireland difficult'. He also suggested that this may not be the appropriate time for de Valera to visit Portugal, citing as a contributory factor the lack of time to change the travel arrangements.[69] He was again warning the department that he was not inclined to draw attention to Ireland's own wartime position with reference to Portugal.[70] This was especially important in the light of de Valera's 'egregious error of judgement' in visiting Hempel to express condolences on the death of Hitler, which cast a shadow over Ireland's post-war foreign policy.[71]

In his annual report for 1945, Cremin wrote that on the political front Portugal was still markedly anti-communist. It was not in a hurry to join the United Nations 'but did reiterate its readiness to co-operate in any work sincerely seeking to promote peace'. Cremin evaluated Portugal's international position at the end of 1945 as solid, 'by reason especially of the support which she enjoyed from the side of Great Britain and the USA'. As Pinto argued, 'Salazarism was no affront to international order'.[72]

In early 1946, for the first time in five years, Cremin was ordered to return to Dublin, where he took up the rank of counsellor in the department. His brother, Fr Frank Cremin, who visited Con's family in Lisbon to celebrate his daughter Ann's first communion, was the first relation he had seen since 1940.[73]

Portugal and Ireland at the end of the Second World War offered an interesting comparison. Portugal made the case that she had been pro-allied throughout the war. Ireland, which had been pro-allied, conversely propagated the myth that she had been impartially neutral.[74] Portugal's case, while shaky, was designed to confirm Salazar and his regime in the post-war world. Ireland's case for impartial neutrality was patently unsupportable and did maximum damage internationally for short-term electoral gains at home. Cremin observed and reported these comparisons.

Cremin's year in Portugal had allowed him to witness the reality of power politics as they affected a small nation. He saw the electoral process being manipulated without challenge or international censure. He witnessed how a constitutional crisis in a large neighbour threatened to destabilise a small nation state. He also had the opportunity to study an 'academic dictator'.[75] It was a lesson in power politics which encouraged him never to subscribe to the belief held by John A. Costello and Seán MacBride that: 'We are sometimes accused of acting as if we were a big nation, in fact we are'.[76]

Cremin's next posting abroad was as ambassador to Paris in 1950. This vantage point provided him with ample opportunity to observe further the role of a small nation state in the rapidly forming bipolar world.

CHAPTER 5

Interlude Counsellor,
1946–50

AFTER A QUIET AND SOMEWHAT UNEVENTFUL
posting in Lisbon, relative to the drama and the challenges of his
time both in Paris/Vichy and in Berlin, Cremin was transferred
back to Dublin in April 1946. His plans to travel overland had to
be changed because the French border with Spain was closed at
the time owing to the execution by the Franco regime of a Spanish
hero of the French Resistance.[1] Cremin recorded that he travelled
home on a B54 to Shannon, which he described as being 'much
bigger than the one on which I had last travelled'.[2]

In recognition of his solid service, Cremin was immediately
promoted to the rank of counsellor. His promotion to assistant
secretary followed in 1949. Having served as secretary of the department of external affairs since the 1920s, Joseph Walshe was
posted to the Holy See in 1946. Both as a sign of respect for
Walshe and of the importance in which the Holy See was held by
the Irish government, the legation in the Holy See was raised to
the status of an embassy. This made Walshe the first envoy to serve
as ambassador in the Irish diplomatic service.[3]

The assistant secretary, F.H. Boland, took over as secretary.
Conor Cruise O'Brien, who was serving as a diplomat in Iveagh
House at the time, has written that Boland's star had been rising since 1940 when he advised against 'tacking tactically closer
to Germany'.[4] He further characterised Boland's diplomatic style
as being of the distinctly unenthusiastic tradition of the French
diplomat, Talleyrand, giving the advice that one should 'Tóg bog é'
and not rush to report.[5]

Boland was forty-two years old and was very different from Walshe in the manner in which he handled the running of the department. Cremin and Boland had very different personalities, were close friends and the former was a strong ally and supporter of administrative reform. Boland and Cremin together were responsible for preparing the department to play its role in the management of Irish policy during a period of European reconstruction and the early years of the Cold War. In 1946, Ireland sought unsuccessfully to join the United Nations. Cremin, who later served as Irish permanent representative to the UN between 1964 and 1974, might have had an entirely different career had the Soviet Union not blocked Irish entry at that stage. In his memoirs Cremin speculated that:

> Ireland's entry in 1946, if it had occurred, would perhaps have marked in notable fashion our return to wider international activities after the relative stagnation which characterised that area in the interval since Mr de Valera had presided over the last more or less normal session of the League of Nations.[6]

In May 1945, the department had faced the challenge of dealing with the diplomatic aftermath of de Valera having offended the allies with his visit of condolence to the German minister in Dublin, Edouard Hempel.[7] Dermot Keogh wrote that 'a sense of foreign policy realism had deserted de Valera on that occasion' and that his visit cast a shadow on early post-war Irish foreign policy.[8] Cremin remained attached to headquarters in Dublin until April 1950, when he was appointed as minister to Paris.

It may be argued that Dublin considered it wise to keep Warnock and Cremin out of circulation for a spell in order not to risk the ire of the victorious allies.[9] It is much more likely, however, that both men were kept in Dublin because they had had a most gruelling experience during the war years and needed time to recuperate. It was also the case that the regular diplomatic pattern of postings had been severely disrupted by the war. Both men would have been given a spell of duty in Dublin much earlier if the circumstances had permitted. Moreover, their acquired diplomatic expertise was needed in the department in order to cope with the new challenges of European recovery and of Cold War diplomacy.[10]

The end of the war did not bring about an improvement in the standards of living of many Irish people. Throughout 1946 and 1947, bread rationing was introduced, the harvests were poor and the teachers were involved in a bitter and protracted dispute.[11] Ireland was also suffering economically, owing to her inability to use the sterling credits to purchase dollar goods.[12]

In 1948, Fianna Fáil lost power for the first time since 1932 and the first inter-party government took power. The leader of Clann na Poblachta, Seán MacBride, replaced de Valera as minister for external affairs. His party was a member of a five-party government, with John A. Costello of Fine Gael as Taoiseach. The three-year period of inter-party government between 1948 and 1951 is noted for two important foreign policy decisions. Costello announced the declaration of the Irish republic during a visit to Canada in the autumn of 1948, and Ireland refused to join NATO in 1949. The department of external affairs was both directly and indirectly involved in the running of an anti-partition campaign. MacBride was responsible for the establishment of the Irish News Agency under the direction of Conor Cruise O'Brien. Boland and Cremin used the pretext of the Anti Partition League (APL) and argued successfully for an increase in the number of staff for the department. The small but significant increase was the last personnel increase until the 1970s.[13]

One of the major historical difficulties in studying Cremin's career during this period is that it is sometimes very difficult to track his distinctive, personal contribution to advising on Irish policy. He was no longer sending regular reports from a legation abroad to headquarters; rather, he was co-ordinating and developing Irish policy as part of a small department active in many distinctive areas. That, of course, meant that he was handling many different files at the same time and was engaged in many different projects, some minor and others of significant importance to the development of the state.

Cremin stated in his memoirs that 'the department had much to do as a result of the decision taken by the government in July 1945, at the end of the war in Europe, to make available for the relief of distress on the continent a sum of £3 million to be provided in the form of goods that were scarce there. The gift was unanimously approved by the dáil'.[14] One aspect of the distribution of this material involved working with various Irish charities, including the Irish Red Cross, and liasing internationally with the continental Catholic charitable organisation, Caritas.

Cremin also had dealings with the Irish-run Save the German Children Society (SGCS) on his return from Lisbon. The SGCS had some good intentions but was also motivated by fascist and anti-Semitic principles which were un-Christian to say the least.[15] The society was co-founded by Liam D. Walsh, and had among its patrons Oliver Flanagan, TD, and Dan Breen, both of whom were anti-Semitic and Anglophobic.[16] In early June 1946, the Irish Red Cross stated that they would pay for the cost of transporting one hundred German children to Ireland. Cremin was given the responsibility to liaise between the SGCS, the Red Cross and the Irish government.

The historian Molohan stated that two officials from the SGCS requested a letter of introduction from the minister for external affairs for a visit to London in the summer of 1946. This was not forthcoming because the 'department feared that this would seem like an official recommendation of the society'.[17] Cremin stated that the society was 'making the present arrangements only because Germany is in such a bad political situation and not primarily because German children are badly off'.[18] Given that Cremin had personally witnessed the destruction of two European nation states and the suffering of their peoples, the crass anti-Semitic sentiments behind the SGCS would not have endeared them to him. Cremin appeared to recommend that the government should not become too closely identified with them, thereby saving the government from potential international embarrassment.

Another project that Cremin was involved in was assisting Irish military intelligence in its efforts to gain possession of a set of maps printed by the Germans in the early war years in preparation for the invasion of Ireland, code-named 'Operation Green'. Dan Bryan, head of G2, Irish military intelligence, was anxious that a set be brought to Dublin.

As it happened, an Irishman serving in the US army, John J. Fleming, offered the Irish consul in New York the maps. Fleming had taken the maps from the Luftwaffe headquarters in Bavaria. Having established that Fleming was the legitimate owner, Cremin accepted his offer.[19]

In 1948, Seán Murphy, who had been made aware of the existence of such maps by Cremin, located a set of the maps in Paris. It was not until February 1948 that Murphy sent on the twenty-five black and white maps to Cremin.[20] The recovery of these maps was important for the department to help dispel any doubts of Nazi intentions towards Irish neutrality.

Protocol matters were also within Cremin's remit.[21] One issue which concerned him was the approval given by Seán MacBride to Aer Lingus for the exportation of two Vickers Vikings planes (adapted from the Wellington bomber). The planes were to go to an 'Egyptian Air Company' in the midst of the second UN truce in Israel, which lasted from 18 July to 15 October 1948.[22] The planes were exported via Italy or Spain, who were not members of the UN, to Egypt. Almost a week later Cremin recorded his unease with the sale of the planes. Paula Wylie speculates that Cremin might have been contemplating whether to make a record in the files at all.[23]

The Economic Recovery of Europe
Most of Cremin's personal energy in these years was directed towards the handling of Ireland's involvement in Marshall Aid. On 5 June 1947, General George Marshall announced the USA's plan to fund in part the economic recovery of Europe so as to act as a bulwark against communism. Each European country had to put together a report to apply for a grant. The possibility of a large grant of dollars led to frantic activity within the department. Cremin was given responsibility for the day-to-day handling of the Marshall plan file. He worked directly under Boland who was also very

active in shaping the government's reaction to the plan. While the initial invitation to join the European Recovery Programme (ERP) – as the Marshall plan became known – revealed:

> … much about the perceptions and attitudes of the US and Britain towards Ireland in 1947, the Irish government reaction to the invitation provides an insight into the decision making process in the Dublin administration. This raises the question of the relative balance of external and internal factors in that process and whether the government had any latitude available to it when considering whether or not to accept the invitation … The political and diplomatic dimensions to the decision were not without significance.[24]

The invitation to participate in the ERP was welcomed by the department of external affairs as it allowed Ireland to co-operate in an international organisation 'in which the members of the British commonwealth were not also participating'.[25] One could further argue that the inclusion of Ireland in European organisations was perceived by the department as Ireland being readmitted to the mainstream of European nations; only Franco's Spain was excluded. Bernadette Whelan states: 'Ireland's involvement in the Marshall Plan began in July 1947. The consequences were immediate for the administration which found itself operating at a European level for the first time ever'.[26] More importantly for the Irish administration:

> Ireland's representatives in Paris and officials in Dublin found themselves producing data for external scrutiny and comment, formulating positions on the removal of barriers to intra-European payments and trade, the raising of European production and productivity levels, the German questions and thus, gradually producing a policy on a nascent European economic union as the CEEC [Committee for European Economic Co-operation] was transformed into the Organisation for European Economic Co-operation (OEEC) in April 1948.[27]

The Marshall Plan was one which, at its inception, attracted little or no public interest in Ireland. This was owing to a combination of factors: the political consensus on participation; a lack of information; a culture of secrecy in decision making circles; and the state of the economy.[28] From June 1947 to February 1948, Boland established his authority over the Irish ERP in Dublin, Paris, Washington and London. The de Valera government supported Boland's policy of keeping the department of external affairs in control of the programme, rather than the department of finance.[29] Boland attended the meetings of the Marshall Plan and Cremin liased with de Valera on matters of everyday concern with the CEEC.

Cremin's involvement went back to the first meeting of the plan:

> Two officials from the department of external affairs played a central role in the development of the Irish strategy in the summer of 1947. Boland had been made the Irish representative on the co-ordinating committee. Con Cremin … worked very closely with his superior to present the relevant documentation to Paris. De Valera had made an important procedural decision in this area. It was external affairs and not finance which took the lead in the preliminary discussions on Marshall Aid. Boland, not his counterpart in finance, represented Ireland in Paris. Documentation came through external affairs and was distributed to the relevant departments. This was a prudent decision on the part of the Taoiseach.[30]

Cremin in his memoirs stated that during the initial meetings of the CEEC in Paris in the summer of 1947:

> The principal Irish delegate was the secretary of the department, Mr Boland, who made quite an impact. The debates and studies proceeded with great despatch to such an extent that a thorough report in two parts covering all the major sectors of the European economies, including agriculture, was ready by early September. A covering letter transmitting the report on the Marshall Plan was signed by ministers at a formal ceremony in the Salle de l'Horloge in the Quai d'Orsay.[31]

Cremin recollected that de Valera, who was also minister for external affairs, went to Paris in September 1947 to sign the report itself.

The entourage consisted of Boland, Maurice Moynihan, secretary to the department of the Taoiseach, and Frank Gallagher, head of the government information bureau. Cremin also attended.[32] He recalled that:

> [De Valera] was received with great friendliness (the [French] prime minister being Ramadier). For me [*sic.*] who had of course been in France in the years immediately before the war I was struck by the contrast of the treatment accorded to [de Valera] then and now. It seemed to me that the French had changed their attitude which before the war was more or less of indifference and in fact the new attitude reflected what I would regard as a more detached position on the part of the French against the background of relations between France and Ireland over the centuries.[33]

The Swedish, Swiss and Irish delegations felt that their neutrality would not allow them to sign the report, which included a statement critical of Germany. Boland felt that it was a political reference; de Valera agreed with Boland's interpretation and stated that Ireland should object to the relevant clause, even if she were to stand alone in doing so. The neutrals were ultimately unsuccessful, but they succeeded in having a piece included at the front of the relevant section stating that the section had only been agreed by those CEEC countries that were at war with Germany.[34]

De Valera was hostile to any suggestion which might impinge on Ireland's reputation as an impartial wartime neutral. In a similar vein, he was also hostile to the idea of a customs union, since it might denigrate Irish sovereignty. Consequently, Irish policy was opposed to the proposed customs union, which would later lead to a reduction in tariffs. Protectionism continued as official government dogma until the late 1950s. Whelan says the Irish position was influenced by de Valera's opposition to integration, the underdeveloped nature of the economy and the British position.[35] Boland, on 31 August, stated that the Irish government's position vis-à-vis tariffs was that it could not consider tariffs in themselves to be evil. Whelan states:

Following consultation with the Danish delegation, [Boland] reported to Dublin that firstly, taking part in the CUSG would not oblige Ireland in any way to a customs union ... Secondly, it would be more useful to be inside rather than outside the discussions which could provide interesting information on intra European trade relations.[36]

It took the combined efforts of Boland and Cremin to stress to de Valera that:

... the creation of the study group would not threaten Ireland because the participating governments had agreed not to form a customs union but only to examine the problems involved in formation. They emphasised that it would provide an opportunity to explain Ireland's special problems associated with early industrial development.[37]

Throughout the summer of 1947, Boland and Cremin fretted over the stance that Ireland should take on neutrality within the CEEC:

While neutrality remained as Ireland's formal status, it could still be bartered with. It was evident from de Valera and Boland's views that the application of neutrality in peacetime was still being worked out over the summer of 1947. There was no agreed Irish line at the beginning of CEEC activities beyond avoiding comment on political issues ... Consequently Boland and his team, who were on the ground in Paris, interpreted de Valera's hard-line instructions on neutrality and formulated a CEEC policy over the summer which was neutral on the surface but in practice was guided by the need to protect national interests, resulting in a general alignment with Britain but temporary alignments with other small powers.[38]

It was this ability to combine realism with idealism in foreign policy that enabled the CEEC to be:

... a great test of the mettle of the emerging external affairs ... Boland and Cremin, directing Irish affairs in Paris and Dublin respectively, co-ordinated the preparation of the Irish report, attended the many CEEC formal and informal meetings and dealt with economic, financial and political matters. The department did not obtain additional resources until 1948, thus CEEC work was added to existing work, and this applied also to the diplomats in all the embassies and missions. With the launch of the Marshall Plan, Ireland once again found herself launching her boat into the surf of international affairs. This coincided with Fianna Fáil losing power in February 1948.[39]

The policy of external affairs retaining control of the plan continued and MacBride helped to outmanoeuvre the department of finance by getting agreement that his department (external affairs) would have control over spending whatever they received.[40] The Marshall Plan was not an unqualified administrative success for Ireland. Whelan argues that:

> … lack of resources … ensured that CEEC experience was confined to certain individuals. External affairs did not obtain additional staff until May 1948 … Until then Ireland was unable to maintain a dedicated delegation at the CEEC; consequently Boland travelled between Dublin and Paris where he worked with the support of the existing staff in both places … In addition, he was concerned about the extra pressure which was imposed on Iveagh House because of the extra work and his own absence.[41]

MacBride brought his own thinking into how the Irish side of the ERP should be run. He visualised and created a small section within the department of external affairs which was run efficiently and administered by capable people.[42] MacBride emphasised that Cremin's ERP committee would determine Ireland's strategy.[43] The result of this administrative battle between finance and external affairs was that the ERP work came under the remit of a specialised section with Cremin as assistant secretary. It was headed by T.V. Cummins, a counsellor, and included Frank Biggar (first secretary) and J. O'Brien (third secretary).[44]

In spite of the increase in staff, the effort and time that the department was putting into the Marshall Plan and the benefits that it could bring to the country, the main efforts of Cremin and his colleagues over the summer of 1947 were directed at developing a Long Term Recovery Programme. In an early draft of his memoirs he admitted that Ireland's balance of payments 'were of course quite irregular. Moreover in our case were extremely relevant in forecasting what the balance of payment might be in the last year'.[45] As a trained economist he saw the weaknesses of the Irish case for claiming aid, owing to the complete lack of statistical infrastructure.

Joe Lee wrote that the Irish 'cobbled together' the Long Term Recovery Programme and 'brutally exposed the inability of Irish governments to devise a coherent long term programme of public expenditure'.[46] This is painfully obvious when one looks at the sophisticated mechanism which the French employed in order to ensure that ninety per cent of their Marshall Aid went into capital investment.[47] This was not the fault of the department of external affairs nor its staff, rather it was a cultural challenge which the Irish state had not faced up to.

On the whole, the Irish efforts at procuring Marshall Aid were less successful than had been hoped. The Irish government eventually extracted only £36 million, seven-eighths on loan, compared with the £120 million grant with which MacBride had hoped to transform the country. They invested in long-term projects because the official mind could not think of short-term ones. Land drainage, forestry and other long-term projects got precedence.[48] If the funds had been invested in industrial development, wealth and employment might have been created.

> MacBride had campaigned vigorously in the first half of 1948 to persuade the ECA [European Currency Association] not to acknowledge the partition of Ireland in the allocation of aid. He had been firmly silenced by Washington lest he endanger the passing of the ERP legislation. Washington in fact showed even less sympathy for the Irish position, awarding the republic no grants during the first year of the programme but only loans, probably because of its neutrality during the war.[49]

Ireland was unprepared economically and socially for the first applications for Marshall Aid. The tradition of state planning had not been developed, being only in its infancy.[50] T. Desmond Williams argued 'the period 1948 to 1951 may be regarded as the end of a political era and the beginning of an economic one'.[51] In his memoirs, Cremin stated:

> The OEEC convention could reasonably be regarded as the first deliberate step on the road to European unification. Its aims as set out in the preamble and in several of its provisions went far beyond the immediate purpose of the Marshall Plan and especially beyond the division of American Aid which was an important function of the Organisation in the years 1947–48.[52]

Declaration of a Republic

On 7 September 1948, the Taoiseach, John A. Costello, on a visit to Canada, declared that Ireland would leave the commonwealth and become a republic. The declaration came much to the surprise of the government who had never authorised such a decision. The minister for health at the time, Noel Browne, argued it was a spontaneous pronouncement by Costello when a replica of 'Roaring Meg' (the cannon) was placed in front of him.[53] The cabinet gave retrospective authorisation to the declaration.[54] The incident, according to Dermot Keogh, showed that: 'Foreign policy continued to provide the best examples of decision making skills more associated with the Marx Brothers than with a government in western democracy'.[55] Bowman argues that de Valera thought the declaration 'the height of political folly' as a bridge to Northern Ireland had been destroyed.[56] The actual events were confusing and it is reasonable to presume that Cremin was not involved in the decision, since Boland 'was certainly taken completely by surprise'.[57] During that time, Cremin was heavily involved in the CEEC committee and in his memoirs he did not even mention the declaration.[58] Cremin's role was confined to that of the damage limitation exercise which followed the announcement.

Dermot Keogh argues that the declaration led to a 'sense of

renewed tension' with Britain.[59] However, Nicholas Mansergh pointed out the complete lack of negative consequences: the British Nationality Act 1948 made British and Irish citizenship reciprocal, and preferential trade with Britain was maintained.[60]

Partition was still a live political issue and after Fianna Fáil lost power in 1948 de Valera took up the anti-partition drive. He went on an anti-partition whistle stop tour of the United States and the commonwealth.[61] However, in spite of all the bluster:

> The anti-partition committee was active for a number of years, without results. Here there was much a-doing about nothing … partition had become one of the greatest clichés of Irish politics; and to preach against it was as obvious as preaching against sin. No one ever really expected much to be achieved.[62]

It is highly unlikely that Cremin would have thought that the Anti-Partition League would be able to influence events in Northern Ireland. He had witnessed at first hand the strength of Anglo-American solidarity in the war. After the war 'de Valera referred less frequently to the north, except for ritualistic purposes … to prevent MacBride stealing his thunder on partition'. He adopted a highly public, almost theatrical anti-partitionism.[63] This 'sore thumb' pose embarrassed Ireland at international meetings. Referring to the historical antecedent of the policy of successive Irish governments on Northern Ireland, Lee stated that:

> Behind its rhetorical smokescreen, Sinn Féin in practice abdicated responsibility for northern Catholics, selling them down the drain in the partition year of 1920. For all practical purposes, it stood idly by. From then on, everything Sinn Féin said or did on partition was a matter of bolting the stable door after the horse had gone.[64]

Irish governments after 1920 did not substantially alter this policy until 1968, but the 'rhetorical smokescreen' did affect Irish foreign policy occasionally. Certainly this happened in 1949 when Ireland was offered the chance to participate in NATO. The department of external affairs responded by producing a file on NATO, which outlined what they felt was American strategy towards Ireland. Cremin probably wrote this in early- to mid-1949 for MacBride and the department.[65] It emphasises Stanley Baldwin's emphasis on 'the [British] isles', and also agrees that if the Russians attacked and were not held at the Rhine then the 'isles' would be used by the Americans to defend north America.[66] Sloan argues that in 1945: 'The geopolitical parameters within which Eire was now interpreted focused on a defence in depth of western Europe'.[67] Cremin noted that the Swedes and the Spaniards were the only non-members in Western Europe of the NATO pact but that both spent much more on defence than Ireland did:

> Ireland is, therefore, in a very exceptional position and, if policy with regard to Spain changes – as there are indications it may – will find herself the only country in western Europe not geographically in contact with Russia (like Sweden), which is not a member of the pact organisation.[68]

The fact that Cremin emphasised the Spanish connection drew a parallel between the Irish state and Franco's Spain. The Irish state had previously attempted to play down such connections. It might be inferred from this that Cremin was in favour of Ireland joining NATO.

Under the heading of 'Partition and the Atlantic pact' Cremin stated that during the last two wars the Americans and the British had bases on the island of Ireland. Cremin argued the British were not worried about the inadequate defences owing to the fact that the British had troops in the north that could be used to counter any threat:

> Now that specific and extensive measures are being taken to organise the defences of western Europe and the north Atlantic, some attention may be directed to the inadequacy of Irish defences even for the protection of the present area of the republic. It may be suggested that a state which has made or is making a limited defence effort in

connection with its present area would not be capable of taking over the more extensive and more important defences of the whole of Ireland on the outbreak of war, if partition were ended. This argument may tend to counterbalance the one that Ireland cannot effectively defend herself while partition lasts. It may also help the pro-partition argument that Northern Ireland is essential to British and American defence. It certainly will appeal to the many people in America and elsewhere who are concerned at present with little except the Russian problem.[69]

Cremin emphasised that the unification of Ireland would hold little attraction for the United States. Nicholas Henderson wrote that before the Irish government were asked to join NATO, the British had argued that the:

> … state department agreed that the question of partition should be regarded as quite distinct from the North Atlantic pact. They would not be prepared to consider any proposals the Irish might make which involved linking the two matters. The state department instructed the US minister in Dublin to make clear to the Irish government the views of the US government on this subject. If the latter raised the partition question in connection with the North Atlantic pact, they would not be consulted further about the pact since it would be assumed that they were not seriously interested.[70]

On 7 January 1949, the US minister, George Garrett, gave an aide-mémoire inviting Ireland to join NATO to MacBride. MacBride, in consultation with his party, felt that this was a golden opportunity to trade off a démarche on partition with NATO membership.[71] When word of the Irish tactic leaked out, MacBride was in Paris for an OEEC meeting. The secretary of external affairs, Boland, received telegrams from Irish-Americans in Washington, the sum total of which was: 'Listen, you're making fools of yourselves.'[72]

This advice against linking NATO membership to partition was owing in part, Troy Davis argues, to the internationalisation of America by the end of the Second World War:

Much of the anti-partition strategy in the United States during the early post-war period was at variance with the basic foreign policy attitudes of the time and was, in fact, reminiscent of the isolationist outlook of the inter-war years, which had included a strong anti-British element.

Davis argues that Irish-Americans were far less interested in Irish affairs in the post-war period than their counterparts of a generation earlier.[73] MacBride did not recognise this change in Irish-America and in the state department which 'did not believe that the question of partition was in any way connected with membership of the North Atlantic pact'.[74] Boland therefore advised strongly against the proposal, but MacBride was not to be dissuaded and pressed it through government. It was a victory for 'vintage old guard nationalism'.[75] US rejection came swiftly: 'MacBride's posturing on NATO was as gauche as it was naïve. It introduced a note of crude horse trading into high-diplomacy'.[76]

MacBride's diplomatic style did not impress the department and Cremin stated that 'relations between the minister and un-named diplomats were not quite perfect'.[77] Lee wrote that MacBride had failed to establish an effective working relationship with his department, or at least with F.H. Boland, the secretary.[78] In interview Cremin admitted 'that he personally got on quite well with MacBride who appeared to like him', but 'did not answer the question when ... asked whether the same could be said for Boland'.[79]

MacBride's failure to establish good relations with Boland is exemplified by his first question to Boland upon arriving in Iveagh House when he asked for a list of British agents in the department.[80] At the end of his first meeting with middle and lower civil servants, MacBride asked: 'Don't you think [foreign affairs] may be rather fun?'[81] This would not have gone down well with professional diplomats, who had successfully steered Ireland through the Second World War.

The interlude in Cremin's career was instructive for Cremin in that he developed his contacts in post-war Paris through the Marshall Plan. He kept the Irish state clear of damaging contact with neo-fascist organisations such as the SGCS. Although he was not involved in the decision to declare an Irish republic, he did prepare a position paper on Ireland and NATO, indicating that he personally was in favour of Ireland's membership of that organisation, which was botched by MacBride's gauche handling of high politics. It was in the aftermath of Ireland's failure to join NATO that Cremin was appointed assistant secretary.[82]

CHAPTER 6

Paris, 1950–54

CREMIN WAS APPOINTED BY SEÁN MacBRIDE to Paris in March 1950, at the age of forty-one. Seán Murphy, who had been Ireland's minister in Paris since 1938, was transferred and promoted to ambassador in Ottawa. Murphy's reassignment was long overdue on two grounds. Firstly, he ought to have been transferred earlier but the unusual circumstances of the war had kept him en poste. Secondly, the French government would have preferred to see this former envoy to Vichy sent elsewhere.[1] The Irish government had deliberately kept him there to emphasise that Dublin appointed ministers to countries, not regimes.[2] By 1950, Dublin's rights were vindicated, even if it was at considerable personal cost to Murphy, who was made to feel uncomfortable and unwelcome in Paris by the Quai d'Orsay and other government authorities.

It was through the development of the first Long Term Recovery Programme (LRP) that the Irish official mind began to think for the first time about planning economic development.[3] One supposes that Cremin's expertise on the Marshall Plan must have had a bearing on his appointment to Paris, where the OEEC convened.

After the disruption caused by the war, Ireland quickly resumed trade with France and its level of exports increased markedly over the period 1949–54. In 1949, imports from France had been valued at £1,807,283. They consisted mostly of foodstuffs, fruit, wines, spirits, glassware, manufactured goods, machinery, fertilisers and chemicals. Exports to France were valued at £218,255 and consisted mostly of cattle, horses, fish, wool and seeds.[4] By 1952, imports from France were valued at £2,059,772 and exports to France had grown to £1,404,984.[5]

The trade gap between imports and exports caused considerable anxiety on the part of the Irish government, which reacted by increasing tariffs on certain goods.[6] The growth of trade between the two countries was hampered by a number of factors: the devaluation of sterling in 1949, the Irish growing concern about the trade deficits in 1950–51 which led to an increase in tariffs, and Irish financial retrenchment in 1952.[7] Trade between Ireland and France continued to grow despite this, although:

> … the great weight of her trading, as of her financial interest, continued to lie not in continental countries but with Britain. The trade agreements of 1947 and 1948, together with the strength of sterling as a currency, were fundamental; economic relations with the continent were still peripheral in their importance.[8]

As trade with France improved, Cremin attempted to give more importance to the role of the legation in the development of Franco-Irish economic relations, with some success.[9]

In 1950, the government decided to raise the status of the legation in Paris to that of an embassy. Cremin therefore presented his credentials twice in six months: in March as minister and in October as ambassador.[10]

Cremin's time in Paris saw one exceptional change at home: de Valera did not retain the portfolio of minister for external affairs. Frank Aiken took over when Fianna Fáil was returned in 1952. The new government was relatively short lived and in May 1954, Liam Cosgrave became Cremin's fourth minister.[11]

'Ireland's Listening Post'

Paris continued to be the main Irish listening post on the continent in the context of the Cold War. Threats of international crises and rumours of imminent war could be tested through contacts at the Quai d'Orsay and by consulting ambassadorial colleagues. The vast majority of these colleagues had served at the highest levels in their respective diplomatic services and were senior diplomats of wide experience. The British ambassador to Paris was Sir Oliver Harvey, the US ambassador was David Bruce and the Italian ambassador was Signor Quaroni. One of Cremin's sources for information on the Catholic Church in France and on international relations in Paris was the papal nuncio, Angelo Roncalli, later John XXIII.[12] Cremin and Roncalli were on close personal terms and often had 'cups of tea together in the kitchen of the Irish embassy', indicating a close informal friendship.[13] Roncalli and Cremin shared a love of the classics and classical antiquity.[14] Cremin recalled that Mgr Roncalli was from 1951 on a regular attendant at the St Patrick's day celebrations:[15]

> [he] was a great friend of Ireland who much enjoyed the St Patrick's day reception at the embassy and had, like so many of his contemporaries on the continent, a high admiration for Daniel O'Connell. By temperament he was very friendly with an easy manner calculated to make one feel at home. And he got on well with all classes of people.[16]

Cremin was to be well placed as minister and then ambassador in Paris. His appointment toned down some of the more extreme rumours coming from Walshe at the Vatican, especially in reference to World War Three which, according to Walshe, was both inevitable and imminent.[17] Walshe's reports 'were read frequently by the Taoiseach, and a summary of their contents would have been accepted by the inter-party government as being authoritative'.[18] This translated itself into Irish attempts to acquire modern weaponry in the early 1950s.[19] Cremin, however, 'knew the art of the diplomatic message'. The first rule was to stifle the urge to write to Dublin about everything.[20] He reported in a much calmer and more reflective manner and acted as a stabilising influence on Irish policy, especially when it came to the stockpiling of raw materials in the early 1950s.[21] After all, Paris was still Ireland's most important listening post on continental Europe and was home to the headquarters of both NATO and the OEEC.

Cremin and Walshe, representing different generations, differed markedly in temperament and professional style. Walshe was volatile and given to exaggeration. He rushed his fences and tended to report breathlessly on what he had heard most recently at the Vatican – albeit from usually very high sources – and was not inclined to cross-check his information.[22] The quality of Cremin's information and his informants was very high. Cremin, unlike Walshe, combined information from several sources and sent comprehensive balanced reports to Dublin.[23] From his first tour in Paris he knew full well the pitfalls of allowing oneself to fall under the influence of a particular party political line as his first superior in Paris, O'Brien, had in the 1930s.[24] His daughter, Aedeen Cremin, said in interview that her parents 'worked very hard in Paris to lobby politicians, [and] this involved having a good cellar and a great cook [called] Gaston, who was a cordon bleu'.[25] They were mindful no doubt of Lord Palmerston's adage that: 'Dining is the soul of diplomacy.'[26] Regardless of the quality of one's table, the political situation in Fourth Republic Paris during the period 1950–54 was one of flux and change.

Cremin's Foreign Policy Concerns

During Cremin's time in Paris between 1950 and 1954 the government of the Fourth Republic was changing constantly. This was owing to 'the inescapable need to form coalitions, despite increasingly divergent programmes, which led the parties to negotiate majorities for specific problems once the position in the assembly had reached deadlock'.[27] The complexity of French domestic politics prevents an in-depth analysis here.

Perhaps Cremin's most important reporting concerned geopolitical developments and France's views thereon. These developments contributed substantially to the collapse of several French governments in the Fourth Republic. The most pressing issue was western European defence. De Gaulle's 'apocalyptic warnings' about a third world war first attracted Cremin's attention in August 1950. Cremin's 'reports became increasingly less concerned with domestic French politics and more troubled with the growing European pre-occupation with defence, as the Cold War intensified, and with the first tentative moves towards European economic co-operation'.[28]

Two aspects of French foreign policy in particular would dominate Cremin's reporting: the European Defence Community

(EDC) or Pleven Plan (a method of integrating Germany into European defence); and, although they seem disparate, the colonial war in Indo-China between the French and the communist Viet-Minh. Although they unravelled at the same time, these two will be dealt with as separate events. Kevin Ruane wrote:

> In the early 1950s, two of the most urgent Cold War problems confronting the western alliance were the attainment of a West German contribution to European defence and, in south-east Asia, the preservation of a non-communist Indo-China. Linking the two issues – the bridge between the Cold War in Europe and Asia – was France.[29]

Cremin's reporting also focused on another of the interests he had developed while working in Dublin in the early post-war years: European integration. Although it did not attract Cremin's attention to the same extent as the EDC, the Schuman Plan, later the European Coal and Steel Community, was 'an immensely practical, "functional" scheme, which sought to build up European co-operation in a limited economic project'.[30] Duchêne argues that the Schuman Plan was the 'one French negotiation of this century taken out of the hands of the diplomats'.[31] This meant that Cremin was at an immediate disadvantage to report on the plan, in that his contacts and sources were in the French government and among his diplomatic colleagues. Also, the Schuman Plan was conducted at the highest level and it is unlikely that Cremin would have been able to add anything to the press reports, which is why there is very little in his diplomatic reports over four years on it. This is clear especially in light of F.H. Boland's, the secretary of external affairs, report on 13 June 1950, where he stated:

> From the point of view of European economic co-operation, the French proposal is obviously one of the highest importance and is a positive step in the right direction. It has the added advantage that it may provide a useful bridge for the development of Franco-German relations which are, of course, vital to Europe. The fact that this initiative was taken by France with great firmness, despite a strong British

opposition, may well prove to be a turning point in European politics. At its minimum, it is a very definite bid by France for the leadership of Europe and a very clear indication that France is not prepared to yield European leadership to Britain.[32]

This indicates the importance that the Schuman Plan took on in the eyes of the department. Paradoxically the missions outside of France were in a much stronger position to report on developments than Cremin who was in the birthplace of the plan.

Domestic French Politics, 1950–54
During his time in France, French politics were in a state of flux; Cremin saw ten governments and one general election. The centre parties of French politics (the MRP [Mouvement Républicain Populaire], radicals, socialists, farmers' parties and independents) came together to form the Third Force. Their overriding aim was to keep the Gaullists and communists out of power. The Gaullist Rassemblement du Peuple Français (RPF) was a constant critic of the Fourth Republic, as were the communists whom all the parties were committed to keep out of power. The Third Force was in favour of the Fourth Republic.

> The republic came to be known for its inertia both domestically and in the foreign arena. The failure of the French parliament, after two years of deliberation, to ratify the 1952 Pinay proposals to join a European Defence Community highlighted such paralysis.[33]

This inertia was owing in no small extent to the list method of election to parliament, which favoured the communists and the liberal Catholic MRP. The MRP were in favour of keeping the communists out of power, but couldn't risk revising the list system in case they themselves then lost seats in the process.

De Gaulle was a constant critic of the Fourth Republic. In the wake of the war, Lacouture believed that: 'the political parties were in a position to entrap the general' and, in January 1946, de Gaulle found his position untenable.[34] The new constitution of the Fourth

Republic, drafted by the Third Force in 1946, was greeted by the French public with

> ... apathy or hostility: only time would show if this was a temporary protest, born for example, of economic hardship, or evidence of an already profound disillusionment and disaffection.[35]

For many, the Fourth Republic resembled the Third Republic which was held responsible for the fall of France in 1940. This disillusionment led de Gaulle in 1948 to form the RPF which was controlled by an extra-parliamentary executive committee, and was 'not concerned to win seats for itself or to form coalitions, but wanted instead to free France from the dictatorships of the political parties'.[36] On 19 August 1950, with the United Nations in full retreat in Korea, de Gaulle stated that: 'the Korean War was merely a prelude to an infinitely wider conflict'.[37] A fortnight later, Cremin summarised de Gaulle's statement in sixteen points, which laid out the situation in a clear concise manner. Cremin wrote that on the whole the press reaction was critical of de Gaulle's attitude, especially *Le Populaire* (socialist).[38] For the Third Force 'the hovering presence of de Gaulle, strongly suspected of Caesarism by the Left, reinforced distrust of authoritarianism and a strong executive'.[39] In the wake of the June 1951 general election, Cremin wrote:

> To date, no government has yet been approved by the French assembly. On 22nd June, General de Gaulle declared the RPF, as the largest party in the national assembly, would be willing to form a government with the support of any other groups prepared to collaborate with it. So far this proposal has not met with any support from other parties.
> RPF representatives in the new assembly, General de Gaulle stated, were pledged to act as a united party, thus excluding the possibility of arrangements with other parties [de Gaulle wanted unconditional support, not a coalition]. He criticised the new Electoral Law which deprived the RPF of many seats. His party's aim was to give France a stronger governmental system by strengthening the executive vis-à-vis the national assembly (rather on the lines of the relationship

between the president and congress in the U.S.) and to foster new labour relationships envisaging the association of capital and labour, especially in nationalised industries.[40]

Cremin stated that with regard to foreign policy, de Gaulle believed that European defence should be based on a Franco-German axis and that Spanish exclusion from NATO was 'ridiculous'. He also argued that de Gaulle believed 'France should advance towards effective European federation with all countries prepared to co-operate in this aim'.[41]

Cremin highlighted the RPF's policy of subsidies for the Catholic schools, an issue which was holding up the formation of a coalition government.[42] On 26 September 1951, de Gaulle objected to the EDC on the grounds that 'one cannot logically conceive the existence of a European army in the absence of a United Europe'.[43] Cremin stated that the RPF could pose serious difficulties to the government, although de Gaulle was adamant that he would not water down his proposals. There was hostility directed at de Gaulle, especially by the socialists and the MRP. 'President Auriol (whether correctly or not it is widely reported) [stated] to the effect that he would in no circumstances call upon General de Gaulle to form a government as he does not wish to be the Hindenburg of the 4th Republic'.[44] Cremin argued that if the next government was relying on support from the RPF 'a radical change in French attitudes towards the European army, the methods and structures of the Atlantic pact and even the Coal-Steel Pool (against which the RPF voted), would seem to follow'.[45]

The RPF's united front did not last and, in March 1952, six RPF deputies defected. Cremin stated that this was seen as a very severe blow to de Gaulle personally.[46] Although Cremin, in his report, outlined the difficulties of predicting the future of the RPF, he also reported 'the average opinion' that de Gaulle was 'finished as a major power in internal French politics except, as already mentioned, in the event of a crisis approaching a disaster'.[47] On 12 July 1952, Cremin reported that there could be a schism within the RPF. About thirty deputies refused to follow the orders of the executive committee. The reason for the discontent was the policy imposed by de Gaulle forbidding the RPF to go into coalition. Cremin stated that owing to the list system, even with electoral reform, the RPF could never achieve more than twenty-five per cent of the seats:

> General de Gaulle's insistence on fundamental reforms in the political system, however well justified his views on this subject may be (and there is much to be said for them), coupled with his refusal to envisage co-operation in government except on his terms, render the participation of his party in a government impossible except in extreme crisis. It is very probable in such a crisis he would be called upon.[48]

Cremin observed that any deputies with aspirations to ministerial rank were likely to join the dissident group, which had thirty members and had stated that it would follow the ideals of the parent group.[49] Subsequently de Gaulle withdrew his support for the RPF.[50]

Cremin related that the electoral system only suited the MRP and the socialists, and that if elections were called under the present system then this would result in the chamber being pentagonal rather than hexagonal; the Gaullists would cease to exist as a group.[51] The other group – that the Third Force were absolutely determined to keep out of government – was the French Communist party. Cremin's treatment of the French Communist party is an example of his objective outlook.

French Communism

The French Communist party was excluded from power in September 1947 and split internally that December. Their union, the Confédération Générale du Travail (CGT), 'was considerably weakened during the Fourth Republic particularly after 1951' when attempts to call general strikes were not heeded and industrial calm prevailed.[52]

In 1951, Cremin reported the president of the International World Bank, Eugene Black's, statement that the standard of living of the people of Paris must be raised if the spectre of communism was to be defeated once and for all. Cremin wrote that the papers that favoured a progressive social policy, *L'Aube* (MRP) and *Le Populaire* (socialist), gave prominence to Black's pronouncements. *Le Populaire* used the statement to launch an attack on the scandalous gap between profits and workers' wages.[53]

On 22 March 1951, Cremin reported that strikes had broken out nationwide, although they were 'not quite complete in any sector'. The purpose of the strikes was to receive higher wages. Cremin wrote that the three main unions involved were the CGT (communist), CGT-FO (split from the CGT, socialist) and CFTC (MRP); the largest being the CGT with 1.5 million members.[54] He rationally argued that the wage increase sought by the workers was justified owing to the fact that the 'wage index ... continually lagged far behind the retail price index, by reference to the position in 1938, and the recent statistics show no appreciable improvement'. Cremin's experience of French politics in the 1930s meant that he never gave into alarmist reports about communism.[55] He argued that there was a consensus that 'there should be some increase in wage levels or, alternatively, some energetic action to stabilise ... prices' and that the government had neglected wage and price controls in favour of electoral reform in the assembly.[56] The strike ended with some of the demands being met.

The economically-inspired strike of March 1951 contrasted strongly with the politically-inspired strike of 7 June 1952. Cremin reported that the communists failed to mobilise significant protests against General Ridgeway, who came from Korea to take over from Eisenhower as supreme commander of NATO.[57] After relatively minor riots, several hundred were arrested, including Jacques Duclos, a communist deputy.[58] By 10 September 1952, Cremin reported a split within the French Communist party, with Duclos criticising them openly for not reading the masses.[59] After the Ridgeway debacle, Cremin wrote, the French Communist party were examining their strategies; they were never really a serious threat to French stability. Cremin concluded that: 'It has generally been felt, however, and the traditional qualities of the French character justify this opinion, that those who vote communist at an election cannot really be classified as communist by conviction'.[60]

Although a communist revolt in metropolitan France was perceived as a remote possibility by Cremin, the threat to France from her colonies was actual. This was against a background of 'the final breakdown of communication between the communist and non-communist powers, and the onset of open fighting in Indo-China and Korea [which] created a worse environment than ever for the development of east-west relations in Europe. The division of the continent into two hostile blocs became ever more marked'.[61]

French Foreign Policy, 1950–54

French foreign policy had many different facets: France had a colonial empire to manage; a rapidly recovering Germany to contend with; and the volatile Cold War left the world unsure whether or not a 'hot war' would break out. French domestic 'instability took a certain toll in both domestic and foreign policy, particularly because it confirmed the impression abroad of France as an unsteady and floundering ally'.[62]

Cremin's posting to France from the period of 1950–54 saw the acceptance of the Schuman Plan of 9 May 1950, which led to the development of the European Coal and Steel Community (ECSC) on 18 April 1951. However, 'as work on the Schuman Plan proceeded public attention shifted to a new problem, which was to dominate the European debate for four years: German rearmament'.[63] This was born out of the following realisation:

> Among the politicians of the Third Force the conviction was gaining ground that the severe policy towards Germany … might be self-defeating, the surest way, in fact of rekindling German nationalism. Furthermore the Cold War had changed the priorities, raising serious doubts as to the wisdom of a prolonged humiliation of a defeated country which was now at the front line of European defence.[64]

In many ways the European Defence Community 'seemed to complement Schuman's European policy, and paralleled the integrative features of the ECSC'.[65] It was widely believed that the 'EDC would in fact neutralise German militarism'.[66] In April 1950, the political department of the Quai d'Orsay wrote to Schuman, and stated:

> … it is none the less essential to involve the Americans in ever-closer cooperation and to freely accept the limitations on our sovereignty which will place us in a better position to safeguard our national independence.[67]

The French were willing to sacrifice some of their sovereignty to preserve their own freedom, with the caveat being the integration of Western European Defence into NATO. This was owing to France's inability to meet her existing commitments because of her involvement in Indo-China, which was sapping France's military strength.[68]

French Colonial Policy

France in the post-war period was determined to hold on to her empire in Africa and Indo-China, however: 'this attempt to regain the trappings of first-class power status while so desperately weak economically … was nothing more than a *folie de grandeur*.'[69] Cremin's reports on French colonial affairs illustrate these preordained defeats against determined communist guerrilla troops in Indo-China. French colonial affairs got off to a difficult start in the post-war world:

> Madagascar, Algeria, and Indo-China: in each case dialogue with the nationalists had been broken; in each case the French Union had started badly. French policy had been shown to be tied to the evolution of domestic policy, an evolution dictated by the logic of anti-communism. The blusters continued to applaud each 'definitive' military pacification, the pessimists worried about the scarcity of possible interlocutors.[70]

Cremin's period in France corresponded with the French defeat at the hands of the Viet-Minh at Dien Bien Phu in Indo-China and the subsequent withdrawal of French troops, orchestrated by the prime minister, Pierre Mendès-France, at the Geneva conference. Cremin reported on events in French Indo-China periodically as they influenced the wider aspects of French foreign policy.[71]

On 25 August 1950, Cremin reported that the Indo-Chinese 'Associated States' of Vietnam, Laos and Cambodia, which were de facto French protectorates, were invited to the commonwealth conference to discuss the economic development of south-east Asia. It had been stated that France was 'not to attend the forthcoming conference but that the question of her participating in later conversations was under discussion'. Cremin reported this was the first stage 'in the development of a scheme in the material improvement of south-east Asia'.[72]

When the Korean War erupted in June 1950, Cremin reported that the French government wanted to see assistance and sympathy for her actions in Indo-China, which the French perceived as a struggle against communism. The French also wanted communist China to replace the nationalist Chinese at the UN.[73] A month later, Cremin reported that this wish was considerably weakened owing to the withdrawal of the other colonial powers from the proposals and the 'emergence of a strong sentiment of continental solidarity among the people of Asia'.[74] On October 1950, Cremin argued that French policy in relation to Indo-China was unclear, if not muddled.[75] On 17 January 1951, Cremin noted that Nehru, the Indian prime minister, was visiting Paris and that conflict might arise out of India's refusal to recognise Vietnam. Nehru stated that 'Vietnam cannot be regarded as independent until all outside influence (i.e. French) is withdrawn'.[76]

Cremin wrote the French were paying 'close attention to the cease-fire negotiations in Korea in the hope that they may be "the first step towards a return of peace in Asia", with particular reference to the war in Indo-China'.[77] As an indication of his concern for the domestic situation in France, Cremin reported:

It is to be sincerely hoped for the sake of France, that the government will last until the end of August as it would be very awkward if there were not to be a government for the various conferences which are to take place in September and October ... the treaty with Japan, are, of course, of vital interest to France and it is clearly desirable that her spokesmen could speak with an authoritative voice.[78]

There was an animated discussion at the announcement that the Soviets were to attend the San Francisco conference for the signing of the Japanese peace treaty. 'The general line of the press is that Russia has decided to go to San Francisco ... for the purpose of making a certain amount of propaganda ... and, possibly, to cause dissension in the western camp', Cremin continued. Another factor in Soviet thinking was that by siding with the Asiatic countries which had suffered at the hands of Japan, the Soviets would appear to be their champion. The USSR would urge that there should be a Five Power conference which included communist China, with the object of establishing a lasting peace. Cremin reported the view of the Quai d'Orsay that: 'Russia's presence at San Francisco might ... give good or bad results – good if general détente resulted from the negotiations, and bad if ... the Russians proved purely obstructive'.[79]

Cremin stated that Tournelle, head of the political division in the Quai d'Orsay, believed 'a policy of "toughness" was the only one that would pay dividends in dealing with Russia'. He expected that the Soviets would come out with a fullscale project for a general settlement in the far east, with the Korean cease-fire negotiations at Kaesong as a pawn in that game.

Seydoux argued that the US would sign the Japanese treaty, creating an independent Japanese polity, since the US did not allow Soviet gestures to deter them from their course of action. Regarding the San Francisco conference, Cremin stated that the French were satisfied because they had succeeded in getting the states of Indo-China included as the signatories to the Japanese peace treaty and if the Russians proposed a settlement in the far east the French would insist that such a settlement would cover Indo-China.[80] Cremin reported:

... the French are glad that their colonies are granted the same dip-lomatic status as the rest and they regard this as acceptance of the French colonial policy. Although they are not happy with the fact that Most Favoured Nation (MFN) status has been granted [to Japan] without significant reparation payments. At the conference itself Schuman stated that it would be dealt with on a bilateral basis.[81]

In early 1952, the Quai d'Orsay announced that French troops would be withdrawn from Indo-China by 1954.[82] That October, Cremin conveyed the shift in French policy that had occurred since the outbreak of the Korean War, which was an attempt to inter-nationalise the war. President Auriol stated that the war in Indo-China was not to defend French interests, but rather to defend the liberty of the Associated States of Indo-China and 'thereby defend the liberty and security of Europe and the world'.[83] However, un-der pressure from the US, and from Britain, who feared commu-nist insurgency spreading to their colonies, in January 1953 the French revised their decision to withdraw from Indo-China the following year.[84] This was in spite of the war reaping an increas-ingly heavy toll.[85]

By July 1953, Cremin reported the strain on the French econ-omy owing to the war. He observed that the Laniel government intended to make a serious effort to resolve the political problems arising in Indo-China, which might then reduce the burden of the military budget. He considered that the ending of the war in Indo-China would solve many of the problems that beset the gov-ernment at that moment, either by releasing revenue or reducing the budget. It would also make the ratification of the EDC more politically palatable, as German troops would no longer outnum-ber French troops in western Europe. Cremin believed that the then cabinet (Paul Reynaud, vice premier, Edgar Faure, minister of finance, and François Mitterrand, delegate to the Council of Eu-rope) was progressive on Indo-China. Reynaud, in his investiture speech at the end of May, stated:

France has accorded the 'reality of independence' to the Associated States but she must go to the logical conclusion of this policy and 'the Associated States will not feel that they have full independence until this war ceases to be one waged by France, aided by Vietnam, to become one waged by Vietnam aided by France'.[86]

Edgar Faure had long made no secret of his plan to end the heavy expenditure associated with the war in Vietnam. Cremin noted that Mitterrand was in favour of 're-definition' of the relationship between France and Indo-China as well as north Africa, and that the prime minister, Laniel, was disposed towards the policies of Reynaud, while Pleven would go a considerable way with Mitterrand.[87]

The three 'Associated States' were demanding full independence. On the assumption that the French government was prepared to entertain those demands, there were two strategies which could be followed. The first was based on the 1949 agreements which set up the French Union, and the second was the abrogating of the 1949 agreements and the granting of total independence to Indo-China. The latter was superficially the line preferred. However, the opposition to the second strategy was from Georges Bidault himself, who was anxious to court certain support in the parliament, primarily ex-RPF. President Auriol was also opposed to the second strategy because of his interpretation of the constitution. Kupchan argued that the 'ruling elite faced two sources of coalition pressure inducing them to adopt ambitious policies in the middle east'.[88]

According to Cremin, the Indian ambassador was urging the French government to adopt a commonwealth solution for Indo-China, Tunisia and Morocco, i.e. that they would become republics or dominions of the French union. The ambassador told Cremin that this policy had met with approval from several members of the government. Cremin believed that it would depend on how far the French government was prepared to back up their recent statements. He reported that there was considerable opposition to the internationalisation of the war. The commander-in-chief still believed that the war could be won. On the other hand there was growing concern at the economic cost and the useless loss of life.[89] Kissinger wrote that the French feared that if the war was internationalised that one of the conditions of US support would be the granting of full independence to the Associated States.[90] With a complete lack of understanding of the conditions, John Foster Dulles, US secretary of state, 'apparently indicated that he could possibly secure more aid if the French could by a few victories show that it would be more fruitful'.[91] The Viet-Minh were not so accommodating and the French were firmly on the defensive, building bases and waiting to be attacked by the Viet-Minh.[92] The largest of these bases was Dien Bien Phu. Meanwhile in Korea on 27 July 1953 an armistice was declared.

On the subject of the Geneva conference, the Vietnamese prime minister 'expressed doubts as to the prospects of reaching a solution there for the Indo-Chinese affair'. Cremin wrote, 'The Vietnamese prime minister is taking the line put forward at the Congress of Hanoi last October, these relations should be fixed at two successive stages: France should first recognise the full independence of Vietnam and the latter would then decide to associate herself with the French Union'.[93] According to Cremin, the French puppet prime minister, Bao Dai, did not have great support in Vietnam and for that reason would not be able to guarantee that the Vietnamese people would honour any deal he made. Teitgen did not mention this factor and felt that a solution to the Indo-China affair was inextricably linked to the Korean questions and, 'as there is no hope of the Russians agreeing to free elections in Korea, there is not prospect of a solution of the kind suggested being adopted for Indo-China'.[94]

In late March 1954 the French asked the US to give strategic air support to the garrison besieged in Dien Bien Phu. This would have had the effect of strengthening the French position at the Geneva conference. The US refused to come to France's aid and insisted that France should fight on to victory.[95] One of the lessons that France took from Indo-China was that a 'weakened and dependant ally could not be assured that the alliance and the United States would support and promote French interests abroad'.[96]

Dien Bien Phu

Military events were to overtake the negotiations when, on 26 April 1954, Cremin reported that the Viet-Minh had encircled Dien Bien Phu, the fortified base next to the Laos border, and had begun their attack.[97] The Indian prime minister, Nehru, called for a cease-fire, which the French prime minister, Laniel, rejected. Laniel stated that the conditions for a cease-fire were the evacuation of Laos and Cambodia and the Delta by the Viet-Minh.[98] A resolution passed in the French assembly was heavily influenced by the Gaullists, who argued that it was necessary to have independent states that remained part of the French Union. The MRP and Pleven group voted against.

Cremin wrote that the Quai d'Orsay was apprehensive of the attitude of the Soviets and the Chinese, and felt that if the Soviets linked any agreement to the recognition of China then nothing would happen. The US also displayed their scepticism at the prospect of anything coming out of the Geneva conference. At the same time, the French could not appear to reject any proposal no matter how improbable.[99] On 30 April 1954, F.H. Boland, ambassador in London, wrote a report that was circulated to Cremin stating that Bidault was 'in a state of nervous collapse' and that 'His views and judgments were changing from one minute to another'. More importantly the Churchill government refused to commit British forces to Indo-China.[100] The ruling out of force by the British weakened the bargaining position of the French. On 7 May 1954, Dien Bien Phu fell and the following day the Geneva conference began.[101] Cremin reported on the fall of Dien Bien Phu, stating that:

> Rightly or wrongly (I personally feel that the French made a political mistake in this), the development of the struggle for the post was given enormous importance here and a symbolic significance of the first order. As a result, its fall was taken very badly, not only by the government, but by much of French public opinion: it almost assumes in the eyes of the government the proportion of a national catastrophe.[102]

Dalloz argued that: 'Dien Bien Phu sounded the knell of the French Union'.[103] Cremin reported that many of the heads of missions were sending letters of sympathy to the prime minister, including the Swiss ambassador, who 'would not stick his neck out in these matters'. Cremin stated that he would send his own letter 'against the background of our own history and our general outlook on such matters' and that he would deal with the matter of Dien Bien Phu in the abstract.[104] Cremin's decision to send a letter of sympathy without reference to Dublin may have been because he decided that it was unpropitious to allow Ireland to be seen to be anti-colonial at a particularly sensitive time for the French state.[105] The fact that Frank Aiken had advised de Valera on his ill-starred visit to Hempel in May 1945 might also have been a factor.[106]

The Mendès-France Solution

On 12 June 1954, Laniel lost a vote of confidence in the French national assembly, the first French government to have fallen on an imperial matter since 1888.[107] Five days later Mendès-France was appointed prime minister.[108] Cremin wrote in his report that the primary factor in the downfall of the Laniel government and the principal factor for the acceptance of Mendès-France was the latter's willingness to call a cease-fire in Indo-China.

Cremin thought that the French foreign minister, Bidault, had overplayed his hand by suggesting that the west might jointly intervene. The British had ruled that out since April, and British exclusion ensured US neutrality. According to Cremin: 'Not only the Quai d'Orsay but some sections of French public opinion were extremely annoyed by what they regarded as a more or less deliberate undermining by the British (for internal political reasons) of the French negotiating position'. The other major factor in the ability of Mendès-France to conclude the negotiations was amply highlighted by Cremin:

> It is abundantly clear in retrospect that the French made a serious military blunder in trying to hold Dien Bien Phu and were guilty of

a psychological error in their propaganda build up about the defence of the post. The fall of the garrison laid bare the military weakness of France in Indo-China and came as a most unpleasant shock to public opinion which was thus led to favour even more strongly a settlement on almost any terms.

Bidault, Cremin wrote, was in favour of mobilising military resources including the US but the average judgement was that Bidault 'was being too clever'.[109]

Mendès-France promised to find a solution by 20 July 1954, after which date he would offer the resignation of his government if a solution had not been found:

> The grounds on which he regards an early settlement as necessary are that the continuation of the campaign has seemed to him for years past to impose 'an intolerable burden on the country' which compromises economic recovery and expansion, and if the conflict is not terminated rapidly there is a 'risk of international and perhaps atomic war'.

Cremin concluded as follows:

> On the nature of the solution which Mendès-France would accept … He declared that France 'does not need to accept', and will not accept conditions incompatible with her most 'vital interests', she 'will remain present in the far east', the conclusion must be 'an honourable one', and the 'safety of the Expeditionary Corps' and the maintenance of 'its strengths are an imperative duty'.[110]

Bottinger argued that Mendès-France succeeded in 'coordinating allied strategy at Geneva'.[111] Mendès-France also gave assurances that if his measures should fail, the situation would be better than when he found it. Cremin wrote that the Mendès-France government had given the Vietnam question its top priority. To that end Mendès-France met with the Chinese prime minister, Chou En Lai, the British foreign secretary, Anthony Eden, Bedell Smith,

US undersecretary of state, and the new Vietnamese prime minister, Ngo Dinh Diem. Cremin went on to write that the press had given the impression that the final solution would result in a French withdrawal from Laos and Cambodia and the partition of Vietnam into a pro-communist state to the north and a pro-western state to the south.

Mendès-France was optimistic of securing a settlement. 'The general impression', Cremin wrote, was that China 'is extremely anxious to see a settlement soon and in time to forestall the risks of an American intervention … it is regarded by most people here as virtually certain that she can influence the Viet-Minh'.[112] China did influence the Viet-Minh although she 'clearly sacrificed Hanoi's interests for its own during the Geneva conference' by urging her not to drive too hard a bargain.[113]

Cremin then stated that although there was goodwill towards Mendès-France by the Soviets, there was a question as to the extent of their influence with the Viet-Minh. He argued that the peace settlement would depend on the Viet-Minh not securing any spectacular victories in the following few weeks. The recently returned commander-in-chief in Indo-China, General Navarre, stated 'before his departure that the alternatives for France were internationalisation of the war or peace'. Cremin observed that there was little evidence that the French military positions had been reinforced.

Cremin reported that opinion was divided on the setting of a date for the conclusion of negotiations; some said that it would strengthen the communists' position, others argued that it had proved productive in the past. Cremin stated that one factor that could have an important effect was the appointment of Ngo Dinh Diem, a Catholic and strong anti-communist, as prime minister. He concluded with the thought that Mendès-France would not have any difficulty in recognising Peking as the official government of China.[114]

At the end of July, Cremin stated that the French press were sympathetic to Mendès-France. Most of the public believed that Mendès-France had achieved more in a short time than any of his predecessors could have, and Cremin believed that no one could have achieved more. Cremin reported a natural disappointment that Vietnam had to be partitioned, and said there were concerns for the Catholic population in the north of the country. There was also a belief that France had given Vietnam to the communists in two instalments.[115] France's involvement in post-war Indo-China was caused 'not so much [by] the fatal logic of a political system as the fatal logic of a colonial perspective'.[116]

Cremin wrote that the financial cost of the war in Indo-China was between £1.135 billion and £2.4 billion. In the economic field France had lost seven per cent of her export market in Vietnam and twenty-five per cent of her source of raw rubber: 'In the financial and economic field the immediate consequence will hardly be very favourable and may be disadvantageous.' The French also lost the military credits that the US supplied.[117] Bottinger argued that it ended 'the longest and most senseless attempt of this century to defeat an anti-colonial movement of national liberation by military means, they ended almost one hundred years of French colonial rule in Indo-China'.[118] The war had cost France the lives of 92,000 soldiers and 140,000 wounded, with 30,000 taken prisoner.[119] Guy de Carmoy argued that France had: 'saved her expeditionary corps, salvaged her economic interests to some extent, lost almost all her political influence in Indo-China, and compromised her position within the French Union. South Vietnam became a protégé of the United States and north Vietnam a satellite of China.'[120] Kissinger wrote that 'ambiguous documents such as the Geneva Accords reflected reality; they settle what it is possible to settle, in the full knowledge that further refinement must await new developments'.[121]

Indo-China was a constant theme of Cremin's reports and it is of historic interest to see how one of Ireland's top diplomats dealt with the complexities of the French in Indo-China. We can see how Cremin treated the war objectively and, importantly, did not antagonise French pride by engaging in anti-colonial rhetoric, especially after Dien Bien Phu when less experienced diplomats might have allowed an emotional rather than a rational response.

Nevertheless Indo-China was geographically and ideologically remote from Irish foreign policy. One thing which was of vital importance to Irish foreign policy was the defence of western Europe. The threat of a Soviet invasion was perceived as real and the developments in western defence were deemed by Cremin to be of vital importance.

European Defence Community

The EDC treaty was signed in May 1952; 'over the next two years, however, successive French governments advanced a range of pretexts to avoid ratifying the EDC treaty and thereby delaying the moment when Germans would once again bear arms'.[122]

The controversial treaty had its origins in North Korea's invasion of South Korea on 24 June 1950, which provoked a 'war for both Asia and Europe'.[123] Dr Konrad Adenauer stated that Korea was a mere 'dress rehearsal' for Europe and brought into sharp contrast the Federal Republic of Germany's defencelessness.[124] By 27 June, Truman had committed US naval and air units to the war, 'because the executive branch of government decided that the invasion signalled a direct threat to American interests in both Asia and Europe'.[125] It also allowed the United States to engage in initiatives that ranked among the most important of the Cold War, including a start at rearming Germany.[126]

On 7 September 1950, Cremin reported Robert Schuman's statements prior to leaving for the USA where he was to hold talks about German rearmament with the secretary of state, Dean Acheson, and the British foreign secretary, Ernest Bevin. At this stage the maximum the French were willing to concede was a West German foreign ministry, a larger police force and non-commitment on the issue of incorporating German troops into the proposed European army. Schuman did not believe that Britain had changed her mind in relation to the Schuman Plan.[127] Britain had refused the invitation to take part in the Schuman conference, and Young argued they 'seemed to "talk past" each other in June 1950, especially on the principle of losing sovereignty'.[128]

On the prospect of peace in Europe, Schuman declared that

'when the explosives are piled high, one should not play with fire'. According to some newspapers, Cremin wrote, Schuman was not opposed to the admission to NATO of Turkey, whose defence would bring NATO's frontier to the near east, but they would not do so at the expense of western European defence.[129] Hitchcock has argued that the French government was worried that a re-armed Germany would shatter 'France's claim to leadership of the continent … German rearmament presented far more than a military threat to France. It placed France's entire post-war strategy at risk'.[130] Rioux has argued conversely that a place under the US military umbrella 'led to serious reflection on the nature of the Atlantic commitment and on national independence; and French fears of German revival prompted initiatives for European Unity rather than a traditional defensive reaction'.[131] In early September 1950, the Turkish ambassador stated to Cremin:

> The French government … was rather in favour of the European army idea, but is anxious to avoid offending the British and on the other hand desires to ensure that nothing is done which will compromise [the] American action under the Atlantic pact.[132]

After the meeting of Acheson, Bevin and Schuman, Cremin set out the apparent French attitude on a number of points. On the issue of rearmament, Cremin stated: 'France has recognised the necessity of rearming the west as quickly as possible'. The issues of troop numbers and organisation of defensive structures were proving problematic. Cremin argued:

> acceptance of the French thesis on the terms proposed by France, i.e. that each country concerned in the defence of western Europe should contribute in accordance with its means, would have for effect that France would contribute considerably less, by reference to her direct interest for an effective defence of western Europe.[133]

This was an effort by France to 'spread the cost of rearmament, and its attendant inflationary impact, equally among the members of

NATO'.[134] This was an understandable preoccupation since a cut in the standard of living by five per cent would mean the difference between white and black bread on European tables, whereas for US households it would mean foregoing a radio.[135] On 12 September 1950, Acheson proposed the rearmament of Germany, to an 'unbelieving Bevin and Schuman'.[136] In reaction to this, Cremin wrote:

> … the French government fully realise the importance of western Germany for the defence of the west. It is not, however, prepared to accept willingly the rearmament of western Germany. The reasons are primarily the fear of what a rearmed Germany might do, and the feeling that she might constitute a threat to France.[137]

Cremin reported that Schuman, de Gaulle and Bidault were against German rearmament. Pleven dissented and stated that whatever threatened the security of western Germany threatened that of France. The French argued that the equipment shortage made German rearmament academic. Cremin observed that the most the French would concede currently was an increase in the police force, a higher production of steel, the utilisation of German manpower in an integrated European army and the creation of a West German ministry of foreign affairs.[138] It was against this background that Monnet, Schuman and Pleven suggested the formation of the EDC, which would prevent Germany joining NATO and prevent German rearmament undermining the Schuman Plan.[139] Guillen argued that French isolation meant she 'was unable to resist the pressure of the other alliance members' to rearm Germany.[140] The US desire to rearm Germany was coupled with the desire to extend NATO to Greece and Turkey. The French believed that it was a very delicate balancing act to close the near east to Soviet expansion by admitting Turkey and weakening western European defence. Cremin accurately suggested that the fear of Persia coming under the Soviet sphere of influence meant that the extension of the Atlantic pact to Turkey was 'an immediate rather than a remote prospect'.[141] This extension was formally proposed by the United States in May 1951.[142] Young maintains that 'the "Pleven Plan" offered to give the Americans what they wanted – German rearmament – without giving the Germans any military independence'.[143]

Cremin reported that the French government feared a massive increase in armaments in Germany would put a strain on the supply of raw materials and so proposed joint purchasing boards to deal with this eventuality.[144] In mid-September 1950, Cremin reported that the chairman of the foreign affairs committee of the national assembly, Edouard Bonnefous, had stated that he was opposed to allowing Germany to develop a strong police force. He feared that it would give her an independent position from which to be able to bargain between NATO and the USSR. The ultimate solution was not to rearm Germany, but rather to integrate western Germany into a European army; otherwise Germany would be the strongest of the countries in central Europe.[145]

Cremin also reported a meeting with Wapler, of the European division of the ministry of foreign affairs, on the question of the talks between Schuman, Bevin and Acheson. On the question of German rearmament, Wapler told him that Acheson was in favour of the creation of German divisions that would be incorporated into the West German defences. The state department believed that their creation was a matter of the greatest urgency. The French government were considering the matter.[146]

Wapler believed the European army would not be created for another twelve to eighteen months, and that adequate defences were two years away. The Soviets would probably attack when they had an adequate supply of atomic weaponry. Cremin inquired whether the USA would make a compromise on the French defence memorandum in order to gain acceptance of the US thesis on defence: 'He thinks that there is a connection but that it is not extremely close'.[147] Cremin concurred with Rioux who believed that militarily western Europe could only:

> … hold the Red army's forces at the Rhine: from the beginning it was clear that only the Americans could inject the Brussels pact with credibility, that in effect a European defence had to be an Atlantic defence.[148]

Western Europe's combined defence spending was one-third that of the Soviets and one-fifth that of the US.[149] Wapler assured Cremin that the increase in the production of armaments in France would not seriously affect the supply of consumer goods to French citizens. Wapler claimed there would be close economic co-operation between the Atlantic pact countries and the OEEC. Deep distrust still remained between France and Germany; Dumaine, head of protocol, believed 'extreme nationalism is an ingrained characteristic of the German people'.[150]

The French reaction to Acheson's proposals for German rearmament was the European Defence Community – the military twin of the Schuman Plan – which allowed France to gain time. Pleven presented the EDC to the national assembly. The EDC's 'fundamental weakness undoubtedly lay in the attempt to create a common European army for a Europe whose political immaturity and disunity was obvious'.[151] The EDC immediately split the French polity. By late October 1950, Cremin reported two divergent views about German rearmament. Schuman argued there should be a compromise with the US and the British over this issue and that German units should be incorporated into a European defence force. He further argued that France should accept the US guarantees about the superiority of allied forces over German and the prohibition of a German general staff. In contrast, Guy Mollet, secretary general of the Socialist party, was implacably opposed to German rearmament. He felt that German units should not be formed until 'such time as effective European political authority exists'.[152] In December 1950, NATO foreign ministers accepted the principle of the incorporation of German troops into a European army at regimental level as long as they did not comprise over twenty per cent of the total, pending the ratification of the EDC.[153] Cremin reported that 'On the question of the rearmament of western Germany, Wapler, of the political directorate, declared, that there was no widespread unease in France'.[154]

In January 1951, Cremin reported on the differing opinions towards the Soviet diplomatic note which suggested a Four Power conference to thrash out the question of German rearmament.

Schuman saw the reply as rather encouraging, although he felt that it would not have quite the same effect as it would have had before Korea when it would have enabled them to 'get out of the impasse where we are condemned to agree about nothing'. The conference would, however, depend on the middle east remaining calm. Cremin concluded by writing that various government sources argued for close analysis of the document and were in favour of the conference. He stated that according to the *Continental Daily Mail*, Pleven described three schools of thought present in the cabinet. First, that it was a Soviet propaganda exercise, second, that the conference would fail and the Soviets would be forced to reveal their hand further, or thirdly, that it would be a partial success. Cremin wrote that Pleven and Jules Moch, the socialist minister for defence, were in favour of a conference as they wanted a demilitarised Germany.[155] Conversely, Cremin's contacts in the Quai d'Orsay were worried that the standing of France would be damaged with London and Washington:

> There is apparently a feeling in certain quarters in the USA that France would be unreliable in a real crisis. This consideration would suggest that Paris must be rather circumspect in pressing Washington to accept participating in a conference on the terms indicated in the Russian note.[156]

The French government, anxious to allay its allies' fears, sought a preliminary conference in Paris.[157]

Cremin recorded the Turkish ambassador as believing that the US spirit was dampened by Korea and that they were unlikely to intervene immediately elsewhere. He felt the French position would fall short of the US one in the Four Power conference, which would make them appear pro-Soviet. The ambassador also believed the Soviets would find it very difficult to withdraw troops from East Germany without provoking a backlash in their satellites. He also believed the French policy in relation to western defence lacked real determination and that France would be neutral if she were strong enough.[158]

Cremin followed up these comments with a detailed critique of French neutrality. Dumaine, the head of protocol, stated that the report in *Le Monde* that France favoured neutrality was false and, furthermore, *Le Monde* did not represent official government policy. Wapler also stated that *Le Monde* was not an official government organ. President Auriol criticised neutrality. Cremin noted:

> Nevertheless one does occasionally see statements or references suggesting that a policy of neutrality might be the right one for France ... The chief consideration behind the opinion expressed by the Turkish ambassador is, of course, that the geographic situation does not permit France to observe a policy of neutrality unless she is in a position to defend them by force of arms, and this she is certainly not capable of doing.[159]

Wapler claimed he did not believe anything could be expected of the Soviets, stating: 'East and west are, as it were, the two ends of a see-saw in Russian policy. For him they have been gaining in the east in recent years, but consistently losing in the west'.[160] Cremin concluded that the French were keen to see the conference take place, 'but will be careful to avoid diverging unduly from the American attitude'.[161]

On 16 March 1951, Cremin reported that Henri Queuille had formed a new government and replaced Pleven as prime minister.

The Four Power conference of France, Britain, the United States and the USSR was to decide the fate of post-war Germany. Cremin wrote there was little he could add about the preliminary meeting of the Four Power foreign ministers, except that after ten days, the French deputies were still arguing over the minutes of the agenda and the actual meeting would not take place until May.[162] On 23 March, Cremin stated that the Four Powers' talks would break down.[163] The Soviets proposed Germany be declared united and independent, with her own army, that foreign troops would be withdrawn and that Germany would be admitted to the United Nations. Acheson, in reaction, declared the Soviet proposals a 'golden apple tactic' designed to sow discord among the western powers. Symbolically, Acheson, Eden and Schuman signed the agreement ending the occupation of Germany and initialled the European Defence Community treaty which placed West Germany firmly in the NATO camp.[164] The French people were cautious about the prospect of a new German army being formed just six years after the liberation of France.

June 1951 saw the election of a new Pleven government.[165] Their foreign policy programme included:

> A continued effort to bring about the unification of Europe, with particular reference to the Schuman Plan and the project for a European army, this latter 'appearing to be the only concept capable of reconciling the necessity of securing a German contribution to western defence and the protection of Europe against a resurrection of German militarism'.[166]

Cremin wrote:

> I got the feeling from both La Tournelle and Seydoux that the Quai d'Orsay expects that the Franco-British-American talks in Washington … will prepare the way for agreement about a European army and the incorporation of German units therein. One of the big points still outstanding is … the size of the German unit.[167]

In September 1951, Cremin conveyed Schuman's opinion before the San Francisco conference on Japan:

> One cannot prevent in the long run a strong people from arming when it is maintained in a state of inferiority. If we wish to maintain such a people from arming against us, we should associate it with us in the work of pacific reconstruction.

Cremin interpreted this statement as applying to Germany as well as Japan.[168]

Following San Francisco, Cremin reported the US being more 'determined and single minded in pushing rearmament than any other member of NATO, with indifference to any gesture on the part of Russia. The British and the French do not see the need to rearm at quite such a quick pace'. Cremin stated Wapler believed the US might risk war when they were sufficiently rearmed. This was based on Acheson's Ottawa speech where he spoke of 'containing' the Soviets and 'the necessity to enforce peace'. François Seydoux, director of the European division, Cremin reported, held the opinion that: 'Acheson takes a calm, long sighted view of the situation' and 'there is no danger of the administration entering a war against Russia'.[169] In early December 1951, Cremin reported that at the Atlantic Council meeting the US gave it to be understood that:

> … if the European army is to be a substitute for a direct form of German rearmament, the whole scheme must be ready by the next session of the Council scheduled to take place in Lisbon at the beginning of February.[170]

Cremin stated the RPF and the communists were against the idea of a European army. On 9 January 1952, Cremin reported the fall of the Pleven government. He stated that if the next government were relying on support from de Gaulle's RPF, 'a radical change in French attitudes towards the European army, the methods and structures of the Atlantic pact and even the Coal-Steel Pool (against which the RPF voted), would seem to follow'. If the socialists were to come to power, the main issues would be in the financial field. Whatever the outcome, Cremin thought France would be without a government for the next few weeks and the European army talks would be thrown out of gear.[171] The EDC's failure to be ratified over the next five years was owing to the fact that 'French policy over Europe had been daring, courageous, but without popular support'.[172] It is against this background that Cremin reported on the treaty debates.

The British, in early 1952, were fearful that a French withdrawal from Indo-China would make a gift of the area to the communist Viet-Minh and endanger British possessions.[173] They therefore asked the French to send three divisions to Indo-China to defeat the Viet-Minh before handing it over to an army of local troops. Kevin Ruane conversely argues that:

> Although Eden agreed on the importance of helping the French, it was for reasons related to the EDC that he rejected the reinforcement thesis. Any approach to Paris seemed certain to produce requests for a quid pro quo, but for Eden, the idea of paying a price for French reinforcements was politically out of the question. The most likely French demand would be for Britain to commit forces to the EDC as insurance against German domination during the absence of French units in Indo-China.[174]

Another possible demand could be the stationing of British forces in Germany, but outside the EDC. 'Britain supported a supra national EDC, but only from the outside, not as a member'.[175] The British refused to go further into Europe than the US.[176] Notwithstanding this, even at this stage the Pleven group were hopeful that the EDC would be ratified and in May 1952 Cremin reported that:

> Britain and the USA are likely to announce some form of guarantee covering the eventuality of the withdrawal of Germany from the European Defence Community after it is established … The 'guarantee' announced by the British last week naturally does not meet this requirement.[177]

In June, la Tournelle, the director general of political affairs, stated the French were in favour of meeting with the Soviets at a Four Power conference, as were the British; the US, however, were reticent. The French did not want the Four Power conference before the instruments of the EDC treaty were signed, as they did not want the Soviets to use the conference as a tactic to delay its signing. Cremin also argued that with the treaty signed, a relaxation of international tensions would be more attractive to the Soviets. Conversely, if the conference failed it would be easier for the assembly to ratify the treaty. Cremin wrote:

These two divergent attitudes are not at all inconsistent with the general lines of French policy. She is still as unenthusiastic as ever about the resurrection of a powerful Germany and in particular of a German army.

The EDC offered France some guarantees against these eventualities. Neither were French officials in favour of the Soviet suggestion of a united Germany with an independent army. The US was persuaded by the Franco-British suggestion of a Four Power conference and the idea of another conference on free elections in Germany.[178] Simultaneously, Britain signed the Anglo-EDC association treaty, which they thought would satisfy French concerns; they refused to temporarily commit troops to the EDC for fear of being entrapped in a federal Europe.[179]

The Saar question meanwhile continued to plague Franco-German relations; the Saar was a small frontier province, rich in coal and iron ore that France controlled economically after the war. Cremin reported that with the coming into existence of the Coal-Steel pact this question was to be dealt with between France and West Germany. Schuman proposed to Walter Hallstein (state secretary of the West German foreign office) that the Saar would be 'Europeanised' politically and would remain in 'Economic Union' with France. Cremin understood from the Quai d'Orsay that the German attitude to this suggestion was altogether not unfavourable. A German colleague had told him he regarded the Schuman proposal as a minimal concession. Cremin stated that the economic reason for this was that France could not afford to pay for the coal and steel of the Saar except in French francs. The response of the national assembly was unpredictable.[180]

By October 1952, Cremin reported that Schuman could be dislodged from the Quai d'Orsay owing to his general European policy, in particular the Coal-Steel pact, and his views towards the Saar. Cremin stated that nobody quite knew what his position was regarding the Saar question, even his cabinet colleagues. The opposition in France to the EDC treaty was broadly based. The RPF was opposed because 'they think it unworkable and as a diminution in the status of France'. Cremin reported that Schuman was unlikely to be moved however, as it would bring down the Pinay government. He stated that the Pinay government had done quite well but would have to do better in the next few months if they were to overcome these difficulties.[181]

Cremin reported the beliefs of Henri Queuille, vice-premier in the Pinay government, that the risk of war was receding; 'The military means on each side are the principal cause of this'. General Ridgeway, commander of the allied forces in Europe, did not, however, agree with those sentiments. Cremin himself argued that Soviet industrial plants were not thought capable of producing sufficient armaments to fight a third world war.[182]

Cremin reported at the end of 1952 that the prime minister, Mayer, had secured support from the RPF, but wrote, 'I have the impression that his concessions to the RPF on the EDC treaty, so as to secure their support, were not based on a carefully prepared scheme of amendment'. Cremin encapsulated the contradictions within the Fourth Republic: 'Insofar as M. Mayer and the RPF are not *ad idem* about the revision of the EDC treaty the former's future is clearly threatened – for without their votes he cannot count on a majority.' Cremin continued: 'The average observer could be excused for thinking that M. Mayer has not only postponed the prospect of the ratification of the EDC treaty, but has in anticipation more or less washed his hands of the final product'.[183] This was to be the attitude of all French governments towards the EDC until 19 June 1954, when Pierre Mendès-France was elected prime minister.[184]

Rioux was probably correct when he argued that the ratification of the EDC was put on hold until 1954 because 'a curious inactivity on the diplomatic front blocked all solution, while the previous favourable majority disintegrated and a vast quarrel came to dominate opinion'. Thus, on the one hand, there were niggardly technical advances, while on the other raged a sensationalised and moralistic controversy as the EDC question became more deeply than ever enmeshed in the conflicts and stalemates of French domestic policy.[185]

This analysis correlates with a report that Cremin sent of an interview he had with Bidault, the minister for foreign affairs, in January 1953. Bidault stated his purpose was to ensure the ratification of the EDC treaty. Cremin stated:

> [the] position here on the whole issue is one of considerable confusion. Although I have talked to quite a few colleagues, including the American ambassador, it is very difficult to get a coherent picture of the situation and, naturally, more difficult to formulate a reasoned forecast as to what will happen.

The situation was rendered more confusing by the inclusion of elements that increased the irritation against the USA and Germany.[186]

Cremin reported that the inclination of the Soviets to appeasement 'deserves the most careful attention, the Quai d'Orsay are not prepared immediately to draw long term optimistic conclusions'. Some observers thought the French were more willing to 'find signs of relaxation in the Cold War' in order to avoid arming Germany. Cremin was informed by a highly placed Quai d'Orsay official that the reports from the French ambassador in Moscow were extremely cautious.[187]

Furthermore, if détente were to continue the French national assembly would find it very difficult to ratify the EDC. Cremin stated, 'It remains true that socialist or RPF support, or at least abstention, will be essential to getting the treaty through'.[188]

The death of Stalin in March 1953 had an effect in the Quai d'Orsay: 'there is, I think, a real measure of optimism in the Quai d'Orsay about events in Moscow.'[189] This was wishful thinking on the part of anti-EDC elements.[190] Churchill called for a Four Power summit conference in May 1953.[191] On the issue of the conference, Maurice Schuman told Cremin he believed that it would be a great mistake to hold the conference before 'London, Paris and Washington had agreed upon a detailed, concerted attitude as to how the conference should be handled'.[192]

In contrast, the department received a report from Walshe in the Vatican who believed that:

The coming war is going to be decidedly more serious in relation to our representatives abroad, and it is a good thing that, so far as one can judge, the outlook of the entire personnel is solidly national.[193]

This was an oblique reference to the presence of Charles Bewley in the Irish service until 1939. One of these 'solidly national' personnel – Cremin – reported on 2 June 1953 that Mayer's attitude towards the Four Power conference was consistent:

with the line advocated by the Quai d'Orsay. I have on previous occasions expressed the belief that it is the deliberate policy of the Quai d'Orsay to show considerable prudence in assessing the prospects of a lasting détente in relations with Russia and that this policy is inspired both by a fundamental scepticism, until the contrary is clearly proved, to the genuineness of apparent benevolence on the part of Moscow, and by the knowledge that French public opinion is only too ready to welcome signs of détente.[194]

Cremin wrote that the Quai d'Orsay believed the key to the Soviet problem lay with the German question and that there was no reason to believe that the Soviets would put forward a scheme that was acceptable to the west. The Soviets wanted to treat Germany as set out in the Potsdam agreement and even if the Soviets put forward the view of an independent, neutral Germany with her own army this would be equally unacceptable to France.

Cremin relayed the Quai d'Orsay's belief that there was a distinct change in the attitude of the Soviet government, in that they would take more cognisance of Soviet public opinion in the post-Stalinist climate:

They think that the Russians are at present playing their hand shrewdly and that the reassuring statements made by the British prime minister on 11th May 1953 have led Moscow to pull in their cards: when and how these cards will be shown depends on how matters develop in the western camp.[195]

On 21 July 1953, Cremin reported on a conversation he had had with the director general of political affairs in the Quai d'Orsay, who said the removal of Lavrentii Beria, head of the NKVD, would not lead to a change in Soviet foreign policy.[196] In a further conversation with the director general of political affairs, Cremin discovered that the proposal for the foreign ministers to meet with the Soviets was put forward by Bidault, with Adenauer's support. Lord Salisbury, the British foreign secretary, and John Foster Dulles were opposed to the idea. Dulles opposed out of principle, Salisbury out of a wish for the EDC treaty to be signed beforehand.[197]

The conference was proposed on the same basis as the preliminary meeting of 23 September and did not represent anything new. This conference did not preclude the type of great power conference put forward by Churchill, but the French felt that such a gathering should only take place after a successful meeting on German reunification. An agreement following such a meeting would allow as much progress as the signing of a peace treaty with Germany. Cremin's informant did not know how the Soviets would react to the idea.[198]

Le Monde called the foreign ministers' meeting a retrograde step, as they could not see why Moscow would now agree to something which they had rejected several months previously. *Le Monde* argued that the Soviets could only refuse the invitation and thus convince those who were wavering on the EDC vote to vote in favour. Cremin commented:

> Although, as I have indicated in another context there are serious doubts about M. Bidault's enthusiasm for European integration, it is very probable that in insisting on a meeting of the four foreign ministers, he was influenced by the feeling that such a meeting would clarify the position here about the ratification of the EDC treaty. From the beginning many influential Frenchmen have held that there is no need to rearm Germany even within the framework of a European army as it is not proved that an understanding cannot be reached with Russia. The attitude of the French parliament towards Germany and hence the EDC is, of course, in many ways unreasoning.

Cremin concluded the whole situation would be clearer 'if it could be shown that the prospects of a lasting détente in relations with Russia are nil'. Cremin doubted that Bidault had many illusions about the Soviets but Bidault said to the foreign affairs committee that he believed Germany could be freed and fully integrated into the western camp. He recorded the new prime minister, Laniel's, belief that the Red army was coming to power in the Soviet Union after Stalin's death, and he doubted that they would want war.[199]

In early September 1953, Cremin reported that Adenauer's victory in the German elections was regarded by the press as a vote of confidence in favour of Adenauer:

> The general reaction to the results seems to be one of satisfaction qualified by a certain degree of anxiety. Satisfaction is felt because Dr Adenauer's triumph is considered as a victory for the policy of European integration, of which he has been a staunch supporter, and because of the severe defeat of the communists, neo-Nazis and neutralists.[200]

Cremin went on to report that a sense of anxiety arose in France concerning the strength of the Adenauer government and the German economy in comparison with the relative weakness of France and Italy. There was the anxiety that it 'may give Germany a dominating position, and the fear that the chancellor may be somewhat carried away by reason of the resources he commands and the solid position he now enjoys'. Cremin stated that he got the same impression from the head of the German desk in the Quai d'Orsay.

Simultaneously the French were wary owing to the context of the relations between the continent and the USA, especially following the elections and the favour which the US was showing towards the Federal Republic of Germany:

> [Fears that the] principal American strong point on the continent being in western Germany rather than in France have clearly been enormously increased by last Sunday's elections. The French are con-

scious of this and they are naturally not happy about the prospects of a development which could make a considerable difference to them both in the material field and in that of prestige.[201]

The success of Adenauer was seen as dissipating the risk posed by the German neutralists. It was also possible that Adenauer's success might convince the Soviets to enter talks with the UK, USA and France, and there were grounds to suggest that this might be the last occasion that they would be able to speak to the three alone.

Cremin wrote that the return of Adenauer meant the matter of the ratification of the EDC was all the more urgent. The French commander of the Supreme Headquarters of Allied Powers in Europe (SHAPE), Marshal Alphonse Juin, declared that the German divisions were indispensable to the defence of western Europe.[202] How the French government would act remained to be seen. Owing to the build-up of pressure by the US and Britain the EDC was now seen as the least unacceptable method of securing a direct German contribution to western defence. Schuman had commented since he left the Quai d'Orsay that the longer the French government postponed ratification, the more it suited Germany, as she could then tinker around with the conclusions.[203]

In early November 1953, Cremin had a conversation with François Seydoux, director of the European division of the Quai d'Orsay, after a Three Power meeting in London. The meeting was attended by Roberts of the foreign office, McArthur, counsellor of the state department and François Seydoux; it was to carry out a detailed review of the subject matter of the talks with the Soviets. Seydoux called the meeting a 'tour d'horizon', 'with particular reference to the organisation of free elections throughout the Federal Republic of Germany and the eastern zone. He did not vouchsafe further details'. Seydoux stated that its immediate utility was to reinforce the image of western unity. Seydoux stated that the Soviet government was at present in a very weak position for a conference with the western powers on Germany, owing to the flux in leadership as Khrushchev slowly overcame his rivals.[204]

In mid-November 1953, Cremin reported on a dinner he had

with Lord Ismay, secretary general of NATO, who 'expressed the conviction that in the final analysis France must ratify the EDC treaty', and held out three possibilities: Germany arming within the EDC; within NATO; or arming independently, and possibly turning to the Soviets at some stage. 'Of these three possibilities the first, he holds, must clearly be the least unacceptable to France.' Ismay personally regarded the EDC as a 'military nonsense' but as a political necessity.[205]

Cremin asked Ismay how he expected the French to ratify the EDC when they would only do so if Britain pledged support on the continent. Lord Ismay referred to 1940 replying that 'no British government will bind itself militarily to the continent', reaffirming the principle that saw the British sign the Anglo-EDC treaty.[206] Cremin recorded that Lord Ismay would obviously prefer the NATO solution to the German question, but it was not one that the assembly would approve and must therefore be excluded. In Ismay's view, Britain and the US must leave troops on the continent for some years to come – he did not think it was a good tactic to press France about ratification and was urging restraint on the US.[207]

Berlin Conference

In early December 1953, Cremin provided a very interesting insight into the calling of the meeting of western foreign ministers. The French regarded the timing as awkward owing to the imminence of the presidential elections and the fact that it could raise tensions towards the EDC. Conversely, they saw the Soviets' agreement to attend the Four Power conference as fortuitous, as agreement with the USSR would make the ratification of the EDC less urgent.

The French government was embarrassed by the persistent hostility of the parliament to the EDC. They realised that the US would not be able to secure the consent of congress unless the Europeans were seen to be moving towards integration. The stationing of US troops in Europe was a further preliminary to the signing of the EDC.[208]

The French were realistic, though unhappy, about the possibility that the US would declare that if the EDC was not ratified they would withdraw the EDC from the Bonn conventions, which would mean that the latter would come into force independently and Germany would be rearmed within the framework of NATO.[209] The French were most anxious about the EDC and the Bonn conventions.[210] They had good cause to be worried when Dulles:

> … tried to force the hand of the French government in mid-December 1953, when he warned that France must ratify [the EDC] or face an 'agonising reappraisal' by Washington of American commitments to Europe. This implied a retreat to 'Fortress America' concept, which would leave Great Britain and France alone to face once again a revitalised Germany. Dulles was playing a risky game but he was deadly serious … for without the EDC Adenauer might well lose interest in his links with the west. The French also seemed expendable because Dulles wondered if they could ever again be a great power.[211]

After this threat was delivered on 11 December 1953, Cremin reported that the French believed the British were in favour of the meeting with the Soviets but that the US did not have any great enthusiasm for it.

Cremin's colleague at the Quai d'Orsay was of the opinion that the only positive result of the meeting was the reply to the 'Soviet note'. The official belief was that the Soviets' response was a series of statements of respective positions, not one of independent policy. For the US it was an attempt to emphasise western solidarity; for the French it was an attempt to satisfy public opinion and to seize any opportunity that would make German rearmament unnecessary; and for the British it was an attempt to develop trade with the east. Cremin concluded that the Soviets might try to delay the talks so as to catch France between governments, thus delaying the EDC and German rearmament further.[212]

On 19 December 1953, Cremin reported on Dulles' comments that the US would have to make an 'agonising reappraisal' of their policies if the EDC was not ratified 'soon'. This statement provoked both astonishment and distress in France.

The view is quite general that for Mr Dulles to speak as he did is extraordinary behaviour on the part of a foreign minister. Objection is taken to the substance of his declaration on several grounds: interference by a foreign state in an issue in which she herself is not involved, failure to appreciate the justification for French hesitation in a matter involving in a fundamental way relations between this country and Germany, the suggestion (nourished by the comment made in Bonn) that the line taken by Mr Dulles was concerted with Dr Adenauer during their meeting here on the previous day, the implication that American views can determine French policy, the contrast between the American desire to have the French ratify the EDC and their unwillingness to give the guarantees which the French government have sought so as to facilitate ratification.[213]

The foreign affairs commission protested against the statement and asserted 'that no intervention "even from France's best friends" will influence the decisions of the commission about ratification of the treaty'.

Ruane argued that:

The reason for the British change in policy [of not committing troops to Europe] came during the Bermuda conference of December 1953, which was based on 'Washington's reaction should the EDC founder'. The British thought that if the EDC foundered that West Germany would be rearmed within NATO. However Eisenhower declared 'it's EDC and we must get it done'. This threat to disengage from the continent was dismissed as bluff by the French and British; it led Eden to believe that the EDC must be pushed through.[214]

Cremin wrote that Bidault, leader of the MRP, spoke unequivocally in favour of the EDC in the assembly subject to certain well-known conditions: the Saar, British involvement and acceptance of the interpretative protocols, to which he added the maintenance of a US force in Europe; the argument being that the EDC represented the best hope of controlling German rearmament. The Quai d'Orsay was upset at the form of Dulles' speech, as it did not take account of French sensibilities. Dulles' statement was unlikely to speed up French ratification of the treaty, and could have jeopardised the success of the proposed Soviet conference.

Alcide de Gasperi, the Italian prime minister, gave a démarche to Eden before the conference, on the subject of British involvement in the EDC. He outlined the general situation that had evolved from that of eighteen months earlier, i.e. the French being perturbed about the suggestion that the US and British troops would be withdrawn from the continent.[215] Eden in his memoirs rejected the suggestion that Britain was threatening to withdraw from Europe.[216] Cremin described the attitude of the Quai d'Orsay as still believing in the necessity of European defence. However, 'there was a definite tendency in French thinking to move away from the concept underlying the EDC towards the idea of creating some kind of more purely technical mechanism which could be integrated into NATO'.

In late December 1953, Cremin relayed his belief that it would be pointless to guess whether the treaty would be ratified. He wrote that it would be difficult to get a majority to vote for the EDC in its present form, especially without Britain. Opponents of the EDC were far more vocal and could more easily appeal to the average citizen. He continued that the vote on the EDC would come in March next and that it would depend on the composition of the next government.[217] 'In 1954, Eden and British diplomacy which had hitherto been less than fulsome in their support of France' showed themselves to be 'effective defenders of French interests' against US pressure for the ratification of the EDC.[218]

On 20 January 1954, the Four Power Berlin conference opened with the issue of resolving the German and Austrian questions and the question of a Five Power conference.[219] The western position towards the EDC was altered by the proposal to hold a conference in Geneva to discuss 'the problem of restoring peace in Indo-China' which held the prospect of France bringing back large numbers of troops from Indo-China.[220] Two days later, Cremin talked with Count Tovar, head of the Portuguese delegation to NATO, whom Cremin knew from Berlin and Lisbon.[221] Count

Tovar believed that in the final context France would ratify the EDC as the least unacceptable method of German rearmament. Tovar did not believe that the conference with the USSR would be without positive results.[222]

At the beginning of February 1954, Cremin reported on the Berlin conference. The French were impressed by the Soviet position which had been presented to Bidault at the conference. The two points which most impressed the press were the freedom of movement of Molotov and the fact that he asked that a Five Power conference be included on the agenda of this conference. A favourable result was most unlikely but the atmosphere was more positive than had been anticipated.[223]

Cremin wrote that the USSR was trying to wean France away from the US and Britain. He reported that the Soviet ambassador in Paris had been assiduously assuring everyone he met in the Quai d'Orsay of the advantages a better understanding between Moscow and Paris would bring. Cremin wrote that Bidault had a very difficult position in Berlin, where the Four Power conference convened, in that he must not be seen to reject any of the Soviets' advances, as this would play into the hands of the 'neutralists' and make the ratification of the EDC very difficult. Rioux stated of the 'neutralists' that their 'arguments lacked concrete objectives and looked unrealistic'.[224]

Even with this comfort, Bidault had entered the conference with a carefully prepared brief that did not envisage a Five Power conference. Cremin wrote that the Quai d'Orsay was unhappy about the amiable atmosphere, as the Soviets might give the impression that something had been achieved in relation to Germany and thus accentuate the atmosphere of uncertainty prevailing in France about the EDC.[225]

Domestic Politics and the EDC

The Berlin conference did not see the resolution of the German question, but it did lead to a realisation in Britain that the Soviet Union was only interested in the break up of NATO, and this helped Westminster to reach a cross-party understanding.[226] On

23 February 1954, Cremin stated that he was not sure when the EDC would come before parliament, but that when it did he was unsure what parliament's response would be: the Berlin conference made it more likely that the EDC would be ratified, although French distrust of the Germans made it less likely.[227]

Cremin felt that British participation and the Saar questions would be the most difficult.[228] Laniel, the prime minister, had agreed to bring the EDC to a vote in the assembly; however, the besieging of the French base at Dien Bien Phu in Indo-China meant that the EDC could not be ratified while France was preoccupied there.[229]

Cremin wrote that Bidault was also in a difficult position since he had agreed in Berlin to the idea that if Germany were reunited she would be free to determine her own status under the Bonn conventions. Schuman and van Zeeland, the Belgian foreign minister, disagreed with this interpretation of the Bonn conventions. They believed that if the position of Germany were changed through reunification, they would have to renegotiate. The Quai d'Orsay believed that Bidault took the article to its specious limit but did not break it, but in the course had given a huge amount of support to the opponents of the EDC and may have fractured the French army who feared a rearmed Germany. The Laniel government was also divided as to whether or not there would be a free vote and whether or not the government would make this a vote of confidence; if they did it might radically change the outcome.[230]

In Cremin's view the RPF would vote against the EDC, but the radicals and socialists would still be able to carry the vote. The MRP might then be alienated as they were strongly in favour of European integration and the EDC. If the EDC did not come into existence then this might seriously threaten the ECSC; this would be the greatest risk to the future of European integration.[231]

The French government hoped to ratify the EDC before the opening of the Geneva conference on 26 April 1954, and this led to intensive debate throughout March 1954. Cremin relayed foreign minister Bidault's statement to the NATO council, that the

Soviets would not accept German reunification 'on the grounds that once the "ebb" begins it is impossible to know where it will stop'. François Seydoux believed the Soviets wanted to remain in eastern Germany and had a loyal East German administration; this precluded the prospect of free elections as that would mean the East German administration would be swept from power.

On 22 March 1954, Cremin reported: 'Some of my colleagues here take the view that the Berlin conference was at least a qualified triumph for Moscow inasmuch as it could be held to have resulted in delaying ratification of the EDC.' For several ministers, the Berlin conference 'was not a failure … as it decisively proved two things – the solidarity of the western powers and the absolute unwillingness of Moscow to make any concessions whatsoever in the matter of Germany'. This thesis was developed strongly by Teitgen, the vice premier. He also believed the Soviets would settle for the EDC rather than for a reestablishment of the Wehrmacht.

Cremin reported Teitgen was 'almost fanatical about European unification' and that his views about the fate of the EDC must be read in light of this fact. Cremin further reported that there was a better chance of the EDC getting through because its advocates were more inclined to push it through at that moment, and because Bidault had thrown his weight behind the ratification. The EDC was being pressed because any other solution would 'create an autonomous German army'. This would be contrary to the views expressed by parliament in February 1952 and to those of the German federal government; 'it would be paradoxical to see France go back in this manner on her original proposals'. The French government was putting pressure on various groups to support the EDC.[232] Cremin opined that Edouard Herriot's influence might be decisive, as he had the reputation of a sort of elder statesman. One thing Teitgen did not speak about, however, was the association of Britain with the EDC: 'As far as I can ascertain, little hope is entertained by most people here that Britain will agree to any kind of indissoluble association with the European Defence Community'. Cremin added, however, that she might co-operate with the community.[233] On 13 April 1954, the British government entered a 'formal agreement on association with the EDC', and promised that a British armoured division would be placed within the EDC.[234]

On 22 April, Cremin reported that the French cabinet had split over the EDC. The government was a coalition of all shades of political opinion, except for the communists, with both Gaullist parties and some of the radicals opposed to the EDC. The Gaullists had threatened to withdraw from government. Laniel had stated that the EDC was conditional upon approval by the parliament and that certain prerequisites would have to be met: the Saar question; the interpretative protocols; and the conclusion of an agreement with Britain.[235] Jules Moch argued that many were 'opposed to the EDC not because it would rearm the Germans but "denationalise" our army'.[236] The radicals were also dissatisfied within the cabinet.

In the meantime the MRP were exercising considerable pressure for a debate, stating that they would withdraw from government if a date was not set. On 15 April, the government gave a commitment to set a date once the 'preliminary conditions to ratification have been concluded'. They also asked on 18 May that all the necessary measures be taken to ensure they would have debates on British and US involvement and ratification of the Bonn and Paris (EDC) treaties. Cremin believed it was likely that Laniel would not be able to maintain his government beyond the end of May. The Gaullists would not stand by a government that ratified the EDC, and the MRP would not support a government that failed to stand over a treaty. Cremin reported that 'It may be as Edgar Faure thinks, that the evolution of the Geneva conference will fundamentally alter the position and render the EDC less actual', with the return of large numbers of French troops from Indo-China. This possibility was at best problematic and there would have to be 'very clear evidence of such an alteration in the overall situation if MRP leaders like Tietgen and Schuman are to accept the ratification issue being further shelved'.

How the socialists would vote on ratification was open to speculation. Guy Mollet was a supporter of ratification; however

fifty-nine socialist deputies were voting against it. *Le Monde* was
hostile to the EDC and had described the British undertakings
as representing 'guarantees for London' rather than 'by London'.
The former president of the republic, Vincent Auriol, came out
strongly against the EDC.[237]

The EDC question fractured the French chamber and the French
people as they tried to reconcile the emotive issue of rearming the
nation which had occupied France for four years, with the fact that
the French needed German manpower to offset the Soviet threat in
the east. It also led to the fall of the Laniel government and the long
reign of the MRP's Schuman and Bidault.[238]

Mendès-France and the Collapse of the EDC

On 10 July 1954, Cremin reported that Mendès-France had replaced Laniel as prime minister on 18 June. As Rioux has memo-
rably perorated:

> the situation was hardly propitious, the prime minister was work-
> ing against the clock from Geneva to Carthage, the EDC was dy-
> ing and he was confronted with the cumulative hatreds of the MRP,
> the right, the communists, the distillers, Pierre Poujade and the anti-
> semites.[239]

Mendès-France stated in the national assembly that he would 'bring
forward proposals designed to end the uncertainty attached to ratification by France of the treaty of the European Defence Community'. The proposals would be based on an agreement reached
between the advocates and adversaries of the treaty.[240] Mendès-
France also came to power with the promise that he would resolve
the Indo-China question within one month.[241]

Cremin stated that Mendès-France might keep the parliament in session throughout August in order to bring the EDC
issue to a conclusion. Mendès-France had stated that the EDC
'had adversely affected France's position in international affairs
and has also been harmful to the Atlantic alliance'. The purpose
of bringing those for and against the scheme together was so that

the proposal would be ratified by a large majority rather than a few votes. Mendès-France stated that the facts of the case meant it was necessary for the west to rearm even though the conditions of German participation in a common defence organisation was 'a painful prospect for all Frenchmen'.

Cremin stated that the EDC had split the Mendès-France cabinet in four different ways:

> Those who don't object to German rearmament but who object to the EDC, Marshal Juin.
>
> Those who are opposed to the EDC because they are opposed to German rearmament, socialists.
>
> Those who are in favour of the EDC as a step towards European integration.
>
> Those who consider the EDC the least objectionable method of German rearmament.[242]

The latter two groups were conscious of the fact that France initiated the EDC and that she would be damaged internationally if she failed to ratify it. Their views were interchangeable.[243] Rioux argued that:

> The quarrel over the EDC, for so long confined to political and diplomatic circles, gradually spread to broader sections of the public. As it did so it became entangled with other issues and conflicts; with, for example, the clerical–anti-clerical argument when the EDC was presented as an instrument of the Europe of the Christian Democrats, or with economic nationalism … Even the French army was contaminated.[244]

Mendès-France asked General Marie-Pierre Koenig (anti-EDC) and Bourgès-Maunoury (pro-EDC) to work out a compromise which would be acceptable to both.[245] They failed to do so.[246]

Cremin stated that one of the major factors of concern for the French since the EDC was promulgated were the remarkable pace of German recovery and the progressive acceptance of the British and US governments of the Adenauer government as an equal, accompanied by the conviction that Germany could not be forbidden to arm indefinitely. Cremin wrote: 'The stage has been reached at which failure on her part to ratify the EDC no longer meant that German rearmament is prevented and upsets her relations with her friends.'[247] This was the nightmare scenario where French rejection of the treaty would allow for an American-German bilateral rearmament and present France with a *fait accompli*.[248]

Another factor which dominated French thinking was the resurgence of the West German economy after the war. The West German 'economic miracle' was built partly on the fact that Potsdam forbade the manufacture of weaponry and so West Germany was 'able to devote almost the entirety of its resources in the early post-war period to internal economic reconstruction and development'.[249] By 1951 West Germany was producing six times the amount of industrial goods as it had in 1948.[250] France, while recovering under the Monet Plan, continued to be dogged by inflation of 5.3% between 1950 and 1957.[251]

On 21 July 1954, Cremin reported a conversation with Guérin de Beaumont, under secretary for foreign affairs, who thought that the EDC would be ratified. 'He stated that in his view France must ratify as otherwise it would be in a most invidious position vis á vis the countries which have done so'. He continued that France would not be able to make major modifications in the EDC treaty and confirmed that the parliament would sit through August in an effort to reach a conclusion. If Mendès-France succeeded in establishing a cease-fire in Indo-China his popularity in the country would mean that the parliament would find it difficult to go against him; however, the parliament did not always represent public opinion.[252] This was one of the central weaknesses of the French Fourth Republic: parliamentarians could act independently of public opinion, knowing that their actions would not precipitate a general election.[253]

On 24 July 1954, the Soviets proposed a conference of 'all European states and the United States to discuss the question of European Collective Security'. This gave fresh hope to those factions that felt that the EDC would be ratified.[254] On 30 July, Cremin reported that Mendès-France might adopt the following procedure to dispose of the matter: the treaty, substantially in its present form, would be submitted to parliament for approval. Parliament would be informed that if ratified, the treaty would not be implemented until the other allies were consulted and the opportunity of peace with the Soviets was exhausted. Cremin stated that the advantage of this method was that it would dispose of the matter and put it on the back burner for a long time.[255] Mendès-France's government's only hope of survival was to shelve the matter.[256]

On 13 August the assembly voted to hold the EDC debate on 28 August. The following day the French press published the details of the French protocols for the EDC, which led to the immediate resignation of the three Gaullist ministers and alienated Germany.[257] In England, at the Chartwell meeting, Mendès-France laid out his proposed protocol: 'asking for a European army for the Germans and a French army for the French'.[258]

At the Brussels conference on 19–22 August 'the Five refused any further modification to the project'.[259] Mendès-France hinted at the possibility that 'France might yet accept something like the NATO solution to West German rearmament in lieu of the doomed EDC'.[260] In the aftermath of the Brussels conference the EDC was considered dead.[261]

Maurice Schuman argued that Mendès-France 'went there to guarantee failure to show France that it was not him but the other countries who were responsible for wrecking it'.[262] He was accused of not approaching the Brussels conference in good faith, which Cremin attributed to the list of demands that he put forward: 'he put forward at least two requests which on an objective analysis were either unnecessary or unreasonable'. The orders concerned the placing of all the budgets of the EDC before the French parliament and the taking into account of French indirect taxes when placing tenders for arms. This would effectively give a subsidy to the French arms industry.[263]

The Aftermath of the EDC and the
Settlement of the German Rearmament Question

At a debate on 30 August 1954, the French national assembly rejected the EDC on a technical question.[264] Writing about the debate itself Cremin wrote that he believed Mendès-France did not think the Brussels compromises went sufficiently far and so the government stayed neutral. The EDC had split all the parties with the exception of the communists. Cremin stated that the fact that the socialists were equally split ensured the motion would be defeated. With the exception of René Mayer, the radical, none of the prominent EDC activists spoke at the debate – Schuman, Pleven and Pinay all stayed away.[265]

The French rejection of the EDC plunged the western alliance into crisis. The cohesion of NATO and the integration of the FDR into the western system were threatened as well as the future of European unity. Also threatened was the US commitment to European security.[266] Cremin believed that Mendès-France was definitely in favour of maintaining and, indeed, reinforcing the Atlantic alliance, and likewise in favour of permitting German rearmament. It is true he was also in favour of bringing about a détente with the Soviets.

Cremin recorded that the charges levelled against Mendès-France were threefold. The first criticisms were the nature of his demands at the Brussels conference; the second his refusal to take part in the debate concerning the EDC; the third was that he was Jewish:

> I have heard men, who can find nothing whatever wrong with his statements of policy on either internal or external matters, express distrust of his real convictions solely because of his being a Jew.[267]

On 15 September 1954, Cremin analysed the approach that Mendès-France took in the national assembly. The criticism of this approach was it meant Mendès-France had to stick strictly to his own amendments, 'and that consequently his behaviour at Brussels was too rigid for the needs of the situation'. Cremin reported there were two divergent views on what happened at the Brussels conference. According to Mendès-France, he was met with 'a united bloc of five countries ... on every issue'. Spaak, the Belgian foreign minister, on the other hand, understood that Mendès-France and his other four colleagues encountered 'a lack of comprehension on the French side which was at times exaggerated'. Cremin wrote:

> As to why Mendès-France should go to Brussels with the intention of torpedoing the EDC, a possible explanation is that he considers the treaty to be unnecessarily elaborate to meet the primary purpose it was designed to serve (i.e. German rearmament) and to have become too much an instrument for bringing about European integration and the extension of the supra-national principle.

Another factor, Cremin stated, might have been his personal antagonism towards Jean Monnet.

François Seydoux told Cremin that 'he was generally astonished at the impression of hostility to the French protocol which was almost tangible from the very outset of the conference'. Seydoux suspected that the Dutch foreign minister, Beyen, was especially hostile for a variety of reasons. Mendès-France's position was also weakened by a series of articles published in the French press by André Philip and Robert Schuman which failed to support him.[268]

One of the substantive effects of the failure of the EDC was to 'establish NATO as the main security defence forum for western Europe. This had the effect of severing western European security cooperation from the wider process of European integration'.[269] The process which brought this about began immediately after the rejection of the EDC by the French national assembly. Eden, the British foreign secretary, recalling Dulles' 'agonising reappraisal' speech, feared that the US might withdraw from NATO and revert to 'peripheral defence'. He therefore began working on a solution to the vexed question of German rearmament.[270] The British plan was the adaptation of the 1948 Brussels treaty (which was a defensive treaty aimed ostensibly against the Germans), to include

West Germany and Italy, and to 'amend [it] to cover not German aggression, its original raison d'être, but aggression from any source'. West Germany could then be admitted to the Brussels Treaty Organisation and NATO, simultaneously, and on a basis of equality. The advantage for France was that the Brussels treaty had no supranational characteristics and Britain would be a full member.[271] The plan was approved by the British cabinet on 8 September.[272] For Eden it came as an opportunity to point the Six (Germany, France, Britain, US, Italy and Benelux) back towards inter-governmental co-operation and 'might also allow Britain to control future developments among the Six'.[273]

On 22 September 1954, Cremin wrote about the proposals for German rearmament:

> The fundamental difference between the French proposals and those canvassed by Mr Eden is, that, whereas the latter intended to adapt the Brussels pact primarily for political purposes, Mendès-France wishes to use it to cover both the political and the military objectives. London wished to make of the Brussels treaty an instrument which would serve to promote the movement towards European Union but intended to use NATO for German rearmament.

Mendès-France, Cremin wrote, wished to deal with German rearmament in a European context:

> The French proposals envisaged a mini-European version of NATO, which would mirror the minimum requirements that NATO imposed. The French proposed a pooling of armaments and the prohibition of the manufacturing of certain armaments in strategically exposed areas (atomic weaponry, teleguided weapons in Germany). The French also propose an absolute ban on weapons manufacture near the Elbe.[274]

The authority that would control this would have certain supranational qualities. Cremin stated that the French were not inflexible about their plan but that Mendès-France was insisting on a European solution to the question of German rearmament.

The Quai d'Orsay felt they would get a better hearing in London than in Brussels, relying on the fact that the Belgian and Dutch ministers were fearful of an EDC without France which would leave them very exposed to being alone with Germany. Cremin stated that Mendès-France was in favour of a 'definite reconciliation between France and Germany' and hoped to settle the Saar question. Mendès-France wanted to create structures that would aid the creation of the Western European Union. Cremin believed Mendès-France surprised people by stating he thought the Brussels pact needed a 'dose of the supra-national'; however, he was still vague about what manner this would take, other than that France 'must take supra-nationalism slowly'. Presumably this is a reference to the fact that the Brussels treaty would not allow for a diminution of sovereignty over the French army.

Cremin mistakenly predicted Britain would probably stay out of the overall structures. He reported that the reaction in the USA had not been favourable to the French proposal, as it would only allow for the minimum of armaments set down by NATO. Cremin wrote:

> Nevertheless, and having regard to his well known scale of priorities which put national economic improvement first, those who regard as the most urgent need the establishment of a strong defence organisation may be led to wonder whether Mendès-France shares their views.

Cremin stated he did not know how the Mendès-France scheme would fare when it came to parliament.[275]

On 28 September 1954, the London Nine Power conference opened to discuss Eden's proposals. Eden had been given sanction the previous day to give a commitment of four divisions of British troops on the continent. Eden argued that for France and Britain's other European 'friends' 'it meant the difference psychologically, between a conviction and a hope'. On 3 October, the conference ended with the unanimous approval on the termination of the Occupation Statute of West Germany, and on the Bonn government being simultaneously admitted to the Brussels Treaty Organisation – renamed the Western European Union (WEU) – and the North Atlantic Treaty Organisation.[276]

This approval echoed Cremin's report on meeting de Moustier, the recently appointed under secretary for foreign affairs, who thought 'that while the Saar problem may be difficult the admission of Germany to NATO will not encounter any major obstacles in parliament'. De Moustier also talked about the results of the discussions between Mendès-France and Adenauer over the Saar question on which de Moustier believed Adenauer was prepared to compromise.

Cremin wrote that Mendès-France had scored a victory with the British commitment to keep troops on the continent. 'This is regarded by everyone here as a major triumph – even the MRP speakers in the debate conceded it'. Cremin went on to write: 'The EDC advocates argue of course that the Brussels pact arrangements are too negative and say that they will lead to the emergence of a German general staff which was something the EDC was especially designed to obviate.' Cremin continued: 'As to the question of where Mendès-France stands, I have met no colleague who is prepared to say categorically that his professions are seriously at variance with his convictions. The most common view is that it is quite sound on the issue of the Atlantic alliance and fidelity to its principles.' Cremin wrote that the one person whom he felt had doubts about this was the US ambassador.[277]

Walter LaFeber has argued that by allowing the French national assembly to defeat the EDC, Mendès-France:

> had miscalculated. Not fully realising how they were being acted upon rather than acting in the unfolding diplomacy, the French believed that defeat of the EDC had scotched, perhaps killed, German rearmament. Instead they had simply exchanged the EDC, which provided for controls upon that rearmament, for perhaps NATO, which had no such controls and would allow the development of a national German army.[278]

Ruane disagrees and states the French were not so much against German rearmament as the supranational element of the EDC. In addition the WEU elicited a reaffirmation of US support for the defence of Europe and, most importantly of all, the British were more deeply involved in the defence of the continent than ever before.[279]

Ireland and the European Defence Community

Given the amount of time and effort that Cremin spent accurately reporting on the EDC, it is arguable that he was in favour of it as a method of countering the Soviet threat. Cremin's reports ensured that the Irish political and diplomatic policy makers were accurately informed on the EDC. Miriam Hederman O'Brien argues that:

> The European Defence Community was regarded with some favour in Irish circles, which followed the debate 'on the mainland'. Apart altogether from the question of Northern Ireland, the idea of 'foreign bases' in Ireland and the political and financial implications of membership of NATO were not acceptable to many Irish people but the new idea of a genuinely multi-national defence force had no particular prejudices to overcome. None of the political parties raised the issue however and the economic and political ties which the European Defence Community required were still considered out of reach, in practical terms, by the Irish. This did not stop 'Irish-European' circles from taking a high moral tone towards the British and French, who were jointly considered the wreckers of the idea.[280]

Essentially Ireland's political and diplomatic elite had emerged sufficiently from Plato's cave to grasp the new world order. Although the diplomatic and professional elites were carefully examining the developments on the continent, Frank Aiken, the minister for external affairs, nevertheless stated to Schuman 'in the event of a war our policy would be similar to that on the last occasion. He explained that as long as partition continues national unity could not be abandoned for any other policy'.[281] Schuman's response is not recorded.

Although the expressed statement of Frank Aiken was that Ireland would remain neutral, that did not prevent him from asking Douglas MacArthur, political advisor to Eisenhower and member of SHAPE staff in Paris, for modern weaponry or 'At least enough for training purposes'. MacArthur replied that there was resentment towards the neutrals which 'was due to the feeling that Ireland although from every aspect a member of the Atlantic community, was nevertheless not within the Atlantic organisation'.[282] It was this reluctance to join NATO and a tendency to bang the partition drum that left Ireland politically out in the cold in Europe in the early 1950s.

Conclusion

As Ireland's first ambassador to Paris and owing to the service which he had given, Cremin was presented with a second Légion d'honneur. Stephen Collins, who interviewed Cremin, stated that one of Cremin's

> proudest possessions were his two Légion d'honneurs from the French government … The officials asked him if he would have any objection to the presentation of the Légion d'honneur and Cremin was too much the diplomat to mention the fact that he had already been presented with one, especially considering that it might cause some embarrassment to Ireland if he did mention it.[283]

One might infer that Cremin never wore his first decoration for fear of offending French sensibilities.

Cremin's four years in Paris were some of the most eventful in post-war French history. He saw the destruction of the French empire in Indo-China, and its impact on de Gaulle who, he accurately predicted, was 'finished as a major power in internal French politics'.[284] He saw the establishment of the Common Market, which, although it was probably the most momentous event in post-war European history, did not impact on many of his reports.[285] The project for European integration was conducted away from the diplomatic circles of Paris however, and Cremin probably felt that he could not have added anything useful, as he was not a diplomat who reported trivialities. In terms of trade, he did help increase Ireland's trade to France during his tenure as ambassador, although it was impossible for him to overcome the fundamental barriers which hampered Ireland's economic expansion at this time.

The greatest concern during his time in Paris was the question of European defence. This was intrinsically linked to the future of Ireland, which Cremin perceived to be with the continent. The reports on the threat from the Soviet Union and the development of the EDC to counter the threat served as the main focus of his reports. The importance of keeping the department current with the thinking from the heart of the EDC was vital in that Cremin, for the second time in his career, was able to counter some of the more alarmist reports from Joseph Walshe. These efforts were vital in keeping Ireland's foreign policy on a stable path in the post-war world.

CHAPTER 7

Vatican, 1954–56

'IN 1954, J.P. WALSHE, SECRETARY OF the department and our first ambassador, decided to retire from his post as ambassador to the Holy See where he ranked as dean of the diplomatic corps.'[1] That ought not to have been a matter of personal professional concern to the Irish ambassador to France. His next posting ought to have been a return to departmental headquarters in Dublin or, more likely, a new assignment to either London or Washington. Keogh has argued:

> It was another posting, and not necessarily one of the more sought after by an Irish diplomat in the fast track. Con Cremin, who succeeded Walshe at the Villa Spada, expressed his great surprise at having been appointed to the post.[2]

Keogh further writes that this ambassadorial position should really have been for a man reaching the age of retirement or on his first posting. Cremin was neither of those but Joseph Walshe still managed to get Cremin to succeed him.[3] Walshe placed 'an inordinate diplomatic importance' on Irish links with the Vatican and on church affairs in general.[4] In an 'Outline of the Duties of the Irish Minister to the Vatican' which Walshe had sent Séan MacBride, he stated:

> More than any post abroad, these call for the highest degree of care and self sacrifice in the representative. His very routine of life must be adapted in no small degree to that of his Vatican environment. Unless he sets out of deliberate purpose to become an observant Churchman in detail, he is courting failure.[5]

Walshe obviously believed that Cremin possessed the necessary qualities of care and self-sacrifice.[6] Cremin himself stated there was 'doubtless much speculation about the succession, given that the post had for four years been our only embassy'.[7]

The second inter-party government had been elected in May 1954 and Liam Cosgrave, the newly appointed minister for external affairs, appointed Cremin to the Vatican.[8] Cremin was well known to both the papal nuncio to France, Roncalli, and his predecessor, Valeri. If they were advised of Cremin's transfer, the Vatican would have received a positive endorsement of his calibre and of his competence.[9]

In geopolitical terms, the perspective of the Irish state on the Vatican had changed and 'by the end of the short-lived Fianna Fáil government, Irish-Vatican relations had become less intimate. While the "Special Relationship" continued, neither de Valera nor Aiken regarded Rome as the epicentre of world power'. The Irish government had come to view the Vatican in a more realistic light and the diplomatic corps found more to occupy their attention in Paris, Bonn, London, Washington and Ottawa.[10]

Cremin, to his surprise, was named Walshe's successor in July 1954. His appointment was reported in the *Irish Independent* on 24 August.[11] In September he made his farewells in Paris and left for Rome the next month.[12] Two weeks later he presented his letters of credence to Pius XII.[13] Cremin was to remain in the Irish embassy, the Villa Spada, for two years, until October 1956, during which time his minister, Cosgrave, and the Taoiseach, Costello, would visit. In his memoirs, Cremin reflected philosophically on the time spent in his new posting:

> It was, however, of very great interest with only very occasional problems of substance but in a setting which had great attractions and where literally no part of the world was alien to the work of the Holy See.[14]

His predecessor, Joseph Walshe, had decided to retire to Rome and had bought an apartment where he intended to live out his remaining years. In 1955, he travelled to South Africa to recuperate from an illness but died in Cairo on his return journey on 6 February 1956.[15]

One of the main contacts for any Irish diplomat was the extensive Irish religious community in Rome. However, Ireland was without high-level nationals in the Curia, the Vatican civil service, and Cremin had to cultivate these contacts.[16] The rector of the Irish College, Mgr Donald Herlihy, had been a close friend of Cremin's since school days at St Brendan's College, Killarney.[17] He was also a source of much information.[18] During Cremin's stint as ambassador an Irishman, Fr Browne, was elected as master general of the Dominican order, the first Hibernian in the 740 years of the order.[19] Cremin's brother, Frank, one of the staff of the Pontifical University, St Patrick's College Maynooth, would also have supplied introductions.

The Cremin family seem to have enjoyed their time in the Vatican. In his memoirs, Cremin stated that Villa Spada was the most attractive of the three embassies in London, Paris and the Vatican.[20] It was also the only residence to boast a swimming pool, which the family greatly enjoyed.[21] Aedeen Cremin said that her parents loved travelling: 'My mother probably preferred Paris, but my father might have enjoyed the Vatican more, given the atmosphere of heavy intrigue.'[22] Cremin also had the opportunity to engage in some serious scholarship: researching the burial place of the O'Neills and the O'Donnells at San Pietro in Montorio, and publishing his results in *The Capuchin Annual* in 1959.[23] For a classics scholar, Rome evinced a great interest. The eternal city's libraries, architecture and classical antiquities were enough to sate the appetite of any bibliophile. He was also interested in history and art and used Latin at the dinner table.[24]

On 24 May 1955, Cremin wrote that he and his family were received by the pope: 'He referred several times to "faithful Ireland" and in giving his blessing at the end of the audience included Ireland in it.'[25] On 31 December 1955, Cremin had a further audience with the pope where he conveyed the greetings of the Irish people. On the issue of partition, Cremin stated there was a certain amount of impatience on the part of some young Irishmen who favoured more direct action:

> The Holy Father remarked that this is a difficult problem which is rendered more difficult and painful by the harsh attitude of the Protestant population. He added that the situation of the Protestants there is strange as we treat those within our jurisdiction very well: 'with you, he said, they get more than they are entitled to.' He used the phrase twice during this part of the conversation. I remarked that it was true that we observed tolerance towards non-Catholics, that I suppose we should practise Christian charity even if others do not adopt a similar attitude towards us, and that I also supposed that the Holy Father was not suggesting that we treat non-Catholics too well. He agreed entirely with these last two propositions, going on to remark that the contrast between the behaviour of the Protestants in the Six Counties and that of Protestants in England is strange and striking.[26]

The internal politics of the Vatican were slightly anomalous and Cremin commented in his memoirs on the interesting situation he found there during his time as ambassador. No secretary of state had been appointed after 1944; instead the post was divided between two sostituti, or under-secretaries of state: Mgrs Tardini and Montini. Although neither was a cardinal, Cremin speculated this was owing to a lack of vacancies in the Sacred College, which was limited to seventy members until John XXIII's pontificate.[27] According to Cremin, both men 'divided the functions between them in a manner which was not quite precisely defined'.[28] Walshe, in a secret memorandum on 3 March 1954, stated there was considerable resentment at the prospect of appointing either of them as secretary of state.[29]

On 4 November 1954, Cremin sent a biographical summary of Montini to Dublin taken from the Catholic Action newspaper, *Il Quotidiano*, from which he concluded: 'it would not be surprising if both Monsignor Montini and Monsignor Tardini were both created cardinals at an early consistory.'[30] Hebblethwaite argues, 'Pius XII wanted to make Tardini and Montini cardinals, but it had to be *both together*'. Tardini refused and his 'refusal meant that Montini could not become a cardinal either'. John XXIII subsequently made Tardini secretary of state and made Montini a cardinal.[31]

The Question of a British Nuncio
It was during Cremin's time in the Vatican that Ireland was finally allowed to join the United Nations.[32] On 17 December 1955, Cremin wrote that *Il Quotidiano* contained the following item on the admission of the new members to the UN. Cremin quotes:

> In particular the entry of nations of old Catholic civilisation like Italy, Spain, Portugal and Ireland will represent, without doubt, an effective contribution for the defence and the development of civilisation.[33]

On 21 December 1955 Cremin reported that Mgr Tardini's (in charge of external affairs), belief that Ireland's joining the UN was a positive development.[34] In March 1956, Tardini stated Ireland at the United Nations 'should ensure the observance of Christian principles in international life'.[35] The three principles Cosgrave enunciated at the UN (fidelity to the charter of the UN, independence, and the preservation of Christianity) included a reference:

> to preserve the Christian civilisation of which we are a part and with that end in view to support wherever possible those powers principally responsible for the defence of the free world in their resistance to the spread of communist power.[36]

With the preservation of Christian civilisation as one tenet of Irish foreign policy, the spectre of Northern Ireland lurked in the background. On 30 September 1955, Cremin reported a visit of the Taoiseach, John A. Costello, to Mgr Tardini, who commented on the 'very favourable' treatment the Irish accorded to non-Catholics:

> He wondered whether the reason for our favourable attitude towards non-Catholics is to secure independence for the north. The Taoi-

seach remarked that we give fair treatment to non-Catholics both on general principles and also in the interest of future unity, that the non-Catholics within our jurisdiction appreciate and acknowledge that they are fairly treated, that it is a fact that Catholics are not well treated in the north where politicians exploit religious differences for political ends, and that partition is a very difficult problem, the solution of which requires time and patience. Mgr Tardini said that he agrees about the need for time and patience but that the favourable treatment accorded by us to non-Catholics is to him a source of great anxiety.[37]

Cremin marked the report 'Secret' owing to the reference to the north; secrecy surrounded all matters relating to Northern Ireland.[38] This was particularly so over the issue of the raising of the status of the apostolic delegate in London to that of nuncio. This posed a major difficulty for Ireland in that: 'Ordinarily, the area of a nuncio's or inter-nuncio's diplomatic accreditation and the area of his ecclesiastical jurisdiction are exactly co-terminous. But … an exception to this rule has been made in the case of the nuncio in Ireland'.[39] Any changing of the status of the apostolic delegate in London would mean that the nuncio would be accredited to the United Kingdom of Great Britain and Northern Ireland. From Ireland's perspective this would convey *de jure* recognition of partition by the Vatican.

Joseph Walshe had already fought a successful rearguard action against any change in the apostolic delegate's position and left Cremin to conclude the battle.[40] In March 1953, Boland reported from London: 'conversations are proceeding from behind the scenes here with a view to the apostolic delegation in this country being raised to the status of an inter-nunciature. The principal steps in the matter are being taken by the Catholic Union'.[41] On 18 December 1953, Walshe had delivered an *appunto* (*aide-mémoire*) to Mgr Dell'Acqua setting out the Irish government's concerns.[42] The perceived danger increased when, in June 1954, Mgr O'Hara was appointed apostolic delegate. Boland thought it 'might be a prelude to the raising of the status of the apostolic delegation to that of an inter-nunciature' owing to the fact that Mgr O'Hara was a US citizen. This meant that there were not any constitutional difficulties with a British commonwealth subject representing a 'foreign state' at the Court of St James.[43] On 3 October 1954, Cremin wrote to Liam Cosgrave, indicating the importance of the issue in the minds of the Irish politicians:[44]

> As to the other matter on which you wrote to me, your predecessor did not give me the impression that there was an immediate danger. It was, however, the one question that he asked me to mention to you.[45]

Cross-party support in foreign policy was rare but the inflexible thirty-two county republic, 'the *Hibernia irredenta* mentality' prevailed on both sides of the dáil.[46] Cremin diplomatically stated to Cosgrave:

> In the crisis I had already decided not to act on the [previous] department's minute, but to leave the matter over until your arrival. For me in my interim capacity – to intervene might easily have results we would not wish for and might also restrict your freedom of movement in the matter later.[47]

Cosgrave asked Cremin to elicit information on the appointment of a nuncio to London and asked Cremin to express 'once again to the Vatican authorities the importance of the issue to the Irish Church and public opinion'.[48]

In early November 1954, Liam Cosgrave himself arrived in Rome. He and Cremin discussed the matter at length and examined the text of the *appunto* which Walshe had left with Mgr Dell'Acqua in December 1953.[49]

Cremin argued there were a number of factors to be taken into account, primarily whether the 'Vatican would be prepared to sacrifice friends of whose loyalty it is sure (like Ireland) to gain elsewhere a political point to which it attaches importance'. Secondly, Cremin stated Churchill had asked the duke of Norfolk, head of the Catholic Union, 'not to add to his difficulties' and leave the matter drop. Thirdly, Cremin argued that if Ireland were seen to 'protest too much, we might give the Vatican the impression that, although opposed to such a step, we were psychologically prepared for it'.

Cremin counselled Cosgrave 'to allude to the matter, but without seeming to press what is ... conjecture'. The minister was to seek a meeting with Montini and to raise the matter on the following lines:

> Mr Walshe was very pre-occupied with the prospect that a nuncio would have jurisdiction over the six counties.
>
> We don't object to the Vatican extending accreditation.
>
> We are only dealing with an eventuality but the government endorses entirely the objections raised in Walshe's *appunto* to extend the jurisdiction of the Vatican representative in London to the six counties.[50]

The meeting went ahead with Mgr Dell'Acqua, not Montini, on 5 November 1954, and he gave the following reassurances:

> There is no real possibility of a nuncio or inter-nuncio being appointed to London.
>
> If the question arose full account would be taken of our views on the point at issue.
>
> Mgr Dell'Acqua affirmed that the Holy See attaches a very special importance to Ireland and will always 'give a preference to Ireland'.[51]

Cremin was further reassured on 7 November 1954, when Mgr Dell'Acqua assured him there were not any new developments.[52] In May 1955, Cremin was asked to ascertain if there were any developments.[53] On 28 July, he replied there was nothing new to report.[54]

When Cremin had an interview with the British minister to the Vatican, Sir Douglas Howard, they discussed the recent audience of John Foster Dulles, the US secretary of the state, with the

Vatican. Neither knew what transpired during the meeting and engaged in diplomatic fencing.

> Sir Douglas Howard wondered whether the question of the appointment of an American representative to the Vatican had been raised. He added immediately that he was quite certain that it would not be raised by the Holy See. I said that I had no information of the point and commented that it is rather anomalous that Washington is still without representation here. The British minister agreed and remarked that there is also an anomaly in the British representation inasmuch as Britain maintains a legation whereas the Vatican representative in London is only an apostolic delegate.

The British minister stated he knew of movements by the Catholic Union to have a nuncio or inter-nuncio appointed to London but 'his government would much prefer that the issue should not be raised', in light of the sensitive jurisdiction question this would raise. He went on to elaborate that this was not owing to any fundamental opposition on the part of the government but owing to the fact that 'various elements throughout the country [would] become vociferous'. He felt quite sure the Vatican would not take any action. On the other hand the 'apostolic delegate suffers no serious inconvenience by not having diplomatic status'. 'Sir Douglas Howard concluded his remarks on the question by again repeating that [her majesty's government] would certainly much prefer that the matter should not be raised'.[55]

Cremin stated: 'I was very glad to get his account of the situation spontaneously. I naturally gave no hint whatever of any particular interest on our part in the question'.[56] On 26 January 1956, F.H. Boland, the Irish ambassador to London, alerted Dublin that an Irish ecclesiast stated the issue of the status was being revived. Boland noted:

> The idea of consistently having a foreigner as papal representative in this country clearly runs counter to the whole policy of the Catholic Church in England which is always leaning over backward to estab-

lish its essential 'Englishness' – so much so that (up to recently at any rate) it has always ignored and deplored the Irish and other alien elements in its ranks and even today it still tends to outdo even the Protestant denominations in protesting its loyalty to the crown and its stout British patriotism.[57]

Boland thought the danger was purely hypothetical. Cremin subsequently met with Dell'Acqua who revealed: 'the position in the matter with which we are concerned has undergone no change.'[58] Cremin arranged for Cosgrave to meet Tardini (secretary of extraordinary affairs) and Dell'Acqua, to emphasise Ireland's specific interest in the matter to Tardini.[59]

On 20 March 1956, Cosgrave and Cremin met with Dell'Acqua and Tardini and explained the Irish difficulty with a London nuncio or inter-nuncio having jurisdiction over the six counties. Tardini replied:

> If the problem should arise … he declared that the Vatican would approach its solution in the light of 'the most friendly dispositions' it entertains for Ireland. The minister thanked Mgr Tardini for this assurance.[60]

But even the appointment of an apostolic delegate to London caused concern in the Irish camp. Cremin was intimately involved in drafting a report which was to be submitted secretly to the Vatican, in relation to Ireland's concerns about the prospective appointment of such a delegate. In a draft of 3 March 1956, Cremin advised:

> I would be inclined to suggest that while we should strongly urge the Vatican to endeavour to secure that the offending phrase [jurisdiction over Northern Ireland] be omitted from the letters of credence we should in fact concentrate our attack on the second point i.e. try to ensure that, whatever the terms in which the credentials are drafted, the ecclesiastical jurisdiction of the representative does not extend to the six counties.[61]

In August, Cremin reported that Mgr Dell'Acqua again assured him that there had not been any 'concrete developments whatsoever'.[62] On 22 September 1956, before Cremin left the Holy See, he sent a note to Mgr Dell'Acqua concerning the status of the apostolic prefecture to London. Of the note, Cremin stated:

> The draft is in some ways a little strong but I don't know whether this is a defect as it may be just as well to make perfectly clear in a written submission our deep opposition to that feature of the change which is of concern to us and so get the Vatican thinking, in time, of how to dispose of the problem.[63]

Cosgrave agreed with Cremin's line and stated that emphasis should be placed on the 'split [of] the ecclesiastical jurisdiction of some of the northern dioceses', as some straddled the border.[64] The final draft was sent on 5 October 1956.[65] The matter did not end there and on 28 January 1957 the question followed Cremin to his new appointment in London.[66] Cremin's successor in the Vatican, Leo T. McCauley, had the honour of quashing the suggestion of a nuncio in London, which he did with a report on 14 February 1957.[67]

The Question of a US Ambassador to the Vatican

The question of raising the diplomatic mission from the United States to that of a full embassy had been suggested by Cardinal Spellman to US President Harry Truman in the early 1950s. The idea had met with vociferous anti-Catholicism and Spellman, cardinal archbishop of New York, gave up hope of establishing diplomatic relations in January of 1953.[68]

Cremin noted: 'It is true that in general conversation between colleagues from time to time surprise is expressed at the USA not filling what most of them regard as a serious gap'. Cremin wrote that Truman had asked General Clarke to allow his name to go forward because he needed 'a Protestant, a 33rd degree mason and a military man, and someone who is known and respected in Italy'. US ecclesiastics believed however that 'as long as the issue provokes heated controversy in the USA it is better not to raise it'.[69]

In May 1956, Cremin wrote that the now former President Truman was visiting Italy and had an audience with Pius XII on 20 May 1956. Cremin reported he had not heard anything of what transpired but: 'in any case Mr Truman has made it clear that his present journey is a purely private one and he has no mandate whatever from the administration.' Cremin suggested, 'It appears however ... that there was some discussion between himself and the Holy Father about [US] diplomatic representation to the Holy See'. Cremin stated:

> There may be perhaps a vague hope in the Vatican ... that the decision of Mr Eisenhower to send a special representative to the recent cere-monies for the anniversaries of the Holy Father may be the prelude to the establishment of formal relations ... I get the impression in fact of a wide divergence of opinion between American clerics both as to the likelihood of diplomatic relations being established and the extent to which Mr Eisenhower personally would desire or be ready to go to bring about such a result. The common view seems to be that he personally would like to have a diplomatic mission here for general reasons ... but he is slow to summon the courage to take such a step.

Cremin concluded by saying that some US clerics were doubtful of the sincerity of Eisenhower's convictions.[70]

On 4 July 1956, Cremin reported that an Italian newspaper claimed Eisenhower would try to establish a US embassy in the Vatican.[71] Finally, on 19 July 1957, Cremin stated that he had an audience with the visiting Irish-American cardinal archbishop of Chicago, Cardinal Stritch. Cremin concluded that the cardinal's visit was not in relation to US-Vatican diplomatic relations.[72]

The campaign to formally establish diplomatic relations be-tween the Vatican and the US was finally scotched in March 1961 when 'John F. Kennedy declared his opposition to the establish-ment of such relations'.[73] It was not until 1983 that a US ambas-sador to the Vatican was appointed.[74]

The Health of Pius XII and the Papal Succession

Throughout Cremin's period as ambassador to the Vatican the health of Pope Pius XII was a subject of much debate, especially in relation to his potential successor.[75] He had been gravely ill since 1954.[76] By 4 March 1954, Walshe reported that neither the Vatican authorities 'nor the pope want the Catholic world to know that the government of the Church has already passed out of his hands'.[77] By November, Cremin speculated there might be a small consistory (an assembly of cardinals and the pope) held to give the 'hat' to Montini, although it would be contrary to Pius XII's policy of not holding consistories.[78]

In December, the ambassador reported Pius XII was suffering from a stomach ailment but cancer was ruled out.[79] The same month Cosgrave said he believed Pius XII looked well during a private audience. Cremin reiterated reports that Montini was going to be made a cardinal and some speculated on who would take over his duties in Milan.[80] Cremin related that Montini had been appointed to the archbishopric of Milan as a 'punishment' for holding 'advanced views'. Cremin learned from a friend that both Montini's allies and enemies were delighted with his appointment; his allies felt he would be the next pope and his enemies were glad he had been removed from the centre of affairs.[81] In January 1955, Cremin confirmed reports that Pius XII's health was improving, but:

> there is little doubt that the Holy Father so conceives his obligations as pope that he must be active to the point of exhaustion. Any pope must of course, as head of the Church 'govern' in a positive manner. Pius XII has always interpreted the principle very strictly. It is, indeed, as you know, a source of grievance on the part of many of the members of the Curia that they are much less involved in the running of the affairs of the Church than they should be by virtue of their position.[82]

The papal historian, Kelly, agrees that Pius XII was: 'authoritarian in style, he acted himself as secretary of state from 1944, and increasingly diminished the role of the cardinals.'[83] This point of view reflected the thinking in a report received by Cremin in Rome on 6 January 1955. F.H. Boland, Ireland's ambassador to London, argued:

> there is likely to be a strong section of opinion in the Sacred College against the appointment of any prelate likely to be tempted to retain the immediate direction of the secretariat of state in his own hands.

Boland further reported there were two schools of thought in the Church: the 'Gospel school' (progressive), led by Montini and the 'Pragmatic school' (conservative), led by Cardinal Ottaviani. Boland stated that the two schools might split the Italian vote in a future election of a successor to Pius XII and thereby exclude the election of an Italian pope.[84]

Cremin soon informed Dublin: 'It is a very common view that the Holy Father will hardly survive more than a few months':

> There are also those who say (and indeed the Holy Father may agree with them) that if he cannot be more active in the discharge of his functions than he has been for some time past his survival would be disadvantageous for the Church as many important affairs depend directly on the present pope to an unusual degree.[85]

Cremin stated he frequently heard criticism of the secretariat of state now that the pope was ill. In April, Cremin returned to the issue of Pius XII's health and reiterated: 'General opinion here is that the next pope will be Italian. Equally it is still thought that it will be Mgr Montini', but his young age might militate against him.[86]

In November 1955, Cremin reported that the Taoiseach, John A. Costello, believed Pius XII was looking well.[87] On 9 June 1956, Cremin reported Mgr Dell'Acqua's statement that Pius XII was 'organically quite well, but he is very tired'. Cremin wrote: 'I got the impression that the monsignor really feels that the pope is overdoing things and he seemed rather more uneasy than on other occasions about the possible consequences of the heavy schedule of work the pope follows.'[88]

With the illness of Pope Pius XII a matter of constant speculation, Cremin discreetly researched all the protocol necessary for the funeral of a pope. On 15 December 1954, he sounded a cautious note:

> It is our intention to check the soundness for the occasion involved of the 'protocol' outlined in these notes. Clearly, however, we must proceed prudently in this if we are to avoid giving the impression of being alarmist.[89]

Throughout December and January Cremin researched the protocol and, having completed the research, proffered the idea of the president calling on the nuncio to offer condolences and the Taoiseach and the minister coming to the coronation.[90] This followed the precedent set by de Valera in 1939 who, as minister for external affairs and Taoiseach, had attended Pius XII's coronation.[91] Despite the continuous concern for Pius XII's health, he survived until 9 October 1958, long after Cremin had moved from the Vatican.[92]

Communism

The English journalist Peter Nichols has argued that Pius XII:

> came to hate communism as a power in the world; as primate of all Italy, he sought to break its power at home.[93] This is not altogether surprising, given the severe provocation he suffered in the form of widespread persecution of the Catholic faithful. He ended by aligning the Vatican closely with the western world against communism: a move away from the Church's traditional neutrality.[94]

This preoccupation with the threat posed by communism to western Christian civilisation dominated many of Cremin's reports. Pius XII saw communism as a seamless political entity from Berlin to Peking, at least until 1956 when Khrushchev denounced Stalin and the fractures within communism became apparent.[95]

As late as 1955, Cremin informed Dublin that the Soviets were receiving demands from the Chinese for equipment.[96] Khrushchev responded generously and gave substantial amounts of military and industrial equipment and technical expertise.[97] However, tensions led to the Sino-Soviet split in 1958, undermining western perceptions of communist solidarity.[98] But during Cremin's tenure in Rome this fragmentation was not apparent. Communism, as Cremin reported in mid-November 1954, was reasserting its ideology of 'communist science against religious faith'.[99] This ideology was modified by Khrushchev, who signed a circular published in *Pravda* in November on anti-religious activity which proclaimed: 'destroy religion but do so in a polite manner'.[100] Naturally such polite professions did not engender Vatican sympathy.

The fall of mainland China to communism in 1948 and the establishment of a nationalist government on the island of Formosa (Taiwan) which was recognised by the west as the legitimate government of China and occupied the seat at the UN until the 1970s presented the Vatican with a diplomatic conundrum.[101] The west supported Chiang-Kai-Shek's nationalist government in Taiwan, as did the Vatican. The Vatican did not wish to antagonise communist China and endanger the position of Chinese Catholics, but on the other hand Pius XII was deeply hostile towards communism.[102]

On 4 January 1955, Cremin reported that an article in *Osservatore Romano* omitted to mention that the nationalist Chinese ambassador had presented his credentials during 1954. Cremin observed that the ambassador 'must regard the article ... as a further indication of a deliberate tendency on the part of the Vatican to write down his presence'.[103] Therefore like the United States the Vatican did not recognise communist China, but the Vatican had to be more circumspect than the United States. The Chinese ambassador's name was on the diplomatic lists but these had a limited circulation within the diplomatic community.[104] On 6 February 1955, J.W. Lennon, first secretary in Iveagh House, asked Cremin to report on whether the Vatican was:

soft pedalling on the recognition of Formosa in order to keep the door open on the recognition of Mao's China or was it the fact that the Chinese ambassador was appointed in 1943 and therefore did not have to be mentioned again.[105]

Cremin reported that Ambassador Sié had first held the position in 1943 and ceased to hold it in 1946-47. 'Owing to a lacuna in our records I cannot say precisely when' (a reference to Walshe's destruction of the records). Cremin explained that when Sié was reappointed he had to present new credentials. The *Osservatore Romano*'s failure to cover the presentation of Sié's credentials was 'significant' and Cremin maintained his earlier assessment that the Vatican was inclined to 'soft pedal on the presence of a Chinese minister from the Formosa government'. Cremin refuted the suggestion by Lennon that the Vatican is 'keeping the door open for recognition of Mao's China', as a misleading interpretation of the Holy See's policy. He added:

> There is obviously a considerable gap between not having a representative accredited by the Formosa authorities and recognising communist China. They are two entirely separate issues and few administrations in the world are more competent or accustomed to distinguish between different things than that of the church.

Cremin continued:

> he had heard from a fairly reliable authority that the Holy See was more concerned with the avoidance of complicating the Church's position in the countries of India and Indonesia, which regard Formosa as a puppet regime.[106]

Of more immediate concern to the Vatican was the establishment of communist regimes throughout central Europe in the wake of the Second World War. Here also the Vatican faced the challenge of how to deal with regimes wishing to destroy the Church. In mid-November 1954, Cremin reported on a visit he made to Mgr Tardini, pro-secretary of state for extraordinary ecclesiastical affairs. Cremin reported that Tardini processed all the nuncio's reports and it was his belief:

The world 'is heading for the abyss'. If asked, he went on, whether there would be war tomorrow or in the near future, he would answer 'no'. If, he said, I were Molotov or Malenkov, I would not dream of going to war as I would risk losing something whereas I am getting everything I want as things are.

On the subject of Indo-China, Tardini stated western governments 'are seriously lacking in authority'. He went on to say he:

> considers it certain that the whole of Indo-China will be communist in the relatively near future. The acceptance by the west at Geneva of a plebiscite for the whole of Vietnam by 1956 was equivalent to handing over the whole country to the Viet-Minh as they are more numerous. He characterised the whole attitude towards Indo-China as a mistake. It should long ago have been recognised that this was not a purely French affair but involved directly all the western world and its standing in the east. When Indo-China has gone entirely communist this will inevitably have the most serious repercussions for the west among the other countries in the east.[107]

The Church was obviously concerned about the situation in Indo-China since it had experienced terrible losses earlier in China when the communists had taken over.[108]

In the Soviet Union on 31 January 1955, Malenkov was dismissed from the post of prime minister at the plenary meeting of the central committee.[109] Khrushchev, as head of the Communist party, replaced Malenkov with Bulganin, thereby safeguarding the Soviet power base both ideologically and militarily.[110] Cremin thought the Vatican could secure valuable information about the workings of the Kremlin from Catholics behind the Iron Curtain. He went on to report that the Catholic Action newspaper *Quotidiano* had an article by 'Diplomaticus' who believed the Red army was 'getting into the saddle'.[111]

On 15 February 1955, after a conversation with Mgr Dell'Acqua, Cremin reported the monsignor thought the changes in Moscow were to be welcomed and recorded:

He was naturally not able to give a categoric opinion but I got the impression that he welcomed these events. He did not think the changes mean an alteration in Russian policy which would make war more likely, and at the same time he feels that they betray the existence of difficulties in the Soviet Union and dissentions, both within the government and between the different directing organs of the state, which are reassuring in as much as they suggest that the whole system is suffering from a certain weakness that may in time become accentuated and lead to a more satisfactory state of affairs from the standpoint of the Church (and of the west). Mgr Dell'Acqua thinks (with indeed those of my colleagues with whom I have had a word on the subject and with most of the press here) that the army played a role in ousting Malenkov and has, with the appointment of Bulganin as prime minister and Zhukov as minister for defence, acquired a much greater direct influence on policy than it enjoyed hitherto.[112]

On 20 September 1955, Cremin had a meeting with the Finnish representative to the Holy See, Knorring. He told Cremin that the Soviet Union 'is suffering from economic difficulties and that there is also some degree of political instability'. Knorring went on to state the USSR's problems stemmed primarily, but not only, from agriculture. There was also a lack of consumer goods and the Soviet population had become more 'exigent in this regard'. Knorring also noted that Finnish citizens who had left during the 1930s or were captured during the war were being allowed back to Finland. Cremin stated:

Mr Knorring's remarks struck me as particularly interesting in the light of certain recent suggestions that the apparent change in the attitudes of the Russian government is due not to internal difficulties but to a deliberate alteration in policy. One may note in the same context statements on the Russian position made at the recent 5th congress in Milan on Cultural freedom.

On an economic note, Cremin quoted Colin Clarke, an Oxford economist, that the Soviet economy was growing by two per cent per annum.[113] This was very poor in relation to the spectacular rates of growth in western Europe and the United States, but was better than Ireland.

On 22 September 1955, Cremin reported on the visit of the Taoiseach, John A. Costello, to Mgr Dell'Acqua. During the meeting Dell'Acqua stated that the Geneva accords, which allowed the French to withdraw from Indo-China, gave the superficial impression of ease in the international situation, but they actually harmed France and Italy. Dell'Acqua argued: 'One cannot precisely assess Russian policies or the motives that inspire them but there seems to be at least some weaknesses in Russia'.[114]

The religious intolerance of the communist regimes in eastern Europe led to the arrest and imprisonment of many religionists and was the focus of several of Cremin's reports. In September 1955 Cremin reported on the continued detention of the Hungarian Cardinal Mindszenty.[115] The following month, he reported that the Polish Cardinal Wyszynski might be released on grounds of ill-health.

An article in the Italian communist newspaper *Unità* stated that the failure of the Vatican to establish dioceses in the former German territories implied the Vatican fundamentally lacked sympathy with the Polish state.[116] Cremin rejected this and stated that the Vatican would not recognise frontiers that were not recognised by any peace treaty.[117] On 19 October 1955, Cremin reported the Vatican was:

in favour of a relaxation of international tension, doubts whether the Russians have any sincere intention of changing their outlook and fears that the only effect of the 'Geneva Spirit', which costs the Russians nothing, will be to undermine western solidarity and the capacity and will to resist communist influence.

The 'Geneva Spirit' was the residual goodwill that existed towards communism after the settlement of the Indo-China question.[118] Cremin quoted Montini, who felt détente was dangerous for countries with strong communist parties such as France and Italy. Montini stated: 'International relations can be modified, can improve and even be reversed from one day to the next, but an internal "yielding" once it had taken place is irremediable'.[119] Montini reflected the fears of Christian Democrats in Italy who predicted that the growth in the strength of the Communist party could not be rolled back once they had achieved success.[120]

In February 1956, Cremin reported Mgr Dell'Acqua's belief that the danger of the new Soviet line of collegiate government, which allowed greater freedom among the satellites, might wed Yugoslavia more firmly to the Soviet bloc. Cremin argued that, militarily, the defection of Greece from the west was all that was required for communism to have a powerful unit in that part of the world. Dell'Acqua thought Britain had a less accommodating attitude than the French towards Russia, because they realised the dangers of the 'Geneva Spirit'.[121] Ruane argues Eden thought positively of France as a 'geographic necessity' to stand against the Soviets.[122] In relation to West Germany, Mgr Dell'Acqua stated he thought the position of Adenauer was very strong.[123]

On 9 March 1956, Quaroni, Italian ambassador to Paris, spoke on the lessons to be taken from the twentieth Soviet congress, which denounced Stalinism. Cremin wrote that Quaroni was 'extremely intelligent (it was commonplace in Paris during my period there to describe him as the most "intelligent" of all the heads of mission)'. Cremin concluded that Quaroni was much more pessimistic than the Finnish minister was regarding the aggressive intentions of the Soviets.[124]

On 26 March 1956, Cremin reported that Mgr Dell'Acqua 'expressed anxiety at the vacillation in America, and to some extent in Britain, in the approach to Russian affairs', especially the suggestion of a Four Power conference to discuss German reunification. Mgr Dell'Acqua believed the fear in France and Italy was that:

> the prospect of effectively dealing with the disruptive influence of communism are already small enough and the process becomes much more arduous when the impression is created that in 'solid' countries like Britain and the USA communism is regarded as something with which one can amicably live.

Cremin wrote that the German ambassador, Jaenicke, regarded the publishing of the Yalta papers as 'bordering on a disaster' owing to the disclosure of the sphere of influence which Churchill agreed with Stalin. Jaenicke believed this owing to a tendency which he deplored for foreign policy 'to be determined by reference to internal political considerations.'[125] Another area that deeply concerned the Vatican was the issue of denominational education.

The Vatican and Denominational Education

The question of denominational education was a recurrent issue in western Europe at this time. On 13 April 1955, Cremin sent a report on the schools crisis in Belgium. He stated that Spaak, the socialist Belgian foreign minister, did not have much enthusiasm for the new schools bill, which would undermine Church control of their schools. The Church was resisting it with a united front. Cremin reported that the more radical members of Spaak's party wanted it to go through.[126] In Austria, the socialist government argued that the 1938 Nazi law superseded the 1922 concordat with the Vatican which gave primacy to denominational education. The resulting tension meant relations between Austria and the Vatican were somewhat strained. Meanwhile, Mendès-France, the French prime minister, was suggesting a concordat with the Vatican.[127]

On 15 February 1955, Cremin wrote of Mendès-France's visit to the Holy Father: '[he is] a Jew and a radical, and is [or was] a freemason, all qualities which in other men would have made him reluctant to seek an audience'. Cremin wrote, with a sense of admiration:

> Here again the French prime minister has given proof of that sense of political realism and freedom from doctrinaire prejudice which is so widely attributed to him. He obviously recognises the Church as a powerful force at the present time. He probably also realises that a normal act of courtesy on his part towards the Holy Father could do him good in France.

Cremin continued:

The Mendès-France gesture is on the other hand calculated to win him some sympathy or at least to diminish hostility among those French Catholics who supported the MRP and the independents and moderates who have hitherto been his strongest adversaries.[128]

Mendès-France's gesture was appropriate as Cremin reported:

I understand that as of two months ago at least the French hierarchy were far from enthusiastic about Mendès-France. Furthermore ... he carries responsibility for the Indo-China agreements which have been interpreted as involving the abandonment of over a million Catholics in the Red River 'bishoprics'; he is likewise held by many influential French politicians to have been responsible for torpedoing the EDC and his most implacable enemies in the French parliament (always excluding the communists) have been the professedly Catholic MRP. The sentiments of regret felt by the Holy Father for the loss of the EDC, and his anxiety about the dangers of the policies which have recently become manifest, are abundantly clear from his Christmas message.

The discussions between the French prime minister and Pius XII were in private, but must have mentioned the fate of the Catholics in Vietnam. Cremin noted:

On the other hand that something was said about the international and in particular the European situation and about that of France; in a press conference prior to his departure from Rome, Mendès-France paid tribute to the Holy Father's 'clarity of ideas and of views, his exposition of international problems and above all the complete knowledge he has of French problems at the present moment', adding 'he follows minutely and day by day the development of France's situations and problems'.[129]

The next time Cremin mentioned Mendès-France was in December 1955, when Mendès-France offered Cardinal Tisserant, the prefect of ceremonies, a concordat with the Vatican to allow for the teaching of the Catholic religion in state schools. While

Cardinal Tisserant was in favour, not all the prominent ecclesiastics shared his faith in Mendès-France.[130] In April 1956 Cremin wrote that most moderate lay Catholics in France were in favour of the proposals brought out by Mendès-France that would settle the issue of the position of Catholic schools once and for all.[131] In order to proceed on the schools issue, the French ambassador to the Vatican, the Count d'Ormesson, was retired and replaced by Roland de Margerie, a career officer, in order to conduct the negotiations on the issue of the Catholic schools. Cremin argued: 'although the fact that he is I believe a good Catholic and is certainly *bien-pensant* means that any proposals submitted by him would hardly be free from the suspicion of "clericalism".'[132] It was perhaps because Mendès-France was Jewish that he felt capable of tackling the Catholic schools issue.

Mendès-France had praised Pius XII's actions towards the Jews during the war, but this did not remove either him or Pius XII from criticism.[133] On 9 February 1955:

> the *Osservatore Romano* ... carried a front page article which purported to answer criticism that the Holy Father and the Vatican had been indifferent to the persecution of the Jews before and during the war. It had little difficulty in showing that such criticism is unfounded.[134]

During a visit by Mendès-France to Italy, Cremin reported 'Pius XII showed considerable personal sympathy to persecuted Jews before and during the war'.[135] In July 1955, the *Osservatore Romano* refuted any suggestions made in an Israeli newspaper that the Holy Father did not do enough to help the Jews. Cremin wrote that the *Osservatore* article refuted 'the charges that the Holy Father did not do everything possible and cites a number of post-war testimonies by Jewish groups to his efforts'. Cremin went on:

> As stated in my earlier report no one here seriously doubts that the Holy Father did as much as he could to help the suffering Jews. That he was less outspoken in public and less direct than his predecessor can be explained by the fact that the circumstances with which he

was confronted were quite different. In his allocution of 2nd June 1943 to the Sacred College of which an extract is given in the article in question he explained indeed that every public utterance of his in favour of those persecuted on racial grounds had to be 'carefully weighed and measured in the very interest of those sufferers so as not to render more grave and intolerable their situation'. It is of course also a fact that Pius XI was notoriously outspoken and incisive when he felt it necessary to attack something to which he objected whereas the present Holy Father adopts a different approach in such cases and is much more nuancé in his declarations.[136]

Cremin argued the present criticism had more to do with Pius XII's position on Jerusalem, which was opposed to Israel's, than on the issue of the Holocaust.[137] Cremin's analysis is interesting in that he had served in Nazi Europe and tried to save Jews in his capacity as a diplomat. He would probably have agreed with the opinion of Robert W. M. Kempner, the former United Nations' delegate at the Tribunal of War Crimes at Nuremburg, who wrote: 'Any propaganda attempt undertaken by the Catholic Church against Hitler's reich would not only have been a provoked suicide, as Rosenberg has now said, but it would have hastened the execution of still more Jews and priests.'[138] Pierre Blet stated:

> Pius XII proceeded silently, with discretion, at the risk of appearing inactive or indifferent. And yet the work of assisting the war's victims was his favourite undertaking … Consequently, he did not nourish any illusions as to the extent of his influence, even if others, supplied with good intentions or, on the contrary, with hostile intentions ascribed to him unlimited power.[139]

It is undoubtedly the case that Cremin would not have agreed with the thesis that Pius XII was 'Hitler's pope'.[140] Cremin also had the advantage that he was writing objectively before Rolf Hochhuth's inflammatory play of 1964, 'The Deputy', which polarised the debate on Pius XII and the Holocaust.[141]

Cremin's Professionalism

In February 1955, Cremin had occasion to defend his profession-alism. On 14 February, he wrote to J.W. Lennon, 'concerning the use of names of persons who have been sources of information'. Cremin wrote:

> I would see serious objection to mentioning the names of members of the Vatican service who may be good enough to furnish us with information or observations of a confidential nature ... [Owing to the] degree of discretion which the Vatican expects from its officers, I would prefer that there should not be even the slightest risk of the names being divulged.

Cremin went on to dismiss the guesswork which some in Iveagh House resorted to in order to determine who was the source of Cremin's information. He continued:

> It may be stated that in speaking thus I am being unduly prudent and perhaps also unduly uneasy about the risks of indiscretion at home. It is evident, however, that where the divulgation of a source of in-formation serves no useful purpose and may be harmful we cannot be too careful in obviating the risks of this happening. You say that the reports in question are confidential. I should like to point out to you that your letter in which you mention specifically two names as being the source of information supplied by me is not marked either 'personal' or 'confidential' and was not even enclosed in a envelope. It reached us open with another minute (313/6a) of 5th February which was marked in manuscript 'confidential'. This means that both of these communications went right through the department and the registry for everyone to see.

Cremin criticised Lennon for trying to identify the sources of his information, arguing it served no purpose and asked that any iden-tifications inserted into his reports be removed.[142]

The Nuncio and the Ballina School Dispute

Diplomatic disputes arising from Ireland's internal politics rarely occurred during Cremin's time in Rome. However, when the nuncio to Dublin was perceived to have exceeded his mandate and intervened in the jurisdiction of one of the Irish bishops, Cremin had to play a part in calming ecclesiastical tempers.

On 18 May 1956, Cremin reported on the Ballina school dispute, where the bishop of Killala wanted to dismiss the lay teachers and hand over the school to the Marist Brothers. The Irish National Teachers Organisation (INTO) went to the nuncio, Levame, in Dublin to ask him to intercede. The nuncio suggested they ask the archbishop of Dublin, John Charles McQuaid, to intercede instead:

> Dr Levame said that this episode is perhaps symptomatic of some dangers inherent in the present situation in Ireland which are not the less serious for not being obvious: the waves he said which do the harm in the Mediterranean are those that are not evident on the surface of the sea and our position is perhaps not dissimilar. He observed that there is a tendency in Ireland 'to rest on our laurels' (obviously he meant from the point of view of Catholicism). In the old days it was not easy to get to Ireland but now people and ideas can be transported with remarkable rapidity.

Levame believed *The Irish Times* featured the Ballina affair so prominently because the editor was a member of the Communist party. Cremin dismissed this idea stating that the *Irish Independent* gave as much coverage to the story.[143]

On 24 May 1956, Cremin wrote that the nuncio 'has been rather outspoken here about the extent to which the hierarchy more or less ignore him'. Cremin mentioned the hierarchy were intending to hold a synod that year, but the nuncio did not know about this. Cremin wrote:

> I am sure that you will appreciate that the only reason I am reporting on what the nuncio has been saying is because I think you might be

interested to have this information and not at all because the matters in question are any direct concern of ours … It is of course notorious that the hierarchy in Ireland have always tended to conduct their affairs more or less as if the nuncio did not exist.

Cremin stated: 'I have a strong impression that Cardinal Feltin of Paris sometimes felt that the nuncio there [Roncalli] tended to encroach into fields which he (Cardinal Feltin) regarded as not coming strictly within the nuncio's domain'.[144] On 30 May 1956, Cosgrave informed Cremin that he had dropped a 'discreet hint' on the issue of Levame to the archbishop of Dublin to the effect that the Irish hierarchy should make an effort to include the nuncio.[145]

European Integration
In comparison with his reports on the intricacies of internal church politics, Cremin dealt superficially with the issues of European integration, as they were perceived from the Vatican. On 9 July 1955, Cremin wrote of the visit of Paul-Henry Spaak, the Belgian foreign minister, to Pius XII:

> Spaak was much impressed by the Holy Father and they had an agreeable conversation. In so far as it bore on one point more than another this was the efforts for European unification which, as you know, are of much interest to the Holy Father and of which Spaak is of course an outstanding protagonist.

Cremin wrote 'Spaak seems to be relatively free from the doctrinaire prejudices which frequently characterise prominent socialists'.[146]

The Catholic Church followed developments in European integration closely and later Cremin reported how Cardinal Tisserant admired Guy Mollet, the leader of the French socialist party, for imposing 'on the Socialist party the policy of "Europeanism" in which he believes but in which most of his party does not'.[147] Undoubtedly the Vatican welcomed such developments as they were seen as an additional bulwark against communism.

The Christian Democrats in western Europe, who played a key role in promoting integration, had interested Cremin in October 1955 when he reported a London *Times* statement. The statement said that the Christian Democratic movement had failed to live up to expectation partly owing to the Vatican's policy which did not permit 'a restatement of Roman Catholic principles in the light of a progressive approach to social problems'. Cremin reported that Mgr Dell'Acqua refuted the accusation stating 'the article in question is superficial and not worthy of serious attention' and arguing that the influence of the Christian Democratic movement was not declining. Mgr Dell'Acqua stated the Vatican was not as closely related to the Christian Democratic movement as the *Times* article implied, which was inspired by English distrust of Catholicism. On the issue of the Church not being progressive, Cremin argued the declarations of Pius XII 'rather suggest that open-mindedness and a progressive approach in the numerous fields on which he touches are a principal characteristic of his outlook'. Cremin stated the Christian Democratic newspaper *Il Popolo* reported the Christian Democrats were not endeavouring to promote an 'ideological coalition between European Catholics'. *Osservatore Romano*, the Vatican newspaper, rejected the charge of being un-progressive.[148]

Conclusion

The issues Cremin dealt with at the Vatican were both complex and eclectic in nature. As ever, he reported professionally and defended his professionalism when he felt it was under threat. Although Cremin had been perplexed as to the reason for his transfer to the Holy See, he was well suited to the posting. He was convinced that Joseph Walshe had been responsible for the decision and had hand-picked Cremin to succeed him. Although he was used to more exacting missions, Cremin rose to the professional challenge during his two-year tour of duty. He adjusted to the different and slower pace of diplomatic life at the Vatican. His reports on the Cold War continued to be of value and he did help in thwarting the initiative of the English Catholics regarding the appointment of a nuncio to the Court of St James. His reports on communism demonstrated the complex path that the Catholic Church had to tread during the 1950s. He also succeeded in smoothing relations between the nuncio in Dublin and the Irish bishops. The question of the papal succession was one of intellectual curiosity for Cremin and his two years in the Vatican helped him develop his interests in the Irish exiles in Rome.

Before Cremin left for London, the *Irish Independent*, on 15 October 1956, carried an article which stated: 'Mr Cremin had been ambassador to the Vatican for more than two years. During his farewell visit to the Vatican the Holy Father bestowed on him the Grand Cross of the Pian Order, third highest Vatican decoration, in recognition of his services at the Vatican'.[149] Aedeen Cremin said her father was particularly proud of the fact that two future popes attended his farewell dinner: Roncalli, who became John XXIII, whom Cremin had known in Paris where he was the papal nuncio, and Montini, who became Paul VI.[150]

CHAPTER 8

London, 1956–58

CREMIN, WHO HAD SERVED TWO YEARS at the Holy See, was next appointed ambassador to the Court of St James. The announcement was made in the press on 15 October 1956.[1] He replaced F.H. Boland who was appointed as Ireland's first ambassador to the UN in New York. Cremin left Rome with his family within a few weeks of receiving his directive from headquarters.

Cremin had been given an anomalous posting in mid-career to the Holy See. He was ranked among the top three envoys serving in the diplomatic service at the time and he might have reasonably expected to be sent to Washington or to London at that point in his career, rather than to the Holy See. His promotion to London was more in keeping with his rank and reputation within the department of external affairs.[2]

And so in professional terms, his new posting appealed to him greatly: London was arguably now Ireland's most important embassy. History, geography, commerce, trade, emigration and the issue of partition were the reasons for its great sensitivity and central significance. There were also rumours of all kinds in London, including rumours of war, owing to the Suez crisis.[3]

During his posting in London, Cremin reported on the aftermath of this Suez crisis, as well as the Soviet invasion of Hungary and the continuing crisis in Cyprus. He also had to deal with the routine of Anglo-Irish relations. His background in the handling of commercial affairs placed him in a strong position to encourage greater Irish exports to Britain.

Following in the footsteps of Boland made his job somewhat easier. The latter had set up a range of high-level contacts, many of which Cremin was in a position to activate; these included Hugh Gaitskell, Ernest Bevin, Aneurin Bevan and Clement Attlee. As well as contacts in the political set Boland had left a network of literary and journalistic contacts and connections with the National University of Ireland clubs and Irish clubs.[4] In his memoirs, Cremin mentioned another contact:

> Ireland of course still stood under the commonwealth relations office and both my predecessor and I were fortunate to find an old and very experienced friend in the office of permanent under secretary Sir Gilbert Laithwaite who had been the first British ambassador in Dublin after our change in status in 1950.[5]

Although the British diplomatic profile of Cremin has not been located by this historian, it is probable that he came highly regarded, considering the cordial relations he had built up with his British colleagues in Lisbon, Dublin, Paris and the Holy See. Reports from the British embassy in Dublin and the British legation to the Holy See would have shown him to be a diplomat held in high professional esteem by his colleagues from other countries.[6]

Suez Crisis

The first major task facing Cremin as he took over his new position was to master the file on the middle east and come to terms with the diplomatic confusion at the end of the Suez Crisis. In his previous posting at the Holy See, he was likely to have followed the crisis in outline but was not in an advantageous position to have inside knowledge about the sequence of events leading to the debacle.[7]

The crisis had begun in 1954 when Britain, under pressure from the United States, had agreed to withdraw its forces from the Suez Canal zone in Egypt.[8] With the failure of the Baghdad Pact (the 1955 alliance in which the nations involved agreed to mutual cooperation and non-intervention in each other's affairs), Egypt's Lieutenant-Colonel Gamal Abdel Nasser struck an arms deal with the Soviet bloc.[9] Kissinger succinctly summarises what happened:

> In 1955, just two months after the Geneva Summit, the Soviet Union made a major arms sale to Egypt … a daring move to extend Soviet

influence into the middle east. In making a bid for influence in Egypt, Khrushchev had in effect leapfrogged the *cordon sanitaire* which the United States had constructed around the Soviet Union, confronting Washington with the task of having to counter the Soviets in areas heretofore considered to be safely within the western sphere.[10]

To counter this move, the British sought United States support for the financing of the Aswan Dam project (which proposed to dam the Nile), rather than risk the Soviets financing it.[11] Already annoyed by the arms sale, on 16 May 1955, John Foster Dulles, the US secretary of state, was further alienated by Nasser's recognition of the People's Republic of China. Dulles responded by cutting all aid to the Aswan Dam.[12] In response, on 26 July 1956 Nasser nationalised the Suez canal, intending to use the revenue accruing from tariffs to pay for the dam. The nationalisation of the canal provoked a crisis in western Europe, as there was almost total dependence upon the canal for the transit of oil.[13]

Dulles responded to the nationalisation by engaging in lengthy conferences with Britain and France and by establishing a users' association to manage the canal: '[N]either Britain or France had any inclination of putting "their vital petroleum imports in the hands of Nasser", and the Egyptians refused to share control of the canal'.[14] The delay allowed Nasser to consolidate his position. Anthony Eden, the British prime minister, and Guy Mollet, the French prime minister, both men absolutely opposed to appeasement, had committed themselves to action.[15] Britain and France jointly developed a plan for an assault on Egypt which, for operational reasons, had to begin before 15 November 1956.[16]

Dulles compounded the crisis when on 2 October he ruled out United States military intervention.[17] On 14 October, Eden met with the French General Maurice Challe and Albert Gazier, France's minister for labour. Challe proposed Israel be encouraged to attack Egypt and thus risk the safety of the canal. This would give a pretext for Britain and France to reoccupy the canal zone.[18] On 22 October, Selwyn Lloyd, the British foreign secretary, met David Ben-Gurion, the Israeli prime minister, to finalise details for the attack.[19] On the evening of 29 October, Israel invaded the Sinai Peninsula. Britain and France demanded both sides withdraw ten miles from either side of the canal.[20] The United States, which had not been consulted, condemned Britain and France in the United Nations.[21] On 2 November, the UN assembly voted sixty-five to five in favour of a resolution urging a cease-fire and the withdrawal of British, French and Israeli forces from Egypt.[22] On 4 November, the Egyptians blocked the canal; by 5 November British and French paratroopers had taken Port Fuad and were on the outskirts of Port Said.[23]

On 6 November, with one third of the canal captured, Britain declared a cease-fire, owing to strong US and Soviet opposition and a run on sterling.[24] The cease-fire was declared 'in the teeth of strong French opposition'.[25]

Cremin approached his reporting on the Suez Crisis with significant background knowledge of the decision-making processes at the Quai d'Orsay from his time there as ambassador. He reported on the issue for the first time on 13 November 1956, within days of his arrival in London. He said the Dutch ambassador, Dr Dirk Stikker, was of the opinion that:

> Eden made a serious gaffe in sending troops into Suez. The decision was, in his view, an emotional one on the part of Sir Anthony Eden who was stung to marked hostility towards Colonel Nasser because of the latter, instead of regarding Eden as a friend for having put through the evacuation of Suez two years ago, only accentuated the nationalistic trends of his people.[26]

Stikker also believed the French had encouraged the British, although their views diverged in significant respects, and militarily, the deployment of troops was too slow.[27] Stikker believed the closure of the canal would disrupt the global economy and be inflationary.

While the world's attention focused on Egypt, the Soviet Union invaded Budapest on 4 November 1956 and crushed the popular anti-Soviet revolution there.[28] Stikker had an open mind on whether the Soviets had taken advantage of the Suez situation to go in or whether they would have gone in anyway.[29] The Russian historians Zubok and Pleshakov argued that Imre Nagy, the Hungarian leader, 'failed' Khrushchev's test by introducing reforms and brought the tanks upon himself.[30]

The day following his meeting with Stikker on 14 November, Cremin called on the French ambassador, Jean Chauvel. The ambassador remarked about Suez that it was a pity the Anglo-French force had not seized the canal and the invasion timetable had not been followed successfully. Chauvel stated that Egypt was planning to attack Israel and that the US secretary of state, Dulles, had been most unhelpful during the canal users' association conference.[31]

Cremin reported Harold Macmillan's (the chancellor of the exchequer) speech that hopefully the canal would be open within six to eight weeks and the pipeline would be restored. Macmillan stated that if the sterling reserves fell, 'that is what they are there for'.[32] The historians Cain and Hopkins argue that the Suez Crisis highlighted 'the contradiction between upholding sterling and funding the military operations needed at times to defend Britain's world role.'[33] Kissinger argues:

> By the time the smoke cleared, the Suez crisis had destroyed the Great Power status of both Great Britain and France. Outside of Europe, America would be obliged to man the ramparts of the Cold War essentially alone.[34]

Kissinger believed Dulles and Eisenhower had humiliated their allies and pandered to militant arab nationalism.[35]

F.H. Boland had left in place an experienced team in London which included Frank Biggar, counsellor of the London embassy, who also reported on the Suez Crisis.[36] Biggar told Dublin on 20 November 1956 that the Australian high commissioner, Sir Eric John Harrisson, believed the opposition leader, Hugh Gaitskell's (Labour), adversarial position enabled the Tories to close ranks, but since the cease-fire the Tories in favour of Suez had become disconcerted and might push Eden.[37] Cremin reported on 21 November 1956 on a meeting with Rab Butler, the leader of the house and lord privy seal, who stated:

> There are risks of difficulties arising and there is a danger of wage claims being pressed when the economic effects begin to be felt. Perhaps, however, this ultimate picture may not be too dark as the economic repercussions may take some of the inflation out of the economy.

Cremin relayed that: 'Butler was aware that we [the Irish] did not approve of the Franco–British action but he remarked that he thought that people are beginning to have a better understanding of what was done'.[38]

Towards the end of November, Cremin devoted a report to the implications of an Anglo-French withdrawal from Suez. He noted that the Tories were worried if they withdrew without the canal being cleared then it was likely there would be a major revolt in the Tory back-benches.[39] Cremin also stated that there was discontent among the British military officers in Suez and dissatisfaction with the manner in which the UN was critical of Britain and France but not the Soviets in Budapest.[40] He reported that 130 Conservative party members had come out in favour of the action in Suez and had deplored the UN resolution which called on the British and French troops to leave Egypt by 22 December and not to take part in the UNEF (United Nations Emergency Force).[41] Cremin wrote:

> Prima facie, therefore, the government is in a very difficult position and is likely to be seriously obstructed by its own followers in conforming with the United Nations resolution. One cannot, however, safely take this protest on the part of so many government supporters at its face value nor assume that they will push their attitude to its logical conclusion. Their agitation is due to complex motives, nostalgia for strong arm policies which paid dividends a generation or two ago, exasperation that such a policy, although adopted against all

reasonable expectations and much to their satisfaction, was rendered
abortive through the abrupt cease-fire, dormant discontent with Britain's dependence on the U.S.A.[42]

Cremin believed these attitudes would affect government policy and
lead to a hardening of government statements.

On 1 December 1956 Cremin reported that the British government had agreed on a phased withdrawal from Suez. Cremin stated
that Macmillan (chancellor), Lloyd (foreign secretary) and Butler
(leader of the house and lord privy seal) had persuaded the dissident
Tories that their objections to conforming with the UN's wishes were
unrealistic. However, with the approach of petrol rationing Cremin
believed public opinion was swinging away from the government.[43]

By the middle of December, Cremin reported that a 'die-hard
group' was trying to remove the prime minister, Anthony Eden.
However, the 'die-hard' element within the Conservatives could
only muster fifteen MPs to abstain in the house of commons; the
other 115 followed the whip. Cremin concluded that the 'die-hards'
could hardly influence the party as a whole. Crucially, Cremin concluded his report with the observation that the party had lost
confidence in Eden's judgement. But he added the 'removal of a
Conservative leader was a slow process'. Regarding possible suc-
cessors, Cremin stated that Butler, Macmillan, Duncan Sandys,
Alan Lennox-Boyd and Derick Heathcoat Amory had all been
mentioned as candidates.[44] Eden had entered the house twice and
received hostile receptions.[45] On 8 January 1957, Eden informed
the queen of his resignation.[46] Macmillan replaced him as Tory
prime minister.

Cremin reported that Macmillan was chosen over Butler
as prime minister on the advice of Lord Salisbury, Sir Winston
Churchill, and perhaps even Sir Anthony Eden himself. Cremin
speculated that Eden might have refused to name a successor and
that was why Salisbury and Churchill were called in.[47] The reasons
were 'alleged to be that Macmillan was anti-Munich and Butler
was "soft on Suez" and, finally, Macmillan … would be acceptable
to the party as a whole'. Some sections of the left wing were dis-

satisfied with Butler on the grounds that he did not resign over Suez. Young argued:

> Suez was the end, of course, of Eden. The pressures, of duplicity and failure alike, were too much … His successor as prime minister had no more honourable a record in the crisis than he did. Of all the ministers around Eden, Harold Macmillan played the most ignominious role, being among the first into the breach and the first to leave it.[48]

Macmillan's official biographer does not agree with that thesis.[49]

Cremin wrote that ill-health was the principal reason for Eden's leaving cabinet. He said the City had taken the appointment of Macmillan well and there would be a lot of changes in the cabinet.[50]

Cremin soon reported on the cabinet reshuffle: in the home office, Major Lloyd George was replaced by Butler, possibly because Macmillan would not risk ostracising him.[51] Anthony Head, the minister of defence, was replaced by Duncan Sandys. Selwyn Lloyd was retained at the foreign office.[52] Senior civil servants were moved and Sir Roger Makins went from the foreign office to the treasury.[53] The fact that Selwyn Lloyd was retained at the foreign office was interpreted by Cremin thus: 'It has generally, and probably rightly, been interpreted to mean that Macmillan wished to make clear he is not hauling down the Suez flag and is not formally capitulating to the wave of domestic and international opinion against recent events'.[54]

Cremin commented that Sir David Eccles was appointed to the board of trade. Eccles had a strong reputation for being European in outlook and was involved in the EFTA project (European Free Trade Area).[55] The clear thrust of Macmillan's appointments was to protect his own position by not alienating the Suez group while positioning British policy towards Europe; this was mirrored by changes in the foreign office.

Britain Turns Towards Europe

Carlton argues that Suez may have been a cause rather than an effect of national decline. He argues, however, that the panic engendered by Suez gave rise to a much more rapid retreat from empire.[56] The Suez debacle had left a deep scar in British relations with the United States and had serious consequences for future British foreign policy. The historian Jeremy Black argued that 'Macmillan's moves towards the EEC owed something to his fear that otherwise he would have less influence with the USA'.[57] Paradoxically, it was Britain's unilateral decision to declare a cease-fire and subsequently inform the French which contributed to a cooling in Anglo-French relations and was one of the causes of a hostile attitude by the French when the British approached the EEC.[58]

Selwyn Lloyd, the British foreign secretary, put forward at a meeting of the NATO council in December 1956 a 'European Grand Design for a new Atlantic Assembly'. Cremin, in an extended report on 3 January 1957, evaluated the proposal. The ambassador believed the suggestion had been a 'three wise men' formation of some kind in order to 'co-ordinate or supervise the work of existing organisations such as NATO, WEU and [the] Council of Europe'. Cremin continued:

> I understand on the other hand that thinking in official circles here has been running more and more in the direction of the need for some kind of a parliamentary body to act as a 'sounding board' for some organisations which are at present without such an organ; OEEC and NATO; and this line of thought has become stronger with the prospect of the creation of a free trade area.[59]

Cremin went on to report that it was a 'considerable change' in official thinking, since the British were very distrustful of proposals which gave OEEC material to the Council of Europe, on the grounds that the latter was not exclusively intergovernmental. Cremin gave the following reasons for the change in thinking amongst British officials:

> The British approach to this and similar questions may have undergone a radical change as a result of the Suez events and the rift they

have created in the entente with the USA. We may well find that henceforth Britain will be more sympathetic towards both strictly European projects and efforts to enlist the participation of the U.S.A. and Canada through joint European action.

Cremin stated this change might have occurred before in the form of a proposed Free Trade Area:

> This trend may receive a powerful impetus from the relative isolation into which the Suez operation has brought this country and the realisation that she can no longer do as much on her own, through commonwealth or through bilateral approach to the USA as she thought she could.[60]

Cremin's statement establishes the thesis that Britain's position was changing in significant areas. Logically it followed that Irish policy must change as well to take account of the change in British thinking. The political journalist, Hugo Young, argued:

> 'Suez' and 'Europe', concepts that billow beyond the words that represent them, are the two motifs twined round Britain's definition of herself in the second half of the century. That the Suez disaster and the Rome Treaty occurred almost simultaneously was an accidental fact. But their repercussions one upon the other were, from the British standpoint, intimate. They shaped the British political realm as it has subsequently existed. Together they raised the question of national identity as a predicament that has perhaps been experienced more acutely in Britain than in any other European nation. Suez, the terminal calamity of empire, infused the British mind at the moment when the European dilemma, which has tormented it ever since, was already beginning to assume massive importance.[61]

In the aftermath of the Suez debacle, Cremin visited the British foreign secretary, Selwyn Lloyd. They had a discussion on the latter's proposal to form a European or Atlantic assembly, which would co-ordinate the work of various bodies: NATO, ECSC, etc.

All the countries that belonged to one or more of the bodies would sit in the assembly but would not sit on the committee. Cremin reported that Lloyd has been working at this since the NATO council.

Cremin then visited Sir Ivone Kirkpatrick, permanent under-secretary at the foreign office. Cremin noted: 'In the course of our talk he said that it is essential to give a "push" to European integration', referring to the need to expand the ECSC. It seemed Britain after Suez was less hostile to Europe. Jean Monnet repeated the joke that Nasser was the federator of Europe.[62] This was to have far reaching consequences for Irish foreign policy, as the country could never have joined the EEC without Britain.[63]

> It was clear, too, from what he said, that he is of the opinion that recent events and, in particular, the repercussions here of the Suez Affair, have made London more disposed than hitherto to co-operate in efforts to bring about European integration.[64]

Cremin further learned from Kirkpatrick that Britain was considering the rationalisation of armament production, suggesting that each NATO country specialise in one type of weapon. Cremin responded by stating this was similar to a French scheme put forward at the WEU. Kirkpatrick said that scheme would have placed France in the position of producing all the important heavy armaments, such as tanks. Cremin said Kirkpatrick:

> obviously regards France, particularly because of the time lost on EDC and its ultimate defeat, as bearing a considerable responsibility for the slow tempo of European integration during the last few years. The late Count Sforza had, he said, once remarked to him that the great defect in the European educational system is that it did not teach that 'the biggest island in Europe is France'![65]

The historian Horne conversely stated that Suez 'did more damage to France's relations with the Anglo-Saxons, especially the Americans, than any other episode in post-war history'.[66] Washington was seen to have betrayed its chief allies, and Britain abjectly deserted France and Israel at the first sign of disapproval in Washington.[67] It was against this background of mistrust that Kirkpatrick believed France was prepared to move forward with European integration, although she did not necessarily trust Britain in this regard.[68]

Cremin reported that the change in prime ministers was also having a radical effect on British policy. The German ambassador, Von Herwarth, believed the reason Sir Fredrick Hoyer Millar, previous ambassador to Bonn, had been appointed to the post of permanent under-secretary of the foreign office was that:

> it is regarded here as essential to have for some years to come ... a man in charge of the foreign office who is familiar with German affairs. The grounds for this feeling are that Germany and her behaviour have been determining factors in European and world politics for the past 50 years and that it is essential in the interests of peace to pay the closest possible attention to her.[69]

Cremin pointed out however that the last two under-secretaries had also been German experts.

Cremin noted that: 'Von Herwarth, who was attached for some time to the German embassy in Moscow before the war, was convinced that significant changes were taking place within the Soviet Union as well as the satellite countries':

> Von Herwarth thinks on the other hand that the changes taking place within the Soviet Union and in the satellite countries are not a reason why the west should remain passive and certainly not a reason for adopting a policy of appeasement. In his view the policy should be the reverse: the western countries should put and maintain pressure on the Russians to liberalise their system and their international policies.

Von Herwarth admired Eisenhower's middle-eastern doctrine (that the US would support any government in resisting communism), but 'his only regret is that the American president did not at the same time make an announcement that similar behaviour to that they adopted recently in Hungary will not be tolerated in future from the Russians'.[70] Cremin continued: 'Von Herwarth thinks that the proposal that eastern Germany be de-militarised within a re-united Germany is quite feasible – just as the Rhineland was de-militarised after the first war'. Cremin concluded by saying that the Germans were prepared to make available £50 million to keep the British divisions in Germany, although Macmillan recounted the British looked for £50 million annually and were offered a once-off payment of just £34 million.[72] Cremin reported that the divisions would be 'stream-lined'.[71]

There was a change of direction in British foreign policy towards Europe in the form of EFTA, a tariff group which included the Scandinavian countries.[73] It was a British attempt to create a European community in its image. Irish demands for 'special treatment' fell flat and she never joined.[74] News of EFTA reached Cremin and he reported on 14 February 1957 rumours within the foreign office of an 'entirely new departure … as a result of the Suez affair', meaning a British move towards Europe, given the perfidity of the United States. Hugh Gaitskell, the Labour party leader, stated in the course of a Harvard lecture that 'one must look on the Suez episode as a temporary affair, an aberration which leaves behind a formidable host of problems but which should not lead us away from old friendships and ideas.' Cremin reported there had been a complete break with Eden's policies, and commented that Eden:

> might have misjudged the degree of general reprobation to be expected as he certainly miscalculated the military aspect of the operation … His decision, however, betrayed an indifference to any reasonable assessment of the situation and of the various factors involved which is the more striking having regard to the care with which the administrative machine normally sieves all important policies.

Cremin continued: 'What seems in any case certain is that the rumours one heard in the past of a rather conspicuous element of instability and impulsiveness in Eden's character were based on fact.' He observed:

> To accept Gaitskell's verdict on the episode, while it means that one must not expect any revolutionary change in the general direction of British foreign policy, does not of course involve assuming that there may not be changes in emphasis and in manner. [75]

Cremin also provided a detailed analysis of the Conservatives' annoyance at the United States for failing to back them up at the UN.[76] He believed Macmillan's statement, in speaking of relations with the United States and of the need for friendship, that 'we don't intend to be satellites', was a reflection of the Conservatives' disenchantment. Cremin reported that there was a reciprocal intention to re-establish a close understanding between Washington and London. Cremin examined the effect of the Suez affair on Britain:

> The repeated appeals the people have had in recent weeks to remember that 'Britain has been great, is great and will stay great' (Macmillan 17th January) were a symptom of the sense of both exasperation and humiliation felt by many after the Suez affair and a recognition of the harm done to the country's prestige and standing in the world.

Cremin may have understated the case when he noted there were some in London who believed the United States was not that great a friend to Britain in her hour of need.[77] For the second time in two years. Cremin reported on great European powers being humiliated by lack of US support.[78] Macmillan's official biographer, Alistair Horne, wrote this on the subject:

> After the last troops left the canal in the wake of the débâcle, Britain – and to a lesser extent France – lost whatever pretensions they still might have had the previous July to be superpowers, capable of manipulating global destinies in the imperial manner of the past.[79]

Returning to the question of a new departure in British foreign policy, Cremin reported a conversation with the Dutch ambassador, Dr Dirk Stikker, on the British idea of a grand umbrella body for the 'European Grand Design'. Cremin stated he did not know if it was Stikker's personal view or that of his government, when he said: 'the scheme is neither feasible nor very desirable', and that he did not believe that an umbrella organisation would be acceptable to all those organisations involved.[80]

Anglo-American Bermuda Conference

In March 1957, Britain and the United States attempted to rebuild the relations that were damaged by Suez. In Horne's view, the neutral venue of Bermuda proved suitable as Macmillan 'would not go grovelling to Washington'.[81] Cremin's reports on the Anglo-American conference quoted the communiqué which stated: 'the discussions were conducted "with the freedom and frankness permitted to old friends in a world of growing inter-dependence".'[82]

Cremin interpreted the outcome as the formal healing of the rift over Suez. He noted though that the first concessions, i.e. 'U.S. participation in the military committee of the Baghdad Pact and the supply of guided missiles', were apparently 'made or at least prepared before the Bermuda conference'. He identified that the British had succeeded in getting the USA to agree to support Britain's H-bomb tests.[83] Eisenhower agreed to amend the 1954 Nuclear Energy Act to allow the US to share nuclear technology with the British.[84] Cremin then turned in his report to the importance of the H-bomb tests to British foreign policy. The *Daily Telegraph*, according to Cremin, had argued that: 'Britain without the H-bomb can never exercise an independent role in foreign affairs' and that 'we cannot be politically at the mercy of the United States and militarily at the mercy of Russia'.[85]

On the issue of China, Cremin reported that the British brought up the question of trade with China and the parties were reported as having agreed to differ. On the UN aspect of China, the British did not make inroads on the US position and the likelihood was that Britain had instead moved closer to her ally, according to the

Times. The final point was the proposed reduction of British forces in West Germany. Cremin commented to Dublin:

> All in all, therefore, it seems improbable that the British delegation brought back any new concrete results of importance from the Bermuda talks with the U.S.A. if the communiqué is what it has been claimed to be. Mr Macmillan has praised it as 'not the usual kind with a lot of highfalutin stuff about all sorts of principles but one which tried to be a business communiqué to say what we had done', and the Washington correspondent of the *Times* has said that it was 'unusually informative'.[86]

Cremin continued:

> There is indeed a risk that, in the short run, the government may be accused both of … [dissatisfaction] on some points of immediate importance (e.g. the future of the Suez Canal) and of having confirmed an attitude of subservience to the U.S.A.

The historians Pearce and Stewart believe the shift in British policy towards the development of an independent nuclear deterrent was designed to slash the cost of conventional defence.[87] Horne argued this was the cornerstone of Macmillan's defence policy.[88]

In conclusion, Cremin informed Dublin that the overriding concern for the immediate future remained Suez and the position for British shipping passing through the canal.[89] The canal was only finally reopened on 24 April 1957, and a triumphant Nasser graciously allowed the British and French to use it on the basis of the conditions that were on offer the previous October, before the invasion.[90]

Cremin received a report from the Irish permanent representative to the United Nations, F.H. Boland, that US policy in the middle east was to isolate Syria and Egypt and leave them to 'wither on the vine', politically and economically. Boland stated the British were trying to pursue an independent policy:

Whether it is for reasons of wounded vanity or national jealousy, the British not only criticise United States policies in the middle east but seem to be looking for means of asserting an independent position for themselves in middle eastern affairs even at the expense of thwarting them.

Boland concluded that while for Britain the middle east was primarily of economic importance (oil supplies), for the US it was geopolitical.[91] As Cremin did not comment on Boland's analysis, it would seem to suggest that he approved of it.

Cremin commented on 13 June 1957 on a speech by Selwyn Lloyd, foreign secretary, that proposed a conference to reform the UN charter:

In the first place you will note that he expressed strong dissatisfaction with the 'double standards' system of the United Nations, as illustrated recently by its action in relation to Suez on the one hand, and on the other in relation to Hungary.

He reported further that:

the British government, and very many people here, have held strongly that Washington has been too prone, and was especially so at the time of Suez, to allow (as they would put it) the United Nations to determine American policy.

The speech was seen as an attack upon the UN, but Lloyd denied this the next day.[92]

Cremin dismissed the opinion that Britain was trying to work out a *modus vivendi* with Nasser in order to counter US influence. He wrote that the unfreezing of some Egyptian assets was to pay for British exports and 'apart from the absence (as far as I know) of good evidence to support the suggestion that Britain is courting Egypt, I feel that any step in that direction by London would run into much political difficulty here'.[93] Cremin stated the government and opposition both opposed Nasser's nationalisation of the canal: 'can find no support here for the theory that Britain is disposed to place its trust in Egypt and Syria as a counter weight to the "Kingdoms".' He suggested that Nasser was trying to re-establish relations with Saudi Arabia, Jordan and Iraq, which were quite weak countries. He did not believe that the current situation would last long:

> [with] the creation of a breach between Egypt and Syria, the most vocal and intransigent 'pan Arabs' on the one side, and the other Arab states on the other, one might wonder whether this new position is even relatively permanent. After all, the five countries [Syria, Saudi, Jordan, Iraq and Egypt] seem to be still *ad idem* on their attitude towards Israel, and perhaps in the long term the Israel factor is that which is really decisive both for the relations of the Arab states inter se and for their attitude toward the west.

Cremin concluded that Britain was not necessarily against US policy in the middle east.[94] Sir Ivone Kirkpatrick, permanent under secretary at the foreign office, was extremely critical of Dulles:

> He described him as 'dishonest' and 'unreliable' and said that he (Kirkpatrick) feels that dissatisfaction and indeed exasperation with the behaviour of Mr Foster Dulles during the conferences held last summer were, to some extent, responsible for Eden's decision about Suez.

Following the commonwealth prime ministers conference Cremin reported that the British would raise various matters at the twelfth session of the UN assembly, including the Suez Canal. The British wanted compensation for the nationalisation of the canal, an international regime to run it, free access for all shipping and 'undertakings given unilaterally some months ago by Egypt made international and irrevocable'. The British also wanted to see free access for Israeli ships through the canal. Cremin reported the British would aggressively pursue these policies. He also reported that Britain favoured the retention of UNEF and the creation of a UN rapid response force.

On the Hungarian uprising, Cremin reported that the British condemned the Soviet action and stressed the double standard applied to Britain and the Soviet Union. Britain would, however, do nothing to remedy the Hungarian situation.[95] Eden was critical of the Indian prime minister, Nehru, voting with the Soviet bloc on the grounds that he could not follow 'the very confusing situation' in Hungary.[96]

Cremin reported the earl of Gosford's opinion that Khrushchev was of great importance in the Soviet power structure and that he would probably continue along the same lines as advocated at the twentieth party congress, which denounced Stalinism.[97] Having conversed with the disarmament sub-committee of NATO members, Cremin reported that neither the French, US nor British delegates were very hopeful of successful détente with the Soviets. The British delegate Stassen was 'hopeful that something may emerge but gave me the impression of being rather doubtful'. The French delegate Moch 'struck [Cremin] as a little sceptical about the prospect of success although he is, of course, very keen, for ideological and other reasons, on some specific result'. Cremin noted the changes in Moscow had not produced any change in Soviet ambassador Zorin's instructions.[98]

Cremin reported that Sir William Hayter, former British ambassador in Moscow, believed: 'while Moscow may continue to smile towards the outside world, it would be rash to anticipate any modification in the fundamentals of Russian foreign policy.' Hayter stated Zhukov and the red army had been instrumental in getting Khrushchev elected.[99]

Cyprus

The Cypriot question was one that was to follow Cremin from 1957 through to his posting to the United Nations in the 1960s, until his retirement in 1974. Cyprus was not of direct importance to Irish foreign policy, however the proposed partitioning of the island did raise the question of the legitimacy of partition as a method of solving territorial disputes.[100] Cyprus had been a British mandate since the First World War; it was, however, ethnically divided along Greek and Turkish lines. The Greek majority favoured *enosis* (union) with the Greek mainland. This was completely unacceptable to Turkey and placed Britain in an increasingly invidious position in trying to resolve the Cypriot question.

Macmillan recorded in his memoirs that partition had been voiced in March 1957.[101] On 1 July 1957, Cremin reported a conversation with Sir Ivone Kirkpatrick, the now former permanent under secretary at the foreign office, who stated he had proposed to cabinet the partition of Cyprus. Kirkpatrick stated that the Turks were anxious that Greece would not obtain Cyprus, as it would only whet Greece's appetite for 'Turkey in Europe', meaning the seizure of Thrace and even Istanbul.[102] Kirkpatrick stated he had discussed partition with Lord Radcliffe 'who conceded that partition … could become a feasible proposition', the Turkish zone being used for British military bases. Cremin stated that in light of Suez, he did not think Cyprus was suitable as a military base.[103] For Macmillan, the Cypriot question was unsolvable.[104] Jim Callaghan, spokesman on colonial affairs, wanted self-government so that the Cypriots could grow up politically. In August 1957, Cremin sent a detailed report on the situation in Cyprus stating:

> As you know, the long term British position has been based on the Radcliffe proposal 'which envisages self government, under British sovereignty, over a certain, unspecified, period, with the right of Cyprus at the end of this period (to be decided by the British authorities) to self determination, partition of the island being one of the 'eventual options' under self determination'.

Cremin stated the opposition was against partition. He said the British government was anxious to see a solution to the problem, which was why they had released the archbishop of Cyprus, Makarios, on condition he exhorted his people to end violence; this he did not do. 'The release of the archbishop, therefore, both put Britain in a weak tactical position and risked upsetting good relations with Turkey "which should be the main basis of British policy in the middle east at the present time".'

Cremin believed the attempt to bring NATO in to negotiate a compromise was a valid one. The British were attempting tripartite talks with Turkey and Greece. The Greeks were willing to consider talks but with some preconditions.[105] Cremin was told by the Greek ambassador Seferiadis that the negotiations 'must exclude partition and not exclude *enosis*'.[106] Conversely Turkey argued 'because the British received the island from the Ottoman empire, Turkey should have a considerable say and that partition was the only acceptable solution'. Britain was in a difficult position 'inasmuch as they do not like the partition concept but Turkey was a staunch member of the Baghdad Pact'.[107]

The Greeks did not want to accept mediation by Lord Ismay as they feared partition might be suggested as a solution. The Belgian foreign minister, Spaak, had also offered his good offices. Cremin concluded:

> The British government is anxious … to see negotiations resumed between Britain, Greece and Turkey and rather hopes that the efforts in this direction may be successful before the item is reached in the United Nations but is doubtful about this as the Greek government is particularly unco-operative. It is, however, not impossible that Greece too may not be very anxious to have the issue discussed again.

Cremin stated that the Greeks' room for manoeuvre was limited because they could not openly break with Archbishop Makarios, the leader of the Greek Cypriots, while Turkey had become extremely stubborn in insisting on partition.[108]

Cremin sent a report on the Labour party's position on Cyprus in which he noted that their spokeswoman, Barbara Castle, had stated 'the next Labour government would complete the freedom of Cyprus during their period in office'. This implied that Labour would propose to have the policy of self-determination applied within a period of five years from their return to power. Cremin added: 'Mrs Castle, of course, also rejected partition as a solution, stating *inter alia* that the Labour party has no intention "of seeing the tragedy of a divided Ireland repeated in Cyprus".' Cremin stated the Greeks were much encouraged by this statement.[109]

By 22 November 1957, Cremin reported that the Labour party were distancing themselves from the statement made by Barbara Castle at the Labour party conference. The *Times* argued:

> The way of solving the Cyprus problem resides in its being established 'within the NATO framework as an independent unitary state under international guarantees and with an international ring-master to protect minority rights'.[110]

In 1960, Cyprus became independent, under the leadership of President Makarios. Three years later, this form of home rule collapsed when civil war broke out. A permanent UN peacekeeping force was set up: the United Nations Force in Cyprus (UNFICYP). This situation continued until 1974 when the Greek military junta engineered a coup to overthrow Makarios. This gave the Turks a spurious pretext to invade, resulting in the de facto partition of the island.[111] Cremin was to deal with this issue at the UN in his later career, which is outside the scope of this work.

NATO, the UN and the German Question

One area where Macmillan resolutely decried partition as a solution was in Bonn in May 1957 where he talked 'about the human suffering caused by [the] partition of Germany and Russian oppression'.[112] Cremin stated Macmillan came under pressure from the *Times* for his comments on German unification. Cremin accurately reported that Macmillan's statements were designed to help Adenauer electorally:

> Some recent press comment suggests, however, that the possible consequences of this particular policy are beginning to cause anxiety. To pay lip service to the principle of German unity as long as it remains an academic question is one thing but that [the] British government should really regard this as a first priority and German unity as an absolute prerequisite to a permanent lessening of tension is not unanimously accepted here.[113]

The second criticism in the *Times* was that Macmillan wanted all agreed about disarmament before anything happened.[114] Cremin stated his information came from Pink of the foreign office who:

> rather effects the role of being 'realistic' which others might sometimes equate with cynicism as far as one can judge, the opinion expressed by Mr Pink then has so far been closer to reality than the more optimistic views emanating from some other quarters.[115]

Macmillan's efforts certainly did not harm Adenauer and British officials were surprised that the Christian Democrats won an overall majority in the German general elections. Cremin reported that the British officials were satisfied with the re-election of the Christian Democrats but there was a growing dissatisfaction amongst officials at Germany's economic progress. He also noticed slight disquiet about Adenauer's age; he was eighty-one.[116] In 1958 the German economy overtook the British economy.[117] However, British officials were satisfied that the links between Britain and the US were being strengthened.

The Irish ambassador in Washington, Hearne, stated the damage done to Atlantic personal relations had not healed, 'but the necessity for a revival of mutual confidence has meantime become imperative and relations are manifestly improving'.[118] This is an indication of the status of the 'special relationship' and the importance the British invested in restoring it.[119] Cremin wrote on 9 November 1957, that the talks between Macmillan and Eisenhower might result in a joint communiqué that would:

> involve some drastic change in the policies of the USA and Britain, although it is right to add that, given the relative weakness of Britain's international position and the predominance of the American role in the Western Alliance only a change in American policies could be of real significance.

Macmillan, according to Cremin's account, was very happy with the idea of a joint communiqué as even if it did not yield fruit it would enhance Britain's position internationally and his own domestically. Yet this supposed rapprochement was offset by Eisenhower's failure to visit London when he was in Europe for the NATO meeting. The official excuse was Mrs Eisenhower's health. Cremin stated:

> Naturally nobody here believes that, if the Americans are now prepared to share scientific knowledge, their attitude has been determined by the Sputnik [the first man made satellite].[120] I am assured indeed that the initiative for the recent talks came not from London but from Washington, a fact which is of course of great consolation to the authorities here.[121]

Cremin argued that Spaak, head of NATO, was behind the initiative to share technologies. When the communiqué was issued, Cremin stated that some of his colleagues believed it was marked strongly by Spaak's character but they were doubtful it represented a new chapter in NATO-US-European relations. One colleague stated that Eisenhower: 'was more a "moral re-armer" than anything else'. The *Daily Mail* argued: 'the Americans are not suffering from a crisis of technology but from a crisis in confidence. It is not their scientists but their politicians who have failed them.'[122] Eisenhower was urged to counter the 'missile gap' that many western commentators believed existed between the US and the Soviet Union. Eisenhower, privy to U2 spy plane photographs, knew the 'missile gap' existed in their favour.[123]

On 22 November 1957, Macmillan, in the wake of Sputnik, urged the United States to repeal the McMahon act and share nuclear secrets.[124] Macmillan spoke of the free world making 'an even more significant contribution of their national sovereignty than hitherto'. Cremin stated:

> The suggestion of a greater pooling of sovereignty naturally provoked interest in many quarters and it was explained from official sources that the prime minister in this speech was really uttering a 'general truth' not necessarily capable of immediate application.

Cremin then summarised Macmillan's speech at London's Guild-hall where he stated Britain:

> could no longer stand aside in 'splendid isolation', 'can no longer think in terms of a complete independent policy, whether in economic matters, in defence or in foreign affairs'. This does not mean, he added, that this country will not continue to play 'a leading part' in the world. 'Our real strength and our real influence lies as partners in the various alliances or groupings of which we are members'.

Macmillan concluded that Britain must play her part and this ability was dependent on a sound economy. Macmillan was also at pains to stress that the declaration of interdependence:

> was not designed to bring about 'some exclusive hegemony of Anglo-Saxon supremacy' – an important point having regard to French sensitiveness about the risk of being treated as an inferior and the revival of the wartime dyarachy.

Cremin argued:

> Macmillan's recent statements suggest that he approaches affairs in a different spirit (in, it is true, changed circumstances of British prestige); by their repetition they cannot be classified as simple *obiter dicta* and neither of the two occasions obliged him to speak of the lines he chose. Indeed, as said above, the first reaction of the press was one of surprise that he should have used such 'loaded' expressions as 'willingness to surrender more sovereignty' which one is more accustomed to hear from continental spokesmen.

Cremin stated:

> As far as I have ascertained (and I have spoken to a number of people interested in the question) there are so far no clear cut ideas behind the statements by Mr Macmillan outlined above. Lord Home told me that they could be regarded as little more at this stage than 'thinking out loud'

and the permanent head of the foreign office was no better informed.

Cremin went on to state that he believed Macmillan had the idea of a European armament board.[125]

On 25 November 1957, Cremin reported on an interview George Kennan, the US academic, made on BBC radio where he stated that the problem with détente was Germany and that:

> [the] prospect of Russia changing her attitude [towards Germany and German rearmament] are minimal and that consequently the west should reconsider the whole matter once more with particular reference to the possibility of accepting the exclusion of a reunited Germany from NATO in return for a correspondent withdrawal of Russian troops from eastern territories.[126]

Kennan's proposals did not find favour with Sir William Hayter, deputy under secretary at the foreign office, who was with Kennan in Moscow before the war stated:

> he does not agree with the thesis of Kennan's last lecture and specifically finds it difficult to see how the suggestion made by him about Germany can represent a feasible solution. He fails to see how if, as Kennan maintains, the adoption of these suggestions would be advantageous to the west, Russia would accept them.

Hayter then went on to say that the foreign office would not allow the proposals to go ahead because:

> 1. Russia's leadership is in a state of flux.
> 2. This country can't rely on a disarmed Germany, not solidly associated with the west, to stand by the west.
> 3. However obnoxious Soviet policies are, there is little real fear of them starting a war and that with time it might resolve itself.[127]

Khrushchev, the Soviet leader, after the launch of Sputnik, 'taking his own boasts seriously, embarked on a protracted diplomatic offensive to translate the supposed superiority of Soviet missiles into some kind of diplomatic breakthrough'.[128] These manoeuvres eventually led to the deployment of missiles to Cuba, which fundamentally undermined Khrushchev's leadership.[129]

Anglo-French and Anglo-Russian Relations
As a former Irish ambassador to Paris, Cremin paid close attention in his reports from London to the evolution of Anglo-French relations, which were of central importance to Europe, NATO and the Atlantic alliance. He provided Dublin with coverage of issues of great importance in that regard and he also did not neglect to report on matters of more minor importance. For example, Cremin wrote on the French concerns regarding the supply of small arms to Tunisia, which the French feared would find their way into the hands of the Algerian arab nationalists' Front de Libération Nationale (FLN). Cremin wrote the kernel of the problem lay with the perception of the Tunisian leadership: 'Bourguiba [the Tunisian president] is regarded by the Anglo-Americans as inspired by goodwill for the west'. The French regarded him as 'an anti-French revolutionary come to power and looked upon by Paris more or less like London looks upon [the Cypriot] Archbishop Makarios'.[130] Cremin and Willam Fay opined that the French might sabotage EFTA as a result of the incident.[131] Macmillan later acknowledged that the supply of arms to Tunisia was a 'serious error' in Franco-British relations.[132]

By December 1957, Cremin stated that Macmillan, a Francophile, had made every effort to improve relations between France and Britain, relations which had been severely damaged by Suez. Cremin argued that in Britain, especially among the top strata, there was a great love for France, although there was exasperation at the way she conducted her colonial policy. Cremin argued:

On the specific problem of Algeria few people here either accept the French view as its exclusively French character or agree with the way it is being tackled. This is hardly surprising in a country which has successively, in the course of a few years, granted full independence to

India ... Nor of course is a country which had to concede a generation ago the disruption of the United Kingdom, as it then was, likely to be impressed by the thesis that Algeria is an integral part of metropolitan France.

Cremin argued that Britain was worried that if France's war in Algeria went on too long it would lead to:

1. The weakening of the French economy.
2. The Egyptianisation of North Africa.
3. The diversion to North Africa of many divisions which should be available to NATO in France.[133]

Britain's worries proved correct however as France eventually deployed 500,000 men in Algeria. The war in Algeria eventually brought about the destruction of the Fourth Republic in May 1958.

Cremin reported that as part of the Anglo-French rapprochement that Macmillan and the French prime minister Gaillard issued a joint communiqué which recorded agreement on the need 'to develop the system of consultation in the NATO alliance'. It remained to be seen whether this will open the door to discussion of Algeria within NATO. Cremin concluded his report, which he based on talks with diplomatic colleagues and foreign office officials, by saying:[134]

Finally the communiqué ... mentioned the 'spirit of equality which underlies the [NATO] treaty'. This phrase perhaps reflects the effort made by the British ministers to convince the French of the lack of substance for French fears of being left outside the inner circle and of the absence of an intention to create 'an Anglo Saxon supremacy'. It must be added that French suspicion of a dyarchy can find some justification here, in particular in the field of nuclear weapons.

Cremin stated the British hoped to circumvent the McMahon act by arguing that sharing nuclear technology was a treaty obligation within NATO. Proposals to co-ordinate bomber commands and strengthen political consultation were causing difficulties with regard to joint-control of nuclear weapons.[135] On 12 December 1957, before a NATO meeting, Cremin reported on a conversation with a French diplomat, Baron de Juniac, who had served in Dublin from 1945 until 1948. De Juniac stated the NATO council would reach agreement on two specific points: 1. The pooling of scientific information, other than information on nuclear technology. 2. The establishment of IRBM (Intermediate Range Ballistic Missiles) sites in Europe, barring West Germany.[136] This was in light of the Soviet launch of the first man-made satellite, Sputnik, in October 1957.[137]

In January 1958, Cremin sent a long report to Dublin on western relations with the Soviet Union, based on a conversation which he had with Klaus Volksmann, London editor of *Die Welt*, of Hamburg. The basis of the conversation was in relation to the idea proposed by Macmillan of a non-aggression pact towards the Soviet Union. Volksmann stated that the foreign office explained to him that if the pact were followed by concrete actions then the British government would feel it worthwhile. This statement, Volksmann believed, was meant for Macmillan's visit to see the Indian prime minister, Nehru, who was non-aligned. The FGR feared any accommodation with the Soviets but Macmillan had inadvertently alienated Bonn, Washington and Paris. Volksmann predicted that Germany might enter into high level talks with the Soviets, if only to prove there was nothing to be gained. Dulles was highly distrustful of any connections with the Soviets.[138] Cremin wrote:

> At NATO the British had found themselves on the horns of a dilemma in view of Mr Dulles' strongly negative attitude towards any suggestion of trying to reach a *modus vivendi* with Moscow. Mr Macmillan had been the last of the national delegates to speak and he had adopted a highly ambiguous line.

Volksmann stated that the Oder-Neisse border had been accepted as the de facto border between Germany and Poland. He opined that a unified neutral Germany with a strong central force should be acceptable:

> In Mr Volksmann's opinion, such a development should prove attractive to the Soviets. He is convinced that the Russians have long ago abandoned any intention of taking over western Europe by force. Their experience with their eastern European satellites has made clear to them the enormous difficulty of holding down unwilling peoples. It is bad enough when the peoples involved are such relatively backward ones as the Poles and the Hungarians.

A neutral zone would allow an immediate relaxing of tensions. He believed we were on the threshold of disengagement.[139] Cremin in a covering letter stated: 'I think that the remarks of Mr Volksmann are extremely interesting for any effort to assess the present prospects of a relaxation in international tensions'.[140]

The subject of proposed NATO talks with the Soviet Union started on the assumption the Soviets were going to continue their advance into Europe. Members of the government and the administration had little faith in the prospects of fruitful talks with the Soviet Union. Cremin argued:

> Britain seems to have been, with the USA, the principal advocate at the NATO meeting of a 'tough' line and found resistance in this regard not only from Denmark and Norway but, rather to the surprise of London, from Canada.[141]

Cremin believed Macmillan's suggestion of a non-aggression pact was a kite, to measure public reaction, but it did: 'represent, of course, a radical departure from the government line in the NATO debate'.[142] The alternative argument was that it may have been a sop for Nehru on Macmillan's Indian trip. Cremin explained that the foreign office stated Macmillan's suggestion had been misconstrued and that a non-aggression pact would be considered after a series of agreements. He further stated:

My impression from talks with various people here (foreign office, C.R.O, colleagues) is that while public opinion is in favour of talks, official opinion remains fundamentally very reserved and holds that (a) there is no good evidence of a prospect of fruitful discussions, (b) there is no prospect of a successful meeting unless there is very careful preparation. Nevertheless, it seems not at all unlikely that the resistance of London to conversations with Moscow will abate – through the force of public opinion; and it should be remarked that some of my colleagues (European and commonwealth) hold that it would be folly, even if one believes that nothing will emerge, to continue to resist a meeting.

Cremin went on to state that there had been a lot of talk about disengagement in Europe. Macmillan rejected the idea of a neutral Germany. He also rejected disengagement owing to the fact that IRBM and long range bombers made disengagement impossible.[143] On 15 January 1958 a Gallup poll reported that the public were in favour of talks with the Soviets. Fifty per cent thought they should enter talks even if the US was unwilling.[144]

At the end of January, Cremin called on a number of people in Whitehall; his reports showed the diversity of opinion within the foreign office. Selwyn Lloyd believed the proposed conference with the Soviet Union would not solve anything and the only alternative was a bilateral negotiation between the USA and the USSR. Butler, the lord privy seal and home secretary, stated Britain was going to argue vigorously that disarmament feature strongly and that there be an agreement on control. He suggested that the Soviets would be against preparatory work at a foreign minister level and it would have to be carried out through diplomatic channels.

Hugh Gaitskell suggested that NATO should beat the Soviets at their own game. Sir William Hayter, first permanent under-secretary, believed little would come of the talks with the Soviets. It was improbable that Khrushchev would provide the final answer. He was also doubtful that his main rival, Suslov, would be able to oust him.

Whitney, the US ambassador, stated he thought a summit conference was likely but only because it would be very difficult for the US to go against 'the current which has set in here'. Although the administration could postpone the conference indefinitely he maintained that it would not be wise. Cremin stated:

> Whitney was clearly not enthusiastic about the recent Kennan lectures. He told me that in America Kennan was regarded as interesting in the theoretical fields but as rather unrealistic when it came to practical matters.[145]

In spite of the high stakes of the Cold War the 'dreary steeples of Fermanagh and Tyrone emerged again', with the emergence of an IRA border campaign which was to mar Anglo-Irish relations.[146]

Anglo-Irish Relations

The resignation of Anthony Eden obliged Cremin to speculate on the attitude of the new British cabinet towards the Irish state. On 30 January 1957 he wrote to Dublin: 'Taking the cabinet as a whole I do not think that its general attitude on Irish affairs, and particularly on the question of partition, was likely to be very different from that of its predecessor [Eden]. The new prime minister [Macmillan] should not be a dis-improvement on his predecessor'. Cremin said of Macmillan: 'I do not think that we could look to Macmillan to reverse recent policies in regard to Ireland but he may conceivably be a little more open minded than was Eden'.[147] Cremin observed that although there was a great deal of continuity in the cabinet, Lord Hailsham, minister for education, might be sympathetic to the Irish nationalist position as he was high Anglican as might be Henry Brooke, the financial secretary, who had connections with the Stopford-Green family.[148] Cremin wrote: 'On the assumption that, outside the prime minister, the principal weight in Irish affairs is carried by the members of the cabinet whose departments are particularly concerned with such affairs, the probability is that there is no great change'. The earl of Home, secretary of state for commonwealth relations, according to Cremin:

From all I hear … is objective, deliberate and independent … He has no particular association with Ireland which would tend to make him a priori sympathetic or unsympathetic. A factor which would tend to make him careful and prudent in his dealings with us … is that he is interested in his department and has no desire to use it as a stepping-stone to something bigger.

Cremin then moved on to Rab Butler who had taken over from Selwyn Lloyd in the home office which dealt with six-county affairs. Cremin observed to Dublin that:

it is doubtful whether we could have got a better successor to him there from the material available than Butler who is free from strong prejudices, has a rather academic turn of mind, is progressive in outlook and free from imperialist prejudices, and would tend to be guided by reason rather than by sentiment. [149]

On 21 November 1956, Cremin had a personal interview with the home secretary, Rab Butler. He paraphrased him as saying:

There are, on the whole, no serious problems between the two countries because neither side is trying 'to be clever'. Having made this remark at an early point in the conversation, Mr Butler seemed to clarify later what he meant by saying after, again, using the same expression, that we are not too vociferous about the unity of the country and that this is a good thing as, while it is legitimate to strive for unity, obstacles in the way are very great and public talk about ending partition does not remove them. He then went on to say that the government here do not intend, at the present time, to restrict immigration, that there is good reason for this as Britain needs labour and that he supposed quite a problem would be created if at any time it were found necessary to impose restrictions.

On the subject of the Irish government, Butler stated he had had contacts with the government but he preferred that these contacts should be informal. [150]

Cremin stated that the other offices had not changed except for 'trade (Sir David Eccles) may have other dispositions but I have no reason to think so'. 'Viscount Kilmer (a Scot) [the lord chancellor] was friendly to us', Cremin observed and 'I have found Salisbury [lord president] gracious but he is, of course, a Cecil'.[151]

Under the inter-party government between 1954 and 1957, Liam Cosgrave held the post of minister for external affairs. Official Irish policy on partition did not differ significantly from that of Fianna Fáil. However, Cosgrave was less inclined to bring the matter up as frequently as de Valera had instructed be done at the international level where it was possible to embarrass the British government. Christened the 'sore thumb' policy approach by Conor Cruise O'Brien, Cosgrave drew back from that practice. When Ireland was admitted to the United Nations in 1956, a conscious decision was made not to pursue that practice and so generally Ireland did not mention Northern Ireland, although Irish diplomats were sensitive about partition being used as a tool for settling territorial disputes.[152] The 'sore thumb' policy on partition was not fully abandoned until the 1980s.[153]

On 13 December 1956, Cremin sent a report on the attitude of British Labour leaders towards partition, based on the content of a meeting between the Tánaiste and Irish Labour party leader, William Norton, with several British Labour leaders. The ambassador stated:

> Lord Pakenham expressed the opinion privately that it might be possible to have seriously examined by a Labour government the possibility of ending partition provided this step is accompanied by the concurrent establishment on the part of a united Ireland of some kind of link with Britain – via the commonwealth or otherwise, but something concrete and formally binding.[154]

The inter-party government cooperated closely with the British governments during its term.

However, on 5 March 1957, de Valera and Fianna Fáil were returned to power with a 'record of 78 seats', and Frank Aiken became minister for external affairs for the second time.[155] It was rumoured at the time that de Valera wanted to bring about a settlement of the partition problem before he left office, although much of that was lip service to the ideal of unity.[156] The historian John Bowman argues that:

> With the resort to propaganda a failure and his [de Valera's] 'bridge' of external association destroyed, his options on partition, as he resumed power in 1951, were severely limited. The then Irish ambassador in London, F.H. Boland, recalls that, diplomatically, the issue was by then 'not active at all'.[157]

Aoife Bhreatnach argues:

> Partition inevitably resurfaced in the final years of de Valera's leadership. Feeling the chill wind of political mortality, de Valera was 'deeply anxious' to find some solution to partition ... Aiken pressed the matter with the British government with an urgency not to be repeated after 1959 ... Aiken insisted that the British government state Irish unity was a British interest. Such a step would 'prevent opinion in the north taking refuge in the argument that in steering clear of the south they were not merely thinking of themselves but were serving the strategic interests of Britain and in effect doing what Britain wanted'.[158]

On 19 November 1956, Cremin recorded the reaction of the British press to an IRA attack on a border post.[159] Subsequently Lord John Hope told Cremin that he hoped the attack was not a precursor of things to come. Cremin agreed.[160] But such expressions of hope proved futile. The IRA began a new cross-border campaign on 12 December 1956 with an attack by 120 'volunteers' on ten different targets in Northern Ireland. 'Operation Harvest', as it was code-named by the IRA, resulted in the deaths of six members of the Royal Ulster Constabulary (RUC) and eleven IRA 'volunteers', the introduction of internment in Northern Ireland and in the south, and the mobilisation of 13,000 B-Specials. The campaign cost Stormont about £11 million between 1956 and 1961.[161]

It 'passed almost unnoticed in the British press and parliament'.[162] However, the Irish government, embarrassed by the incidents, informed Sir Gilbert Laithwaite, permanent under-secretary of state for commonwealth relations, through Cremin, that they were doing their utmost to meet the situation. Laithwaite replied he could understand there would be some feeling with the young men in Ireland. Cremin wrote:

> We can assume, I think, that Laithwaite's weight is thrown against impulsive action by London or Belfast, but equally that his advice is not always taken even though his secretary of state, the earl of Home, takes apparently, as I have mentioned in an early report, a calm and level headed view.[163]

In the context of the renewed campaign Cardinal John Francis D'Alton of Armagh brought forward proposals to end partition (just before the February 1957 general election). The proposals consisted of a united federal Ireland rejoining the commonwealth, joining NATO and offering bases on Irish territory. On 4 March 1957, Cremin's second in command, Biggar, reported on the reactions in the British press to the cardinal's proposals. The *Manchester Guardian* commented:

> the cardinal's suggestions have created great interest in Northern Ireland. Unionists were unwilling as they realise that opposition from Belfast might be interpreted as opposing the wide interests not only of the commonwealth but of NATO, for the cardinal suggested that a reunited Ireland should offer bases to NATO. On the other hand nationalists, the *Guardian* correspondent reports, 'greeted the cardinal's plan as a statesmanlike one designed to break the deadlock of partition and also to end the dangerous situation caused by the IRA attacks in Northern Ireland which they fear may eventually lead to civil war'.[164]

On 6 March 1957, Cremin reported the London edition of the *Manchester Guardian* was particularly struck by the cardinal's proposals.[165] William P. Fay, secretary at the Irish embassy, commented that no Irish politician 'could be expected to commit themselves in regard to the proposals so short a time before polling in the general election' and his ideas might have lost a good deal of their freshness by the time of the incoming government.[166] Cremin stated he was surprised the proposals were published in the *Observer*, 'partly because of the *Observer*'s anti-Catholic bias'. Cremin stated there was a theory on Fleet Street that:

> the cardinal's statement had its origins in suggestions from American political and ecclesiastical sources. According to this theory, the statement did not come as any great surprise to the American embassy in Dublin or to St Patrick's in New York.

Cremin stated:

> the cardinal's proposals, which I gathered when in Manchester, were also shared by at least the more moderate section of Irish opinion in London ... the 800,000 odd Irish in this country ... would be glad to see the disappearance of this sole remaining source of possible acrimony between the two countries.

He concluded:

> So far the only criticism of the proposals that any of us in the embassy has heard is that they do not offer sufficient advantages from the British point of view to induce a British government to put pressure on the northern unionists that would undoubtedly be necessary to get the latter to agree even to negotiate on the basis of the cardinal's suggestions.[167]

Following on from the cardinal's proposals that Ireland rejoin the commonwealth, on 8 March 1957 Cremin reported that the conservative MP, Bell, asked a question in the house of commons about Ireland rejoining the commonwealth. Cremin considered it was interesting that a conservative had tabled the question.[168]

Lord Pakenham referred generally to the cardinal's statement when he reviewed a book by a close friend of Éamon de Valera's, Frank Gallagher, entitled *The Indivisible Isle*. Pakenham believed Gallagher would throw himself behind the proposals put forward by Cardinal d'Alton. Cremin stated of articles in the *Daily Telegraph* concerning the Irish general election:

> ... although they do not refer at all to the cardinal's proposals [they] constitute a significant comment coming from this paper on partition ... 'they (the Irish people) hope, too, that something will be done by the new and veteran Irish prime minister to improve the republic's relations – at once tragic and ludicrous – with the Ulstermen to the north'.

Cremin quoted further from the article:

> It will take much time and effort, after the recent troubles to improve official relations with the north, but efforts should be made both in London and Belfast to find ways of helping. Sometimes it looks and sounds as if British ministers had given up thinking about Ireland.[169]

This view is supported by J.J. Lee, who wrote that de facto successive British governments had abandoned the north to its own fate.[170] Cremin reminded Dublin that the *Daily Telegraph* was extremely Tory and the reference to the 'ludicrous relations' between Ireland and the north and the need for British ministers to think about it was all the more interesting.[171] The *Scotsman*, another newspaper of significance, picked up Cardinal d'Alton's proposals for a united Ireland. Cremin told Dublin on 9 March 1957 that the article was entitled: 'Irish Unity Plan, High U.S. Church Backing'. The article stated Cardinal d'Alton 'proposed that Éire and Northern Ireland federate, and that a united Ireland join the commonwealth and offer bases to NATO'. The article made a number of interesting assertions. Firstly, the Irish government had approached the CRO [commonwealth relations office] and discussed the question of unity in relation to the commonwealth. Secondly, the cardinal's proposals, while 'purely personal', were known to have 'high American ecclesiastical backing'. Thirdly, the U.S. administration 'is known to be disturbed at the way Éire's economy fails to prosper. It would like to help, but cannot persuade congress to agree unless some military benefits were to result'.

Cremin reminded Dublin that he had already reported the suggestion of US ecclesiastical involvement. 'There is, of course, no truth in the statement that we have approached the CRO in recent weeks on the question of unity'.[172] It is noteworthy that Cremin did not suggest discussions be initiated on the basis of Cardinal d'Alton's proposals. On 9 March 1957, Cremin reported:

> It is probable that it was Pakenham's brother-in-law, Donald McLachlan, deputy editor of the *Daily Telegraph*, who was responsible for the leading article in yesterday's issue of the paper. You will remember that McLachlan went to Dublin several years ago and that you arranged some interviews for him.[173]

Cremin subsequently had lunch with Lord Pakenham, who was quite excited about the proposals and who:

> in particular, feels that the cardinal was sound in making the entry of a united Ireland into NATO one of the two props of his scheme. Pakenham realises that [it] is a delicate point from the angle of official policy inasmuch as our line hitherto has been that one cannot prejudice the possible decisions in such matters as defence agreements by a unified country. While he appreciates the logic of this attitude, he thinks that in the practical sphere, it is not realistic and for this reason approves the way in which the cardinal has treated the matter.

Pakenham would be happy, Cremin relayed, to provoke a debate in the House of Lords on the cardinal's proposals.[174]

On 16 March 1957, Cremin commented to Seán Murphy on the need to send a letter to the *Tablet* that:

> it would be really ironical if a professedly Catholic organ like the *Tablet*, which enjoys, even in non-Catholic circles, a considerable reputa-

tion for sound and sober views, and although it is of course anti-Irish, could be quoted, without some voice being raised in opposition, to justify both partition and the behaviour of the Six County Administration. I have, therefore, discussed the matter with Mr Tadgh Feehan, secretary of the Anti-Partition League, and we have drafted a letter which we propose to send from his personal address.[175]

The letter refuted the suggestion that northern Protestants would be mistreated in a united Ireland: 'This would be entirely at variance with the actual experience of the Protestant minority in the 26 counties over the past 35 years,' the letter read. The text quoted Professor Joseph Bigger, who believed if anything the Protestants in Ireland had been too fairly treated. The letter concluded that Catholic majorities were forced to live under a Belfast parliament in two of the six-counties.[176] On 19 March 1957, Murphy gave permission for Cremin's draft to be sent to the *Tablet*.[177] On 12 April 1957, the *Liberal News* came out in favour of d'Alton's proposals.[178] De Valera's response to Cardinal d'Alton's proposals was less enthusiastic.

Cremin reported on 2 May 1957 that there had been reports in the newspapers in London that some Labour MPs might visit Dublin in the near future to discuss the question of partition. However, the Tánaiste and leader of the Irish Labour party, William Norton, had discouraged such a move on the grounds of recent IRA activity.[179]

In the same report, Cremin reported meeting the former ambassador to Dublin, permanent under secretary of the CRO, Sir Gilbert Laithwaite, and recorded the latter's argument, 'No government here would, he feels, ever be prepared to put pressure on, or "coerce", the north. If an arrangement satisfactory to both Dublin and Belfast could be found London would be very happy to consider it'. Cremin offered the view that while the British government could not coerce the north, 'it is difficult for Irish people to understand how Britain subscribes in certain areas the principal of unity but holds that this does not apply in the case of Ireland'. Cremin pointed out that in Germany and Laos, Britain was opposed to partition. Cremin stated that Laithwaite was not impressed by this argument.[180]

On 24 May 1957, Cremin had a conversation with Alport, under secretary of state for commonwealth relations, on recent IRA activity. Cremin assured him that the Irish government was doing everything to prevent the violence, however, 'as long as the border remained young men would try and do something about it'.[181]

Earlier in May 1957, Cremin had a meeting with Lord Home, secretary of state for commonwealth relations. Cremin told Home that the minister for external affairs, Frank Aiken, was planning to stop off in London on his way to Europe in order to see him and to discuss partition. Lord Home replied he would be delighted to meet Aiken. However, the secretary of state did not show any willingness to undergo several hours discussing partition with Frank Aiken and, 'he wondered whether we had considered talks with Belfast'. Cremin replied:

> as far as we can see, there is no point whatever in considering talks between ourselves and Belfast as they are simply not prepared to talk. On the other hand we have always maintained that London in many ways holds the key to a solution and we very definitely feel that a word from London could have considerable influence in Belfast.

Home suggested that Ireland might rejoin the commonwealth as a first step towards reunification. To this suggestion, Cremin cautiously replied:

> that I really could not say at this stage what we would be prepared to do. The attitude of the Taoiseach and the minister was that there is no point in envisaging specific or detailed formulae as a means of solving the problem until there is a disposition on the other side to consider a solution. Once such a disposition exists the alternatives could be examined. On the specific question put to me, however (viz. return to the commonwealth) I said that I do not know how we would regard such a suggestion but that my personal opinion is that there is no prospect at all of our entertaining it except as a step simultaneous

with the ending of partition. Lord Home agreed that the existence of a disposition to consider a solution of the problem is fundamental and remarked that he might perhaps have a talk with Mr Butler.

However, in a further report on the same meeting Cremin commented that he believed, 'Lord Home's reaction to what I had to say was not discouraging'. Cremin had been preparing the ground for Aiken's visit and in this respect the outcome was at least a little positive:

> assessing the conversation at its lowest, it is something that Lord Home did not reject, as unprofitable, the idea of the minister's discussing the problem with him and that he likewise did not reject the suggestion that London could appropriately, and should, speak to Belfast.[182]

It was in such small semantic victories that Ireland's Anglo-Irish policy was grounded in the mid-1950s.

On 22 May 1957, Cremin reported on a meeting with secretary of state for the home office, Rab Butler:

> On this occasion he spoke warmly of his acquaintance with the minister and also with the Taoiseach, with whom he had, he said, the pleasure of negotiating, when he was under secretary of state for foreign affairs, in 1938, 1939 and 1940. Quite obviously Mr Butler retains a very lively impression of his meetings with the Taoiseach and the fact that he is perhaps the only member of government officially associated with foreign and Irish affairs in those years is an added reason for his being interested in talking about Irish matters today. You will be aware that Mr Butler is the only member of the House of Commons who has never, as far as I know, disavowed Chamberlain's policies.[183]

Perhaps the implication for Cremin was that Butler might not be opposed to the policy of 'appeasing' Ireland. In the course of the meeting the question of the six counties arose:

Mr Butler remarked that 'the six counties come within his jurisdiction'. And that he and Lord Home were both 'very interested'. However he stated that 'I have no locus standi as [*sic*] the attitude of Belfast is entirely non possumus' ... There could be no question of London going back on any undertaking given to Belfast and there is no evidence of any disposition there to envisage a change. He (Mr Butler) must be very careful, as any move on his part might be misinterpreted and the six-county people, who are 'pretty outspoken', might 'cut up rough'. He would at the same time, be most happy to talk to Mr Aiken and 'exchange notes'. Dublin had, of course, he went on, moved very far from the position now prevailing in the six counties and he did not see easily how it would be possible to get back to a position where a solution could be reached.

Butler obviously did not want to provoke a backbench revolt as a result of incautious actions. In reply, Cremin told Butler that:

we are well aware of the intransigent and apparently immovable attitude adopted by Belfast but that we have always maintained, and we feel confident, that an intervention by London could bring about considerable changes in Belfast ... Mr de Valera's position is that there is no point in speaking of detailed proposals until there is a disposition on the part of all concerned to talk but that, given such a disposition, one could envisage various solutions, although there might be some which we would find impossible to accept.

Cremin suggested Butler pay a visit to Dublin. Butler replied he could pay a private visit and hoped to avoid 'harmful press publicity'. Given the cautious nature of Aiken, Cremin did not feel untoward in remarking that:

the minister fully appreciates this aspect and that it was indeed for that reason that he intends to call on ministers here when he is on his way to, or from, another destination, rather than to make an express journey to London which could hardly avoid being noticed.[184]

Next, on 7 July 1957, Cremin reported on meeting again with Lord Home. Home expressed satisfaction at the emergency powers act, which allowed for internment without trial and was decisive in dealing with the IRA threat during the Second World War. Cremin replied that the emergency powers would not prevent another resurgence in such activities. Home said the presence of a strong stable government in the Republic of Ireland was indispensable, and 'went on to say that a difficulty confronting the British government in considering a solution to partition is that any action it might take could expose it to fire from several sides, including both Dublin and Belfast'. Home then suggested that the council of Ireland might form such a forum for discussion, but Cremin demurred that he 'doubted whether de Valera could have constructive talks with anyone in Belfast'.[185]

In late August Cremin reported the results of an exchange between Pakenham and Macmillan. Pakenham took the opportunity to suggest that a wider discussion on partition should be undertaken. According to Cremin:

> it would seem that Lord Pakenham spoke of a change on the basis generally of Cardinal d'Alton's proposals ... and that the P.M. made some allusions to, on the one hand, the question of our joining the commonwealth, even independently of any solution of the partition problem, and on the other the difficulties of finding a solution which would take account of the views of the six county people.

Macmillan then sent Lord Pakenham a letter that stated:

> With regard to the other matter, I would like to think over what you have said. What I am anxious to avoid is something going off half-cock. Nothing would be worse than creating the atmosphere in favour of Éire rejoining the commonwealth, and terms being asked or a formula being insisted upon which we should have to refuse out of loyalty to our friends in Northern Ireland. Rather than that, it would be better to stick to Walpole's favourite motto 'Quieta non movere'. If on the other hand we felt that this could all come about with general

approval, that would be quite another thing. As I say, I will think it over and perhaps write again.

Cremin believed Macmillan was giving a warning 'to Lord Pakenham himself or to some other party (e.g. to us) as it does not contain any restrictive heading' and therefore Lord Pakenham could show the letter to others. Cremin believed the letter only represented Macmillan's personal views, but that Macmillan would not be adverse to having talks about the problem of partition.[186]

On 18 September 1957, Cremin had a meeting with Lord Pakenham, on the issue of Pakenham having lunch with the Taoiseach. Cremin relayed that the Taoiseach was not planning on taking the initiative on ending partition, but would not object to rejoining the commonwealth on the basis of a united Ireland. To advance matters Lord Pakenham suggested that de Valera might write one or more articles in reputable papers.[187]

On 21 September 1957, Cremin suggested to Seán Murphy that the Taoiseach might visit Macmillan on his return from Rome, on the basis that the Taoiseach rarely travelled abroad and it might be a good opportunity.[188] It would also have the added advantage that it would not attract undue publicity.[189] On 27 October, Cremin had another conversation with Lord Home.[190] Home communicated the British request that the Taoiseach would not raise the issue of partition. However, as a result of pressure from the Dublin government, Clutterbuck, the British ambassador in Dublin, agreed to raise the whole partition question with London again.[191] On 16 March 1958, Aiken, accompanied by Cremin, called on Lord Home. Having exchanged the usual courtesies, the minister brought up the question of partition and gave a brief history of it.[192] However, nothing came of the meeting.

Cremin went on to report opinions on the reception Cardinal d'Alton's proposals would receive from de Valera. The *Observer* correspondent believed de Valera was in favour of the proposals but they: 'have aroused interest rather than enthusiasm in the south.' Cremin quoted the paper's Belfast correspondent's argument that:

'opinion in Northern Ireland has been unmoved' by the proposals and that 'all theorising becomes vain in face of the fact that parliament at Stormont, which has the last word, will not tolerate any interference whatever with the present settlement. In this correspondent's view, the division of Ireland turns more and more on economics'.

The Sunday Times took the view that Northern Ireland would only reunite with the south under the crown and commonwealth, that the republic had rejected those, and that only de Valera could break the deadlock and he was unlikely to do so.[193] Bowman argued that in 1957 and 1958, de Valera obfuscated on whether a united Ireland should rejoin the commonwealth:

> *The Times* made the complaint that even 'the most diligent questioning' had not led de Valera 'to break new ground'. In fact his reply – making allowances for the ratchet pulling in the opposite direction – was a significantly open one.[194]

Throughout March and April Cremin did the round of the St Patrick's day dinners in Birmingham and Sheffield.[195] Biggar reported that he attended a dinner at the Liberal club where Montgomery Hyde, MP, Ulster unionist, spoke on partition, and 'was remarkably moderate'. Cremin's hosts felt this might have been due to his presence, but Cremin stated: 'I am inclined to think that the more likely explanation is that unionist speakers when putting their case to an English audience are now cultivating, as a matter of deliberate policy, an air of reasonableness and commonsense'.[196] This is an interesting indication of Cremin's mindset on partition. Cremin realised that partition could not be ended arbitrarily and rather it would be better to concentrate on improving the lot of the nationalists in the north so that they could receive their fair share of resources.

On 28 May 1957, Cremin reported that Ivon Pink was going on holidays to Dublin and he might call in on the department of external affairs.[197] On 12 June, he reported a suggestion by Lord Pakenham that an Anglo-Irish society be formed in the same vein as the

Anglo-German society. Cremin stated he personally was in favour of the project.[198]

The Anti-Partition League

On 5 July 1957, Cremin reported that the Anti-Partition league was opposed to Cardinal d'Alton's proposals. However, Cremin commented that the league intended to publish 10,000 copies of the d'Alton statement and explained that they planned to enclose a covering letter which would state the cardinal's suggestions were a basis for discussion.[199] On 8 July, Cremin reported on the Fethard-on-Sea boycott (where the refusal of a Protestant, Sheila Cloney, married to a Catholic, to send her children to the local Catholic school led to a boycott of local Protestant businesses). He stated it received very little coverage except in the *Manchester Guardian*, which was full and accurate in its reporting. Cremin explained why the Anti-Partition league was dismayed:

> The reason, of course, is that the league has always used, as one of its strongest arguments, the contrast between the toleration extended to the religious minority in the twenty-six counties and the constant discrimination practised by the majority against the minority in the six counties.[200]

The effects of the Fethard boycott were still being felt when Biggar received a letter from Harold A. Phillips, from the political and economic circle of the National Liberal club, on 10 December 1957. Phillips wrote:

> Also, you may be interested to know that among us your cause suffers more harm from Irish censorship and memories of the Noel Browne case than it does from I.R.A. activities and the attitude of the republic during the war.[201]

On 24 October 1957, an article appeared in the *Irish Press* on a letter of protest by Brian Gallagher, Irish ambassador in the Netherlands. Gallagher was protesting about an article in a leading Dutch newspaper which stated that Ireland had followed a rather pro-German policy during the war. Cremin quoted Clement Attlee's term, the 'benevolence' of Irish neutrality during the war.[202] There can be no doubt Cremin had a repertoire of rebukes ready for such accusations, most of which stemmed from de Valera's visit to Hempel.[203]

One group that attempted to make trouble for the embassy was the Irish National Union, which protested at internment in the Curragh and discrimination against the Irish in Britain. In the 1950s, alongside improved employment prospects there was a noticeable lessening of anti-British feeling, a potent confirmation of change. This was noted with some alarm in a confidential report of the Anti-Partition league in 1957.[204] On 28 October 1957, Cremin reported a meeting with a delegation from the Irish National Union. O'Callaghan (leader), Nolan (secretary), and three others, William Burke, Kierans and Mr X. (unknown). Cremin reported that the following points were raised:

(a) This meeting was in connection with their wish for a delegation 'to visit the Curragh, see the internees and examine conditions'; they also wished to bring a press reporter.

(b) They also wished to send food parcels and comforts and wished to know the rules governing the above and conditions governing correspondence with the internees.

(c) They also told Cremin about a protest outside a film about Ireland.

(d) The attitude of some London magistrates towards the Irish.

(e) They asked about their resolution they handed in on 14 July, Cremin said they got their reply, they stated that they were not satisfied with it.

Cremin continued:

At no point during the interview was any reference made by the delegation to the demonstrations that have taken place, to the picketing of the embassy from July to mid-September, and to the removal of the pickets since then. The conversation was, as I have said, affable and the delegation spoke in a reasonable manner. However, we have been informed this morning that another parade to present a petition is to take place next Sunday afternoon.

In conclusion Cremin asked a reply be given to the first two points raised.[205]

On 8 November, Cremin sent a follow-up report on the Irish National Union, which was a rather damning attack on the movement and the personalities involved. The union was going to parade to the embassy the following Sunday. Cremin said he was not worried since he would not be there that Sunday, but an officer would take the protest. That officer, O'Meara, duly received the protest at the door of the embassy. After this occasion a bomb warning was received by the embassy.

Cremin delivered a scathing attack on the personality of O'Callaghan, stating that: 'I have very little doubt that the primary, and indeed perhaps the sole, objective of O'Callaghan is to secure publicity for himself'. Cremin analysed the following of the Irish National Union thus:

> Although to say that 600 or 1000 people have staged a march of protest to the embassy may in the abstract suggest a powerful movement, this impression would, in the circumstances prevailing here, be false. It is, as you know, reliably estimated that there may be up to 250,000 Irish people resident in Greater London … Put briefly, the movement cannot, in my opinion, be considered significant.[206]

O'Connor argued that in the late fifties, among the Irish born immigrants:

> a 'striking absence of national sentiment' may have been no more than more pragmatic attitudes [*sic*.] of those who came in the late fifties, and who were more intent on investigating and exploiting the new opportunities in Britain. Tricolour flag-waving and lip-service to the sacred cows of the republic, after all, had not provided them with the means to earn a living there, and many of the younger immigrants were impatient with such rhetoric.[207]

Observations on the Irish in Britain

It was perhaps in response to the Irish National Union that Cremin engaged in a large piece of work entitled 'The Irish in Britain and some observations on Anglo-Irish Relations'. This was completed on 29 January 1958.[208] The report was twenty-nine pages long and Cremin wrote that it was part of a broad report. In it he estimated that there were 722,000 Irish born residents in Britain, of whom 200,000 were in London, and that there were possibly an extra 150,000 more Irish than in the 1951 census, making the figure probably 900,000. Cremin stated there were more Irish born in Britain than there were in the United States and that from 1851 to 1951, the average number of Irish in Britain was always over 500,000. In the 1950s, 373,848 Irish citizens emigrated from Ireland. Indeed, 'emigration remained a fact of life for the Irish political elite'.[209]

Cremin believed the total number of Catholics in Britain was 3.3 million, but the figure might be as high as 5 million. Of these, Cremin wrote, sixty-six to seventy-five per cent were of Irish extraction. Cremin stated the majority were employed in unskilled or semi-skilled labour; 'Generally speaking, Irish workers have a better reputation than their English fellows for hard manual work over long hours'. The men worked in building, transport and bar work, while the 'girls are mainly employed in manual work, factories, waitresses, domestic servants'. However, 'nursing is a characteristic profession of the better educated type of Irish girl'.[210] O'Connor has written:

> By contrast with the previous decades, immigrant girls began to move away from domestic service and to receive training as nurses, and to a lesser extent as teachers. Men who in previous decades were content to remain as navvies now sought opportunities to become sub-contractors. Barmen served with an eye to the day when they might become landlord of their own premises. Greater numbers of both sexes were to be found in white-collar employment, attending evening classes in search of marketable credentials, and residing in middle-class districts. Higher and more widespread education in Ireland gave rise to new initiative which grafted on to the old émigré tradition a more positive approach to life in the new country.[211]

Cremin went on to state, 'For Irish university graduates the most typical profession is of course medicine, working as a GP. Engineers and scientists are rare as are lawyers'. The Irish element was strong in the armed forces, but officers were generally from Anglo-Irish families.[212] He concluded, 'Irish born people are not prominent in business'.[213]

Cremin reported on the social position of the Irish in Britain. Socially the Irish were not regarded as foreign, but as one of the family. Catholicism 'does not on the whole operate to their disadvantage' and 'religious tolerance in England is virtually complete'. Indeed, 'One ... sometimes detects a certain reluctant admiration for people who take their religion sufficiently seriously to endeavour to actually practise it'. Paradoxically he stated:

> Resentment to the Irish on religious grounds is far more likely to be found amongst their English co-religionists than among non-Catholics, the ostensible reason being the alleged non-intellectual and narrow character of the Irish church but jealousy of their distinctive position as a select minority and mere social snobbery also play a part.[214]

This correlates with a report sent by Boland several years earlier when he was ambassador:

> ... the Catholic Church in England ... is always leaning over backward to establish its essential 'Englishness' – so much so that (up to recently at any rate) it has always ignored and deplored the Irish and other alien elements in its ranks and even today it still tends to outdo even the Protestant denominations in protesting its loyalty to the crown and its stout British patriotism.[215]

Cremin wrote the Irish socially were accepted, but 'at the highest professional levels, where competition is keenest, the position of the Irishman is not so easy. Here the religious factor begins to be of importance and to some extent the 'old school tie' mentality'.[216] He argued the failure of anti-partitionists to receive little more than a handful of votes demonstrated that: 'the Irish in England vote in accordance with their interests as English residents and not as Irish nationalists'; 'it seems improbable that the Irish in Britain ever achieve a position of political importance comparable to that which their brothers reached in America'. This contrasted with Parnell's era when he could even control English parliamentary seats.[217] O'Connor wrote on this trend:

> This was noted with some alarm in a confidential report of the Anti-Partition league in 1957. The league had been active in Britain in the earlier years of the decade, attempting to mobilise the 850,000 Irish to influence the Ulster question as an electoral issue.[218]

Cremin reasoned that was because: 'There was lacking in England ... the highly fluid situation which permitted the intensive organisation for political purposes of racial groups in the newer countries.'[219] This had the further effect: 'One result of the powerlessness of the Irish electorate as such is the paucity of Irish MPs whether by birth or decent in the House of Commons'. Cremin stated that in politics the Irish did not carry a weight commensurate with their numbers.[220] Cremin's report was sent to Canada, Australia and Argentina, and Seán Nunan requested similar surveys be undertaken.[221] This was a prescient piece of thinking in that it allowed Irish foreign policy to develop the diplomatic diaspora card with finesse.

Conclusion

Cremin's appointment to the Court of St James came at a pivotal moment in post-war British history. The retreat of the British at Suez was the death knell of Britain as a world power. The illusion of empire which she had maintained after the Second World War had been eclipsed by the US as a rising global power. He kept Dublin informed of the thinking of top officials within the cabinet and the foreign office and he reported the shift in foreign office thinking towards the EEC in the wake of Suez. The political reports that he sent on the launch of Sputnik and the Cypriot question, the frosty relations between Britain and France in the wake of Suez and the belief that Britain would attempt to improve relations with Germany were all prescient and cogent.

Cremin's main task in London was to develop better Anglo-Irish relations. This he did through the development of contacts with British cabinet members, often acting as a 'fire-brigade' to explain IRA outrages during the early stages of their 'border campaign' in the mid-1950s. He diligently worked on the vexed and emotional question of anti-partition. However, intellectually he did not display a strong conviction for this policy area, regarding the development of nationalist participation in the northern Irish state to be more practical and fruitful. A major report on the Irish in Britain sought to examine how the Irish were integrating into British society and also emphasised that the Irish in Britain could not be mobilised to vote on an exclusively Irish issue. The days when Parnell could command ten seats in the English (British) parliament were long over.

Cremin's Last Appointments

Cremin's stay in London was relatively short. In 1958, his career as an ambassador ended temporarily. He was recalled to Dublin to take over from Séan Murphy as secretary of the department of external affairs. His new position meant that he could directly advise the minister and cabinet on the direction of Irish foreign policy. Among other issues, this enabled him to play a leading role, with the secretary of the department of finance, Dr T.K. Whitaker, in Ireland's first application to join the EEC. However, de Gaulle's vetoing of Britain derailed the Irish application as well.

After his tenure as secretary he returned to London as ambassador in 1963 where he reported on the aftermath of the French vetoing of the British application to join the EEC, sending back analysis on where the British policy failed. These analyses were of major assistance as background for the preparation of further bids to join the EEC, culminating in the success of 1973.

In 1964, he was appointed to the permanent mission at the United Nations, which meant he became one of the most visible faces of Irish diplomacy. He held that position until his retirement in 1974. The United Nations in the mid-1960s produced a more measured diplomacy than the days of the 'Red China' vote in 1958, and this was a time when Ireland was making real progress in building up bilateral and multilateral policies. Irish participation in the various peacekeeping missions of the 1960s earned the Irish state respect if not the admiration of her peers.

With the outbreak of the troubles in Northern Ireland in 1968–69, Cremin helped guide Ireland through one of the most difficult periods in Anglo-Irish relations. This was one of the most dangerous periods in post-war Irish history when civil war was a distinct possibility. Among Cremin's major success at the UN was his manoeuvring in 1969 to find a means for the minister for external affairs, Dr Patrick Hillery, to address the security council. Realising that the Irish minister would be blocked if he tried to make a formal statement, Cremin, with the support of the Spaniards, found a formula which allowed Dr Hillery to put a statement of the Irish position on the record. The British, in turn, read into the record a commitment to reform.

Cremin brought his considerable experience and good judgement to bear in his UN posting. He used it to the full throughout his time to help inject an element of realism into Dublin's sometimes wayward expectations of what was possible for Irish policy in that multilateral forum. This nuanced approach gave Ireland some necessary breathing space and allowed passions to be tempered by realism.

From the 1930s and the Second World War to the early 1970s, Cremin played a very important role in the development of a professional diplomatic service. He was a strong influence on a younger cohort of diplomats in whose recruitment he had also played an active part. In his time, Cremin was an outstanding member of the Irish diplomatic community. He showed diligence in the face of extreme adversity and was respected for his calmness and for his courage. During his postings he was noted for being able to develop contacts, some less palatable than others, but all of help in his position.

The most outstanding feature of Cremin's work was that while he influenced Irish policy throughout his career, he did so quietly and selflessly. He did not seek out the notoriety which many crave.[222] In the files, Cremin showed an acute dislike of any lack of professionalism and of grandstanding. He was a model of the professional diplomat, achieving his results through careful and painstaking research and through the checking and cross-checking of sources.

His reporting was never dramatic. It revealed an approach that was steady, disciplined, professional and dependent on empirical research and layers of sources. He did not allow his passions to blind him to his duty. He was a public servant dedicated to the promotion of the interests of the Irish state, which he served diligently for thirty-nine years.

Cremin was known to be a Francophile. He had a deep love for the Irish language and Irish culture, especially the role played by Irishmen on the continent. He also had a great love of the classical world of archaeology, and might have made his profession in archaeology had not the opportunity of a cadetship arisen in the department of external affairs.

It is not an easy task to write a diplomatic biography of as complex a figure as Con Cremin. As a diplomat, he was among the best that Ireland produced in his generation. Professional, discreet, an accomplished linguist, he was able to penetrate the upper echelons of the administrations of Britain, France, the Vatican and even Nazi Germany.

At the UN in the 1960s and 1970s, junior diplomats would remark on his ability to circulate with ease around a crowded room. He left nobody out. According to people who knew him, as a man he was witty, charming and urbane, and was able to deal easily with people from all walks of life. This is not something which comes across in departmental files, which were the primary source for this book.

The Irish historian is somewhat handicapped by the paucity of memoirs left by senior civil servants, ministers and Taoisigh. The tradition of the neighbouring island is to produce memoirs and diaries as soon as possible having retired from public office. If one looks at the history of Churchill's memoirs by David Reynolds, it relates that Churchill's memoirs were close to being an official history. Figures in Irish public life do not have that tradition, which is a pity, as many historians have to rely in that vacuum on the biased memoirs of British politicians, especially on the issue of Northern Ireland. But that reticence to go into print is changing.

Cremin was an exception in his generation. He did, unlike other Irish diplomats, put pen to paper. His memoirs may appear to be a disappointing read at one level. However, the unpublished manuscript has laid out a chronological structure and provided some interesting anecdotes. It has left a scaffolding which has helped very much in the writing of this diplomatic biography. Owing to restrictions on space and my desire to deal comprehensively with Cremin's early career I have chosen to finish this book in 1958, the year that Cremin was appointed as secretary general of the Department of External Affairs, replacing Seán Murphy. This work therefore is an attempt to re-evaluate the role of the professional diplomat in the development of the history of the Irish state. The work itself is not an exhaustive treatment of the man himself but it will provide the reader with a study of the professional career of an exemplary diplomat who lived in extraordinary times.

Endnotes

CHAPTER 1

1 Cremin's parents married on 13 January 1907 in Kenmare. On their marriage certificate Daniel Cremin (son of James Cremin), lists his profession as farmer. The priest who married them was Fr Cornelius McCarthy. Births, marriages and deaths office. Cissy Crussell interview, 10 March 2001.

2 J.J. Lee, *Ireland 1912-85* (Cambridge University Press, Cambridge, 1989), p. 73.

3 Conor Cruise O'Brien interview, 11 June 2001. Dr Conor Cruise O'Brien stated that he did not know if Cremin had any political leanings at all, but assumed that he was Fianna Fáil. Cissy Crussell told me that her father was adamantly anti-Fianna Fáil and anti-de Valera throughout his life. When he died in the early 1960s, de Valera attended his removal. This provoked some amused comment among Cissy and her cousins. Cissy Crussell interview, 10 March 2001.

4 Cissy Crussell interview, 10 March 2001.

5 Playing cricket would have meant that he was not allowed to play with the Gaelic Athletics Association (GAA) owing to Rule 26: the ban on the playing of foreign sports.

6 Cissy Crussell interview, 10 March 2001 and information given by Dermot Keogh.

7 University College Cork Calendars 1926–34 and Cremin, 'Memoirs', p. 8.

8 Cremin, 'Memoirs', p. 8.

9 C.C. Cremin, 'Phases of Corcyraean History' (MA thesis, University College Cork, 1931)

10 Cremin, 'Memoirs', p. 10. See also C.C. Cremin, 'Archaeology and History', in *Ireland To-day*, Vol. II, No. 4 (April 1937). In 1937 Cremin reviewed Plutarch's *Life of Aratus* by W.H. Porter. See Cremin, C.C., 'Review of *Plutarch's Life of Aratus*, edited by W.H. Porter', in *Ireland Today*, Vol. II, No. 4 (September 1937).

11 *Ibid.*

12 Early draft of Con Cremin's 'Memoirs' compiled by Mgr Frank Cremin.

13 Cissy Crussell interview, 10 March 2001; Cremin, 'Memoirs', p. 9.

14 Interview with Dr Patrick O'Donoghue, November 2000.

15 Patricia O'Mahony's father was the secretary of the Board of Health in Killarney, Co. Kerry. He had fought on the anti-treaty side in Kerry and was said to be a friend of de Valera.

16 Early draft of Con Cremin's 'Memoirs' compiled by Mgr Frank Cremin. F.H. Boland remembered tripping over bags of seed potatoes, fertilisers and veterinary medicine in the passageways of the department of external affairs. F.H. Boland, 'Unpublished Memoir', p. 14.

17 Dermot Keogh, *Ireland and Europe 1919-1989* (Hibernian University Press, Cork and Dublin, 1989), p. 54.

18 Cissy Crussell interview, 10 March 2001.

19 Early draft of Con Cremin's 'Memoirs' compiled by Mgr Frank Cremin.

20 Cremin and Boland always referred to each other on first name terms in their

correspondence. Anne Cremin stated that Boland and her father were friends (Ann Cremin interview).

21 Keogh, *Ireland and Europe,* p. 65.

22 William L. Shirer, *The Collapse of the Third Republic* (Simon and Schuster, New York, 1969), pp. 326-331.

23 Paul Kennedy, *The Rise and Fall of Great Powers* (Unwin Hyman, London, 1988), p. 337.

24 Cremin, 'Memoirs', p. 10.

25 Cissy Crussell interview, 10 March 2001. It is not my intention to examine the role that Patricia Cremin played in the diplomatic career of Con Cremin. Katie Hickman argues that diplomatic wives represented a lacuna in history (Katie Hickman, *Daughters of Britainnia, the lives and times of diplomatic wives* [Harper Collins, London, 1999], p. xxiii and 51).

26 Keogh, *Ireland and Europe*, p. 53.

27 *Ibid.*

28 Robert J. Patterson, 'Ireland and France, An analysis of Diplomatic Relations, 1929-50' (MA thesis, University College Cork, 1993), p. 61. Robert Patterson states O'Brien was 'an unhappy choice' to be the Irish representative in Paris.

29 Keogh, *Ireland and Europe*, pp. 63-64.

30 Cissy Crussell records that Cremin was more interested in cars when he was young and asked the local garage owner to teach him about them. It produced mirth when a colleague, looking to pay his respects to Cremin, called in for petrol and was told that he used to worked there. Cissy Crussell interview, 10 March 2001.

31 De Valera later disciplined Art O'Brien. See J.P. Duggan, *An Undiplomatic Diplomat – C. H. Bewley (1888-1969)*, Summer 2001, Vol. 90, No. 358.

32 Patterson, 'Ireland and France, 1929-50', p. 70. Art O'Brien repatriated six destitute Irishmen who were intending to go to Spain in mid-1937 and suggested that the 'Irish Nationals be excluded from the weekend ticket system' which allowed them to travel to Paris without a passport. See Ferghal McGarry, *Irish Politics and the Spanish Civil War* (Cork University Press, Cork, 1999) p. 56.

33 NAI, DFA 119/49, O'Brien to Walshe, 31 January 1939 and Keogh, *Ireland and Europe*, p. 81.

34 Patterson, 'Ireland and France, 1929-50', p. 70.

35 *Ibid.,* p. 66.

36 NAI, DFA 107/189, O'Brien to Walshe, 25 November 1937.

37 Keogh, *Ireland and Europe,* p. 63.

38 NAI, DFA 107/189, O'Brien to Walshe, 25 November 1937.

39 *Ibid.*

40 O'Brien's diplomatic experience was inadequate and he was blinded by his personal hostility to the Popular Front. See Keogh, *Ireland and Europe*, pp. 63-64.

41 *Ibid.*, p. 105.

42 *Ibid.*, p.65.

43 Charles Bewley suggested that there was something sinister about O'Brien's retirement. However, O'Brien *was* sixty-six years of age and Bewley is not a reliable source. Charles Bewley, *Memoirs of a Wild Goose* (Lilliput Press, Dublin, 1989), pp. 171-73.

44 Cremin, 'Memoirs', p. 40a.

45 Cremin, 'Memoirs', p. 36.

46 Keogh, *Ireland and Europe*, p. 65.

47 Cremin, 'Memoirs', p. 10.

48 However, this would be in keeping with the character of Cremin who would not speak ill of his colleagues or ministers. In his memoirs he does not mention the policy rift of 1940 nor the declaration of the republic in 1949 nor the professional relationship between Boland and MacBride, events in which he was in a prime position to provide authorative commentaries.

49 Dr Garret FitzGerald interview, 2 December 2000.

50 Garret FitzGerald, *All in a Life, an autobiography* (Gill and Macmillan, Dublin, 1991), p. 127.

51 NAI, DFA 313/3/33, Annual report of Irish legation in Paris, between 1 April and 30 September 1938, signed 7 October 1938, drafted by Cremin. Cremin's style is distinctive.

52 Cissy Crussell interview, 10 March 2001. Lacouture argues that in mid-1938, de Gaulle 'had been living in a state of war for months'. Jean Lacouture, *De Gaulle* (Hutchinson, London, 1970), p. 55.

53 Maurice Manning, *The Blueshirts* (Gill and Macmillan, Dublin, 1970), pp. 206-7. Only 9 of 663 of O'Duffy's Irish brigade opted to stay beyond their six-month contract, which ended in June 1937 and the others left through Lisbon (Keogh, *Ireland and Europe*, p. 80). The Irish that went to fight on the republican side never numbered more than 150. Keogh's figure is similar to the figure suggested by O'Riordan (Michael O'Riordan, *Connolly's Column* [New Books, Dublin, 1979] pp. 162–65). Fergal McGarry disagrees with this figure and suggests that a figure of 200 first generation Irishmen fought with the republican forces (Fergal McGarry, *Irish Politics and the Spanish Civil War*, p. 56). The Connolly Column left Spain on 7 December 1938 and were placed on a sealed train for Dieppe, thus not coming into contact with the Irish legation at all (O'Riordan, *Connolly's Column*, p. 137).

54 O'Brien retired in 1938 and Charles Bewley retired from the service in 1939 (Keogh, *Ireland and Europe*, pp. 65-105).

55 Dermot Keogh 'Ireland, de Gaulle and World War II' in Pierre Joannon, *De Gaulle and Ireland* (Institute of Public Administration, Dublin, 1991), p. 25.

56 Ian Kershaw, *Hitler, 1936-45, Nemesis* (Allen Lane, London, 2000), pp. 181-231. The obverse of that is that the allies could not afford to fight the war any later than 1939 as their peacetime economies would not be able to sustain the strain.

57 Patterson, 'Ireland and France, 1929–50', p. 95. I was not able to locate this file in the National Archives of Ireland. It was misplaced at the time of writing.

58 *Ibid*.

59 Keogh, *Ireland and Europe*, p. 117.

60 F.S.L. Lyons, *Ireland since the Famine* (Weidenfeld and Nicolson, London, 1971), p. 548.

61 Keogh, *Ireland and Europe*, p. 118. De Valera had instructed Walshe to find out the Vatican's thinking on the matter. See also Dermot Keogh, 'Profile of Joseph Walshe, secretary, department of foreign affairs, 1922-46', *Irish Studies in International Affairs*, Vol. 3, No. 2 (1990), p. 60.

62 T. Ryle Dwyer, *Strained Relations, Ireland at peace and the USA at war 1941-*

45 (Gill and Macmillan, Dublin, 1988), p. 4. Dwyer also argues that de Valera used neutrality to demonstrate Irish independence and would not risk involvement in the war even to end partition.

63 Robert Fisk, *In Time of War, Ireland, Ulster and the Price of Neutrality, 1939-45* (Paladin Grafton Books, London, 1983), p. 76. 'Chanak was a small seaport on the Dardanelles in Turkey. The Versailles treaty kept some British soldiers on duty in Turkey. In 1922, some Turkish nationalists took over Chanak territory and endangered British troops. Britain called upon Canada and the rest of its dominions for help. The prime minister, Mackenzie King, told Britain that he would have to consult parliament before he could send in Canadian troops. The crisis ended before Canada could make a decision on the issue. This was the first time that Canada had refused a direct request to protect the empire'. http://www.swil.ocdsb.edu.on.ca/SWLCanMu/cnfrnc.html

64 Ireland had no indigenous arms industry and the majority of the weapons that the state possessed dated from the Civil War. Lee argues that Ireland had a comfortable war owing to the fact that she economised on defence and at best our neutrality was 'half-armed' compared to Sweden or Switzerland (Lee, *Ireland,* pp. 234-6).

65 Keogh, *Ireland and Europe,* pp. 118–19.

66 Lee, *Ireland,* p. 221.

67 T. Desmond Williams, 'Ireland and the War' in K.B. Nolan, and T. Desmond Williams (eds.) *Ireland in the War Years and after 1939-1951* (Gill and Macmillan, Dublin, 1969), p. 21.

68 Kathleen Burk, *Troublemaker, the life and history of A.J.P. Taylor* (Yale University Press, London, 2000), p. 99.

69 This is arguably so, in that de Valera did not discuss foreign policy with his cabinet, nor did he bring the opposition into government.

70 *Ibid.*, p. 246.

71 John Keegan, *The Second World War* (Hutchinson, London, 1989), p. 112.

72 Cremin, 'Memoirs', p. 11. The Maginot line was the static system of frontier defences on the Franco-German frontier which fatally did not extend to the Belgian frontier.

73 Knowlson, *Damned to Fame, The Life of Samuel Beckett* (Bloomsbury, London, 1996), p. 762.

74 Early draft of Con Cremin's 'Memoirs' compiled by Mgr Frank Cremin.

75 Cremin, 'Memoirs', p. 12. It was rendered uninhabitable so that it could not be requisitioned.

76 Early draft of Con Cremin's 'Memoirs', compiled by Mgr Frank Cremin.

77 It is interesting to note that the US embassy did not leave following the precedent that the US ambassador did not leave during the Paris Commune of 1870-71, see Robert Murphy, *Diplomat among Warriors* (Doubleday, New York, 1964), pp. 40–41. Bill Bullitt had the idea that the Germans would allow the communists to run riot in Paris for a few days and was prepared to defend the embassy with Thompson guns.

78 W.D. Halls, *Politics, Society and Christianity in Vichy France* (Berg, London, 1995), p. 226.

79 Cremin, 'Memoirs', p. 13.

CHAPTER 2

1 Cremin, 'Memoirs', p. 13. Bill Bullitt's aunt, Frau Grabisch, of Munich, was connected with Casement's activities in Germany during the first war.

2 Fr Patrick Travers, 'Some Experiences During the War Years: The Irish College in Paris 1939–45'. Copy of a paper delivered in Dublin in 1947. I would like to thank Professor Keogh for this reference.

3 Cremin, 'Memoirs', p. 13.

4 William L. Shirer, *The Collapse of the Third Republic* (Simon and Schuster, New York, 1969), p. 780.

5 Cremin reported the cost of using his car in connection with the evacuation from Paris was £26.15.0 and asked that that amount be credited to his account in Switzerland. This amount was based on a rate of 6d per mile based on a journey of 1,070 miles. NAI, DFA 246/118, Cremin to Walshe, 12 May 1941.

6 Cremin, 'Memoirs', p. 14.

7 Robert Murphy, *Diplomat among Warriors* (Doubleday, New York, 1964), p. 40.

8 Fr Patrick Travers 'Some Experiences'.

9 *Ibid.*

10 *Ibid.* He grew vegetables with considerable success and a report by Murphy in 1942 stated that while the other Irish priests looked thinner, Fr Travers never looked better. NAI, DFA P 12/1, Murphy to Walshe, 22 June 1942.

11 Shirer, *The Collapse of the Third Republic*, p. 788.

12 *Ibid.*, p. 800.

13 *Ibid.*, p. 835.

14 Cremin, 'Memoirs', p. 16.

15 Shirer, *The Collapse of the Third Republic*, p. 854.

16 *Ibid.*, p. 862. Mussolini wanted the French fleet and the Loire Valley, Franco wanted French north Africa.

17 *Ibid.*, p. 903.

18 Cremin, 'Memoirs', p. 16.

19 Shirer, *The Collapse of the Third Republic*, p. 911. De Gaulle described it as 'lamentable and hateful' (Jean Lacouture, *De Gaulle, the Rebel 1945–1970* [Collins, London, 1991], p. 249). Operation Catapult was the attack on Mers-el-Kébir/Oran, the two naval bases, close to each other, where the French fleet was harboured. The two names were used interchangeably in Irish reports and in subsequent histories.

20 NAI, DFA P 12/1, Murphy to Walshe, 13 July 1940.

21 *Ibid.*, 15 July 1940.

22 NAI, DFA 19/34, Murphy to Walshe, 8 July 1940.

23 Lord Casey, *Personal Experiences, 1939-1946* (Constable and Company, London, 1962), p. 48.

24 Cremin, 'Memoirs', p. 17.

25 *Ibid.*

26 Shirer, *The Collapse of the Third Republic*, p. 942.

27 J.P. Azéma, *From Munich to the Liberation* (Cambridge UP), p. 55.

28 NAI, DFA 119/49, Murphy to Walshe, 31 January 1939.

29 Cremin, 'Memoirs', p. 20.

30 NAI, DFA P12/1, Murphy to Walshe, 29 September 1940.

31 Cremin, 'Memoirs', p. 18.

32 NAI, DFA Paris 100/2, Murphy to Walshe, 24 November 1942. For further

analysis see Mary Daly, 'Irish Nationality and Citizenship since 1922', in *Irish Historical Studies*, xxxii, No. 127 (May 2001).

33 Patrick Keatinge, *The Formulation of Irish Foreign Policy* (Institute of Public Administration, Dublin, 1973), p. 142. It is also without question that this tradition continues, with Irish diplomats sometimes risking their personal safety to assist Irish citizens in distress.

34 Count O'Kelly was the minister in Paris in the 1920s and early 1930s. In keeping with the tradition of the time, as O'Kelly had been a minister he still retained his title, even in semi-retirement. Hence there is some confusion in the literature when O'Kelly is ascribed the title of minister, although he was strictly a chargé d'affaires. This ambiguity was probably promoted to enhance O'Kelly's standing with the German authorities. This tradition continued with Charles Bewley being issued a diplomatic passport during the first inter-party government.

35 Dermot Keogh 'Ireland, de Gaulle and World War II' in Pierre Joannon, *De Gaulle and Ireland* (Institute of Public Administration, Dublin, 1991), p. 25.

36 Dermot Keogh, *Ireland and Europe 1919-1989* (Hibernian University Press, Cork and Dublin, 1989), p. 52.

37 *Ibid.*, p. 139.

38 NAI, DFA Paris 100/2, Murphy to Walshe, 24 November 1942.

39 Cremin, 'Memoirs', p. 20.

40 *Ibid.*, p. 21.

41 NAI, DFA 19/34, Murphy to Walshe, 27 August 1940.

42 Fr Patrick Travers 'Some Experiences'. They affixed certificates around the building to ensure that the Germans would not attempt to requisition the building during the war.

43 Cissy Crussell interview, 10 March 2001.

44 Garret FitzGerald, *All in a Life, an autobiography* (Gill and Macmillan, Dublin, 1991), p. 127.

45 NAI, DFA P12/1, Murphy to Walshe, 24 August 1940.

46 *Ibid.*

47 *Ibid.*, Walshe to Murphy, 29 August 1940.

48 *Ibid.*, Warnock to Walshe, 6 September 1940.

49 *Ibid.*, 13 September 1940.

50 NAI, DFA P12/1, Murphy to Walshe, 15 September 1940.

51 *Ibid.*, 28 September 1940.

52 NAI, DFA P12/1, Walshe to Murphy, 1 October 1940.

53 *Ibid.*, 3 December 1940.

54 *Ibid.*, Walshe to Warnock, 7 December 1940.

55 *Ibid.*, Warnock to Walshe, 11 December 1940.

56 *Ibid.*, 17 December 1940.

57 *Ibid.*, Murphy to Walshe, 16 February 1941.

58 The Nazis had occupied two-thirds of France including all the industrialised north and west Atlantic coasts.

59 NAI, DFA P12/1, Murphy to Walshe, 16 February 1941. This would also have the effect of giving some diplomatic protection to his business.

60 *Ibid.*, 11 March 1942 and 20 April 1942.

61 NAI, DFA 49/20a, (Shelf 4/305/4) Correspondence from Jews in France concerning exit visas, 21 September 1942.

62 *Ibid.*

63 *Ibid.*

64 Interview with Ann Cremin.

65 Richard Ellman, *James Joyce* (Oxford University Press, Oxford, 1983), p. 738.

66 James Knowlson, *Damned to Fame, The Life of Samuel Beckett* (Bloomsbury, London, 1996), p. 762.

67 *Ibid.*, p. 302.

68 *Ibid.*, p. 302.

69 NAI, DFA P12/1, Confidential reports from Berlin, August 1942; NAI, DFA 49/20a, Correspondence from Jews in France concerning exit visas, September 1942, Shelf 4/305/4; see the Fay Abusch case.

70 Deirdre Bair, *Samuel Beckett* (Jonathan Cape, London, 1978), p. 335.

71 Donal Ó Drisceoil, *Censorship in Ireland, 1939-1945: neutrality, politics and society* (Cork University Press, Cork, 1996). Ó Drisceoil stated 'A 100% censorship was applied to correspondence to and from the continent of Europe for the entire duration of the Emergency', p. 62. In correspondence with the military archives, 16 October 2003, Comdt. Brennan informed me that there is 'no material in the G2 (Intelligence) or office of the controller of censorship 1939–46 collections relating to Con Cremin. There is mention of his name, which indicates that his correspondence was being examined. However, this was standard practice and a file was opened if any material or information came to notice. Quite clearly, this did not occur'.

72 Cissy Crussell interview, 10 March 2001.

73 Earlier draft of Con Cremin's 'Memoirs' compiled by Mgr Frank Cremin.

74 R.T. Thomas, *Britain and Vichy, the dilemma of Anglo-French Relations 1940-42* (Macmillan, London, 1979), p. 215.

75 http://www.dfait-maeci.gc.ca/hist/Dupuy-e.asp. Churchill was 'deeply grateful … for Dupuy's magnificent work … The Canadian channel is invaluable and indeed at the moment our only line'.

76 Cremin, 'Memoirs', p. 18.

77 William Leahy, *I Was There* (London, Victor Gollancz, 1950), p. 15.

78 Correspondence with Dr Aedeen Cremin, 16 March 2001.

79 Azéma, *From Munich to the Liberation*, p. 93.

80 Keogh, *Ireland and Europe,* p. 139; Mahon Hayes interview, 31 October 2003.

81 Maurice Martin DuGard, *La Chronique de Vichy: 1940–1944* (Flammarion, Paris, 1975). This indicates an anti-fascist mentality. (I am very grateful to Prof. M. MacNamara for this reference.)

82 Cremin, 'Memoirs', p. 22.

83 Early draft of Con Cremin's 'Memoirs' compiled by Mgr Frank Cremin.

84 Cremin, 'Memoirs', p. 23; Creeda FitzGibbon interview, 29 March 2001.

85 NAI, DFA P12/1, Murphy to Walshe, 29 September 1940.

86 Leahy, *I Was There,* p. 23.

87 Early draft of Con Cremin's 'Memoirs' compiled by Mgr Frank Cremin.

88 Cremin, 'Memoirs', p. 23.

89 *Ibid.*, p. 24. Romania was the main producer of oil in Europe at this time.

90 NAI, DFA Paris 48/11, Murphy to Walshe, 17 May 1941.

91 NAI, DFA P12/1, Murphy to Walshe, 11 December 1942.

92 *Ibid.*, 25 January 1943.

93 *Ibid.*, 4 February 1943.

94 *Ibid.*, 2 June 1943.

95 Azéma, *From Munich to Liberation*, p. 93.

96 Dermot Keogh, *Twentieth Century Ireland, Nation and State* (Gill and Macmillan, Dublin, 1994), p. 115.

97 Lee, *Ireland*, p. 247.

98 Keogh, *Twentieth Century Ireland*, p. 115.

99 Dr Garret FitzGerald interview, 2 December 2000.

100 Dermot Keogh, 'Profile of Joseph Walshe, secretary, department of foreign affairs, 1922-46', *Irish Studies in International Affairs*, Vol. 3, No. 2 (1990), p. 61. It needs to be said that Cremin did not view himself as anything 'more than a civil servant' and never pursued an ideological party line.

101 Dermot Keogh, *Ireland and the Vatican* (Cork University Press, Cork, 1994), p. 9.

102 Keogh, 'Ireland, de Gaulle and World War II', p. 24.

103 Lee, *Ireland*, p. 246.

104 The Earl of Longford and T.P. O'Neill, *Éamon de Valera* (Houghton Mifflin Company, Boston, 1971), p. 370.

105 NAI, DFA P12/1, Murphy to Walshe, July to December 1940.

106 Cremin, 'Memoirs', p. 12; Keogh, *Ireland and Europe,* p. 140.

107 Cremin, 'Memoirs', p. 140.

108 NAI, DFA P12/1, Walshe to Murphy, 22 July 1940.

109 Cremin, 'Memoirs', p. 20.

110 Keogh, *Ireland and Europe,* p. 140; One can see the vehemence with which Cremin defended his professionalism during his stay in the Vatican. See Chapter 7.

111 NAI, DFA A2 & A2.1, 'Britain's inevitable defeat', Walshe to de Valera, June 1940. Keogh, *Ireland and Europe,* p. 156. In interview (2 December 2000), Dr FitzGerald agreed with this thesis.

112 Dermot Keogh, 'Profile of Joseph Walshe', p. 76. Boland, Moynihan and the chief-of-staff of the defence forces did not support Walshe's viewpoint according to Keogh. See also Keogh, *Twentieth Century Ireland*, p. 115. In interview, Conor Cruise O'Brien told me that de Valera did not keep an office in Iveagh House and most of the business was done over the phone or by messengers (Conor Cruise O'Brien interview, 11 June 2001). One might suggest that this distance helped de Valera not to give into panic owing to the fact that he was physically one step removed.

113 NAI, DFA P12/1, Walshe to Murphy, 12 November 1940.

114 *Ibid.*, Murphy to Walshe, 19 November 1940

115 *Ibid.*, Murphy to Walshe, 19 November 1940.

116 *Ibid.*, Walshe to Murphy, 25 November 1940.

117 Keogh, *Ireland and Europe,* p. 159.

118 NAI, DFA P12/1, Murphy to Walshe, 4 December 1940.

119 Cremin, 'Memoirs', p. 18.

120 Murphy, *Diplomat among Warriors*, p. 49.

121 The meeting took place on 22 October 1940 at the railway station of Montoire. Herbert R. Lottman, *Pétain, Hero or Traitor?* (Viking, Harmondsworth, 1985), pp. 210–16.

122 NAI, DFA P12/1, Murphy to Walshe, 4 December 1940. The Irish diplomats

never complained about their personal food situation in Vichy; Admiral Leahy, the US ambassador, did extensively in *I Was There*.

123 Keogh, *Ireland and Europe*, p. 160.

124 NAI, DFA P12/1, Walshe to Murphy, 7 January 1941.

125 NAI, DFA P12/1, Murphy to Walshe, 13 January 1941.

126 In March 1941, Cremin brought back his wife, Patsy and their daughter, Ann (Cremin, 'Memoirs', p. 20). Cissy Crussell interview, 10 March 2001.

127 Keogh, *Ireland and Europe*, p. 160.

128 *Ibid.*

129 Cissy Crussell interview, 10 March 2001. Cremin, 'Memoirs', p. 22.

130 Keogh, 'Ireland, de Gaulle and World War II', p. 28.

131 He did not visit his family in Kenmare on this occasion, and only saw them subsequently, after a period of five years, in 1946. Cissy Crussell interview, 10 March 2001.

132 The skill of the allied and Nazi intelligence services in intercepting diplomatic pouches should not be underestimated, see Enno Stephanson, *A Man Called Intrepid* (Book Club Associates, London, 1976), p. 309. Even when diplomatic pouches were on Irish ships they were not safe (Boland, 'Memoirs'). The Irish code 'dearg' was a low grade cipher; this will be discussed further in the next chapter.

133 NAI, DFA P12/1, Walshe to Murphy, 19 February 1942.

134 NAI, DFA P12/1, Murphy to Walshe, 21 February 1942.

135 Lottman, *Pétain*, pp. 295–96.

136 Conor Cruise O'Brien interview, 11 June 2001.

137 NAI, DFA 205/124. F.T. Cremins to Walshe, 20 February 1945. The Swiss 'had sometimes been more evenhanded toward the one rather than the other, according to the way the tide of war was flowing'. They also wanted the war in northern Italy brought to an end quickly and without the distruction of the port of Turin (Leonard Mosley, *Dulles* [The Dial Press, New York, 1978]).

138 Keogh, *Twentieth Century Ireland*, p. 154.

139 *Ibid.*

140 NAI, DFA A2 & A2.1, 'Britain's inevitable defeat', Walshe to de Valera, June 1940 (no specific date in June given, although from context it must be late June).

141 O'Kelly was in Paris until all diplomats were expelled, but owing to the difficulty in communications his input into confidential reports would have been minimal. NAI, DFA P12/1, Murphy to Walshe, 19 November 1940. This report gives a hint of this.

142 *Ibid.*, 19 July 1940.

143 *Ibid.*, 28 July 1940.

144 *Ibid.*, 26 August 1940.

145 *Ibid.*, 3 July 1940. The majority of the French fleet was destroyed by the British navy in order to prevent it falling into the hands of the axis. Leahy, *I Was There*, p. 23.

146 NAI, DFA P12/1, Murphy to Walshe, 26 November 1940. Turkey only joined the war in 1944.

147 Martin Gilbert, *A History of the Twentieth Century, Vol. II* (Harper Collins, London, 1998), p. 347.

148 NAI, DFA P12/1, Murphy to Walshe, 21 November 1940.

149 The Germans expelled 100,000 French citizens from Lorraine and sent them to the unoccupied zone. The Italians had invaded Greece from Albania and were held back by the Greek army.

150 NAI, DFA P12/1, Murphy to Walshe, 2 December 1940.

151 Leahy, *I Was There*, p. 522. Leahy wrote on 25 January 1941 that Pétain called Laval 'dishonest and unpatriotic, a bad Frenchman'. 'Laval was a traitor, a Jew, a rat, a gangster, a scoundrel, a pig – so said the letter writers, the main reproach being that he favoured collaboration with the Germans' (Lottman, *Pétain*, p. 231).

152 On 18 June 1940 de Gaulle was 'supported only by an elderly jurist, three colonels, a dozen captains, an unskilful secretary, a few journalists, three battalions of legionaries and the confidence of a prime minister'. Lacouture, *De Gaulle, the Rebel*, p. 244. NAI, DFA P12/1, Murphy to Walshe, 2 December 1940.

153 Lacouture, *De Gaulle*, p. 256.

154 NAI, DFA 219/1d, Murphy to Walshe, 11 December 1940.

155 NAI, DFA P12/1, Murphy to Walshe, 13 December 1940.

156 *Ibid.*, 16 December 1940.

157 Lottman, *Pétain*, p. 225. This was the 1,751 gold ingots worth $223 million entrusted to the French national bank for safe keeping and laundered by the Swiss for the Nazis. Tom Bower, *Nazi Gold* (Harper Collins, New York, 1997), p. 52.

158 Lottman, *Pétain*, p. 231.

159 NAI, DFA 219/1d, Murphy to Walshe, 17 December 1940.

160 NAI, DFA P12/1, Murphy to Walshe, 18 December 1940.

161 *Ibid.*, 23 December 1940; and Lottman, *Pétain*, p. 233. This took place on 20 December 1940.

162 NAI, DFA 219/1d, Murphy to Walshe, 3 January 1941.

163 *Ibid.*, 10 January 1941.

164 NAI, DFA P12/1, Murphy to Walshe, 20 January 1941.

165 *Ibid.*, 27 January 1941.

166 *Ibid.*, 3 February 1941, The RNP never attracted more than 20,000 members.

167 *Ibid.*, 6 February 1941.

168 *Ibid.*

169 Leahy, *I Was There*, p. 28. This occurred on 8 February 1941.

170 NAI, DFA P12/1, Murphy to Walshe, 12 February 1941. Leahy argued in a meeting on 24 February, 'I found him (Darlan) frankly in favour of economic collaboration with Germany' (Leahy, *I Was There*, p. 30).

171 NAI, DFA P12/1, Murphy to Walshe, 19 February 1941.

172 Lottman, *Pétain*, p. 199.

173 NAI, DFA P12/1, Murphy to Walshe, 1 March 1941.

174 *Ibid.*

175 *Ibid.*, 2 April 1941.

176 Syria was where Vichy made concessions and allowed Nazi planes to refuel in French Syria so that they could bring arms to the General Rashid Ali in Iraq who had revolted against British rule. NAI, DFA P12/1, Murphy to Walshe, 3 April 1941.

177 The Paris press was controlled by the Nazis and in that regard was used as an instrument of Nazi policy.

178 The Balkan situation was a reference to the Nazi annexation of Yugoslavia and Greece that was completed by 27 April 1941.

179 NAI, DFA P12/1, Murphy to Walshe, 22 April 1941.

180 Leahy, *I Was There*, p. 39.

181 Lottman, *Pétain*, p. 251.

182 NAI, DFA P12/1, Murphy to Walshe, 16 May 1941.

183 Leahy, *I Was There*, p. 45.

184 H.R. Kedward, *Occupied France, Collaboration and Resistance 1940-44* (Basil Blackwell, Oxford, 1985), p. 38.

185 Lottman, *Pétain*, p. 251.

186 NAI, DFA P12/1, Murphy to Walshe, 24 May 1941.

187 Lottman, *Pétain*, p. 251.

188 NAI, DFA P12/1, Murphy to Walshe, 6 June 1941.

189 This thinking did not take into account that the German army marched into Russia with 700,000 horses and 600,000 vehicles. Also the majority of German troops had not been issued with winter clothing by the autumn of 1941 (Richard Overy, *Russia's War* [Penguin, London, 1997], p. 88).

190 NAI, DFA P12/1, Murphy to Walshe, 4 July 1941.

191 Overy, *Russia's War*, p. 327.

192 NAI, DFA P12/1, Murphy to Walshe, 11 July 1941.

193 *Ibid.*, 16 July 1941.

194 Lacouture, *De Gaulle*, p. 302.

195 J.F. Sweets, *Choices in Vichy France* (Oxford University Press, Oxford, 1986), pp. 53–58. The history of the French church during the war is full of internal contradictions, however this applied to all institutions in France. W.D. Halls, *Politics, Society and Christianity in Vichy France* (Berg, London, 1995), Chapter 10.

196 NAI, DFA P12/1, Murphy to Walshe, 28 July 1941. The cleric's name would have been withheld for reasons of security and confidentiality.

197 *Ibid.*, 6 August 1941. The accuracy of this report shows the high quality of the Irish information. Weygand visited Vichy on 9 August and according to Leahy steeled Vichy's resolve into not surrendering the bases. (See Leahy, *I Was There*, p. 71.)

198 Kedward, *Occupied France*, p. 40.

199 NAI, DFA P12/1, Murphy to Walshe, 27 August 1941.

200 NAI, DFA P12/1, Murphy to Walshe, 25 October 1941.

201 R. Aron, *The Vichy Regime 1940-44* (Putnam, London, 1958), p. 292.

202 Halls, *Politics, Society and Christianity*, p. 231.

203 Peter Calvocoressi and Guy Wint, *Total War*, (Viking, London, 1989) p. 202.

204 Kennedy, *The Rise and Fall of Great Powers*, p. 342.

205 NAI, DFA, P12/1, Murphy to Walshe, 17 December 1941.

206 *Ibid.*, 5 January 1942.

207 Lottman, *Pétain*, p. 269.

208 NAI, DFA 219/1d, Murphy to Walshe, 31 December 1941.

209 *Ibid.*, 7 March 1942.

210 *Ibid.*, 30 March 1942.

211 Leahy, *I Was There*, p. 109.

212 NAI, DFA P12/1, Murphy to Walshe, 18 April 1942.

213 *Ibid.*, 21 April 1942; Leahy, *I Was There*, p. 112.

214 *Ibid.*, 7 May 1942

215 Leahy, *I Was There*, p. 113. French diplomatic practice requires that ministers of state make the first calls on ambassadors.

216 NAI, DFA P12/1, Murphy to Walshe, 10 May 1942.

217 *Ibid.*, 5 June 1942.

218 Leahy, *I Was There*, p. 116.

219 *Ibid.*, p. 117.

220 NAI, DFA P12/1, Murphy to Walshe, 25 July 1942.

221 *Ibid.*, 22 June 1942.

222 Leahy, *I Was There*, p. 378.

223 *Ibid.*, 30 June 1942.

224 *Ibid.*, 10 October 1942.

225 Albert Speer, *Inside the Third Reich* (Phoenix, New York, 1970), p. 422–26.

226 NAI, DFA P12/1, Murphy to Walshe, 8 November 1942.

227 *Ibid.*, 13 November 1942.

228 *Ibid.*, 17 November 1942.

229 *Ibid.*, Murphy to Walshe, 27 November 1942. Marshal Pétain had given orders that the fleet was to be scuttled if it was in danger of being captured (Lottman, *Pétain*, p. 295). Gilbert, *A History of the Twentieth Century Vol. II*, p. 474. Three U-boats escaped and joined the Free French in north Africa.

230 Lottman, *Pétain*, p. 294. On 16 November 1942, Pétain broke with Darlan.

231 Cointet, Jean-Paul, *Pierre Laval* (Fayard, Paris, 1993) p. 535. Laval was executed, by a French firing squad, on 15 October 1945. De Gaulle refused all requests for clemency.

232 NAI, DFA P12/1, Murphy to Walshe, 19 December 1942. The Irish code was never secure.

233 Lacouture gives five pages to the assassination, the responsibility for which belongs to either the royalists or Gaullists. Darlan's death removed all obstacles for the Gaullists to form the provisional government. Lacouture, *De Gaulle*, pp. 409–14.

234 NAI, DFA 359/8, Murphy to Walshe, 15 February 1943.

235 Leahy, *I Was There*, see Chapter 'Darlan Delivers'.

236 Cremin, 'Memoirs', p. 18.

237 *Ibid.*, 2 August 1943.

238 *Ibid.*, 23 August 1943.

239 *Ibid.*, 23 August 1943.

240 *Ibid.*, 5 October 1943.

241 *Ibid.*, 28 November 1943.

242 NAI, DFA P12/1, Walshe to Murphy, 6 January 1943.

243 NAI, DFA 119/49, Murphy to Walshe, 31 January 1939.

244 Keogh, *Ireland and Europe*, p. 105.

245 Dermot Keogh, *Jews in Twentieth Century Ireland* (Cork University Press, Cork, 1999), p. 119.

246 *Ibid.*, p. 158.

247 NAI, DFA 219/1d, Murphy to Walshe, 8 January 1941.

248 Dermot Keogh, *Jews in Twentieth Century Ireland*, p. 194.

249 *Ibid.*, p. 208.

250 NAI, DFA 49/20a, Cremin to Walshe, 21 September 1942.

251 NAI, DFA P12/1, Murphy to Walshe, 22 September 1942.

252 NAI, DFA 49/20a, Cremin to Walshe, 25 September 1942.

253 *Ibid.*, 26 September 1942.

254 Hilberg, *The Destruction of European Jews,* p. 409.

255 Paula E. Hyman, *The Jews of Modern France* (University of California Press, London, 1998), p. 162.

256 NAI, DFA P12/1, Murphy to Walshe, 23 August 1943.

257 NAI, DFA 49/20a, Briscoe to Murphy, early September 1942.

258 *Ibid.*, Cremin to US official, 15 September 1942.

259 *Ibid.*, Abusch to Murphy, 15–21 September 1942; Murphy to Briscoe, 21 September 1942.

260 *Ibid.*, Cremin to Abusch, 23 September 1942.

261 *Ibid.*, Abusch to Murphy, 24 September 1942.

262 *Ibid.*, unknown US consul in Nice to Cremin, September 1942.

263 *Ibid.*, Cremin to Abusch, 6 October 1942 and 21 October 1942.

264 *Ibid.*, Walshe to Murphy, 13 November 1942.

265 *Ibid.*, Murphy to Abusch, 4 January 1943.

266 *Ibid.*, Walshe to Murphy, 27 August 1943.

267 *Ibid.*, Murphy to Walshe, 27 August 1943.

268 NAI D/T S16671A, 20 July 1959.

269 Stephan Collins interview, 4 December 1999; Creeda FitzGibbon interview, 29 March 2001 and Prof. Dermot Keogh, 4 December 1999. All three confirmed that Cremin had been awarded two Légion d'honneurs. Creeda FitzGibbon stated that Cremin had intervened with the Germans to prevent a group of French hostages being shot. Interview with Creeda FitzGibbon, née Cremin, 29 March 2001.

270 I have made inquiries with numerous historians (Dr D. McMahon, Dr C. Crowe, Dr M. O'Driscoll, R. Patterson, Prof. D. Keogh) and none have come across a record of this. According to article 40.2.2 of Bunreacht na hÉireann Cremin should have sought the permission of the government. However owing to the expediencies of wartime they probably took an executive decision not to request sanction (see Leonard Mosley, *Dulles* [The Dial Press, New York, 1978] pp. 174–88). It is also arguable that the negative propaganda that could have been created if Cremin did request permission would have been considerable.

CHAPTER 3

1. NAI, DFA 17/1, Warnock to Walshe, 12 August 1943. 'Die Billige Gesandtschaft' (the cheap legation) was the title given to the Irish legation by auswärtiges amt (foreign office) officials, owing to the small size of the legation.

2 *Ibid.,* p. 18.

3 T. Desmond-Williams, 'A Study in Neutrality' in *The Leader,* 14 March 1953.

4 Patrick Keatinge, *The Formulation of Irish Foreign Policy* (Institute of Public Administration, Dublin, 1973), p. 111.

5 Fisk, *In Time of War,* p. 372.

6 Correspondence with Dr Aedeen Cremin, 16 March 2001.

7 Keogh, *Ireland and Europe,* p. 105.

8 Cremin was certainly a Francophile in that he admired their culture and civilisation, however he was not sycophantic about his admiration of French civilisation.

9 Cremin, 'Memoirs', p. 24.

10 Keogh, *Ireland and Europe*, p. 139.

11 Lee, *Ireland*, p. 248.

12 Walshe personally penned an undated report in early July 1940 entitled 'Britain's inevitable defeat'.

13 *Ibid.*, p. 247.

14 Geoffrey Elborn, *Francis Stuart, a life* (The Raven Arts Press, Dublin, 1990), p. 126.

15 Early draft of Con Cremin's 'Memoirs' compiled by Mgr Frank Cremin.

16 Gilbert, *A History of the Twentieth Century, Vol. II*, pp. 465–66. Germany had penetrated through to the Caucasus, Rommel was readying to attack Egypt, and the Japanese had taken Kokoda in New Guinea.

17 David O'Donoghue, *Hitler's Irish Voices* (Beyond the Pale Publications, Belfast, 1998), pp. 25, 35 and 167.

18 Lottman, *Pétain*, p. 284. The allies had attempted to take the fortified port of Dieppe without close tank-infantry support and failed with heavy casualties. Duggan argues in his work on Hempel that an Irishman informed the German minister that the allies were to invade Dieppe and that Hempel broadcast this information.

19 NAI, DFA 219/4, Cremin to Walshe, August 1942.

20 NAI, DFA 17/1, Warnock to Walshe, 1 April 1943.

21 *Ibid.*, Walshe to Warnock, 27 April 1943.

22 *Ibid.*, Warnock to Walshe, 18 June 1943.

23 *Ibid.*, Walshe to Warnock, 5 July 1943.

24 NAI, DFA P12/3, Walshe to Warnock, probably 1–11 August 1943.

25 Owing to a lapse in judgement Warnock showed the newspapers to Francis Stuart who used them to make Irland-Redaktion sound more authentic. See O'Donoghue, *Hitler's Irish Voices*, p. 105.

26 NAI, DFA 17/1, Warnock to Walshe, 12 August 1943. Warnock feared the opening of the second front, which would make it impossible to get out of Germany.

27 *Ibid.*

28 Ellic Howe, *The Black Game* (Queen Ann Press, London, 1982), pp. 102–26.

29 NAI, DFA 17/1, Warnock to Walshe, 12 August 1943.

30 *Ibid.*, Walshe to Warnock, October 1943.

31 Italy by August 1943 was *de facto* out of the war. The puppet fascist state in the north had simply provoked a civil war, which led to the further destruction of property and the fabric of Italian life; NAI, DFA 17/4, Walshe to Warnock, 2 June 1944.

32 NAI, DFA 17/1, Walshe to Warnock, 24 November 1943.

33 NAI, DFA P12/3, Warnock to Walshe, March 1943.

34 Keegan, *The Second World War*, p. 428.

35 Gilbert, *A History of the 20th Century*, Vol. II, p. 531.

36 Fisk, *In Time of War,* p. 371. Ironically the reason the legation caught fire so easily was owing to a phosphorous bomb setting fire to the workmen's wooden huts. The workmen were building a bomb shelter for the legation.

37 NAI, DFA 46/14, Warnock to Walshe, 16 December 1943.

38 Cremin, 'Memoirs', p. 25.

39 *Ibid.*, p. 25. Charlie Mills was a trotting pony breeder and ran a stud farm.

NAI, DFA 17/1, Walshe to Cremin and Warnock, 16 December 1943. In his memoirs Cremin related that the editor of *The Irish Times,* Robert Smyllie, had been interned in August 1914 with Charlie Mills (Cremin, 'Memoirs', p.26).

40 Cremin, 'Memoirs', p. 26.

41 Cissy Crussell interview, 10 March 2001.

42 NAI, DFA 17/1, Warnock to Walshe, 29 November 1943.

43 NAI, DFA 353/21 (Original File 246/247, then changed to 241/396) 1943–45, Warnock to Walshe, 3 December 1943.

44 Keogh, *Ireland and Europe,* p. 303. NAI, DFA 313/4, Fay to Nunan, October 1954. Conor Cruise O'Brien and William Fay received telegrams in 'dearg' but they could not find out where the key for the code was kept.

45 Eunan O'Halpin, *Defending Ireland* (Oxford University Press, Oxford, 1999), pp. 184–85, see endnote 104.

46 Keogh, *Ireland and Europe*, p. 311.

47 O'Halpin, *Defending Ireland*, p. 185.

48 MacWhite in Rome had long since lost faith in the code and it is unlikely that Cremin would have thought the code would deter any but casual observers (Keogh, *Ireland and Europe,* p. 309).

49 NAI, DFA 17/1, Walshe to Cremin and Warnock, 16 December 1943.

50 NAI, DFA 17/1, Cremin and Warnock to Walshe, 18 December 1943. The response of the department of finance is not recorded in the files.

51 *Ibid*. Requests for motorcar allowances to the department of finance were not generally well received. Conor Cruise O'Brien, *Memoir, My life and themes* (Profile, London, 1999), p. 93.

52 NAI, DFA 17/1, Warnock to Walshe, 13 January 1944.

53 *Ibid.*, F.T. Cremins to Walshe, 26 January 1944.

54 Madeleine Kent, *I Married a German* (George Allen and Unwin Ltd, London, 1938), p. 222.

55 Although the damage was inflicted by the RAF, the German government was liable for the damage.

56 NAI, DFA 353/21, 1943–45, Veale to Cremin, 11 December 1943.

57 *Ibid.*, (original file 246/247, then changed to 241/396) 1943–45, Walshe to Cremin and Warnock, January 1943.

58 PRO, FO 371/104086. Gustav Adolf Steengracht von Moyland survived the Soviet onslaught and was eventually sentenced to seven years' imprisonment http://encyclopedia.thefreedictionary.com/Ministeries+Trial

59 Keogh, *Twentieth Century Ireland*, p. 123. This also included the destruction caused by the bombing of the North Strand and the destruction of other Irish property, including some of the ships belonging to Irish Shipping.

60 The RAF committed themselves to the 'Battle of Berlin' on 18–19 November 1943 (see Keegan, *The Second World War,* p. 428).

61 NAI, DFA 19/3, Cremin to Walshe, February 1945.

62 Early draft of Con Cremin's 'Memoirs' compiled by Mgr Frank Cremin.

63 Cremin, 'Memoirs', p. 28.

64 *Ibid.*, p. 29.

65 Alexandra Richie, *Fausts Metropolis* (Harper-Collins Publishers, London, 1998), p. 533.

66 NAI, DFA 2/10, Cremin to Walshe, 24 June 1944.

67 Creeda FitzGibbon interview, 29 March 2001. Dr Deirdre MacMahon, who

interviewed Cremin in the 1980s, stated that she had the opinion that he felt he was experiencing history being made, 27 February 2000.

68 Correspondence with Dr Aedeen Cremin, 16 March 2001.

69 Cremin, 'Memoirs', p. 40a.

70 I remain to be convinced by T. Ryle Dwyer's suggestion that de Valera and Walshe allowed OSS (Office of Strategic Services) questions to be put to Cremin, Warnock, Murphy and MacWhyte after September 1943, which they unwittingly answered. Their reports were of use to the allies, but I think it unlikely that De Valera and Walshe would have risked Ireland's reputation and the lives of its diplomats by engaging in overtly unneutral behaviour (T. Ryle Dwyer, *The Examiner*, 12 July 2000).

71 NAI, DFA P12/3, Cremin to Walshe, 7 March 1944.

72 *Ibid.*, 13 March 1944. After Italy declared an armistice, loyal Italian units were disarmed and imprisoned. The Finns feared that this would happen to them.

73 NAI, DFA P12/3, Cremin to Walshe, 22 March 1944. In all of Cremin's reporting throughout his career the term 'Russians' is used for the 'Soviets' and 'Russia' for the 'Soviet Union'. In his reports the terms are interchangeable.

74 For an account of Finnish diplomacy during the war see Gripenberg, *Finland and the Great Powers* (Nabraska University Press, Lincoln, 1965). See also Stig Jagerskiold, *Mannerheim, Marshal of Finland* (Minnesota University Press, Minnesota, 1986).

75 NAI, DFA P12/3 27, Cremin to Walshe, March 1944.

76 Jörg K. Hoensch, *A History of Modern Hungary, 1867-1994* (Longman, London and New York, 1996), p. 157.

77 NAI, DFA P12/3, Cremin to Walshe, 27 March 1944.

78 O'Donoghue, *Hitler's Irish Voices*, p. 155.

79 Keogh, *Ireland and the Vatican*, p. 178.

80 NAI, DFA P77, Cremin to Walshe, 18 April 1944.

81 *Ibid.*, 20 April 1944.

82 Keogh, *Ireland and the Vatican*, p. 186. NAI, DFA P77, Cremin to Walshe, 4 June 1944.

83 Anthony Beevor, *Stalingrad* (Penguin, London, 1998), pp. 148-49.

84 Keogh, *Ireland and the Vatican*, p. 188.

85 NAI, DFA P12/3, Cremin to Walshe, 17 April 1944 and 9 May 1944.

86 *Ibid.*

87 Early draft of Con Cremin's 'Memoirs' compiled by Mgr Frank Cremin.

88 NAI, DFA P12/3, Cremin to Walshe, 14 June 1944.

89 Kershaw, *Hitler 1936-1945*, p. 642.

90 NAI, DFA P12/3, Cremin to Walshe, 19 June 1944 and Gilbert Martin, *A History of the Twentieth Century, Vol. II*, p. 578.

91 Kennedy, *The Rise and Fall of Great Power*. Kennedy argues that Germany had lost the war of production. Even though German production peaked in 1944, she was defeated in that the material resources of the allies far outstripped Germany's. Defeat was therefore inevitable in a war of attrition.

92 NAI, DFA P12/3, Cremin to Walshe, 4 July 1944.

93 *Ibid.*, 8 July 1944.

94 NAI, DFA P12/3, Cremin to Walshe, 24 July 1944.

95 Peter Grose, *Gentleman Spy, the life of Allen Dulles* (University of Massachusetts Press, Amherst, 1996), p. 198.

96 Kershaw, *Hitler 1936-1945*, p. 675.

97 NAI, DFA P12/3, Cremin to Walshe, 22 July 1944.

98 PRO, HW 1/3124. Sent on 22 July 1944, not seen by Churchill until 29 July 1944. (NAI, DFA P12/3, Cremin to Walshe, 24 July 1944.)

99 Grose, *Gentleman Spy*, p. 200.

100 I came across a reference to a personal profile of Cremin from 1944 in the PRO. Upon inquiring, I was informed that the file was probably destroyed. It is possible that the file is still classified. From its existence one can infer that a dossier had been built up on Cremin, probably using Oxford, UCC and diplomatic contacts.

101 NAI, DFA P12/3, Cremin to Walshe, 29 July 1944.

102 Major-General F.W. Von Mellenthin, *Panzer Battles* (Cassell, London, 1955), p. 194.

103 NAI, DFA P12/3, Cremin to Walshe, 29 July 1944.

104 *Ibid.*, 11 August 1944.

105 *Ibid.*, 18 September 1944.

106 Donald S. Detwiler, *World War II, German Military Studies, Vol. 24* (New York, Garland, 1975), Appendix A. Eisenhower, in particular, feared that he would leave his flanks vulnerable.

107 PRO HW 1/3124, 21 September 1944.

108 NAI, DFA P12/3, Cremin to Walshe, 21 September 1944. The words in brackets were put in by the telegraph operator who decoded the message.

109 PRO, HW1/3265, sent 8 October 1944, seen on 12 October 1944.

110 NAI, DFA P12/3, Cremin to Walshe, 19 November 1944.

111 *Ibid.*, 29 November 1944.

112 *Ibid.*, 20 December 1940.

113 *Ibid.*, 24 December 1944.

114 See MacDonald, *Battle of the Bulge* (Phoenix, London, 1998), pp. 7-14 and Mellenthin, *Panzer Battles*, p. 406. Also Hildebrand, *The Foreign Policy of the Third Reich*, p. 132.

115 NAI, DFA P12/3, Cremin to Walshe, 24 December 1944.

116 *Ibid.*, 14 January 1945.

117 NAI, DFA 2/12 (Berlin legation), Walshe to Cremin, 1 November 1943.

118 NAI, DFA 49/20A, Correspondence from Jews in France concerning exit visas, Murphy to Walshe, 28 December 1943.

119 NAI, DFA 2/12 (Berlin legation), Walshe to Cremin and Warnock, 5 January 1944.

120 *Ibid.*, Cremin and Warnock to Walshe, 10 January 1944. Needless to say Murphy and Cremin did not know the genocidal nature of the Nazis' Jewish policy.

121 *Ibid.*, Cremin and Warnock to Walshe, 17 February 1944.

122 *Ibid.*, Cremin to Walshe, 14 March 1944.

123 *Ibid.*, Cremin to Walshe, 16 March 1944.

124 *Ibid.*, 24 March 1944.

125 *Ibid.*

126 *Ibid.*, department II of the German foreign office was responsible for the crushing of attempts to obtain visas for Jews or for information about the Holocaust leaking out (Weitz, John, *Hitler's Diplomat, Joachim von Ribbentrop* (Phoenix Giant, London, 1992), p. 289).

127 NAI, DFA 2/12 (Berlin legation), Walshe to Cremin, 27 March 1944.

128 *Ibid.*, 20 April 1944.

129 *Ibid.*, 22 April 1944.

130 *Ibid.*, 27 April 1944.

131 *Ibid.*, 12 May 1944.

132 *Ibid.*, Walshe to Cremin, 6 June 1944; Lottman, *Pétain*, p. 307.

133 *Ibid.*, Cremin to Walshe, 7 July 1944.

134 Weitz, John, *Hitler's Diplomat*, p. 289; NAI, DFA 2/12 (Berlin legation), Cremin to Walshe, 7 June 1944.

135 NAI, DFA 2/12 (Berlin legation), Cremin to Walshe, 27 August 1944.

136 *Ibid.*, 29 August 1944.

137 *Ibid.*, 5 October 1944.

138 Ninety per cent of men and ninety-five per cent of women were murdered immediately upon arrival at Auschwitz. Theo Tschuy, *Dangerous Diplomacy, the story of Carl Lutz, Rescuer of 62,000 Hungarian Jews* (Eerdmansm Grand Rapids, Michigan, 2000), pp. 76-78.

139 NAI, DFA 2/12 (Berlin legation), Walshe to Cremin, 21 October 1944.

140 *Ibid.*, Cremin to Walshe, 27 October 1944.

141 NAI, DFA A20 Berlin legation file on Frank Ryan, Cremin to department, 21 December 1944.

142 NAI, DFA 2/12 (Berlin legation), Cremin to Walshe, 23 December 1944.

143 *Ibid.*, 28 December 1944.

144 Keogh, *Ireland and Europe*, p. 303.

145 Williams, 'Aspects of Neutrality', *The Leader*, 14 March 1953.

146 Keogh, *Twentieth Century Ireland*, p. 96.

147 Keogh, *Ireland and Europe*, pp. 151–55.

148 Francis Stuart, 'Frank Ryan in Germany, Part I', *The Bell*, Vol. XVI, No. 2, November 1950, p. 42.

149 Francis Stuart, 'Frank Ryan in Germany, Part II', *The Bell*, Vol. XVI, No. 3, December 1950, p. 40.

150 NAI, DFA A20, Walshe to Cremin, 6 April 1944.

151 *Ibid.*, Cremin to Walshe, 13 April 1944.

152 Seán Cronin, *Frank Ryan* (Repsol Publishing, Dublin, 1980), p. 232.

153 Enno Stephan, *Spies in Ireland* (Stackpole, Harrisburg, 1965), p. 287.

154 NAI, DFA A20, Cremin to Walshe, 15 July 1944.

155 *Ibid.*, Walshe to Cremin, 20 December 1944.

156 *Ibid.*, Cremin to Walshe, 4 January 1945.

157 *Ibid.*, Stuart to Cremin, 18 February 1945.

158 *Ibid.*, Cremin to Walshe, 20 February 1945. Immediately after the end of the war Cremin sent on all the relevant documentation, indicating the urgency which it had assumed in Walshe's mind (NAI, DFA A20, Cremin to Walshe, 28 June 1945).

159 O'Donoghue, *Hitler's Irish Voices*, p. 42.

160 Geoffrey Elborn, *Francis Stuart, a life* (The Raven Arts Press, Dublin, 1990), p. 126. Warnock's company in the summer of 1940 may have contributed to his poor judgement with regard to the reports he sent back that year (Lee, *Ireland*, p. 246).

161 NAI, DFA A72, Bryan to Walshe, 17 August 1945.

162 *Ibid.*, Cremin to Walshe, 27 August 1942. Cremin replaced Warnock while the

latter recovered from a car crash.

163 *Ibid.*

164 Ryle T. Dwyer, *Nice Fellow, a biography of Jack Lynch* (Mercier Press, Cork, 2001), p. 162. 'Internment without trial was implemented, while six IRA men were executed and four others were allowed to die on hunger strike.'

165 NAI, DFA 2/6s, Stuart to Cremin, April 1944.

166 *Ibid.*, Walshe to Cremin, 1 June 1944. Walshe further stated that Stuart's Irish citizenship was of a rather technical nature. David O'Donoghue, 'Berlin's Irish Radio', p. 105: Stuart was born in Australia to Northern Irish parents and was brought up in Co. Antrim. William Joyce was born in Brooklyn, NY, and raised in Galway.

167 Natterstad, *Francis Stuart*, p. 66.

168 NAI, DFA A20, Stuart to Cremin, 24 February 1945.

169 NAI, DFA 2/6s, Stuart to Cremin, 7 March 1945. No copy of that note exists within the National Archives of Ireland.

170 Elborn, *Francis Stuart*, p. 171.

171 Fisk, *In Time of War*, p. 406.

172 NAI, DFA 2/6s, 1 June 1944.

173 Natterstad, *Francis Stuart*, p. 66.

174 Keogh, *Twentieth Century Ireland*, p. 155.

175 Natterstad, *Francis Stuart*, p. 67.

176 Anne McCartney, *Francis Stuart, face to face: a critical study* (Institute of Irish Studies, Queens University Belfast, 2000), p. 158.

177 NAI, DFA A72, Bryan to Boland, 17 August 1945.

178 *Ibid.*

179 *Ibid.* Stuart was a brother in law to MacBride and 'when he was director of intelligence of the IRA he was largely responsible for their contacts with the Germans'. A second factor was that Goertz consulted with him in Berlin and he went to Stuart's house in Ireland.

180 Kevin Myers, *The Irish Times*, 22 October 1997.

181 Cremin, 'Memoirs', p. 29.

182 NAI, DFA 44, Annual report for 1944, written in May 1945. Some of the consular cases given assistance were: the Smith Sisters, who fled Warsaw in July 1944 (NAI, DFA 10/14, 6 July 1944); May Finucane, who was repatriated (NAI, DFA 10/1); Mrs Coyle (whose husband Vincent Coyle was killed in a air raid on Berlin in August 1943) and her two children (NAI, DFA 10/2); Fr Williams (NAI, DFA 2/10 German exit and transit visas); and John Vickers (NAI, DFA 10/5). These are just a sample of the consular cases; each case required a heavy volume of correspondence. The Irish religious houses served as an auxiliary arm, giving succour and shelter.

183 NAI, DFA 44/6, Cremin to Walshe, September 1944.

184 Cremin, 'Memoirs', p. 31.

185 NAI, DFA 44/6, Warnock to Walshe, 1 February 1943.

186 *Ibid.*, 12 May 1943.

187 *Ibid.*, 24 July 1944.

188 *Ibid.*, Cremin to Cummins, 20 April 1944.

189 *Ibid.*, Cremin to Walshe, 28 April 1944.

190 *Ibid.*, 17 May 1944.

191 *Ibid.*, 12 September 1944.

192 *Ibid.*, 29 September 1944.

193 *Ibid.*, 5 October 1944.

194 *Ibid.*, 16 November 1944.

195 *Ibid.*, 29 November 1944.

196 *Ibid.*, 16 January 1945.

197 *Ibid.*, 17 January 1945.

198 NAI, DFA 2/12 (Berlin legation), German Exit Visas in Special Cases (Jews etc), Cremin to Walshe, 1 February 1945.

199 NAI, DFA 44/6, Cremin to Walshe, 9 May 1945.

200 Bill Bullitt, the US ambassador to Paris, brought two English friends across the Spanish frontier in the guise of 'domestics'. When a Spanish police officer saw the ladies' hands and did not believe that the lady in question was a chambermaid, he was promptly told that she was the ambassador's mistress.

201 NAI, DFA 44/3, Warnock to Walshe, 13 September 1943.

202 *Ibid.*, Warnock and Cremin to Walshe, 7 October 1943.

203 *Ibid.*, 7 December 1943.

204 *Ibid.*, 2 January 1944.

205 On 29 December 1943 the *Kerlogue* rescued 168 German sailors who were the survivors of a naval battle in the Bay of Biscay (Fisk, *In Time of War*, pp. 319–20). The *Kerlogue* did not enter British territorial waters and proceeded to Cobh where the sailors were interned for the duration of the war, although Dwyer maintains that they should have been released because they were survivors from a shipwrecked ship. The legality was, however, overlooked and the Germans were eventually repatriated. Second World War conference, UCC, 19 May 2000. NAI, DFA 44/3, Warnock and Cremin to Walshe, 11 January 1944.

206 NAI, DFA 44/3, Warnock and Cremin to Walshe, 7 March 1944.

207 *Ibid.*, 10 May 1944.

208 *Ibid.*, 7 June 1944.

209 *Ibid.*, Vernon to Cremin, 12 July 1944.

210 *Ibid.*, Walshe to Cremin, 14 September 1944.

211 *Ibid.*, Cremin to Walshe, 19 September 1944.

212 *Ibid.*, 19 December 1944.

213 *Ibid.*, 15 January 1945.

214 *Ibid.*, 26 February 1945.

215 Cremin, 'Memoirs', p. 31.

216 NAI, DFA P12/3, Walshe to Cremin, August 1944.

217 *Ibid.*, 28 October 1944.

218 *Ibid.*, Cremin to Walshe, 31 October 1944. He requested permission to send the children to Switzerland 'when the situation merited it'.

219 Peter Hebblethwaite, *John XXIII* (Geoffrey Chapman, London, 1984), p. 209. NAI, DFA P12/3, Cremin to Walshe, 2 November 1944.

220 See Chapter 1.

221 An interesting aspect of Irish 'neutrality' was the practical flexibility and ideological rigidity that was displayed. Ireland's policy of friendly neutrality is well documented (Keogh, *Ireland and Europe*, pp. 165–96) While having diplomatic relations with Nazi Germany until the end of the war was entirely proper for a 'neutral' country (the Swiss and the Swedes also kept up diplomatic relations), the blunder of attempting to appear 'ideologically neutral' was disastrous when it came to de Valera extending condolences to

Hempel on Hitler's death and brought much unwanted attention to Ireland's policy of neutrality (Lee, *Ireland*, p. 269).

222 De Valera said to the dáil that 'There are over 2,050 of our citizens whom we know of, living in the different countries of [continental] Europe. Most of these are resident in the larger countries, Italy, France, Spain, Germany and so on, but we have also had requests for assistance of various kinds from our citizens in countries such as the Netherlands, Sweden, Hungary, Finland, Yugoslavia, Romania and other parts of Europe'. *Dáil Debates*, 28 June 1944, Columns: 1329–56.

223 The Spanish ambassador had an added reason of wanting to get out of the path of the Soviets because he was on their black list.

224 Cremin, 'Memoirs', p. 32.

225 NAI, DFA P12/3, Cremin to Walshe, 16 November 1945.

226 Conversation with Ann Cremin, 3 May 2001.

227 NAI, DFA P12/3, Walshe to Cremin, 23 November 1944.

228 Overy, *Russia's War*, p. 257.

229 NAI, DFA P12/3, Cremin to department, 19 January 1945.

230 *Ibid.*, Cremin to Walshe, 27 January 1945.

231 *Ibid.*, Cremin to Walshe, 1 February 1945.

232 Cremin, 'Memoirs', p. 33.

233 Overy, *Russia's War*, pp. 261-62.

234 NAI, DFA 10/179, Cremin to Mullally, 9 March 1945.

235 NAI, DFA P12/3, Cremin to Walshe, 7 February 1945.

236 *Ibid.*, 11 February 1945. Cremin was to meet Count Tovar again when the latter was appointed as ambassador to NATO in Paris in the early 1950s.

237 Cremin, 'Memoirs', p. 35.

238 NAI, DFA P12/3, Cremin to department, 19 and 23 February 1945.

239 *Ibid.*, Walshe to F.T. Cremins, 12 March 1945.

240 *Ibid.*, 15 March 1945.

241 Cremin, 'Memoirs', p. 38.

242 NAI, DFA P12/3, Cremin to Walshe, 30 March 1945.

243 *Ibid.*, 5 April 1945.

244 Cremin, 'Memoirs', p. 38.

245 *Ibid.*

246 NAI, DFA P12/3, Walshe to F.T. Cremins, 17 April 1945.

247 Cremin, 'Memoirs', p. 39.

248 NAI, DFA P12/3, Cremin to Walshe, 25 April 1945. See also: James Bacque, *Crimes and Mercies, The Fate of German Civilians under Allied Occupation, 1944–50* (Warner Books, London, 1997), see chapter 7.

249 NAI, DFA P12/3, Cremin to department, 25 April 1945.

250 Walter LaFeber, *America, Russia and the Cold War, 1945-92* (McGraw-Hill, inc., New York, [7th edition]), pp. 8–9. Gilbert, *A History of the Twentieth Century, Vol. II*, pp. 538–39.

251 Cremin, 'Memoirs', p. 39.

252 NAI, DFA P12/3, Cremin to Walshe, 1 May 1945.

253 *Ibid.*, 15 May 1945.

254 *Ibid.*

255 *Ibid.*, 17 May 1945.

256 NAI, DFA P12/3, Walshe to Cremin, 19 May 1945.

257 *Ibid.*, Cremin to Walshe, 21 May 1945.

258 *Ibid.*, Walshe to Cremin, 7 June 1945.

259 *Ibid.*, Cremin to Walshe, 26 June 1945.

CHAPTER 4

1 The British, under the duke of Wellington, had driven the French out of Portugal during the Napoleonic Wars and restored the Portuguese king to his throne. Elizabeth Longford, *Wellington* (Abacus, London, 1992) pp. 93–116.

2 Hugh Kay, *Salazar and Modern Portugal* (Eyre and Spottiswoode, London, 1970), p. 120. The British did not need the wolfram, having adequate supplies from the commonwealth, but it was necessary to keep it out of the hands of the Nazis.

3 *Ibid.*, p. 181.

4 *Ibid.*, pp. 121–27. Franco was pro-axis during the war, but he did not allow German troops to take Gibraltar, which would have closed the eastern Mediterranean to the allies. Franco had allied himself to the axis by a treaty of friendship with Germany in March 1939 and by joining the anti-Comintern pact. In June 1940 he had seemed on the verge of joining the war a few days after Mussolini did so and Franco sent 18,000 men to share in the anti-communist crusade. (Calvocoressi and Wint, *Total War*, p. 146.)

5 *Ibid.*

6 D.L. Raby, *Fascism and Resistance in Portugal; communist, liberals and military dissidents in the opposition to Salazar, 1941-1974* (Manchester University Press, Manchester, 1988), p. 20.

7 *Ibid.*, p. 23.

8 *Ibid.*, p. 33.

9 Murphy had been in France since 1938, Kerney in Spain since before the Spanish Civil War and MacWhyte in Rome was at the point of physical exhaustion and wanted to retire from the service. Walshe pursuaded him to stay on so that he would be entitled to the full pension. Warnock in August 1943 was in 'desperate need of a break'. See, Keogh, *Ireland and Europe.*

10 Rome would have been a very difficult position owing to the relatively large number of Irish citizens in the country.

11 Cremin, 'Memoirs', p. 42.

12 NAI, DFA 359/4, Cremin to Walshe, 1 March 1946. Most of Ireland's continental imports during the war came via Lisbon. Irish ships would load up with goods in Lisbon before sailing for Ireland.

13 Kay, *Salazar and Modern Portugal*, p. 182. Ireland is interesting in that she too was excluded from the UN which was mainly due to the desire to reduce the number of 'Catholic' non-Soviet voting nation states.

14 Tom Gallagher, *Portugal, a twentieth century interpretation* (Manchester University Press, 1983), p. 107.

15 The Soviet Union had established a control commission in Finland, which was perceived as a precursor to the taking over of the country. See Stig Jägerskiöld, *Mannerheim, Marshal of Finland* (Minnesota Press, Minnesota, 1986), pp. 175–96.

16 NAI, DFA 313/11, Cremin to Walshe, 27 July 1945.

17 *Ibid.*, 2 August 1945.

18 *Ibid.*, 8 August 1945.

19 See Chapter 2.

20 NAI, DFA 313/11, Cremin to Walshe, 21 September 1945. Brazil had declared war on the axis in response to German u-boats sinking their merchant shipping. Admiral Donnitz, *Ten Years and Ten Days* (Cassell, London, 2000) p. 252.

21 Raby, *Fascism and Resistance in Portugal,* p. 23.

22 *Ibid.*, p. 22

23 Gallagher, *Portugal*, p. 114.

24 NAI, DFA 313/11, Cremin to Walshe, 7 October 1945.

25 *Ibid.*, 11 October 1945.

26 *Ibid.*, 18 October 1945.

27 Raby, *Fascism and Resistance in Portugal,* p. 24.

28 *Ibid.*, p. 25.

29 *Ibid.*, p. 22.

30 NAI, DFA 313/11, Cremin to Walshe, 27 October 1945.

31 *Ibid.*, 30 October 1945.

32 António Costa Pinto, *Salazar's Dictatorship and European Fascism* (Columbia University Press, New York, 1995), p. 168.

33 NAI, DFA 313/11, Cremin to Walshe, 2 November 1945.

34 Early draft of Con Cremin's memoirs compiled by Mgr Frank Cremin.

35 Gallagher, *Portugal,* p. 102.

36 NAI, DFA 313/11, Cremin to Walshe, 3 November 1945.

37 *Ibid.*, 10 November 1945.

38 *Ibid.*, 16 November 1945.

39 Raby, *Fascism and Resistance in Portugal,* p. 25.

40 NAI, DFA 313/11, Cremin to Walshe, 16 November 1945.

41 *Ibid.*

42 *Ibid.* Some high ranking officers were against the regime, but they were not in a position to influence the army.

43 *Ibid.*, 22 November 1945.

44 The contact was probably Owen O'Malley, the British ambassador. In his memoirs, Cremin stated that O'Malley was a Hibernophile. The statement takes a long term viewpoint and displayed a complete lack of concern with communism.

45 NAI, DFA 313/11, Cremin to Walshe, 24 November 1945.

46 NAI, DFA 359/4, Cremin to Walshe, annual report for 1945.

47 Cremin, 'Memoirs', p. 44. Pinto argued, 'Salazar was an "academic dictator" who closely followed international politics and the ideas of the times … He was ultra-conservative in the most literal sense of the term. He steadfastly defended his rejection of democracy and its ideological heritage.' Pinto, *Salazar's Dictatorship and European Fascism*, p. 170.

48 Cremin, 'Memoirs', p. 44.

49 NAI, DFA 313/11, Cremin to Walshe, 18 December 1945.

50 *Ibid.* Doherty gave a figure of 120,000 Irishmen serving in the British forces from both sides of the border. Richard Doherty, *Irishmen and Women in the Second World War* (Four Courts Press, Dublin, 1999), p. 25.

51 NAI, DFA 313/11, Cremin to Walshe, 21 December 1945.

52 NAI, DFA 359/4, Cremin to Walshe, annual report of the Irish legation in Lisbon 1945–55 (Box 2296), annual report for 1945, 1 March 1946.

53 Stanley G. Payne, *The Franco Regime 1936-75* (University of Wisconsin Press, London and Wisconsin, 1986), p. 348.

54 NAI, DFA 313/11, Cremin to Walshe, 18 September 1945.

55 *Ibid.*, 21 September 1945.

56 The pretender to the throne was Juan, the second surviving son of Alfonso XIII, who had abdicated in Juan's favour in January 1941. After November 1942 Juan threw his hat in the ring. He advocated complete neutrality during the war. During 1943 he broadened the basis of his appeal by convincing Rodezno that he was sufficiently traditionalist and the veteran liberal Romanones that he was sufficiently constitutionalist. J.W.D. Tryhall, *Franco* (Repert Hart-Davis, London, 1970), p. 195. NAI, DFA 313/11, Cremin to Walshe, 9 October 1945.

57 NAI, DFA 313/11, Cremin to Walshe, 18 January 1946.

58 *Ibid.*, 29 January 1946.

59 *Ibid.*, 30 January 1946.

60 *Ibid.*, 9 February 1946.

61 Paul Preston, *Franco* (Harper Collins, London, 1993), p. 535.

62 NAI, DFA 313/11, Cremin to Walshe, 9 February 1946.

63 *Ibid.*, 19 February 1946.

64 Preston, *Franco,* p. 373.

65 NAI, DFA 313/11, Cremin to Walshe, 3 March 1946.

66 *Ibid.*

67 Gerald P. Fogarty, 'Francis J. Spellman, American and Roman', in G.P. Fogarty, *Patterns of Episcopal Leadership* (Macmillan, New York, 1989), p. 229.

68 NAI, DFA 313/11, Cremin to Walshe, 3 March 1946.

69 *Ibid.*, 25 March 1946.

70 *Ibid.*, 27 March 1946.

71 Keogh, *Ireland and Europe,* pp. 191 and 198.

72 Pinto, *Salazar's Dictatorship and European Fascism*, p. 168: 'Its nationalism was based on the legacy of the past and on its colonial patrimony. Its system of alliances was based on the Anglo-Portuguese alliance which was never questioned and which ensured the English government's discreet support of the dictatorship. The geography and progress of the Second World War determined Portugal's non-involvement. Salazarism focused on maintaining neutrality and continuing the old system of alliances.'

73 Cissy Crussell interview, 10 March 2001.

74 All the major histories of Ireland during the war demonstrate how the country was not in fact neutral: see Fisk, *In Time of War;* Keogh, *Twentieth Century Ireland;* and Lee, *Ireland 1912-85.*

75 Pinto, *Salazar's Dictatorship and European Fascism*, p. 170.

76 Keogh, *Ireland and Europe,* p. 214.

CHAPTER 5

1 Cremin, 'Memoirs', p. 45 and Preston, *Franco*, p. 553.

2 Cremin, 'Memoirs', p. 45.

3 Keogh, *Ireland and Europe,* pp. 200–201. Before the Second World War, ambassadors were only exchanged between great powers of equal rank.

4 Conor Cruise O'Brien interview, 11 June 2001.

5 Keogh, *Ireland and Europe*, p. 200.

6 Cremin, 'Memoirs', p. 47.

7 Ronan Fanning, 'Raison d'État and the Evolution of Irish Foreign Policy' in Michael Kennedy and Joseph M. Skelly (eds), *Irish Foreign Policy 1919–1966* (Four Courts Press, Dublin, 2000), p. 317.

8 Keogh, *Ireland and Europe*, pp. 196–97.

9 Cremin was not posted abroad until March 1950 and Warnock was posted abroad in 1947 to Stockholm, also a neutral during the war. Count Tovar, the Portuguese minister to Berlin, stayed in Lisbon until 1946 and was appointed to the Vatican in 1946 until 1950 (NAI, DFA 313/4a, Cremin to Nunan, 12 May 1952).

10 The Irish department of foreign affairs generally brings diplomats home every three to five years; Cremin had been abroad for eight.

11 Keogh, *Twentieth Century Ireland*, pp. 164–67.

12 Haughton argues that: 'By 1946 residents had external assets totalling £260 million, approximately equivalent to GNP that year'. John Haughton, 'The Historical Background', J.W. O'Hagan (ed.), *The Economy of Ireland, Policy and Performance of a European Region, 8th edition* (Gill and Macmillan, Dublin, 2000), p. 33.

13 Keatinge, *The Formation of Irish Foreign Policy*, p. 115.

14 Cremin, 'Memoirs', p. 45.

15 Cathy Molohan, *Germany and Ireland 1945–55, two nations friendship* (Irish Academic Press, Dublin, 1999), p. 45.

16 Donal Ó Drisceoil, *Censorship in Ireland*, p. 76. Liam D. Walsh was a member of the Irish fascist group the People's National Party which he had tried to merge with the IRA before being interned in the Curragh Camp 'for subversive activities'. Cathy Molohan, *Germany and Ireland 1945-55*, p. 46.

17 Cathy Molohan, *Germany and Ireland 1945-55*, p. 54.

18 NAI, DFA 366/20, Cremin to McLaulen, consul in New York, 4 May 1946.

19 *Ibid.*, Bryan to Cremin, 6 November 1946. Owing to shortages after the war the maps had been used to make envelopes.

20 *Ibid.*

21 UN sanctions forbade the export of arms or civil aircraft to either of the belligerents.

22 Paula Wylie, 'Ireland's decision for de facto recognition of Israel', in Kennedy and Skelly, *Irish Foreign Policy 1919-1966*, p. 146.

23 Bernadette Whelan, *Ireland and the Marshall Plan, 1947-57* (Four Courts Press, Dublin, 2000), p. 17.

24 *Ibid.*, p. 42.

25 *Ibid.*, p. 17.

26 *Ibid.*, p. 17.

27 *Ibid.*, p. 49.

28 Ronan Fanning, *The Irish Department of Finance 1922-58* (Institute of Public Administration, Dublin, 1978), p. 110.

29 Keogh, *Ireland and Europe*, p. 210.

30 Cremin, 'Memoirs', p. 48.

31 *Ibid.*, p. 48.

32 *Ibid.*, p. 49.

33 Whelan, *Ireland and the Marshall Plan*, p. 63.

34 *Ibid.*, p. 70.

35 *Ibid.*, p. 74.

36 *Ibid.*

37 *Ibid.*

38 *Ibid.*, p. 75.

39 Keogh, *Twentieth Century Ireland*, p. 185.

40 *Ibid.*, p. 196.

41 Whelan, *Ireland and the Marshall Plan*, p.62.

42 One of the difficulties with MacBride was his 'republican' background. As a former head of staff of the IRA he brought with him the 'paranoid world of revolutionary politics which had an influence on his administrative style' (Keogh, *Ireland and Europe*, p. 213).

43 Fanning, *Department of Finance*, p. 110.

44 *Ibid.*, p. 121.

45 Cremin, 'Memoirs', p. 121.

46 Lee, *Ireland*, p. 305.

47 Jean Monnet, *Memoirs* (Collins Press, London, 1978) pp. 271–77.

48 *Ibid.*, p. 304. If Ireland had a large active Communist party, US funding would have flowed in, as occurred in Italy.

49 Alan S. Milward, *The Reconstruction of Western Europe* (Methuen and Co., London, 1984) p. 184

50 Keogh, *Twentieth Century Ireland*, p. 197.

51 T. Desmond Williams, 'Conclusion', in Noland, K.B., and Williams, T. Desmond, *Ireland in the War Years and After, 1939-1951* (Gill and Macmillan, Dublin, 1969), p. 206.

52 Cremin, 'Memoirs', p. 48.

53 'Roaring Meg' was a cannon that was used to defend the City of Derry during the siege of 1689.

54 Noel Browne, *Against the Tide* (Gill and Macmillan, Dublin, 1986), pp. 127-32.

55 Keogh, *Twentieth Century Ireland*, p. 189.

56 John Bowman, *De Valera and the Ulster Question* (Claredon Press, Oxford, 1982), p. 273.

57 Keogh, *Twentieth Century Ireland*, p. 190.

58 Cremin, 'Memoirs', pp. 45–54.

59 Keogh, *Twentieth Century Ireland*, p. 191.

60 Nicholas Mansergh, 'Ireland in the War Years and After' in Noland and Williams, *Ireland in the War Years and After, 1939-1951*, p. 143.

61 Keogh, *Twentieth Century Ireland*, p. 191.

62 T. Desmond Williams, 'Conclusion', in Noland and Williams, *Ireland in the War Years and After, 1939-1951*, p. 209.

63 Joseph Lee and Gearóid Ó Tuathaigh, *The Age of de Valera* (Ward River Press, Dublin, 1982) p. 109.

64 *Ibid.*, p. 90.

65 Possibly before Ireland's second *aide mémoire* of 25 May 1949 (Keogh, *Twentieth Century Ireland*, p. 195).

66 NAI, DFA A89, *The North Atlantic Pact and Ireland 1949-1952*, undated and unsigned.

67 G.R. Sloan, *The Geopolitics of Anglo-Irish relations in the twentieth century* (Leicester University Press, London, 1997), p. 244.

68 NAI, DFA A89.

69 *Ibid.*

70 Sir Nicholas Henderson, *The Birth of NATO* (Weidenfeld and Nicolson, London, 1982), p. 77.

71 Keogh, *Twentieth Century Ireland,* p. 192.

72 *Ibid.*

73 Troy Davis, 'Anti-partitionism, Irish American and Anglo-American Relations, 1945-51' in Kennedy and Skelly, *Irish Foreign Policy 1919-1966*, p. 201.

74 Henderson, *The Birth of NATO*, p. 105. See also Ronan Fanning, 'The United States and Irish Participation in NATO: the Debate of 1950', *Irish Studies in International Affairs*, Vol. 1, No. 1, 1979, p. 38.

75 Keogh, *Twentieth Century Ireland*, p. 193.

76 *Ibid.*, p. 194.

77 Keogh, *Ireland and Europe*, p. 313.

78 Lee, *Ireland*, p. 307.

79 Keogh, *Ireland and Europe*, p. 313.

80 Keogh, *Twentieth Century Ireland*, p. 186.

81 Whelan, *Ireland and the Marshall Plan*, p. 103.

82 Cremin, 'Memoirs', p. 55.

CHAPTER 6

1 Keogh, Dermot, *Twentieth Century Ireland*, p. 154.

2 Ireland was the only mission that was able to keep its diplomat who had been accredited to Vichy. The Vatican recalled Valerio Valeri in December 1944, fearing loss of prestige if the Soviet ambassador presented the New Year's greetings, instead of the nuncio; the nuncio was traditionally the dean of the diplomatic corps, if the nuncio was not *en poste* the most senior diplomat would deliver the New Year's greetings – this would have fallen to the Soviet ambassador. Peter Hebblethwaite, *John XXIII* (Geoffrey Chapman, London, 1984), p. 200.

3 Lee, *Ireland*, p. 305.

4 NAI, DFA 348/1A, Cremin to Nunan, 18 April 1950.

5 *Ibid.*, 8 December 1953.

6 *Ibid.*

7 Lee, *Ireland*, p. 323.

8 Nicholas Mansergh, 'Ireland in the War Years and After' in K.B. Noland, T. Desmond Williams, *Ireland in the War Years and after 1939-1951*, p. 138.

9 See Annual Reports of the Paris legation 1950-54, NAI, DFA 359/8, Cremin to Nunan.

10 Cremin, 'Memoirs', p. 55.

11 Liam Cosgrave was the son of W.T. Cosgrave.

12 Monnet stated of Harvey that 'he repeats everything'. François Duchêne, *Jean Monnet, the first statesman of interdependence* (Norton, London, 1994), p. 187.

Nelson D. Lankford, *The Last American Aristocrat* (Little Brown and Company, Boston, 1996). Bruce, from a well-connected Old Virginian family, served in the OSS during the war, was appointed the US head of the Marshall Plan to France and was also appointed ambassador to France. He was later assistant secretary of the state department.

NAI, DFA 14/113 (Vatican Files), 9 March 1956. Cremin stated that: 'Quaroni is however extremely intelligent (it was commonplace in Paris during my period there to describe him as the most "intelligent" of all the heads of mission)'.

Roncalli was appointed to Paris to resolve the post-war issues within the Catholic Church which he did with extreme skill. Roncalli was a close friend of Cremin and attended his farewell party in the Vatican in 1956 (Aedeen Cremin correspondence, 16 March 2001).

13 Cissy Crussell interview, 10 March 2001.

14 *Ibid.*, and Hebblethwaite, *John XXIII*, p. 172.

15 Cremin, 'Memoirs', p. 59.

16 *Ibid.*, p. 57.

17 Dermot Keogh, *Ireland and the Vatican* (Cork University Press, Cork, 1995), p. 321; and NAI, DFA P12/2a, Walshe to Boland, 20 June 1950. Walshe believed 'that the Russians may start in 1951, if the Americans, who are ready that year, do not take the initiative'. See also NAI, DFA P202, Walshe to Boland, 1 December 1950.

18 *Ibid.*, p. 322.

19 UCDA Aiken Papers, P104/5807, Cremin to Nunan, 30 August 1951.

20 Lankford, *The Last American Aristocrat*, p. 303.

21 Keogh, *Twentieth Century Ireland*, p. 205; Nigel Moriarty, 'Ireland's reaction to the Cold War: Aspects of Emergency Planning, 1947–63' (M.Phil thesis, University College Cork, 1995). With the outbreak of the Korean War in 1950, the price of raw materials went up substantially owing to the fear that the war was a preliminary to an invasion of western Europe. See Lacouture, *De Gaulle, the Ruler*, p. 147.

22 NAI, DFA 14/55 (Vatican Series), Walshe to department, 1 December 1950. Walshe quoted Montini, one of the two sostituti, who jointly fulfilled the function of a secretary of state: '[he] has always felt that the Russians would one day cross the Rubicon. He has never had any real belief in American or modern British diplomacy.'

23 Cremin would frequently wait two or three days before submitting a report in order to consult colleagues and cross-check information.

24 See Chapter 1.

25 Correspondence with Dr Aedeen Cremin, 16 March 2001.

26 Lankford, *The Last American Aristocrat*, p. 225.

27 Jean Pierre Rioux, *The French Fourth Republic 1944-58* (Cambridge University Press, Cambridge, 1987), p. 159.

28 Ronan Fanning, 'Charles de Gaulle, 1946–58, from resignation to return, the Irish Diplomatic Perspective', in Pierre Joannon, *De Gaulle and Ireland* (Institute of Public Administration, Dublin, 1991), p. 71.

29 Kevin Ruane, 'Anthony Eden, the Foreign Office and Anglo French Relations, 1951–54' in Alan Sharp and Glyn Stone, *Anglo-French Relations in the Twentieth Century, Rivalry and Cooperation* (Routledge, London, 2000), p. 280.

30 J.W. Young, *Britain, France and the unity of Europe* (Leicester University Press, Bath, 1984), p. 153.

31 Duchêne, *Jean Monnet*, p. 206.

32 NAI, DFA 14/71 (Vatican Series) Nunan to Walshe, also circulated to Vatican, 13 June 1950.

33 R. Aldrich and J. Connell (eds.), *France in World Politics* (Routledge, London and New York, 1989), p. 196.

34 Jean Lacouture, *De Gaulle, the Ruler, 1945-1970* (Collins Harvill, London, 1991), p. 105.

35 Rioux, *The French Fourth Republic 1944-58*, p. 106.

36 *Ibid.*, p. 156.

37 Lacouture, *De Gaulle, the Ruler*, p. 147.

38 NAI, DFA 313/4a, Cremin to Nunan, 2 September 1950.

39 Rioux, *The French Fourth Republic*, p. 99.

40 NAI, DFA 313/4a, Cremin to Nunan, 26 July 1951.

41 *Ibid.*

42 *Ibid.*

43 *Ibid.*, 26 September 1951.

44 *Ibid.*, 30 October 1951.

45 *Ibid.*, 9 January 1952.

46 *Ibid.*, 8 March 1952.

47 *Ibid.*, 12 July 1952.

48 *Ibid.*, 8 March 1952.

49 *Ibid.*

50 Brian Crozier, *De Gaulle, The Statesman* (Eyre Methuen, London, 1973), p. 440.

51 NAI, DFA 313/4B, Cremin to Nunan, 27 September 1954.

52 Ronald Tiersky, *French Communism* (Columbia University Press, New York, 1974), p. 192.

53 *Ibid.*

54 CGT (Confédération Générale du Travail), CGT-OF (Confédération Générale du Travail – Force Ouvrière), CFTC (Confédération Française des Travailleurs Chrétiens).

55 Cremin did have to moderate the reports of Walshe in the Vatican, one of the differences was that Walshe had very little field experience. Walshe had been posted as a 'revolutionary diplomat' to the Versailles conference in 1919 before taking up the role of secretary in 1922 (Keogh, *Ireland and Europe*, pp. 8-11).

56 NAI, DFA 313/4A, Cremin to Nunan, 22 March 1951.

57 *Ibid.*, 7 June 1952.

58 Tiersky, *French Communism*, p. 209. Although minor riots did occur the Communist party did not succeed in bringing about a general strike. This is significant in that it demonstrated how low the stock in the Communist party had fallen.

59 NAI, DFA 313/4A, Cremin to Nunan, 10 September 1952. Duclos stated that the political bureau had not read the masses and argued for a 'United National Front', which would work to end the Schuman Plan, German rearmament, the war in Indo-China, and 're-establish the independence of France'.

60 *Ibid.*

61 Roger Morgan, *The United States and West Germany, 1945-1973* (Oxford University Press, Oxford, 1974), p. 33.

62 Michael M. Harrison, *The Reluctant Ally, France and Atlantic Security* (The John Hopkins University Press, Baltimore, 1981), p. 15.

63 J.W. Young, *Britain and European Unity* (Macmillan, London, 2000), p. 32.

64 Rioux, *The French Fourth Republic*, p. 141.

65 William L. Hitchcock, *France Restored, Cold War Diplomacy and the Quest for Leadership in Europe 1944-1954* (The University of North Carolina Press, Chapel Hill and London, 1999), p. 134.

66 Rioux, *The French Fourth Republic*, p. 207.

67 Pierre Guillen, 'France and the Defence of Western Europe' in N. Wiggershaus, and R.G. Foerster (eds.) *The Western Security Community* (Berg, Oxford, 1993), p. 137.

68 *Ibid.*, p. 139.

69 Kennedy, *The Rise and Fall of Great Powers*, p. 367.

70 Rioux, *The French Fourth Republic*, p. 121.

71 NAI, DFA 313/4 A-B, Cremin to Nunan, 1950–54.

72 NAI, DFA 313/4A, Cremin to Nunan, 25 August 1950.

73 *Ibid.*, 12 September 1950.

74 *Ibid.*, 13 October 1950.

75 NAI, DFA 313/4B, Cremin to Nunan, 19 October 1950.

76 NAI, DFA 313/4A, Cremin to Nunan, 17 January 1951.

77 *Ibid.*, 14 August 1951.

78 *Ibid.*

79 *Ibid.*

80 *Ibid.*

81 *Ibid.*, 11 September 1951.

82 Ruane, 'Anthony Eden, the Foreign Office and Anglo French Relations', p. 284.

83 NAI, DFA 313/4A, Cremin to Nunan, 28 October 1952.

84 Ruane, 'Anthony Eden, the Foreign Office and Anglo French Relations', p. 286.

85 The Indo-China war was costing France the entire class of St Cyr, the French military academy, in casualties between 1945 and 1950.

86 NAI, DFA 313/4B, Cremin to Nunan, 16 July 1953. This was a precursor of Nixon's 'Vietnamisation' of the war in 1969. (LaFeber, *America, Russia and the Cold War*, p. 143).

87 *Ibid.*

88 Kupchan, *The Vulnerability of Empire*, p. 292.

89 NAI, DFA 313/4B, Cremin to Nunan, 16 July 1953.

90 Kissinger, *Diplomacy* (Simon and Schuster, London, 1995), p. 626.

91 NAI, DFA 313/4B, Cremin to Nunan, 16 July 1953.

92 Jacques Dalloz, *The War in Indo-China, 1945-1954* (Gill and Macmillan, Dublin, 1990), p. 105.

93 NAI, DFA 313/4B, Cremin to Nunan, 22 March 1954.

94 *Ibid.*

95 Harrison, *The Reluctant Ally*, p. 39.

96 *Ibid.*, p.39.

97 The logic was to protect Laos, the reality was that the best French battalions were in a hollow, surrounded by mountains. The Viet-Minh entrenched single guns on the reverse slopes of the mountains. The French were dependent on one airstrip, which was put out of action on 15 March 1954. Rioux, *The French Fourth Republic*, pp. 217-8.

98 This would involve the surrender of all the Viet-Minh gains over the last four

years. Joseph Bottinger, *Vietnam, a Political History* (Andre Deutsch, London, 1969), pp. 133–48.

99 NAI, DFA 313/4B, Cremin to Nunan, 26 April 1954.

100 *Ibid.*, 30 April 1954.

101 Dalloz, *The War in Indo-China*, p. 175.

102 NAI, DFA 313/4B, Cremin to Nunan, 13 May 1954.

103 Dalloz, *The War in Indo-China*, p. 173.

104 NAI, DFA 313/4B, Cremin to Nunan, 13 May 1954.

105 Cremin would have been aware of how sensitive France was at this stage. She lost 1,500 dead, 4,000 wounded and 12,000 prisoners at Dien Bien Phu. (Rioux, *The Fourth French Republic*, p. 217.)

106 Frank Aiken may have advised de Valera to pay his condolences to Hempel on the death of Hitler. Keogh, *Ireland and Europe*, p. 191.

107 Larkin, Murphy, *France since the Popular Front*, p. 175.

108 Dalloz, *The War in Indo-China*, p. 177.

109 NAI, DFA 313/4B, Cremin to Nunan, 30 June 1954.

110 *Ibid.*, 30 June 1954.

111 Bottinger, *Vietnam, a Political history*, p. 375.

112 NAI, DFA 313/4B, Cremin to Nunan, 30 June 1954.

113 Denny Roy, *China's Foreign Policy* (Macmillan, London, 1998), p. 31.

114 NAI, DFA 313/4B, Cremin to Nunan, 30 June 1954.

115 *Ibid.*, 29 July 1954.

116 Smith, *French Colonial Consensus*, p. 220. Quoted in Kupchan, *The Vulnerability of Empire*, p. 293.

117 NAI, DFA 313/4B, Cremin to Nunan, 29 July 1954.

118 Bottinger, *Vietnam, a Political history*, p. 382.

119 John Talbott, *The War Without Victors, France in Algeria, 1954-1962* (Faber and Faber, London, 1981) p. 8.

120 Guy de Carmoy, *The Foreign Policy of France, 1944-1968* (The University of Chicago Press, Chicago, 1970), p. 147.

121 Kissinger, *Diplomacy*, p. 635.

122 Kevin Ruane, 'Anthony Eden, the Foreign Office and Anglo French Relations', p. 281.

123 LaFeber, *America, Russia*, p. 99.

124 Aybet, *The Dynamics of European Security Cooperation*, p. 71.

125 LaFeber, *America, Russia*, p. 105.

126 *Ibid.*, pp. 105–6.

127 NAI, DFA 313/4A, Cremin to Nunan, 7 September 1950.

128 Young, *Britain and European Unity 1945-99*, p. 31.

129 NAI, DFA 313/4A, Cremin to Nunan, 7 September 1950.

130 Hitchcock, *France Restored*, p. 135.

131 Rioux, *The French Fourth Republic*, p. 133.

132 NAI, DFA 313/4A, Cremin to Nunan, 9 September 1950. Cremin rarely used the names of colleagues whom he contacted.

133 NAI, DFA 313/4A, Cremin to Nunan, 12 September 1950.

134 Hitchcock, *France Restored*, p. 148.

135 Dean Acheson, *Present at the Creation* (W.W. Norton and Co., New York, 1987), p. 559.

136 LaFeber, *America, Russia*, p. 109.

137 NAI, DFA 313/4A, Cremin to Nunan, 12 September 1950.

138 *Ibid.*

139 Aybet, *The Dynamics of European Security Cooperation*, p. 73.

140 Guillen, *France and the Defence of Western Europe*, p. 144.

141 NAI, DFA 313/4A, Cremin to Nunan, 12 September 1950.

142 LaFeber, *America, Russia*, p. 127. Greece and Turkey joined NATO in 1952. Richard Clogg, *A Concise History of Greece* (Cambridge University Press, Cambridge, 1992) p. 150.

143 Young, *Britain and European Unity 1945-99,* p. 33.

144 NAI, DFA 313/4A, Cremin to Nunan, 12 September 1950; see also François Duchêne, *Jean Monnet*, pp. 27–63.

145 *Ibid.*, 15 September 1950.

146 *Ibid.*

147 *Ibid.*

148 Rioux, *The French Fourth Republic*, p. 136.

149 Kennedy, *The Rise and Fall*, p. 369.

150 NAI, DFA 313/4A, Cremin to Nunan, 15 September 1950.

151 Rioux, *The French Fourth Republic*, p. 144.

152 NAI, DFA 313/4A, Cremin to Nunan, 23 October 1950.

153 LaFeber, *America, Russia*, p. 110.

154 *Ibid.*, 12 December 1950.

155 Adenauer was not in favour of a unified demilitarised Germany because it left Germany without the ability to control her destiny (Kissinger, *Diplomacy,* p. 503).

156 NAI, DFA 313/4A, Cremin to Nunan, 7 January 1951.

157 *Ibid.*, 15 January 1951.

158 *Ibid.*, 18 January 1951.

159 *Ibid.*

160 *Ibid.*, 20 January 1951.

161 *Ibid.*, 10 February 1951.

162 *Ibid.*, 16 March 1951.

163 *Ibid.*, 23 March 1951.

164 LaFeber, *America, Russia*, p. 130.

165 NAI, DFA 313/4A, Cremin to Nunan, 23 June 1951. The number of MRP and communist seats was drastically reduced owing to the electoral reforms which were designed to prop up the Third Force and marginalise the communists and Gaullists.

166 NAI, DFA 313/4A, Cremin to Nunan, 14 August 1951.

167 *Ibid.*, Cremin to Nunan, 16 August 1951. A combat team would only have allowed for companies of German infantry, not for large armoured formations; this would have ensured that the Germans could not pursue an independent foreign policy line.

168 NAI, DFA 313/4A, Cremin to Nunan, 11 September 1951.

169 *Ibid.*, 4 October 1951.

170 *Ibid.*, 6 December 1951.

171 *Ibid.*, 9 January 1952.

172 Rioux, *The French Fourth Republic,* p. 145.

173 The British fought a successful anti-insurgency war against communist guerrillas in the Malaya peninsula in the late 1940s. (Lawrence James, *The Rise*

and Fall of the British Empire [Abacus, London, 1998], pp. 542-43.) Crucially, the difference was that the supply of arms to the Malaysian peninsula could be cut; this could not be done in Indo-China. Greece was a similar scenario.

174 Kevin Ruane, 'Anthony Eden, the Foreign Office and Anglo French Relations, 1951–54', p. 284.

175 *Ibid.*, p. 285.

176 *Ibid.*, p. 285.

177 NAI, DFA 313/4A, Cremin to Nunan, 26 April 1952.

178 *Ibid.*, 19 June 1952.

179 Ruane, 'Anthony Eden, the Foreign Office and Anglo French Relations', p. 286.

180 NAI, DFA 313/4A, Cremin to Nunan, 22 August 1952.

181 *Ibid.*, 4 October 1952.

182 *Ibid.*, 31 December 1952.

183 *Ibid.*, 16 January 1953.

184 LaFeber, *America, Russia,* p. 168.

185 Rioux, *The French Fourth Republic*, p. 201.

186 NAI, DFA 313/4A, Cremin to Nunan, 30 January 1953. French hostility to the USA was based on a complex love and loathing of the US (Langford, *The Last American Aristocrat*, p. 218).

187 NAI, DFA 313/4AII, Cremin to Nunan, 2 April 1953.

188 *Ibid.*

189 *Ibid.*, 14 April 1953.

190 Edward Fursdon, *The European Defence Community, a history* (Macmillan, London, 1980), p. 228.

191 *Ibid.*, p. 228.

192 NAI, DFA 313/4AII, Cremin to Nunan, 21 May 1953.

193 NAI, DFA 14/23/1, Holy See Files, Walshe to department, 21 May 1953.

194 NAI, DFA 313/4AII, Cremin to Nunan, 2 June 1953.

195 *Ibid.*

196 Beria was removed by a plot organised by Malenkov and Khrushchev who both feared for their personal safety (R. Craig Nation, *Black Earth, Red Star, A History of Soviet Security Policy, 1917-1991* [Cornell University Press, Ithaca, 1992], p. 205). NAI, DFA 313/4B, Cremin to Nunan, 21 July 1953.

197 NAI, DFA 313/4B, Cremin to Nunan, 21 July 1953.

198 *Ibid.*

199 *Ibid.*, 24 July 1953.

200 *Ibid.*, 9 September 1953.

201 *Ibid.*

202 *Ibid.*

203 *Ibid.*

204 *Ibid.*, 5 November 1953.

205 *Ibid.*, 18 November 1953.

206 *Ibid.* See also Ruane, 'Anthony Eden, the Foreign Office and Anglo French Relations', p. 286.

207 NAI, DFA 313/4B, Cremin to Nunan, 18 November 1953.

208 *Ibid.*, 4 December 1953.

209 *Ibid.*

210 *Ibid.*

211 LaFeber, *America, Russia*, p. 168.

212 NAI, DFA 313/4B, Cremin to Nunan, 11 December 1953.

213 *Ibid.*, 19 December 1953.

214 Ruane, 'Anthony Eden, the Foreign Office and Anglo French Relations, 1951–54', p. 288.

215 Eden was opposed to British involvement in the EDC from 28 November 1951, See Hugo Young, *This Blessed Plot* (Papermac, London, 1998), p. 76.

216 Anthony Eden, *Memoirs, Full Circle* (Cassell, London, 1960), p. 33.

217 NAI, DFA 313/4B, Cremin to Nunan, 19 December 1953.

218 Ruane, 'Anthony Eden, the Foreign Office and Anglo French Relations', p. 286.

219 Fursdon, *The European Defence Community*, p. 235.

220 *Ibid.*, p. 238.

221 See Chapter 3.

222 NAI, DFA 313/4B, Cremin to Nunan, 22 January 1954.

223 *Ibid.*, 1 February 1954.

224 Rioux, *The French Fourth Republic*, p. 139.

225 NAI, DFA 313/4B, Cremin to Nunan, 1 February 1954.

226 Fursdon, *The European Defence Community*, p. 243.

227 NAI, DFA 313/4B, Cremin to Nunan, 23 February 1954.

228 *Ibid.*

229 Ruane, 'Anthony Eden, the Foreign Office and Anglo French Relations', p. 288.

230 NAI, DFA 313/4B, Cremin to Nunan, 23 February 1954.

231 *Ibid.*

232 NAI, DFA 313/4B, Cremin to Nunan, 22 March 1954. Coercion was used: 'One deputy who owned an aeroplane factory was told that he would have his contracts cancelled should the EDC not pass.'

233 *Ibid.*

234 Ruane, 'Anthony Eden, the Foreign Office and Anglo French Relations', p. 288.

235 NAI, DFA 313/4B, Cremin to Nunan, 22 April 1954.

236 Quoted in Herbert Tint, *French Foreign Policy since the Second World War* (Foreign Policy Studies, Weidenfeld and Nicolson, London, 1972), p. 59.

237 NAI, DFA 313/4B, Cremin to Nunan, 22 April 1954.

238 Fursdon, *The European Defence Community*, p. 263.

239 Jean-Pierre Rioux, 'The Moderniser: Pierre Mendès-France' in John Gaffney (ed.), *France and Modernisation* (Avebury, Aldershot, 1988), p. 104.

240 NAI, DFA 313/4B, Cremin to Nunan, 10 July 1954.

241 Ruane, 'Anthony Eden, the Foreign Office and Anglo French Relations', p. 289.

242 NAI, DFA 313/4B, Cremin to Nunan, 10 July 1954.

243 *Ibid.*

244 Rioux, *The French Fourth Republic*, p. 206.

245 Fursdon, *The European Defence Community*, p. 275. General Koenig was the minister for defence and Bourgès-Maunoury was the minister for industry and commerce. General Koenig was also the *rapporteur* for the national assembly committee.

246 *Ibid.*, p. 276.

247 NAI, DFA 313/4B, Cremin to Nunan, 10 July 1954.
248 Fursdon, *The European Defence Community*, p. 276.
249 Sima Liberman, *The Growth of the European Mixed Economies* (Schenkman Publishing Co., Cambridge, Massachusetts, 1977), p. 51.
250 *Ibid.*, p. 49.
251 *Ibid.*, p. 7.
252 NAI, DFA 313/4B, Cremin to Nunan, 21 July 1954.
253 Rioux, *The French Fourth Republic,* p. 449.
254 Fursdon, *The European Defence Community*, p. 275.
255 NAI, DFA 313/4B, Cremin to Nunan, 30 July 1954.
256 Rioux, *The French Fourth Republic,* p. 204.
257 Fursdon, *The European Defence Community*, p. 278.
258 *Ibid.*, p. 285.
259 *Ibid.*, p. 229.
260 *Ibid.*, p. 290.
261 *Ibid.*, p. 294.
262 *Ibid.*, p. 288.
263 NAI, DFA 313/4B, Cremin to Nunan, 14 September 1954.
264 Ruane, 'Anthony Eden, the Foreign Office and Anglo French Relations', p. 290.
265 NAI, DFA 313/4B, Cremin to Nunan, 14 September 1954.
266 Ruane, 'Anthony Eden, the Foreign Office and Anglo French Relations', p. 290.
267 NAI, DFA 313/4B, Cremin to Nunan, 14 September 1954.
268 *Ibid.*, 15 September 1954.
269 Gülnur Aybet, *The Dynamics of European Security Cooperation, 1945-91* (Macmillan, London, 1991), p. 69.
270 Ruane, 'Anthony Eden, the Foreign Office and Anglo French Relations', p. 291.
271 *Ibid.*
272 *Ibid.*, p. 292.
273 Young, *Britain and European Unity,* p. 39.
274 *Ibid.*, p. 39. Adenauer committed West Germany 'not to manufacture certain armaments including atomic, bacteriological and chemical weapons'.
275 NAI, DFA 313/4B, Cremin to Nunan, 22 September 1954.
276 Ruane, 'Anthony Eden, the Foreign Office and Anglo French Relations', p. 295.
277 NAI, DFA 313/4B, Cremin to Nunan, 7 October 1954.
278 LaFeber, *America, Russia*, p. 169.
279 Ruane, 'Anthony Eden, the Foreign Office and Anglo French Relations', p. 295.
280 Miriam Hederman, *The Road to Europe, Irish Attitudes 1948-61* (Institute of Public Administration, Dublin, 1983), p. 47.
281 NAI, DFA P12/19, Cremin to Nunan 13 July 1951. The meeting took place in Paris on 13 May 1951.
282 Aiken Papers, P104/5807, 30 August 1951.
283 Interview with Stephen Collins, 4 December 1999. Interview with Creeda FitzGibbon, 29 March 2001. Creeda Fitzgibbon told me that both the parchments were signed by the same unknown official.

284 NAI, DFA 313/4a, Cremin to Nunan, 12 July 1952.

285 Charles Williams, *Adenauer* (Little Brown, London, 2000), p. 371.

CHAPTER 7

1 Cremin, 'Memoirs', p. 73.

2 Keogh, *Ireland and the Vatican*, p. 342.

3 *Ibid.*

4 *Ibid.*, p. 9.

5 *Ibid.*, p. 357.

6 Paddy MacKernan stated that Cremin would assiduously proofread a document as many times as was necessary in order to get it right (Interview, 3 May 2001).

7 Cremin, 'Memoirs', p. 73.

8 Keogh, *Twentieth Century Ireland,* p. 227.

9 See Chapters 2 and 6.

10 Keogh, *Ireland and the Vatican*, p. 342.

11 NAI, DFA 313/6a, Cremin to Nunan, 25 August 1954; *Irish Independent*, 24 August 1954.

12 Cremin, 'Memoirs', p. 73.

13 *Ibid.*, p. 74.

14 *Ibid.*, p. 76.

15 Keogh, *Ireland and the Vatican,* p. 347.

16 *Ibid.*, p. 165.

17 Donald Herlihy was rector of the Irish College from 1951 until 1964 when he was appointed bishop of Ferns. I am grateful to Professor Keogh for this information. Cissy Crussell interview, 10 March 2001.

18 NAI, DFA 14/63, Cremin to Murphy, 14 June 1955.

19 NAI, DFA 313/6, Cremin to Nunan, 12 April 1955.

20 Cremin, 'Memoirs', p. 76. See also Cornelius C. Cremin, 'Some Irish Associations in Rome' in Fr Virgilius, OFM Cap. and Fr Henry, OFM Cap. *The Capuchin Annual* (Dollard, Dublin, 1959), pp. 257–64.

21 Interview Ann Cremin, September 2001.

22 Correspondence, Dr Aedeen Cremin, 16 March 2001.

23 Cremin, 'Memoirs', p. 77.

24 Interview Ann Cremin, September 2000.

25 NAI, DFA 313/6, Cremin to Murphy, 24 May 1955.

26 *Ibid.*, 31 December 1955. The Northern Ireland state had effectively institutionalised sectarianism, which was to continue until the civil rights movement of the 1960s.

27 Cremin, 'Memoirs', p. 73.

28 *Ibid.*

29 NAI, DFA 313/6, Walshe to Nunan, 3 March 1954.

30 DFA 313/6, Cremin to Nunan, 4 November 1954.

31 Hebblethwaite, *John XXIII*, p. 289 and 293.

32 This was part of the so-called 'bloc deal' of 1955.

33 NAI, DFA 417/129, Cremin to Murphy, 17 December 1955.

34 *Ibid.*, 21 December 1955.

35 NAI, DFA 14/81 (Vatican Series) Cremin to Nunan, 20 March 1956.

36 Conor Cruise O'Brien, 'Ireland in International Affairs' in Conor Cruise O'Brien, *States of Ireland* (Panther, London, 1974), p. 126. The three principles were as follows:
  1. Scrupulous fidelity to the obligations of the charter;
  2. 'We should try and maintain a position of independence, judging the various questions on which we have to adopt an attitude or cast a vote strictly on their merits, in a just and disinterested way.' This implied an effort 'to avoid becoming associated with particular blocs or groups in so far as possible';
  3. 'To do whatever we can as a member of the United Nations to preserve the Christian civilisation … [and resist the] spread of communist power and influence … We belong to the great community of states, made up of the United States of America, Canada and western Europe.'

37 NAI, DFA P12/2(a), Cremin to Murphy, 30 September 1955.

38 *Ibid.*, 30 December 1955.

39 NAI, DFA 14/21 (Vatican Series), Boland to Murphy, 26 January 1956.

40 Keogh, *Ireland and the Vatican*, p. 346.

41 NAI, DFA 14/21 (Vatican Series), Boland to Nunan, 28 March 1953.

42 *Ibid.*, Cremin to Nunan, 6 November 1954.

43 *Ibid.*, 15 June 1954.

44 On 2 June 1954, the second inter-party government took office by a majority of 79 votes to 66 (Keogh, *Twentieth Century Ireland*, p. 227).

45 NAI, DFA 14/21 (Vatican Series), Cremin to Nunan, 3 October 1954.

46 Keogh, *Twentieth Century Ireland*, p. 229.

47 NAI, DFA 14/21 (Vatican Series), Cremin to Nunan, 3 October 1954.

48 *Ibid.*, Cosgrave to Cremin, 4 October 1954.

49 *Ibid.*, Cremin to Nunan, 6 November 1954.

50 *Ibid.*

51 *Ibid.*

52 *Ibid.*, 7 November 1954.

53 *Ibid.*, department to Cremin, 6 May 1955.

54 *Ibid.*, Cremin to Murphy, 28 July 1955.

55 *Ibid.*, 31 October 1955.

56 NAI, DFA 14/21 (Vatican Series), Cremin to Murphy, 3 November 1955.

57 *Ibid.*, F.H. Boland to Murphy, 26 January 1956. Forwarded to Cremin on 1 February 1956.

58 *Ibid.*, Cremin to Murphy, 18 February 1956.

59 *Ibid.*, 18 February 1956.

60 *Ibid.*, 20 March 1956.

61 *Ibid.*, 3 March 1956.

62 *Ibid.*, 7 August 1956.

63 *Ibid.*, 22 September 1956.

64 *Ibid.*, Cosgrave to Cremin, 26 September 1956. The dioceses of Clogher, Kilmore, Raphoe, Derry and Armagh all straddle the border. Armagh is the ecclesiastical capital of Ireland. Oliver P. Raftery, *Catholics in Ulster, 1603-1983, An Interpretative History* (Hurst and Company, London, 1994), pp. xiii-xiv.

65 NAI, DFA 14/21 (Vatican Series), Cremin to Murphy, 5 October 1956.

66 *Ibid.*, 28 January 1957.

67 *Ibid.*, Leo T. McCauley to Murphy, 14 February 1957.

68 Gerald P. Fogarty, *The Vatican and the American Hierarchy from 1870 to 1965* (Michael Glazier, Collegeville, Minnesota, 1982), p. 323.

69 NAI, DFA 313/6, Cremin to Murphy, 4 October 1955.

70 NAI, DFA 14/56 (Vatican Series), Cremin to Murphy, 26 May 1956.

71 *Ibid.*, Cremin to Murphy, 4 July 1956.

72 *Ibid.*, Cremin to Murphy, 19 July 1957.

73 Fogarty, *The Vatican and the American Hierarchy,* p. 331. 'Thus the movement begun in 1935 by Spellman with the aid of Joseph P. Kennedy was now ended with the opposition of Kennedy's son.'

74 Thomas J. Reese, S.J., 'Diplomatic Relations with Holy See' in *America*, 16 March 1985. See http://www.georgetown.edu/centera/woodstock/reese/america/a-wilson.htm

75 J.N.D Kelly, *The Oxford Dictionary of the Popes* (Oxford University Press, Oxford, 1986), p. 318.

76 NAI, DFA 14/48/4 (Vatican Series), Walshe to Nunan, 2 February 1954.

77 *Ibid.*, 4 March 1954.

78 NAI, DFA 313/6a, Cremin to Nunan, 11 November 1954.

79 NAI, DFA 313/6, Cremin to Nunan, 13 December 1954.

80 NAI, DFA 313/6a, Cremin to Nunan, 21 December 1954.

81 NAI, DFA 313/6b, Cremin to Nunan, 3 January 1955. Montini became Paul VI after John XXIII.

82 NAI, DFA 14/48/4 (Vatican Series), Cremin to Nunan, 3 January 1955.

83 Kelly, *The Oxford Dictionary of the Popes*, p. 320. Kelly went on to argue: 'In his latter years when he was frequently prostrate with serious illness, this solitary bent placed undue power in the hands of the narrow not always scrupulous, circle on which he was forced to depend.'

84 NAI, DFA 313/6b, Cremin to Nunan, 3 January 1955.

85 *Ibid.*, 9 February 1955.

86 NAI, DFA 14/48/4 (Vatican Series), Cremin to Nunan, 28 April 1955.

87 *Ibid.*, Cremin to Murphy, 15 November 1955.

88 *Ibid.*, 9 June 1956.

89 NAI, DFA 14/48 (Vatican Series), Cremin to T.J. Horan in the department, 15 December 1954.

90 *Ibid.*, T.J. Horan in the department to Cremin, 14 December 1954. Cremin to T.J. Horan in the department, 23 December 1954 and T.J. Horan to Cremin, 19 January 1955.

91 NAI, DFA 14/48 (Vatican Series) Cremin to T.J. Horan in the department, 2 February 1955.

92 *Ibid.*, Fay to Cremin, 9 October 1958.

93 'In July 1949, Pius XII issued a collective excommunication against the millions of Italians who continued to vote for the Communist party, and subsequently opined that socialism, having the same materialistic philosophy as communism, was irreconcilable with Christianity'. Denis Mack Smith, *A Political History* (Yale University Press, New Haven and London, 1997) p. 437.

94 Peter Nichols, *The Politics of the Vatican* (Pall Mall Press, London, 1968) p. 100.

95 LaFeber, *America, Russia*, p. 199.

96 NAI, DFA 313/6, Cremin to Nunan, 29 April 1955.

97 V. Zubok and P. Pleshakov, *Inside the Kremlin's Cold War, From Stalin to Khrushchev* (Harvard University Press, London, 1996) p. 170.

98 LaFeber, *America, Russia*, p. 199.

99 NAI, DFA 313/6a, Cremin to Nunan, 13 November 1954.

100 NAI, DFA 14/113 (Vatican Series), Cremin to Nunan, 15 Feb 1955.

101 Roy, *China's Foreign Policy*, pp. 1–10.

102 NAI, DFA 313/6a, Cremin to Nunan, 30 October 1954.

103 NAI, DFA 14/63 (Vatican Series), Cremin to Nunan, 4 January 1955.

104 *Ibid.*, Cremin to Nunan, 21 January 1955.

105 *Ibid.*, Lennon to Cremin, 6 February 1955.

106 *Ibid.*, Cremin to Nunan, 14 February 1955.

107 NAI, DFA 313/6a, Cremin to Nunan, 22 November 1954. This is the nascent thinking that went into the domino theory in relation to Vietnam.

108 NAI, DFA 313/6a, Cremin to Nunan, 23 December 1954.

109 Zubok and Pleshakov, *Inside the Cold War*, p. 168.

110 LaFeber, *America, Russia*, p. 173.

111 NAI, DFA 313/6, Cremin to Nunan, 14 February 1955. Khrushchev did move against Malenkov with the backing of the Red army. (LaFeber, *America, Russia*, p. 172.)

112 NAI, DFA 313/6a, Cremin to Nunan, 15 February 1955.

113 NAI, DFA 14/113 (Vatican Series), Cremin to Nunan, 20 September 1955.

114 NAI, DFA 14/81 (Vatican Series), Cremin to Nunan, 22 September 1955.

115 NAI, DFA 313/6, Cremin to Murphy, 21 September 1955. Cardinal Mindszenty was arrested in 1949 and not released until the uprising of 1956 whereupon he had to seek refuge with the US embassy. (Peter Nichols, *The Politics of the Vatican* [Pall Mall Press, London, 1968]), p. 241.

116 These were the areas that Poland had taken control of after their borders were moved 200 kilometres westward.

117 NAI, DFA 313/6, Cremin to Murphy, 14 October 1955.

118 See Chapter 6.

119 NAI, DFA 313/6, Cremin to Murphy, 19 October 1955.

120 This was spectacularly seen in 1948 when the Italian Communist party achieved thirty-one per cent of the vote. See Keogh, *Ireland and the Vatican*, p. 246.

121 NAI, DFA 14/113 (Vatican Series), Cremin to Nunan, 27 February 1956.

122 Ruane, 'Anthony Eden, the Foreign Office and Anglo French Relations', p. 297.

123 NAI, DFA 14/113 (Vatican Series), Cremin to Nunan, 27 February 1956.

124 *Ibid.*, Cremin to Nunan, 9 March 1956.

125 NAI, DFA 313/6, Cremin to Nunan, 26 March 1955.

126 *Ibid.*, Cremin to Nunan, 13 April 1955.

127 *Ibid.*, Cremin to Murphy, 20 December 1955. The socialists, although they were in coalition with the Christian Democrats, were very anti-clerical.

128 NAI, DFA 313/6, Cremin to Nunan, 16 February 1955.

129 NAI, DFA 15/92 (Vatican Series), Cremin to Nunan, 15 February 1955.

130 NAI, DFA 313/6, Cremin to Murphy, 24 December 1955.

131 NAI, DFA 14/97 (Vatican Series), Cremin to Nunan, 25 April 1956.

132 *Ibid.*, 13 July 1956.

133 De Gaulle and Mendès-France praised the actions of Pius XII during the war.

134 NAI, DFA 313/6b, Cremin to Nunan, 9 February 1955.

135 NAI, DFA 313/6, Cremin to Nunan, 16 February 1955.

136 *Ibid.*, Cremin to Murphy, 20 July 1955.

137 *Ibid.*

138 Pierre Blet, *Pius XII and the Second World War, according to the archives of the Vatican* (Paulist Press, New Jersey, 1999), p. 285.

139 *Ibid.*, p. 288.

140 Carlo Falconi, *The Silence of Pius XII* (Faber and Faber, London, 1965); John Cornwall, *Hitler's Pope* (Viking, London, 1999). The thesis of Kertzer would similarly have been dismissed; David I. Kertzer, *Unholy War, the Catholic Church and the rise of anti-Semitism*, or as named in the USA, *The Pope Against the Jews* (Robert Wilde, London, 2002).

141 Peter Novick, *The Holocaust and Collective Memory* (Bloomsbury, London, 1999), p. 143.

142 NAI, DFA 313/6, Cremin to Nunan, 14 February 1955. This was similar to the attack which Seán Murphy's professionalism suffered from Walshe in 1940.

143 NAI, DFA 14/45/2 (Vatican Series), Cremin to Murphy, 18 May 1956.

144 *Ibid.*, 24 May 1956.

145 *Ibid.*, 30 May 1956.

146 NAI, DFA 313/6, Cremin to Murphy, 9 July 1955.

147 *Ibid.*, 24 December 1955.

148 *Ibid.*, 15 October 1955.

149 NAI, D/T S16099, Press cuttings, 15 October 1956.

150 Correspondence with Dr Aedeen Cremin, 16 March 2001.

CHAPTER 8

1 NAI, D/T S1196099, Cremin to Murphy, 15 October 1956.

2 The top diplomatic postings were Paris, London, Washington and Permanent Mission UN.

3 Cremin, 'Memoirs', p. 81.

4 F.H. Boland, 'Memoirs', p. 18. Most of the political figures mentioned were from the Labour party.

5 Cremin, Memoirs, p. 81.

6 While in the Public Record Office in 1998 I located a file on Cremin from 1943. Upon enquiring I was told that the file was probably destroyed. Very few files survive on Ireland within the PRO for the period. It is my personal belief that after the outbreak of the Troubles in 1968 many files were withheld or destroyed.

7 David Dutton, *Anthony Eden, A Life and Reputation* (Arnold, London, 1997), p. 419.

8 Kissinger, *Diplomacy* p. 528. For a more in-depth analysis of Suez see: David Carlton, *Britian and the Suez Crisis* (Institute of Contemporary British History, Basil Blackwell, 1988), W. Scott Lucas, *Divided We Stand, Britain US and the Suez Crisis* (Hodder and Stoughton, London, 1991) Roy Fullick and Geoffrey Powell, *Suez, the Double War* (Leo Cooper, London 1979). It also gave rise to a raft of personal reminiscences including those by many of the

principal characters Selwyn Lloyd, Macmillan, Eden and Evelyn Shuck-burgh.

9 In 1955, the British and the USA tried to find a solution to the Arab-Is-raeli conflict, the Alpha project. This was destroyed in September 1956 when Nasser purchased a huge amount of arms from the Soviets destablising the balance of power in the middle east. Carlton, *Britain and the Suez Crisis,* pp. 26-27.

10 Kissinger, *Diplomacy* p. 523.

11 Carlton, *Britain and the Suez Crisis,* p. 28. By December 1955 Anthony Eden, the British prime minister persuaded the USA in association with the World Bank to finance the Aswan Dam project (the dam was to dam the Nile and harness its power to electrify Egypt).

12 *Ibid.*, p. 33. The recognition of the Peoples' Republic of China allowed an al-liance on Capitol Hill of the China Lobby and the Southern Congressmen, who did not want competition for southern cotton. (LaFeber, *America, Russia,* p. 185).

13 Jean Monnet, *Memoirs,* p. 421. Monnet spoke of 'the whole world trading system was at the mercy of one of its vital arteries being cut off, and our oil imports were under constant threat'.

14 LaFeber, *America, Russia,* p. 187.

15 David Dutton, *Anthony Eden,* p. 385. This was especially true of Eden who took personal umbrage at Nasser's perfidity and bad faith. Eden was also defined by Munich, which made him adamantly anti-appeasement and col-oured his judgment.

16 David Carlton, *Britain and the Suez Crisis*, p. 44. Storms were expected by this time which would have made any landing problematic.

17 Kissinger, *Diplomacy,* p. 530. The ruling out of the use of force meant that the Western Powers had no effective means of answering Nasser's challenge in that the canal could not be blockaded without inflicting considerable damage on the west itself.

18 David Carlton, *Britain and the Suez Crisis*, p. 57.

29 *Ibid.*, p. 65. The details were finalised on the 24 October that the Israeli's would attack Egypt on the 29 October 1955.

20 Trevor N Dupuy, *Elusive Victory, the Arab-Israeli Wars 1947-1974* (Macdonald and James, London, 1978), pp. 137-148. Israel played a cautious diplomatic hand. The attack on the Sinai had its origins in July 1956 when the Israeli prime minister Ben Gurion gave permission to seize the Straits of Tiran (which gave Israel access to the Red Sea). This plan was adapted to Opera-tion Musketeer at the Sèvres Meeting. The Israeli's planned to capture the heights to the east of Suez, to capture the Straits of Tiran, to bring about the collapse of the Egyptian Army on the Sinai and to destroy the Fedayeen base on the Gaza strip and Sinai border. The British and French were to destroy the Egyptian air force.

21 David Carlton, *Britain and the Suez Crisis*, p. 71. The most amazing feature of this condemnation was that the US voted with the Soviet Union.

22 *Ibid.*, p. 72.

23 *Ibid.*, p. 75. The rapid advance was possible due to Nasser withdrawing most of the Egyptian Army to defend Cairo.

24 *Ibid.*, pp. 76-78. 'Macmillan felt a cease-fire was necessary in order to prevent

a run on the pound, Eden while 'dimly' aware of the sterlin crisis was also in receipt of Eisenhower's 'sulphurous communications' Bulganin's threats of rocket attacks on London, thirdly he was in receipt of 'unusually vigorous messages from Dixon spelling out just how damaging the operation was proving to Great Britain's reputation in the UN' and finally Dag Hammarsklöld had sent a message that the Israeli's had agreed to a cease-fire'.

25 Alistair Horne, *Macmillan 1894-1956* (Macmillan, London, 1998), p. 440. Carlton argues that the recriminations over who allowed the cease-fire be called and who lacked resolve, have dominated much of the subsequent debate. David Carlton, *Britain and the Suez Crisis*, pp. 77-79.

26 NAI, DFA 313/31B, Cremin to Murphy, 13 November 1956.

27 *Ibid.*

28 LaFeber, *America, Russia*, p. 192.

29 NAI, DFA 313/31B, Cremin to Murphy, 13 November 1956.

30 Zubok and Pleshakov, *Inside the Kremlin's Cold War, From Stalin to Khrushchev* (Harvard University Press, London, 1996), p. 186.

31 NAI, DFA 313/31B, Cremin to Murphy, 14 November 1956.

32 *Ibid.*, 17 November 1956.

33 P.J. Cain and A.G. Hopkins, *British Imperialism, 1914-1990* (Longman, New York and London, 1995), p. 289.

34 Kissinger, *Diplomacy* p. 523.

35 *Ibid.*, p. 533. Kissinger further argued that the US had succeeded in destroying Britain's self image which destroyed 'its willingness to play a major role in international affairs'.

36 Biggar was counsellor at the embassy from 1954 to 1959.

37 NAI, DFA 313/31B, Cremin to Murphy, 20 November 1956.

38 *Ibid.*, 21 November 1956.

39 *Ibid.*, 13 November 1956.

40 *Ibid.*, 26 November 1956. The Security Council had met on 28 October to discuss Hungary, without resolution, on the 3 November 1956 the Soviets vetoed a Security Council resolution. By 9 November Hungarian opposition had been substantially crushed.

41 David Carlton, *Britain and the Suez Crisis*, p. 90. UNEF is the United Nations Emergency Force.

42 NAI, DFA 313/31B, Cremin to Murphy, 1 December 1956.

43 *Ibid.*

44 *Ibid.*, 18 December 1956.

45 David Carlton, *Britain and the Suez Crisis*, p. 92. Eden entered the House on the 17, 18 and 22 December. On the 17th he was greeted by a distinct lack of cheers. On the 18th he was unable to answer questions in front of the 1922 Committee and on the 22nd he lied to the house about whether there was a conspiracy with Israel.

46 *Ibid.*, p. 93.

47 *Ibid.*, 11 January 1957.

48 Young, *This Blessed Plot*, p. 112.

49 Horne, *Macmillan*, p. 455.

50 NAI, DFA 313/31C, Cremin to Murphy, 12 January 1957.

51 *Ibid.*, 14 January 1957.

52 *Ibid.*, 18 January 1957.

53 Alistair Horne, *Macmillan,* p. 6.
54 NAI, DFA 313/31C, Cremin to Murphy, 18 January1957 see also Alistair Horne, *Macmillan,* p. 6.
55 *Ibid.,* 23 January 1957.
56 *Ibid.,* pp. 98-99. Carlton also argues that the British retreat from Africa can also be seen to have its roots in local conditions without reference to Suez. He states that a rejoinder to that argument is that 'we should not overlook the unspoken assumptions that influence any generation of leaders: they are as much part of the furniture of a period that elaborating them is simply rendered otiose'.
57 Jeremy Black, *Convergence of Divergence? Britain and the Continent* (University of Durham, Centre for European Studies, Durham), p. 16.
58 David Carlton, *Britain and the Suez Crisis,* pp. 104-105. Carlton argues that it was not Suez or the actions of the 6 November 1956 so much as Macmillan's strongly pro-American standpoint after Suez which led to the French rejecting Britain in 1963.
59 NAI, DFA 313/31C, Cremin to Murphy, 3 January 1957.
60 *Ibid.*
61 Hugo Young, *This Blessed Plot* (Papermac, London, 1999), p. 100.
62 Jean Monnet, *Memoirs,* p. 112.
63 Since Ireland's trade with Britain during the 1950s was running at close on seventy per cent, it would have been economically impossible for Ireland to join independently of Britain.
64 NAI, DFA 313/31C, Cremin to Murphy, 8 January 1957.
65 NAI, DFA 313/31C, Cremin to Murphy, 8 January 1957.
66 'Anglo-Saxons' referred to the United States of America and the United Kingdom.
67 Horne, *Macmillan,* p. 446.
68 *Ibid.,* 10 January 1957.
69 *Ibid.,* 11 February 1957.
70 Although the Soviets had learned as early as 1953 that 'US calls to "roll back" Communism were mere radio histrionics' (Hobsbawm, *Age of Extremes,* p. 228).
71 NAI, DFA 313/31C, Cremin to Murphy, 11 February 1957.
72 Harold Macmillan, *Riding the Storm,* p. 54. The divisions cost £64 million per annum and were eating heavily into the British balance of payments.
73 Horne, *Macmillan,* pp. 30-35.
74 Lee, *Ireland,* p. 352.
75 NAI, DFA 313/31C, Cremin to Murphy, 14 February 1957.
76 David Carlton, *Britain and the Suez Crisis,* p. 103. Throughout the Suez crisis, the United States failed to support Britain and France in Suez and even arranged to vote with the Soviet Union to condemn Britain, France and Israel on the 4 November 1955.
77 NAI, DFA 313/31C, Cremin to Murphy, 14 February 1957. Domestically the Conservatives lost a by-election and saw support drop by 14%. See: NAI, DFA 313/31C, Cremin to Murphy, 22 February 1957.
78 The French defeat at Dien Bien Phu could be ascribed to a reluctance on the part of the United States to give the French air support. As at Suez lack of US support compelled withdrawal by two powers which had fought two total wars in thirty years.

79 Horne, *Macmillan*, p. 445.

80 NAI, DFA 313/31C, Cremin to Murphy, 12 March 1957.

81 Horne, *Macmillan*, p. 21.

82 NAI, DFA 313/31C, Cremin to Murphy, 29 March 1957.

83 *Ibid.*

84 David Carlton, *Britain and the Suez Crisis,* p. 104. France was not granted such a consolation prize and did not join the nuclear club until 13 February 1960, this may have contributed to a cooling of Anglo-French relations (Lacouture, de Gaulle, Ruler, p. 423).

85 NAI, DFA 313/31C, Cremin to Murphy, 29 March 1957.

86 *Ibid.*

87 Pearce and Stewart, *British Political History, 1867–1995, democracy and decline* (Routledge, London, 1996), p. 478.

88 Horne, *Macmillan*, p. 45.

89 NAI, DFA 313/31C, Cremin to Murphy, 29 March 1957.

90 David Carlton, *Britain and the Suez Crisis*, p. 95.

91 *Ibid.*, Boland to Murphy, 28 May 1957.

92 *Ibid.*, Cremin to Murphy, 13 June 1957.

93 *Ibid.*, 29 June 1957.

94 NAI, DFA 313/31C, Cremin to Murphy, 29 June 1957.

95 *Ibid.,* 27 July 1957.

96 Eden, *Full Circle*, p. 545

97 NAI, DFA 313/31C, Cremin to Murphy, 9 July 1957.

98 *Ibid.,* 19 July 1957.

99 *Ibid.,* 26 July 1957.

100 See the Vatican chapter to see what huge proportions these issues took on within Irish foreign policy.

101 Harold Macmillan, *Riding the Storm 1956-1959* (Macmillan, London, 1971), p. 224.

102 NAI, DFA 313/31C, Cremin to Murphy, 1 July 1957.

103 *Ibid.*

104 Macmillan, *Riding the Storm*, p. 663.

105 The conditions were 'recognition of the right of the Cypriot people to exercise self determination, a project for settlement if the problem acceptable to both Greeks and Cypriots, and an undertaking that the conference will elaborate details of the project accepted' (NAI, DFA 313/31C, Cremin to Murphy, 23 August 1957).

106 *Ibid. Enosis* was the Greek concept of uniting Cyprus with mainland Greece.

107 NAI, DFA 313/31C, Cremin to Murphy, 23 August 1957.

108 *Ibid.*

109 *Ibid.,* 7 October 1957.

110 *Ibid.,* 22 November 1957.

111 Martin Gilbert, *Challenge to Civilisation, a history of the twentieth century, 1952-1999* (Harper Collins, London, 1999), pp. 481-82.

112 Horne, *Macmillan*, p. 33.

113 NAI, DFA 313/31C, Cremin to Murphy, 20 June 1957.

114 *Ibid.*

115 NAI, DFA 313/31C, Cremin to Murphy, 18 September 1957.

116 *Ibid.*, 21 September 1957. Adenauer was to remain as chancellor until 15 October 1963, aged 87 (Williams, Adenauer, p. 523).

117 Young, *This Blessed Plot*, p. 106. In 1958 the German economy relentless trend of German growth produced the cross-over between the economies of the war winners and losers: that was the year the German economy grew bigger than the British, and German exports first exceeded British exports. It was the climax of a period, 1950-8, in which the annual percentage growth rates for manufactured exports were as follows: West Germany 15.0, Netherlands 9.8, Italy 8.9, Britain 8.5 Annual average growth rates overall, 1950-60, were: West Germany 7.8 per cent, Italy 5.8, France 4.6, Britain 2.7. Of course, the continentals had started from a lower base. But this was the establishment of a pattern of which obliged the economist Peter Oppenheimer to write in 1970: 'It was estimated that all the other countries of north-western Europe [except Ireland] had surpassed Britain in output per head by the time the Conservatives left office' in 1964.

118 NAI, DFA 313/31C, Cremin to Murphy, 18 September 1957.

119 Horne, *Macmillan*, p. 23.

120 Sputnik was the launch of the first manmade satellite. It opened up to the United States the prospect of attack by intercontinental ballistic missiles.

121 NAI, DFA 313/31C, Cremin to Murphy, 9 November 1957.

122 *Ibid.*

123 LaFeber, *America, Russia and the Cold War*, p. 196.

124 Horn, *Macmillan, 1956-86*, p. 55. The McMahon act forbade the US sharing atomic technology with any second parties. This particularly irked Britain and France because they had to invest fortunes developing technologies which the United States had done already.

125 NAI, DFA 313/31C, Cremin to Murphy, 22 November 1957.

126 *Ibid.*, 25 November 1957.

127 *Ibid.*, 28 November 1957.

128 Kissinger, *Diplomacy*, p. 570.

129 Eric Hobsbawn, *The Age of Extremes*, p. 230, Khrushchev's memoirs are replete with remarks about how powerful Soviet rockets were. 'We were simply trying to remind other countries that we were powerful and deserved respect', (Khrushchev, N., *Khrushchev Remembers*, Little Brown, London, 1970, p. 405).

130 NAI, DFA 313/31C, Cremin to Murphy, 16 November 1957.

131 *Ibid.*, 30 November 1957.

132 Horne, *Macmillan 1956-86*, p. 33.

133 NAI, DFA 313/31C, Cremin to Murphy, 10 December 1957.

134 *Ibid.*

135 *Ibid.*

136 *Ibid.*, 12 December 1957.

137 Kissinger, *Diplomacy*, p. 570.

138 Dulles, John Foster, *Present at the Creation*, p. 230

139 NAI, DFA 313/31D, Cremin to Murphy, 11 January 1958.

140 *Ibid.*

141 *Ibid.*

142 *Ibid.*

143 *Ibid.*

144 *Ibid.*, 15 January 1958.

145 *Ibid.*, 31 January 1958.

146 Churchill, W.S., *Hansard*, 150, 16 February 1922, col. 1270, quoted in Lee, *Ireland*, p. 46.

147 NAI, DFA 313/31C, Cremin to Murphy, 30 January 1957.

148 Harold Macmillan, *Riding the Storm* (Macmillan, London, 1971), p. 2. Macmillan stated that he was sound rather than brilliant and absolutely loyal.

149 NAI, DFA 313/31C, Cremin to Murphy, 30 January 1957.

150 NAI, DFA 313/31B, Cremin to Murphy, 21 November 1956.

151 NAI, DFA 313/31C, Cremin to Murphy, 30 January 1957, Cecil is short hand for Cecil Rhodes, one of Britain's greatest imperialists.

152 O'Brien, Conor Cruise, *States of Ireland*, p. 128.

153 Interview with Dr Garret FitzGerald, 2 December 2000.

154 NAI, DFA P203/2A, Cremin to Murphy, 13 December 1956.

155 Keogh, *Twentieth Century Ireland*, p. 233.

156 *Ibid.*

157 John Bowman, *De Valera and the Ulster Question, 1917–1973* (Clarendon Press, Oxford, 1982), p. 281.

158 Aoife Bhreatnach, *Frank Aiken and the Formulation of Foreign Policy*, M.Phil Thesis, UCC 1999, pp. 30-31.

159 NAI, DFA, Secretaries Office File Series A12/1a, Cremin to Murphy, 19 November 1956.

160 *Ibid.*, 22 November 1956.

161 Keogh, *Twentieth Century Ireland*, p. 229.

162 Boyce, George, *The Irish Question and British Politics, 1868-1996* (Palgrave, Macmillan, London, 1996), p. 107.

163 NAI, DFA 313/31C, Cremin to Murphy, 17 January 1957.

164 NAI, DFA 305/14/299, Biggar to Murphy, 4 March 1957.

165 *Ibid.*, Cremin to Murphy, 6 March 1957.

166 *Ibid.*, Fay to Murphy, 4 March 1957.

167 *Ibid.*, Cremin to Murphy, 6 March 1957.

168 *Ibid.* The question appeared in Hansard, 14 March 1957, Col. 1308. However, Cremin noted that Bell's constituency had a considerable Irish element and it may have been that he was looking after his seat.

169 NAI, DFA 305/14/299, Cremin to Murphy, 8 March 1957.

170 Lee, *Ireland*, p. 430.

171 NAI, DFA 305/14/299, Cremin to Murphy, 8 March 1957.

172 *Ibid.*, Cremin was not in the habit of going freelance unlike some Irish ministers.

173 NAI, DFA 305/14/299, Cremin to Murphy, 9 March 1957.

174 *Ibid.*

175 *Ibid.*, 6 March 1957.

176 *Ibid.*, 14 March 1957.

177 *Ibid.*, Murphy to Cremin, 19 March 1957.

178 *Ibid.*, Cremin to Murphy, 12 April 1957.

179 NAI, DFA P203/2A, Cremin to Murphy, 2 May 1957.

180 *Ibid.*

181 NAI, DFA, Secretaries Office File Series A12/1a, Cremin to Murphy, 24 May 1957.

182 NAI, DFA P203/2A, Cremin to Murphy, 9 May 1957.

183 *Ibid.*, 22 May 1957.

184 *Ibid.* This is reminiscent of de Valera's visit to Churchill in the 1951 when F.H. Boland told de Valera that he would have to go to lunch with Churchill and could not drop in his card, since the reason for his visit to London was to see his ophthalmologist (F.H. Boland 'Memoirs', p. 15).

185 NAI, DFA P203/2A, Cremin to Murphy, 27 July 1957.

186 *Ibid.*, 20 August 1957.

187 *Ibid.*, 18 September 1957.

188 *Ibid.*, 21 September 1957.

189 Aiken and deValera shared the same belief that an Irish minister should only visit London on his way somewhere else.

190 NAI, DFA P203/2A, Cremin to Murphy, 23 October 1957.

191 *Ibid.*, 3 March 1958.

192 *Ibid.*, 2 March 1958.

193 NAI, DFA 313/31C, Cremin to Murphy, 12 March 1957.

194 John Bowman, *De Valera and the Ulster Question*, p. 292.

195 NAI, DFA 313/31C, Cremin to Murphy, 13 March 1957 Creeda Fitzgibbon recalls that Cremin would prepare new speeches for each dinner and not recycle them (Creeda FitzGibbon interview).

196 NAI, DFA 313/31C, Cremin to Murphy, 17 April 1957.

197 *Ibid.*, 28 May 1957.

198 *Ibid.*, 12 June 1957.

199 NAI, DFA 305/14/299, Cremin to Murphy, 5 July 1957 and NAI, DFA 313/31C, Cremin to Murphy, 5 July 1957.

200 NAI, DFA 313/31C, Cremin to Murphy, 8 August 1957.

201 *Ibid.*, 10 December 1957.

202 *Ibid.*, 24 October 1957.

203 Keogh, *Ireland and Europe*, p. 196. 'No single event episode did more to distort the role played by Ireland during the war than de Valera's visit to the German legation. International reaction, particularly in the United States was vigorous and uncomprehending'.

204 O'Connor, *The Irish in Britain*, p. 67.

205 NAI, DFA 313/31C, Cremin to Murphy, 28 October 1957.

206 *Ibid.*, 8 November 1957.

207 Kevin O'Connor, *The Irish in Britain* (Torc Books, Dublin, 1972), p. 68.

208 NAI, DFA 313/31C, 29 January 1958, see also DFA 14/29/1 Vatican Files

209 Keogh, *Twentieth Century Ireland*, pp. 216-17.

210 NAI, DFA 313/31C, 29 January 1958, see also DFA 14/29/1 Vatican Files

211 O'Connor, *The Irish in Britain*, p. 64.

212 Keogh, *Twentieth Century Ireland*, p. 216. Keogh wrote that among the Dublin working classes the tradition of joining the British forces had not been broken.

213 NAI, DFA 313/31C, 29 January 1958, see also DFA 14/29/1 Vatican Files.

214 *Ibid.*

215 NAI, DFA 14/21 (Vatican Files), Boland to Murphy, 26 January 1956.

216 NAI, DFA 313/31C, 29 January 1958, see also DFA 14/29/1 Vatican Files.

217 George Boyce, *Ireland 1828 – 1923, from Ascendancy to Democracy* (Blackwell, Oxford, 1992), p. 52.

218 O'Connor, *The Irish in Britain,* p. 67.

219 NAI, DFA 313/31C, 29 January 1958, see also NAI, DFA 14/29/1 Vatican Files.

220 *Ibid.*

221 NAI, DFA 313/31D, Cremin to Murphy, 29 January 1958. As secretary Cremin commissioned reports on the Irish Diaspora in all the major Irish population centres including, Argentina (DFA 14/114, Vatican Series), the US (DFA 14/115, Vatican Series), Canada (DFA 14/116 Vatican Series). All the reports were circulated in February 1960. This was a wise policy in that it gave a cohesion to Irish policy in relation to Diasporas and allowed policy to be properly formulated.

222 Cremin had an active dislike for Charles Bewley and commented unfavourably on his book *Memoirs of a Wild Goose.* Dr Crussell interview, 10 March 2001.

223 Shakespeare, *Othello,* Act V, sc IV.

Bibliography

Primary Sources

Cremin's unpublished memoirs in possession of Cremin family
Department of Finance
Department of Foreign Affairs
    Confidential reports from Paris, Berlin, Lisbon, the Vatican, London and Permanent Mission United Nations (PMUN)
    Mission files from Paris, Berlin, Lisbon, the Holy See and London
    Secretaries' files in the Department of Foreign Affairs
Department of Industry and Commerce (for the period dealing with OEEC)
Department of the Taoiseach
Irish Military Archives, Dublin
    G2 (Intelligence) Files
    Office of the Controller of Censorship 1939-46 collections
National Archives, Dublin
National Library of Ireland
    Denis Devlin papers
Public Record Office, Kew Gardens, London
'Save the German children': scrapbook compiled by John Sheedy, Mount Shannon, Co. Clare
The Irish Times Photographic Archives
Trinity College, Dublin
    Frederick Boland papers
University College Cork
    College calendars 1926–34
    Minute books of the Commerce, Debating and Law societies
University College Dublin
    Frank Aiken papers, UCD (De Valera papers were not open)

Interviews
Stephen Collins, 4 December 1999
Anne Cremin, September 2000
Conor Cruise O'Brien 11 June 2001

Cissy Crussel, 10 March 2001

Dr Emma Cunningham, 10 May 2001

Dr Garret FitzGerald, 2 December 2000

A. O'Brien, October 1998

Dr Patrick O'Donoghue, November 2000

Interviews with retired and serving Irish diplomats (confidential sources)

Secondary Sources

Abi-Saab, Georges, *The United Nations Operation in the Congo 1960-1964* (Oxford University Press, Oxford, 1978)

Acheson, Dean, *Power and Diplomacy* (Harvard University Press, Cambridge, Massachusetts, 1958)

— *Present at the Creation* (W.W. Norton and Co., New York, 1987)

Akenson, Donald Harman, *Conor, a Biography of Conor Cruise O'Brien, Volume 1 Narrative* (McGill, Queens University Press, 1994)

— *The United States and Ireland* (Harvard University Press, Cambridge, Massachusetts, 1973)

Aldous, Richard and Lee, Sabine (eds), *Harold Macmillan and Britain's World Role* (Macmillan, London, 1996)

Aldrich, R. and J. Connell (eds), *France in World Politics* (Routledge, London and New York, 1989)

Aron, R., *The Vichy Regime 1940-44* (Putnam, London, 1958)

Aybet, Gülnur, *The Dynamics of European Security Cooperation, 1945-91* (Macmillan, London, 1991)

Azéma, J.P., *From Munich to the Liberation* (Cambridge University Press, Cambridge, 1984)

Bacque, James, *Crimes and Mercies, the Fate of German Civilians under Allied Occupation, 1944-50* (Warner Books, London, 1997)

Bair, Deirdre, *Samuel Beckett. a Biography* (Cape, London, 1978)

Ball, George W., *Diplomacy for a Crowded World, an American Foreign Policy* (Bodley Head, London, 1976)

Beevor, Anthony, *Stalingrad* (Penguin, London, 1998)

Bew, Paul and Patterson, Henry, *Seán Lemass and the Making of Modern Ireland 1945-66* (Gill and Macmillan, Dublin, 1982)

Bewley, Charles, *Memoirs of a Wild Goose* (Lilliput Press, Dublin, 1989)

Blet, Pierre, *Pius XII and the Second World War, According to the Archives of the Vatican* (Paulist Press, New Jersey, 1999)

Bonnet, Georges, *Quai d'Orsay* (Times Press, Isle of Man, 1965)

Bottinger, Joseph, *Vietnam, a Political History* (Andre Deutsch, London, 1969)

Bower, Tom, *Nazi Gold* (Harper Collins, New York, 1997)

Bowman, John, *De Valera and the Ulster Question* (Claredon Press, Oxford, 1982)

Boyce, George, and O'Day, Alan, *The Making of Modern Irish History* (Routledge, London, 1996)

Boyce, George, *Ireland 1828–1923, from Ascendancy to Democracy* (Blackwell, Oxford, 1992)

— *The Irish Question and British Politics, 1868–1996* (Palgrave, Macmillan, London, 1996)

Brennan, Robert, *Ireland Standing Firm, My Wartime Mission in Washington and Eamon de Valera, a Memoir* (UCD Press, Dublin, 2002)

Browne, Noel, *Against the Tide* (Gill and Macmillan, Dublin, 1986)

Bunreacht na hÉireann, Constitution of Ireland (Dublin, 1938)

Burk, Kathleen, *Troublemaker, the Life and History of A.J.P. Taylor* (Yale University Press, London, 2000)

Cain, P.J., and Hopkins, A.G., *British Imperialism, 1914-1990* (Longman, New York and London, 1995)

Callaghan, James, *A House Divided, the Dilemma of Northern Ireland* (Collins, London, 1973)

Canning, Paul, *British Policy towards Ireland 1921-1941* (Oxford University Press, Oxford, 1985)

Carlton, David, *Britian and the Suez Crisis* (Institute of Contemporary British History, Basil Blackwell, 1988)

Carrol, Joseph T., *Ireland in the War Years* (Newton Abbot, London, 1975)

Casey, Lord, *Personal Experiences, 1939-1946* (Constable and Company, London, 1962)

Catchpole, Brian, *The Korean War* (Constable, London, 2000)

Clogg, Richard, *A Concise History of Greece* (Cambridge University Press, Cambridge, 1992)

Cointet, Jean-Paul, *Pierre Laval* (Fayard, Paris, 1993)

Coogan, Tim Pat, *Wherever Green is Worn, the Story of the Irish Diaspora* (Hutchinson, London, 2000)

Cooney, John, *John Charles McQuaid* (O'Brien Press, Dublin, 1999)

— *The Crozier and the Dáil* (Mercier Press, Cork, 1986)

Cornwall, John, *Hitler's Pope* (Viking, London, 1999)

Cronin, Anthony, *Samuel Beckett: the Last Modernist* (HarperCollins, London, 1996)

Cronin, Seán, *Frank Ryan* (Repsol Publishing, Dublin, 1980)

Crozier, Brian, *De Gaulle, the Statesman* (Eyre Methuen, London, 1973)

Dalloz, Jacques, *The War in Indo-China, 1945-1954* (Gill and Macmillan, Dublin, 1990)

de Carmoy, Guy *The Foreign Policy of France, 1944-1968* (University of Chicago Press, Chicago, 1970)

De Gaulle, Charles, *The Complete War Memoirs of Charles de Gaulle* (Carroll and Graf, New York, 1998)

Deighton, Len, *Overlord, D-Day and the Battle for Normandy* (Pan Books, London, 1984)

Delaney, Eamon, *An Accidental Diplomat* (New Ireland, Dublin, 2001)

Denis, Mack, *Smith, a Political History* (Yale University Press, New Haven and London, 1997)

Detwiler, Donald S., *World War II, German Military Studies, Vol. 24* (Garland, New York, 1975)

Doherty, Richard, *Irishmen and Women in the Second World War* (Four Courts Press, Dublin, 1999)

Doll, Mary A. and Mary Aswell, *Beckett and Myth* (Syracuse University Press, 1988)

Donnitz, Admiral Karl, *Ten Years and Ten Days* (Cassell, London, 2000)

Downey, James, *Lenihan, his Life and Loyalties* (New Island Book, Dublin, 1998)

Du Moulin de Labarthete, H., *Les Temps de Illusions, Souvenirs (Juillet 1940 – Avril 1942)* (A L'Enseigne du Cheval Ailé, Paris, 1946)

Duchêne, François, *Jean Monnet, the First Statesman of Interdependence* (Norton, London, 1994)

DuGard, Maurice Martin, *La Chronique de Vichy: 1940-1944* (Flammarion, Paris, 1975)

Duggan, John P., *Neutral Ireland and the Third Reich* (Lilliput Press, Dublin, 1989)

Dupuy, Trevor N., *Elusive Victory, the Arab-Israeli Wars 1947-1974* (MacDonald and James, London, 1978)

Dutton, David, *Anthony Eden, a Life and Reputation* (Arnold, London, 1997)

Dwyer, T. Ryle, *Irish Neutrality and the USA 1939-1947* (Gill and Macmillan, Dublin, 1977)

— *Strained Relations, Ireland at Peace and the USA at War 1941-45* (Gill and Macmillan, Dublin, 1988)

— *De Valera's Finest Hour: in Search of National Independence, 1932-1959* (Mercier Press, Cork, 1982)

— *De Valera: the Man and the Myth* (Poolbeg, Dublin, 1991)

— *Guests of the State: the Story of Allied and Axis Servicemen Interned in Ireland during World War II* (Brandon, Dingle, 1994)

Dyer, Louise, *Machiavelli and the Modern State* (Ginn, Boston, 1904)

Eden, Anthony, *Memoirs, Full Circle* (Cassell, London, 1960)

— *Days for Decision* (Faber and Faber, London, 1949)

Edwards, Owen Dudley, *Conor Cruise O'Brien Introduces Ireland* (University of Wales, Cardiff, 1967)

Elborn, Geoffrey, *Francis Stuart, a Life* (The Raven Arts Press, Dublin, 1990)

Falconi, Carlo, *The Silence of Pius XII* (Faber and Faber, London, 1965)

Fanning, Ronan, *Independent Ireland* (Helicon Limited, Dublin, 1983)

— *The Irish Department of Finance 1922-58* (Institute of Public Administration, Dublin, 1978)

Farrel, Brian, *Seán Lemass* (Gill and Macmillan, Dublin, 1983)

Fisk, Robert, *In Time of War, Ireland, Ulster and the Price of Neutrality, 1939–45* (Paladin Grafton Books, London, 1983)

FitzGerald, Garret, *All in a Life, an autobiography* (Gill and Macmillan, Dublin, 1991)

Fogarty, Gerald P., *The Vatican and the American Hierarchy from 1870 to 1965* (Michael Glazier, Collegeville, Minnesota, 1982)

Foster, R.F., *Modern Ireland* (Allen Lane, London, 1988)

Freidel, Frank, *Franklin D. Roosevelt, a Rendezvous with Destiny* (Little Brown, Boston, 1990)

Fullick, Roy, and Geoffrey Powell, *Suez, the Double War* (Leo Cooper, London 1979)

Fursdon, Edward, *The European Defence Community, a History* (Macmillan, London, 1980)

Gallagher, Frank, *The Indivisible Island* (Gollancz, London, 1956)

Gallagher, Tom, *Portugal, a Twentieth Century Interpretation* (Manchester University Press, 1983)

Gilbert, Martin, *A History of the Twentieth Century, Vol. II., 1933-1951* (Harper Collins, London, 1998)

— *Challenge to Civilisation, a History of the Twentieth Century, 1952-1999* (Harper Collins, London, 1999)

Girvin, Brian, *From Union to Union, Nationalism, Democracy and Religion in Ireland – Act of Union to EU* (Gill and Macmillan, Dublin, 2002)

— *The Emergency, Neutral Ireland 1939–45* (Macmillan, Dublin, 2006)

Gripenberd, G.A., *Finland and the Great Powers* (Nabraska University Press, Lincoln, 1965)

Grose, Peter, *Gentleman Spy, the life of Allen Dulles* (University of Massachusetts Press, Amherst, 1996)

Halls, W.D., *Politics, Society and Christianity in Vichy France* (Berg, London, 1995)

Harkness, David, *The Restless Dominion, the Irish Free State and the British Commonwealth of Nations, 1921-1931* (Macmillan, London, 1969)

Harrison, Michael M., *The Reluctant Ally, France and Atlantic Security* (The John Hopkins University Press, Baltimore, 1981)

Hayes, Carlton J. H., *Wartime Mission in Spain* (Macmillan, New York, 1946)

Hebblethwaite, Peter, *John XXIII* (Geoffrey Chapman, London, 1984)

Hederman, Miriam, *The Road to Europe, Irish Attitudes 1948-61* (Institute of Public Administration, Dublin, 1983)

Henderson, Sir Nevile, *Failure of a Mission, by the British Ambassador to Berlin 1937-1939* (Putnam, New York, 1940)

Henderson, Sir Nicholas, *The Birth of NATO* (Weidenfeld and Nicolson, London, 1982)

Hickman, Katie, *Daughters of Britainnia, the Lives and Times of Diplomatic Wives* (Harper Collins, London, 1999)

Hilberg, Raul, *The Destruction of European Jews* (Quadrangle Books, Chicago, 1961)

Hildebrand, Klaus, *The Foreign Policy of the Third Reich* (Batsford, London, 1973)

Hitchcock, William L., *France Restored, Cold War Diplomacy and the Quest for Leadership in Europe 1944-1954* (The University of North Carolina Press, Chapel Hill and London, 1999)

Hoare, Sir Samuel, Viscount Templewood, *Ambassador on a Special Mission* (Collins, London, 1946)

Hobsbawn, Eric, *Age of Extremes, the Short History of the Twentieth Century, 1914-1991* (Michael Joseph, London, 1994)

Hoensch, Jörg K., *A History of Modern Hungary, 1867-1994* (Longman, London and New York, 1996)

Hogan, Michael J., *The Marshall Plan* (Cambridge University Press, Cambridge, 1987)

Horgan, John, *Lemass, the Enigmatic Patriot* (Gill and Macmillan, Dublin, 1997)

Horne, Alistair, *Macmillan 1894-1956*, Vol. 1 (Macmillan, London, 1988)

— *Macmillan, 1957-1986*, Vol. 2 (Macmillan, London, 1989)

Howe, Ellic, *The Black Game* (Queen Ann Press, London, 1982)

Howe, Stephen, *Ireland and Empire* (Oxford University Press, Oxford, 2000)

Hyman, Paula E., *The Jews of Modern France* (University of California Press, London, 1998)

Jackson, Julian, *The Popular Front in France, Defending Democracy, 1934-38* (Cambridge University Press, Cambridge, 1990)

James, Lawrence, *The Rise and Fall of the British Empire* (Abacus, London, 1998)

Jenkins, Roy, *Churchill* (Macmillan, London, 2001)

Kay, Hugh, *Salazar and Modern Portugal* (Eyre and Spottiswoode, London, 1970)

Keatinge, Patrick, *A Place among the Nations, Issues of Irish Foreign Policy* (Institute of Public Administration, Dublin, 1978)

— *The Formulation of Irish Foreign Policy* (Institute of Public Administration, Dublin, 1973)

Kedward, H.R., *Occupied France, Collaboration and Resistance 1940-44* (Basil Blackwell, Oxford, 1985)

Keegan, John, *The Second World War* (Hutchinson, London, 1989)

Kelly, J.N.D., *The Oxford Dictionary of the Popes* (Oxford University Press, Oxford, 1986)

Kennedy, Michael and Joseph M. Skelly (eds), *Irish Foreign Policy 1919–1966* (Four Courts Press, Dublin, 2000)

Kennedy, Paul, *The Rise and Fall of Great Powers* (Unwin Hyman, London, 1988)

Kent, Madeleine, *I Married a German* (George Allen and Unwin, London, 1938)

Keogh, Dermot, *Ireland and the Vatican* (Cork University Press, Cork, 1995)

— *Ireland and Europe 1919-1989* (Hibernian University Press, Cork and Dublin, 1989)

— *Jews in Twentieth Century Ireland* (Cork University Press, Cork, 1999)

— *The Vatican the Bishops and Irish Politics* (Cambridge University Press, Cambridge, 1985)

— *Twentieth Century Ireland, Nation and State* (Gill and Macmillan, Dublin, 1994)

Kershaw, Ian, *Hitler, 1936-45, Nemesis* (Allen Lane, London, 2000)

Kertzer, David I., *Unholy War the Catholic Church and the Rise of Anti-Semitism* (Robert Wilde, London, 2002)

Kissinger, Henry, *Diplomacy* (Touchstone, New York, 1994)

Kupchan, Charles A., *The Vulnerability of Empire* (Cornell University Press, Ithaca, 1994)

Lacouture, Jean, *De Gaulle, the Rebel 1890-1944* (Collins Harvill, London, 1991)

— *De Gaulle, the Ruler, 1945-1970* (Collins Harvill, London, 1991)

— *De Gaulle* (Hutchinson, London, 1970)

LaFeber, Walter, *America, Russia and the Cold War, 1945-92* (McGraw-Hill, New York, 7th edn, 1993)

Lankford, Nelson D., *The Last American Aristocrat* (Little Brown and Company, Boston, 1996)

Leahy, William, *I Was There* (Victor Gollancz, London, 1950)

Lee, J.J., *Ireland 1912-85* (Cambridge University Press, Cambridge, 1989)

Lee, Joseph and Gearóid Ó Tuathaigh (eds.) *The Age of de Valera* (Ward River Press, Dublin, 1982)

Levi, Anthony, *Cardinal Richelieu and the Making of France* (Robinson, London, 2000)

Liberman, Sima, *The Growth of the European Mixed Economies* (Schenkman Publishing Co., Cambridge, Massachusetts, 1977)

Lloyd, Selwyn, *Suez 1956: a Personal Account* (Credito Italiano, Milan, 1978)

Lochner, Louis P. (ed.), *The Goebbels Diaries, 1942-1943* (Doubleday, New York, 1948)

Longford, Earl of and T.P. O'Neill, *Eamon de Valera* (Houghton Mifflin Company, Boston, 1971)

Longford, Lord, and McHardy, Anne, *Ulster* (Weidenfeld and Nicolson, London, 1981)

Lottman, Herbert R., *Pétain, Hero or Traitor?* (Viking, Harmondsworth, 1985)

Lucas, W. Scott, *Divided We Stand, Britain, US and the Suez Crisis* (Hodder and Stoughton, London, 1991)

MacDermott, Eithne, *Clann na Poblachta* (Cork University Press, Cork, 1998)

MacDonald, Charles B., *The Battle of the Bulge* (Phoenix, London, 1998)

Machiavelli, Niccolo (edited with an introduction by Bernard Crick), *The Discourses* (Penguin, Harmondsworth, 1970)

— *The Prince* (Humphrey Milford, London, 1903)

Macmillan, Harold, *Riding the Storm 1956-1959* (Macmillan, London, 1971)

Maher, D.J., *The Tortuous Path, the Course of Ireland's Entry into the EEC* (Institute of Public Administration, Dublin, 1986)

Manning, Maurice, *The Blueshirts* (Gill and Macmillan, Dublin, 1970)

McCartney, Anne, *Francis Stuart, Face to Face, a Critical Study* (Institute of Irish Studies, Queens University, Belfast, 2000)

McGarry, Fergal, *Irish Politics and the Spanish Civil War* (Cork University Press, Cork, 1999)

Milward, Alan S., *The European Rescue of the Nation State* (Routledge, London, 1992)

— *The Reconstruction of Western Europe* (Methuen and Co., London, 1984)

Molohan, Cathy, *Germany and Ireland 1945-55, Two Nations Friendship* (Irish Academic Press, Dublin, 1999)

Monnet, Jean, *Memoirs* (Collins Press, London, 1978)

Morgan, Roger, *The United States and West Germany, 1945-1973* (Oxford University Press, Oxford, 1974)

Mosley, Leonard, *Dulles* (The Dial Press, New York, 1978)

Murphy, John A., *Ireland in the Twentieth Century* (Gill and Macmillan, Dublin, 1975)

Murphy, Robert, *Diplomat among Warriors* (Doubleday, New York, 1964)

Nation, R. Craig, *Black Earth, Red Star, A History of Soviet Security Policy, 1917-1991* (Cornell University Press, Ithaca, 1992)

Natterstad, J.H., *Francis Stuart* (Bucknell University Press, London, 1974)

Nichols, Peter, *The Politics of the Vatican* (Pall Mall Press, London, 1968)

Noland, K.B., and T. Desmond Williams (eds.), *Ireland in the War Years and After 1939-1951* (Gill and Macmillan, Dublin, 1969)

Norman, Edward, *Roman Catholicism in England* (Oxford University Press, Oxford, 1985)

Novick, Peter, *The Holocaust and Collective Memory* (Bloomsbury, London, 1999)

O'Brien, Conor Cruise, *Memoir, my Life and Themes* (Poolbeg, Dublin, 1998)

— *To Kantanga and Back* (Four Square Books, London, 1962)

O'Brien, Máire Cruise and Conor Cruise O'Brien, *Ireland, a Concise History* (Thames and Hudson, London, 1994)

O'Brien, Miriam Hederman, *The Road to Europe – Irish Attitudes 1948-1961* (Institute of Public Administration, Dublin, 1983)

O'Connor, Joseph, *Even the Olives are Bleeding, the Life and Times of Charles Donnolly* (New Island Books, Dublin, 1992)

O'Connor, Kevin, *The Irish in Britain* (Torc, Dublin, 1974)

O'Donoghue, David, *Hitler's Irish Voices* (Beyond the Pale Publications, Belfast, 1998)

Ó Drisceoil, Donal, *Censorship in Ireland, 1939-1945: Neutrality, Politics and Society* (Cork University Press, Cork, 1996)

O'Halpin, Eunan, *Defending Ireland* (Oxford University Press, Oxford, 1999)

O'Riordan, Michael, *Connolly's Column* (New Books, Dublin, 1979)

O'Sullivan, Michael, *Seán Lemass, a Biography* (Blackwater Press, Dublin 1994)

Ovendale, Ritchie, *Anglo-American Relations in the Twentieth Century* (Macmillan, Basingstoke, 1998)

Overy, Richard, *Russia's War* (Penguin, London, 1997)

Payne, Stanley G., *The Franco Regime 1936-75* (The University of Wisconsin Press, London and Wisconsin, 1986)

Pearce, Malcolm and Geoffrey Stewart, *British Political History, 1867-1995, Democracy and Decline* (Routledge, London, 1996)

Peck, John, *Dublin from Downing Street* (Gill and Macmillan, Dublin, 1979)

Pierre, Joannon (ed.), *De Gaulle and Ireland* (Institute of Public Administration, Dublin, 1991)

Pinto, António Costa, *Salazar's Dictatorship and European Fascism* (Columbia University Press, New York, 1995)

Preston, Paul, *Franco* (Harper Collins, London, 1993)

Raby, D.L., *Fascism and Resistance in Portugal, Communist Liberals and Military*

Dissidents in the Opposition to Salazar, 1941-1974 (Manchester University Press, Manchester, 1988)

Raftery, Oliver P., *Catholics in Ulster, 1603-1983, An Interpretative History* (Hurst and Company, London, 1994)

Richie, Alexandra, *Fausts Metropolis* (Harper-Collins, London, 1998)

Rioux, Jean Pierre, *The French Fourth Republic 1944-58* (Cambridge University Press, Cambridge, 1987)

Roth, Philip, *Bewley in Berlin: Aspects of the Career of an Irish Diplomat, 1933-1939* (Four Courts Press, Dublin, 2000)

Roy, Denny, *China's Foreign Policy* (Rowman and Littlefield, Boston, 1998)

Ryan, Cornelius, *The Last Battle* (New English Library, London, 1979)

Shirer, William L., *The Collapse of the Third Republic* (Simon and Schuster, New York, 1969)

Shuckburgh, Evelyn, *Descent to Suez: Diaries 1951-1956* (Weidenfeld and Nicolson, London, 1986)

Skelly, Joseph Morrison, *Irish Diplomacy at the United Nations, 1945-1965* (Irish Academic Press, Dublin, 1997)

Sloan, G.R., *The Geopolitics of Anglo-Irish Relations in the Twentieth Century* (Leicester University Press, London, 1997)

Smith, Denis Mack, *Mussolini* (Weidenfeld and Nicolson, London, 1982)

Smith, Walter Bedell, *Moscow Mission, 1946-1949* (Heinemann, Melbourne, 1950)

Smyth, Denis, *Diplomacy and the Strategy of Survival, British Policy and Franco's Spain, 1940-1941* (Cambridge University Press, Cambridge, 1986)

Soares, Mário, *Portugal's Struggle for Liberty* (George Allen and Unwin, London, 1975)

Speer, Albert, *Inside the Third Reich* (Weidenfeld and Nicolson, London, 1970)

Stephan, Enno, *Spies in Ireland* (Stackpole, Harrisburg, 1965)

— *A Man Called Intrepid* (Book Club Associates, London, 1976)

Stuart, Francis, *Black List, Section H* (Brian and O'Keeffe, London, 1975)

Sweets, John F., *Choices in Vichy France* (Oxford University Press, Oxford, 1986)

Talbott, John, *The War Without Victors, France in Algeria, 1954-1962* (Faber and Faber, London, 1981)

Thatcher, Margaret, *The Downing Street Years* (Harper Collins, London, 1993)

Thomas, R.T., *Britain and Vichy, the Dilemma of Anglo-French Relations 1940-42* (Macmillan, London, 1979)

Thorpe, D. R., *Alec Douglas-Home* (Sinclair-Stevenson, London, 1996)

Tiersky, Ronald, *French Communism* (Columbia University Press, New York, 1974)

Tint, Herbert, *French Foreign Policy since the Second World War* (Foreign Policy Studies, Weidenfeld and Nicolson, London, 1972)

Tryhall, J.W.D., *Franco* (Repert Hart-Davis, London, 1970)

Tschuy, Theo, *Dangerous Diplomacy, the Story of Carl Lutz, Rescuer of 62,000 Hungarian Jews* (Eerdmansm Grand Rapids, Michigan, 2000)

Von Clausewitz, Carl, *On War* (Wordsworth, London, 1997)

Von Mellenthin, Major-General F.W, *Panzer Battles* (Cassell, London, 1955)

Weitz, John, *Hitler's Diplomat, Joachim von Ribbentrop* (Phoenix Giant, London, 1992)

Whelan, Bernadette, *Ireland and the Marshall Plan: 1947-51* (Four Courts Press, Dublin, 2000)

Whitaker, T.K., *Interests* (Institute of Public Administration, Dublin, 1983)

Whyte, J.H., *Church and State in Modern Ireland, 1923-1979* (Gill and Macmillan, Dublin, 2nd edn, 1980)

Williams, Charles, *Adenauer* (Little, Brown and Company, London, 2000)

Williams, Philip M., *The Diary of Hugh Gaitskell, 1945-1956* (Jonathan Cape, London, 1983)

Young, Hugo, *This Blessed Plot* (Papermac, London, 1998)

Young, J.W., *Britain and European Unity* (Macmillan, London, 2000)

— *Britain, France and the Unity of Europe* (Leicester University Press, Bath, 1984)

Zubok, V. and P. Pleshakov, *Inside the Kremlin's Cold War, From Stalin to Khrushchev* (Harvard University Press, London, 1996)

Articles

Boyce, George, 'Revisionism and the Northern Ireland Troubles' in George Boyce and Alan O'Day (eds.), *The Making of Modern Irish History* (Routledge, London, 1996)

Cremin, Con, 'Archaeology and History' in *Ireland To-day, Vol. II, No. 4.* April 1937

— 'Review of Plutarch's Life of Aratus', edited by W.H. Porter, in *Ireland To-day, Vol. II, No. 4,* September 1937

— 'Northern Ireland at the United Nations', *Irish Studies in International Affairs*, Vol. 1, No. 2, 1980

— 'The United Nations Conference on the Law of the Sea', *Irish Studies in International Affairs*, Vol. 1, No. 1, 1979

— 'United Nations Peace Keeping Operations: an Irish Initiative 1961-68', *Irish Studies in International Affairs*, Vol. 1, No. 2, 1980

— 'Some Irish Associations in Rome' in Fr Virgilius, OFM Cap. and Fr Henry,

OFM Cap. (eds.) *The Capuchin Annual* (Dollard, Dublin, 1959)

Daly, Mary, 'Irish Nationality and Citizenship since 1922', in *Irish Historical Studies*, xxxii, No. 127 (May 2001)

Davis, Troy 'Anti-partitionism, Irish American and Anglo-American Relations, 1945-51' in Michael Kennedy and Joseph M. Skelly (eds), *Irish Foreign Policy 1919–1966* (Four Courts Press, Dublin, 2000)

Dinan, D., 'After the Emergency, Ireland in the Post-war World' in *Eire Ireland* Autumn 1989

Fanning, Ronan 'Raison d'État and the Evolution of Irish Foreign Policy' in Michael Kennedy and Joseph M. Skelly (eds), *Irish Foreign Policy 1919–1966* (Four Courts Press, Dublin, 2000)

— 'Charles de Gaulle, 1946-1958, from Resignation to Return, the Irish Diplomatic Perspective' in Pierre Joannon (ed.), *De Gaulle and Ireland* (Institute of Public Administration, Dublin, 1991)

— 'Irish Neutrality – an Historical Review', *Irish Studies in International Affairs*, Vol. 1, No. 1, 1979.

— 'The Evolution of Irish Foreign Policy', in Michael Kennedy and Joseph M. Skelly (eds), *Irish Foreign Policy 1919–1966* (Four Courts Press, Dublin, 2000)

— 'The United States and Irish Participation in NATO: the Debate of 1950', *Irish Studies in International Affairs*, Vol. 1, No. 1, 1979.

Fogarty, Gerald P., 'Francis J. Spellman, American and Roman', in G.P. Fogarty, *Patterns of Episcopal Leadership* (Macmillan, New York, 1989)

Geiger, Till, 'The Enthusiastic Response of a Reluctant Supporter: Ireland and the Committee for European Economic Cooperation in 1947' in Michael Kennedy and Joseph M. Skelly (eds), *Irish Foreign Policy 1919–1966* (Four Courts Press, Dublin, 2000)

Goldstone, Katrina, '"Benevolent Helpfulness"? Ireland and the International Reaction to Jewish Refugees, 1933-39' in Michael Kennedy and Joseph M. Skelly (eds), *Irish Foreign Policy 1919–1966* (Four Courts Press, Dublin, 2000)

Guillen, Pierre, 'France and the Defence of Western Europe' in N. Wiggershaus and R.G. Foerster (eds.) *The Western Security Community* (Berg, Oxford, 1993)

Haughton, John, 'The Historical Background' in J.W. O'Hagan (ed.) *The Economy of Ireland, Policy and Performance of a European Region, 8th edition* (Gill and Macmillan, Dublin, 2000)

Kennedy, Michael, '"Publishing a Secret History": the Documents on Irish Foreign Policy Project', *Irish Studies in International Affairs*, Vol. 9, 1998.

Kennedy, Michael and Skelly, Joseph, 'The Study of Irish Foreign Policy from Independence to Internationalism' in Michael Kennedy and Joseph M. Skelly (eds), *Irish Foreign Policy 1919–1966* (Four Courts Press, Dublin, 2000)

Keogh, Dermot, 'Eamon de Valera and Hitler: An Analysis of International Reaction to the Visit to the German Minister, May 1945' in *Irish Studies in International Affairs*, Vol. 3, No. 1, 1989

— 'Ireland, the Vatican and the Cold War' in *Irish Studies in International Affairs*, Vol. 3, No. 3, 1991

— 'Ireland, de Gaulle and World War II' in Pierre Joannon (ed.) *De Gaulle and Ireland* (Institute of Public Administration, Dublin, 1991)

— 'Irish Neutrality and the first application for membership of the EEC, 1961–63' in Michael Kennedy and Joseph M. Skelly (eds), *Irish Foreign Policy 1919–1966* (Four Courts Press, Dublin, 2000)

— 'Profile of Joseph Walshe, Secretary, Department of Foreign Affairs, 1922-46', *Irish Studies in International Affairs*, Vol. 3, No. 2, 1990

— 'The Department of External Affairs, Ireland', in Zara Steiner (ed.), *The Times Survey of Foreign Ministries of the World* (Times Books, London, 1982)

Lee, J.J., 'Seán Lemass' in J.J. Lee (ed.) *Ireland 1945-1970* (Gill and Macmillan, Dublin, 1979)

Murphy, Gary, '"A Wider Perspective": Ireland's View of Western Europe in the 1950s' in Michael Kennedy and Joseph M. Skelly (eds), *Irish Foreign Policy 1919–1966* (Four Courts Press, Dublin, 2000)

Myers, Kevin, 'An Irishman's Diary', *The Irish Times*, 22 October 1997

O'Brien, Conor Cruise, 'Ireland in International Affairs' in Owen Dudley Edwards (ed.), *Conor Cruise O'Brien Introduces Ireland* (Deutsch, London, 1969)

O'Driscoll, Mervyn, 'Inter-war Irish-German Diplomacy: Continuity, Ambiguity and Appeasement in Irish Foreign Policy' in Michael Kennedy and Joseph M. Skelly (eds) *Irish Foreign Policy 1919–1966* (Four Courts Press, Dublin, 2000)

— 'Irish-German relations 1929-39: Irish Reactions to the Nazis' in *Cambridge Review of International Affairs*, 11:1, 1997

— 'The Political Economy of Irish-German Trade, 1932-39', *Irish Studies in International Affairs* (RIA, Dublin, 1999)

O'Halpin, Eunan, '"According to the Irish Minister in Rome…": British decrypts and Irish Diplomacy in the Second World War', *Irish Studies in International Affairs*, Vol. 6, 1995.

Patterson, Robert, 'Ireland, Vichy and Post Liberation France, 1938-1950', in Michael Kennedy and Joseph M. Skelly (eds), *Irish Foreign Policy 1919–1966* (Four Courts Press, Dublin, 2000)

Rioux, Jean-Pierre, 'The Moderniser: Pierre Mendès-France' in John Gaffney (ed.), *France and Modernisation* (Avebury, Aldershot, 1988)

Ruane, Kevin, 'Anthony Eden, the Foreign Office and Anglo French Relations, 1951-1954' in Alan Sharp and Glyn Stone (eds.), *Anglo-French Relations in the Twentieth Century, Rivalry and cooperation* (Routledge, London, 2000)

Skelly, Joseph M., 'Ireland, the Department of External Affairs, and the United Nations, 1957-59: a New Look', *Irish Studies in International Affairs*, Vol. 7, 1996.

Smith, 'French Colonial Consensus' in Charles A. Kupchan, *The Vulnerability of Empire* (Cornell University Press, Ithaca, 1994)

Stuart, Francis, 'Frank Ryan in Germany, Part I' in *The Bell*, Vol. XVI, No. 2, November 1950

— 'Frank Ryan in Germany, Part II', in *The Bell*, Vol. XVI, No. 3, December 1950

Travers, Fr Patrick, 'Some Experiences During the War Years: The Irish College in Paris 1939-45', privately published article.

Whelan, Bernadette, 'Integration or Isolation? Ireland and the Invitation to join the Marshall Plan', in Michael Kennedy and Joseph M. Skelly (eds), *Irish Foreign Policy 1919–1966* (Four Courts Press, Dublin, 2000)

Williams, T. Desmond, 'Aspects of Neutrality', in *The Leader*, 14 March 1953.

— 'Ireland and the War' in K.B. Noland and T Desmond Williams (eds.) *Ireland in the War Years and After, 1939-1951* (Gill and Macmillan, Dublin, 1969)

— 'Irish Foreign Policy 1949-1969' in J.J. Lee (ed.) *Ireland 1945-1970* (Gill and Macmillan, Dublin, 1979)

— 'Conclusion' in K.B. Noland and T Desmond Williams (eds.) *Ireland in the War Years and After, 1939-1951* (Gill and Macmillan, Dublin, 1969)

Wylie, Paula, 'Ireland's decision for de facto recognition of Israel' in Michael Kennedy and Joseph M. Skelly (eds), *Irish Foreign Policy 1919–1966* (Four Courts Press, Dublin, 2000)

Theses

Barry, Lisa, 'The Evolution of Irish Diplomatic Relations with Israel' (Thesis, University College Cork, 2000)

Bhreatnach, Aoife, 'Frank Aiken and the Formulation of Foreign Policy, 1951-54, 57-69' (MPhil Thesis, University College Cork, 1999)

Casserly, Tara, 'Irish-German Relations, 1949-1972' (MA Thesis, University College Cork, 1994)

Cremin, C.C., 'Phases of Corcyraean History' (MA Thesis, University College Cork, 1931)

Cunningham, Emma, 'Irish-Canadian Diplomatic Relations 1939-1950' (PhD Thesis, University College Cork, 2001)

Daly, Maria, 'Sean MacBride and the Management of Irish Foreign Policy during the First Inter-party Government 1948–1951' (MPhil Thesis, University College Cork, 2000)

FitzGerald, Maurice, 'Irish-American Diplomatic Relations, 1948–1963' (MA Thesis, University College Cork, 1997)

Keane, Damien, 'Irish–US Relations during World War Two' (MA Thesis, University College Cork, 1995)

Lavin, Brian J. 'Ireland's Neutrality and the USA: 1939–1945' (MA Thesis, University College Cork, 2000)

Logan, Paul, 'Ireland's Diplomatic Links with Spain: 1920–1950' (MA Thesis, University College Cork, 1997)

Moriarty, Nigel, 'Ireland's Reaction to the Cold War: Aspects of Emergency Planning, 1947–1963' (MPhil Thesis, University College Cork, 1995)

Nolan, Aengus, 'Joseph Walshe and the Management of Irish Foreign Policy, 1922–1946: a Study in Diplomatic and Administrative History' (PhD Thesis, University College Cork, 1997)

O'Driscoll, Mervyn, 'Irish-German Diplomatic Relations, 1922–39: an Examination of Irish Diplomats' Performances in Berlin, 1922–39' (MA Thesis, University College Cork, 1992)

O'Shea, Nuala, 'Frederick H. Boland and Irish Diplomacy 1950–1964' (MA Thesis, University College Cork, 1995)

Patterson, Robert, 'Ireland and France: an Analysis of Diplomatic Relations, 1929–1950' (MA Thesis, University College Cork, 1992)

Power, Michele S., 'European Political Cooperation: Ireland and Neutrality' (MA Thesis, University College Cork, 1994)

Walsh, Col. Maurice, 'The Politics of Irish Defence: from the Civil War to the Congo, 1923–1964' (MA Thesis, University College Cork)

Wylie, Paula L., 'Diplomatic Recognition in Irish Foreign Policy 1949-63' (PhD Thesis, University College Cork, 2001)

Websites

www.nationalarchives.ie National Archives of Ireland website

www.dfait-maeci.gc.ca/hist/Dupuy-en.asp

http://europeanhistory.about.com/library/readyref/blfrancestatesmen.htm

Index

A

A Voz, 96, 103
Abusch, Mrs Fay, 56–7
Acheson, Dean, 151–2, 153, 154, 155, 159
    Four Power conference, 157–8
Adenauer, Dr Konrad, 151, 165, 177–8, 208, 239–40
    election win, 166–7
    and USA, 169, 170
Aer Lingus, 116
Aiken, Frank, 130, 147, 189, 251–2
    and Home, 258–9, 260, 262
    and neutrality, 185–6
Algeria, 140, 244–5
Amory, Derick Heathcoat, 224
Anglo-EDC association treaty, 161
Anglo-French Union, 20
Anglo-German society, 264
anti-partition campaign, 114, 124–8
Anti-Partition League, 257, 264–9
anti-Semitism, 54–7, 115, 180
    pope accused of, 211–12
Antwerp, 72–3
Aosdána, 83–7
archaeology, 8, 272
Argentina, 269
Armstrong, 86–7
Arnhem, battle of, 72
Attlee, Clement, 218, 265
Auriol, Vincent, 136, 143, 144, 157, 176
Auschwitz, 77
Australia, 269
Austria, 81, 171, 209
Azéma, J.P., 28

B

B-Specials, 252
Baghdad Pact, 219, 232, 238
Baldwin, Stanley, 125
Ballina schools dispute, 214–15
Ballyglass, Co. Mayo, 7
Bao Dai, 145
Baruch, Hermann, 108
Battle of the Bulge, 72–3, 77
Bavaria, 71–2
Beckett, Samuel, 26–7
Belgium, 16, 40, 74, 96, 173, 181, 183, 238
    schools crisis, 209
Bell, Ronald, 255
Belton, John A., 10–11
Ben-Gurion, David, 221
Beria, Lavrentii, 165
Berlin, 31, 89, 91. *see also* Irish legation, Berlin
    bombing, 63, 66
    conference, 171–2, 174
    Cremin in, 27
Bermuda conference, 168–71, 232–6
Berne, 65
Besançon internment camp, 25
Bevan, Aneurin, 218
Bevin, Ernest, 151–2, 153, 154, 218
Bewley, Charles, 14, 78, 164
Bhreatnach, Aoife, 252
Bidault, Georges, 144, 146, 147–8, 153, 165, 176
    Berlin conference, 172
    Cremin interview, 163
    and EDC, 170, 173
    and German reunification, 173–4

and USSR, 166
Biggar, Frank, 121, 222–3, 253, 263, 264
Bigger, Professor Joseph, 257
Black, Eugene, 137–8
Black, Jeremy, 226
Blet, Pierre, 212
Blum, Léon, 10, 11
Boland, F.H., 9, 33, 37, 114
    and British nuncio plan, 193–4, 196–7
    Cremin succeeds, 218–19
    in London, 146, 201, 222, 252, 268
    and Marshall Aid, 116–17, 118–21
    and NATO, 126, 127
    republic declared, 123
    secretary, 112–13
    UN representative, 233–4
Bolivia, 30
Bonn, 189, 229, 239
    conventions, 169, 173
    treaty, 175
Bonnefous, Edouard, 154
Bordeaux, 20
Bottinger, Joseph, 148, 150
Bourgès-Maunoury, Maurice, 177
Bourguiba, president, 244
Bowman, John, 123, 252, 263
Brazil, 30, 96, 99
Breen, Dan, 115
Bridges, Ann, 100
Briscoe, Robert, 56–7
Britain, 12, 14, 15, 60, 62, 96, 130, 272
    Anglo-American relations, 240–1
    Anglo-French relations, 36, 39, 40, 44, 53, 244–6, 269–70
    Anglo-Irish relations, 117, 249–64
        and Irish diplomacy, 59
        and Irish neutrality, 15–16
        reports intercepted, 70, 72
        republic declared, 124
    Bermuda conference, 232–3
    and EDC, 159–60, 172–3, 174–5,

176, 179
    EEC veto, 270
    Four Power conference, 156–8, 160–1, 163–4, 168, 171–2
    and German rearmament, 151–2, 153, 155, 177–8, 181–5
    and Indo-China, 143, 146, 147
    Irish emigrants in, 267–9
    papal nuncio question, 192–8, 217
    passports, 23
    Portuguese ally, 94–5, 97, 98, 100, 102, 104–5, 110–11
    rearmament, 159
    relations with USSR, 246–9
    and Spain, 106–7, 108
    Suez crisis, 219–25, 228–9
    Three Power meeting, 167–9
    trade agreements, 130
    turns towards Europe, 225–32
    and USSR, 208, 236
    wartime, 20, 21, 31, 32, 33, 69, 73, 85, 92
        African front, 45
        Berlin bombings, 63, 64, 65, 66
        Irish troops, 104–5
        Southern Redoubt, 71–2
British embassy, Dublin, 219
British Nationality Act, 124
British School, Athens, 8
Brooke, Henry, 249
Browne, Fr, OP, 190
Browne, Noel, 123, 264
Bruce, David, 130
Brussels Treaty Organisation, 179, 180–1, 181–2, 182, 183, 184
Bryan, Dan, 81, 82–3, 115–16
Bulganin, Nikolai, 205, 206
Bulgaria, 39, 98
Bullitt, Bill, 17, 18
Burke, William, 265–6
Busteed, Professor John, 8
Butler, Rab, 223, 224, 225, 248, 250, 259–60

C

Cain, P.J. and Hopkins, A.G., 222
Callaghan, Jim, 237
Cambodia, 141, 146, 149
Canada, 28, 114, 123, 129, 227, 247, 269
Capuchin Annual, The, 190
Caritas, 115
Carmona, President General António de Fragoso, 99, 107
Caro, Mr, 106–7
Castle, Barbara, 238–9
Catholic Action, 205
Catholic Church, 101, 131. *see also* Holy See
   communist threat to, 204–9
   and denominational education, 209–11
   and Vichy, 35, 45–6
Catholic Union, 193, 195, 196
censorship, 16
Centre for European Economic Co-operation (CEEC), 117, 118, 119, 120–1, 123
Cerejeira, Cardianl Manual Gonçalves, 101
Challe, General Maurice, 220
Chanak incident, 15
Chauvel, Jean, 222
Chiang Kai-Shek, 203
China, 30, 105, 141, 142, 146, 271
   Catholicism in, 205
   Egyptian recognition, 220
   and Indo-China war, 148, 149
   trade with, 232
   and USSR, 202–3
Chou En Lai, 148
Churchill, Winston, 20, 21, 163, 165, 194–5, 273
   and Indo-China, 146
   and Irish codes, 64, 70, 72
   and USSR, 209
Civil War, Irish, 10

Clann na Poblachta, 114
Clarke, Colin, 206–7
Clarke, General, 198
Clissmann, Elizabeth, 79, 80
Cloney, Sheila, 264
Clutterbuck, British ambassador, 262
codes, 64
Cold War, 132–3, 139, 151, 163, 217, 249
   Irish policy, 113, 114, 130
   origins, 91–2
Collins, Stephen, 186
Colombia, 30
commonwealth
   conference, 1950, 141
   Irish return proposed, 253–9, 263
communism, 79–80, 96, 102, 110, 141, 217
   and European integration, 215–16
   in France, 137–9, 180
   and USA, 229–30
   and the Vatican, 202–9
   Vietnam, 149–50
Compagnons de France, 47
Confédération Générale du Travail (CGT), 11, 137–8
Conservative party, 222–5, 231, 254
Continental Daily Mail, 156
Continuation War, 67
Cosgrave, Liam, 130, 189, 192, 251
   British nuncio question, 194–5, 197, 198
   papal audience, 200
Costello, John A., 111, 114, 189, 192–3, 201
   Dell'Acqua meeting, 207
   republic declared, 123–4
Council of Europe, 143, 226
Cremin, Aedeen, 59–60, 132, 190, 217
Cremin, Ann, 10, 13, 17, 88, 110
Cremin, Cissy, 7, 14, 64
Cremin, Cornelius (Con). *see also* Irish embassies; Irish legations

assessment of, 271–3
economic thinking of, 12–13
education, 7–8
in external affairs department,
    112–28
head of mission, 59
and Jewish question, 74–8
languages, 59–60
Légion d'Honneur, 186
postings
    Berlin, 58–93
    Lisbon, 94–128
    London, 218–70
    Paris, 9–17, 129–87
    UN, 270–1
    Vatican, 188–217
    Vichy, 18–58
professionalism defended, 213
style of reports, 131–2
Cremin, Creeda, 66
Cremin, Daniel J., 7
Cremin, Fr Frank, 7–8, 110, 190
Cremin, James, 7
Cremin, Patricia (wife), 10, 13, 17,
    29, 190
Cremin family, 29, 85, 88
Cremins, F.T., 65, 89, 90
Cronin, Seán, 79
Cuba, 50, 244
Cumann na nGaedheal, 7, 10
Cummins, Mary, 83–5, 92
Cummins, T.V., 121
Curragh camp, 265
Cush, Co. Limerick, 8
customs union, 119–20
Cyprus, 218, 236–9, 269
Czechoslovakia, 14

D

Dáil Éireann, 10, 15, 115
Daily Mail, 241
Daily Telegraph, 232, 255, 256
Dalloz, Jacques, 147

d'Alton, Cardinal John Francis, 253–
    7, 261, 262–2, 264
Darlan, Admiral, 20, 39, 41–2, 43,
    44, 46
    assassination, 52
    and Pétain, 50–1
Davis, Troy, 126–7
de Beaumont, Guérin, 178
de Carmoy, Guy, 150
de Gasperi, Alcide, 171
de Gaulle, General Charles, 20, 34,
    40, 45, 52, 132, 186, 270
    and EDC, 175
    and Fourth Republic, 134–7
    and German rearmament, 153
    opposes European army, 159
    recognised by US, 38
de Juniac, Baron, 246
de Margerie, Roland, 211
de Valera, Éamon, 14, 23, 25, 81, 94,
    97, 113, 123, 130, 202, 255,
    257
    Anglo-Irish relations, 251–2
    and Cremin, 9
    and customs union, 119–20
    Hitler condolences, 105, 110, 113,
        147
    Jewish question, 74, 76
    and Marshall Aid, 118–19
    neutrality, 15–16, 59, 87, 120
    and partition, 124, 259, 260, 262–3
    and Portugal, 104–5, 110
    and Vatican, 68, 189
    and Vichy, 31, 32, 36–7
Déat, fascist, 41, 47
Dell'Acqua, Mgr, 193, 194–5, 197,
    198, 201, 216
    Costello meeting, 207
    on USSR, 205–6, 208
Denmark, 16, 247
Dentz, General, 43
Devlin, Denis, 9
Diario da Manha, 96, 97, 101, 103

Diario de Lisboa, 102

Die Welt, 246

Dien Bien Phu, 140, 145–8, 150, 173

Dohna, Countess, 69

Dominican order, 104, 190

d'Ormesson, Count, 211

Drancy transit camp, 76

Duchêne, François, 133

Duclos, Jacques, 138

Dulles, John Foster, 145, 195–6, 235, 246

　　and EDC, 169–71, 181

　　Suez crisis, 220, 222

　　and USSR, 165

Dumaine, 155, 157

Dupuy, Pierre, 28

Dwyer, T. Ryle, 15

E

East Germany, 174, 230

Eccles, Sir David, 225, 251

Ecuador, 30

Eden, Sir Anthony, 148, 171, 208, 236, 249

　　and EDC, 158, 160

　　and German rearmament, 181–3

　　Suez crisis, 220–5, 230

education, denominational, 209–11

Egypt, 116, 233–5

　　Suez crisis, 219–25

Eisenhower, General Dwight D., 138, 170, 186, 199, 222, 229–30

　　Anglo-American relations, 232, 240–1

Electricity Supply Board (ESB), 8

emergency powers act, 261

European Coal and Steel Community (ECSC), 133–4, 139, 173, 227, 228

European Coal and Steel Pact, 159, 161

European Currency Association, 122

European Defence Community

(EDC), 132–3, 134, 136, 139–40, 143, 187, 210

　　Bermuda conference, 168–71

　　collapse of, 176–9

　　and domestic politics, 172–9

　　establishment of, 151–72

　　and Ireland, 185–6

　　proposed, 153–5

　　and RPF, 161–2

　　treaty debates, 158, 159–68

European Economic Community (EEC), 186, 226, 269, 270

European Free Trade Area (EFTA), 225, 227, 230, 244

European Recovery Programme (ERP), 116–23

external affairs, department of, 38, 114, 203–4

　　Cremin counsellor, 111, 112–28

　　Cremin joins, 8–9

　　Cremin secretary, 270

　　and Cremin's professionalism, 213

　　and Marshall Plan, 117, 121

　　and NATO, 124–8

　　neutrality, 15, 25

　　republic declared, 123–4

F

fascism, 94, 95, 115

Faure, Edgar, 143, 144, 175

Fay, William P., 244, 254

Feehan, Tadgh, 257

Feltin, Cardinal, 215

Fethard boycott, 264

Fianna Fáil, 10, 81, 114, 121, 130, 251–2

　　and Vatican, 189

finance, department of, 64–5, 118, 121

　　and Marshall Aid, 121

Fine Gael, 14, 114

Finland, 67, 96, 206, 208

FitzGerald, Desmond, 14, 31

FitzGerald, Mrs Desmond, 31

FitzGerald, Garret, 13, 31
Five Power conference, 171, 172
Flanagan, Oliver, 115
Fleming, John J., 116
Foreign Affairs Commission, 170
Formosa. *see* Taiwan
Four Power conference, 155–8, 160–1,
      163–4, 168, 171–2, 208
franc, valuation of, 11–12
France, 45, 96, 129, 157, 272. *see also*
      Indo-China; Irish legation,
      Vichy; Second World War
   1937-40, 9–17
   Anglo-French relations, 35, 39, 40,
      44, 53, 244–6, 269–70
   arms industry, 179, 228
   colonial policy, 140–7
   communism in, 137–9, 207–8
   denominational education, 209–11
   and EDC, 151–79
   foreign policy, 1950-54, 139–40
   Four Power conference, 160–1,
      163–4, 168, 171–2
   Franco-German relations, 33–4,
      39–43, 47–50
   and German rearmament, 151–6,
      180–5
   Irish trade with, 129–30
   politics, 1950-54, 134–7
   post-war economy, 178
   rearmament, 159
   Saar question, 161–2, 173, 175,
      183, 184
   and Spain, 106, 112
   and Suez crisis, 220–1, 226
   Three Power meeting, 167–9
   and USA, 47–9, 50, 53, 231
   and USSR, 72, 236
Franco, General F., 11, 94, 95, 112,
      117, 125
   opposition to, 105–10
Franco, Nicolás, 95–6, 106
Franz Joseph, Prince, 91

Free French, 30, 38, 45, 52
French Legion of Veterans, 42
Front de Libération Nationale (FLN),
      244
Fugger, Princess, 90

G

G2, 81, 116
Gaitskell, Hugh, 218, 222–3, 230–1,
      248
Gallagher, Brian, 264–5
Gallagher, Frank, 119, 255
Gallagher, Tom, 96–7
Garrett, George, 126
Gazier, Albert, 220
Geneva, 110, 141, 145, 146, 148, 171
Geneva Accords, 149–50, 207
Geneva Convention, 59
'Geneva Spirit,' 207–8
Germany, 16–17, 119, 143, 270, 272.
      see also Irish legation, Berlin;
      Second World War; West
      Germany
   Irish collaborators, 78–83
   and Jews, 55
   July Bomb Plot, 69, 70–1
   maps of Ireland, 115–16
   post-war, 133–4, 136, 139
   rearmament, 139–40, 151–6,
      160–1
   Walshe attitude to, 30–1
Goebbels, Joseph, 69
Gosford, earl of, 236
government information bureau, 119
Gray, David, 13
Greece, 8, 39, 40, 153, 208
   and Cyprus, 236–9
Griffin, Fr, 24
Guatemala, 50

H

H-bomb tests, 232
Hailsham, Lord, 249

Hallstein, Walter, 161–2
Harris, Air Marshal, 63
Harvey, Sir Oliver, 130
Hayter, Sir William, 236, 243–4, 248
Head, Anthony, 225
Hearne, John J., 240
Hebblethwaite, Peter, 191–2
Hempel, Edouard, 110, 113, 147, 265
Henderson, Nicholas, 126
Herlihy, Mgr Donald, bishop of Ferns, 7, 190
Herriot, Edouard, 174
Herwarth, Von, German ambassador, 229–30
Herzog, Isaac, 74
Hillery, Dr Patrick, 271
Himmler, Heinrich, 72, 78
Hitchcock, W.L., 152
Hitler, Adolf, 10, 14–15, 31, 50, 66, 73, 212
   de Valera condolences, 105, 110, 113, 147
   declares war on USA, 47
   and France, 36, 41–2, 43, 69
   and Franco, 107
   July Bomb Plot, 69, 70–1
   Southern Redoubt, 71–2
   Warnock support for, 60
Hochhuth, Rolf, 212
Holy See, 46, 88, 272. *see also* Irish embassy, Vatican
   and communist regimes, 204–9
   US representative to Vatican, 198–9
Home, earl of, 242–3, 249–50, 253
   Cremin meetings, 258–9, 260, 261, 262
Honduras, 30
Hope, Lord John, 252
Horne, Alistair, 228, 231, 232, 233
Howard, Sir Douglas, 195–6
Hungary, 67–8, 77, 207, 247
   Soviet invasion, 218, 221–2, 223, 229–30, 235–6
Hyde, Montgomery, 263

I

Il Popolo, 216
Il Quotidiano, 191, 192
India, 141, 144, 146, 236, 245, 246–7
Indo-China, 133, 140–1, 160, 173, 176, 178, 186
   communism, 205
   French withdrawal, 143–4, 171, 175, 207, 210
   Mendès-France solution, 147–51
inter-party government, 1948, 114
inter-party government, 1954, 189, 251
internment, 252, 265
Iraq, 43, 235
Ireland, 38, 68, 114, 187
   Anglo-Irish relations, 218, 249–64
   and commonwealth, 253–7, 258–9, 263
   diplomatic codes, 64
   economic development, 122–3, 129–30
   and European integration, 185–6, 228, 230
   German maps of, 115–16
   Irish collaboration with Nazis, 78–83
   and Jewish question, 74–6
   joins UN, 192
   and Marshall Aid, 116–23
   neutrality, 59, 110–11, 265
   Protestants in, 191, 192–3, 257, 264
   republic declared, 123–4, 128
   and Vichy, 28, 30
Irish Brigade, 11
Irish College, Paris, 18, 20, 24
Irish College, Rome, 7, 190
Irish embassy, London, 198, 218–70
   Anglo-Irish relations, 249–64

Britain and Europe, 225–32
Cyprus question, 236–9
report on Irish in Britain, 267–9
Suez crisis, 218, 219–25
Irish embassy, Paris, 111, 189, 190,
    208, 217, 219
communism, 137–9
Cremin in, 129–87
foreign policy concerns, 132–4
French colonial policy, 140–7
French politics, 134–7
Irish embassy, Vatican, 112, 163–4,
    198–9, 219
Ballina schools dispute, 214–15
British nuncio question, 192–8
and communism, 202–9
Cremin in, 188–217
Cremin succeeds Walshe, 188–92
criticisms of Cremin, 213
denominational education, 209–11
European integration, 215–16
Walshe reports, 131–2
Irish Independent, 214, 217
Irish legation, Berlin, 112, 172
allowances, 64–5
bombing, 63, 64, 65
Cremin in, 57, 58–93
and Irish collaborators, 78–83
and Irish nationals, 83
Jewish question, 74–8
life in, 65–6
political reports, 66–9
withdrawal from, 87–93
Irish legation, Lisbon, 62, 94–128,
    112, 172
Cremin sent to, 92
elections, 1945, 96–103
Spanish monarchy restoration,
    105–10
Irish legation, Paris, 26, 82, 116,
    127–8
Cremin in, 128
EDC, 151–72

evacuated, 17
'listening post,' 130–2
Murphy report, 1942, 49
Irish legation, Vichy, 60, 112, 129
assessment of Pétain, 42
Cremin in, 18–58
end of regime, 50–7
French government to, 17
Irish colony support, 22–6
Jewish question, 54–7, 74
reports from, 32–50
wartime life, 28–30
Irish National Teachers' Organisation
    (INTO), 214
Irish National Union, 265–6, 267
Irish News Agency (INA), 114
Irish Press, 189, 264
Irish Red Cross, 27, 115
Irish Republican Army (IRA), 68, 78,
    80, 81, 82, 257, 261, 264
border campaign, 249, 252–3, 258,
    270
Irish Times, The, 214
Irland-Redaktion, 81, 82
Ismay, Lord, 168, 238
Israel, 116, 212, 235
Suez crisis, 220–2
Italy, 34, 50, 52, 67, 105, 116, 130,
    166, 182
Bewley in, 78
communism in, 207–8
and EDC, 171
wartime, 53, 68
Iveagh House. *see* external affairs,
    department of

J

Japan, 61, 142–3, 143, 158
Pearl Harbour, 46–7
Jewish question, 67–8
Berlin, 74–8
France, 54–7
John XXIII, Pope, 131, 191, 192, 217

Jordan, 235
Joyce, James, 26–7
Joyce, William ('Lord Haw-Haw'), 80
Juan, Don, 106–7, 108
Juin, Marshal Alphonse, 167, 177

K

Kallay, Nicholas, 67
Kay, Hugh, 94
Keatinge, P., 59
Kedward, Harry, 46
Kelly, J.N.D., 200
Kempner, Robert W.M., 212
Kenmare, Co. Kerry, 7, 28
Kennan, George, 243, 249
Kennedy, John F., 199
Keogh, Dermot, 9, 10, 30–1, 32–3, 34,
    36–7, 82, 188
    republic declaration, 123, 124
Kerlogue (coaster), 86
Kerney, Leopold, 78, 79
Khrushchev, Nikita, 167, 202–3, 205,
    220, 236, 243–4, 248
Kierans (INU), 265–6
Kiernan, Thomas, 59
Kilmer, Viscount, 251
Kirkpatrick, Sir Ivone, 228–9, 235,
    237
Kissinger, Henry, 145, 150, 222
Knorring, 206
Koenig, General Marie-Pierre, 177
Korean War, 135, 141, 143, 145, 151,
    156
Kupchan, C.A., 144

L

Labour party, UK, 96, 222–3, 238–9,
    251, 257
Lacouture, Jean, 40, 134
LaFeber, Walter, 184
Laithwaite, Sir Gilbert, 219, 253,
    257–8
Laniel, J., 143, 144, 146, 147, 166, 173

and EDC, 175, 176
Laos, 141, 146, 149
L'Aube, 138
Laval, Pierre, 33–4, 39, 43, 47–8, 48,
    51, 53
    anti-Semitic, 55–6
    dismissal, 40–2
    French workers offer, 49–50
Le Monde, 157, 165, 175–6
Le Populaire, 135, 138
Le Temps, 44
League of Nations, 9, 110, 113
Leahy, Admiral William D., 43, 47,
    48
Lee, J.J., 31, 32, 122, 124, 127, 255
Leger, Alex St L., 21
Lennon, J.W., 203–4, 213
Lennox-Boyd, Alan, 224
Léon, Alexis, 27
Léon, Paul, 26–7
Levame, Alberto, 214–15
Liberal News, 257
Libya, 49
Lisbon, 29, 54, 65, 219. *see also* Irish
    legation, Lisbon
Lloyd, Selwyn, 220–1, 224–8, 234,
    248, 250
Lloyd George, Major, 225
London, 188, 189. *see also* Irish
    embassy, London
Long Term Recovery Programme,
    122, 129
Luxembourg, 16

M

MacArthur, Douglas, 186
MacBride, Seán, 111, 114, 116, 121,
    124, 129, 188
    and ERP, 121, 122
    and NATO, 125–8
McCauley, Leo T., 198
MacDonald, Denis Roland, 57, 62
Mack, Harry Bradshaw, 17

McLachlan, Donald, 256
McMahon act, 241, 245–6
Macmillan, Harold, 222, 224–5, 226,
    230, 232
    Cyprus, 237
    and Eisenhower, 240–1
    and France, 244–6
    on German reunification, 239–40
    in India, 246–7
    and Ireland, 249
    on nuclear power, 241–3
    and Pakenham proposal, 261–2
    on US relations, 231
McQuaid, John Charles, 214, 215
MacWhite, Michael, 92
Madagascar, 140
Mahr, Dr Adolf, 61
Makarios, archbishop of Cyprus, 237,
    238, 239, 244
Makins, Sir Roger, 225
Malenkov, G.M., 205, 206
Manchester Guardian, 253–4, 264
Mansergh, Nicholas, 124
Mao Tse-Tung, 204
Marist Brothers, 214
Marquietout, Mlle, 25–6
Marshall, General George, 116
Marshall Plan, 116–23, 129
Mayer, René, 162, 164, 180
Meissner, Miss, 81, 82
Mellenthin, Major-General F.W.
    von, 71
Mendès-France, Pierre, 141, 147–51,
    162
    collapse of EDC, 176–9
    and denominational education,
        209–11
    and German rearmament, 180–5
    and WEU, 184–5
Mexico, 50
Millar, Sir Fredrick Hoyer, 229
Mills, Charlie, 63, 89
Mindszenty, Cardinal, 207

Mitterand, François, 143, 144
Moch, Jules, 156, 175, 236
Mollet, Guy, 155, 175, 215, 220
Molohan, Cathy, 115
Molotov, V.M., 172
Monet Plan, 178
Monnet, Jean, 153, 181, 228
Montgomery, General B.L., 72
Montini, Mgr (Pope Paul VI), 191–2,
    195, 207–8, 217
    as papal successor, 200, 201
Morocco, 144
Mouvement Républicain Populaire
    (MRP), 134–7, 138, 184, 210
    and EDC, 170, 173, 175, 176
Movimento de Unidade Demócratia
    (MUD), 97, 98, 101
Movimento de Unidade Nacional
    Anti-Fascista (MUNAF), 94,
    96, 97
Moynihan, Maurice, 33, 37, 119
Mulally, Liam, 89
Munich, 8, 24, 59, 66, 81
    agreement, 14
Murphy, Robert, 35
Murphy, Seán, 17, 54, 62, 82, 92,
    256–7, 262, 270
    and Cremin, 13–15, 128, 129
    Jewish question, 74
    and Joyce, 27
    on Laval, 51
    in occupied zond, 116
    in occupied zone, 23–5, 26
    reports from, 39–50
    in Vichy, 18–21, 24–6, 29, 30, 56–8
    and Walshe, 30–9, 88
Mussolini, Benito, 39, 53

N

Nagy, Imre, 222
Nasser, Lt-Colonel Gamal Abdel,
    219–20, 228, 233–4
National Liberal club, 264

National University of Ireland, 219
Nationality Act 1935, 22
Navare, General, 149
Nehru, Jawaharlal, 141, 146, 236, 246, 247
Netherlands, 16, 74, 105, 181, 183, 264–5
neutrality, 119, 157, 186
    within CEEC, 120–1
    Ireland, 110–11, 122
    Irish, 15–16, 59, 74, 87, 88
    Nazi intentions, 116
    Portugal, 94, 105, 110–11
Ngo Dinh Diem, 148
Nicaragua, 50
Nichols, Peter, 202
Nine Power conference, 183–4
Nolan (INU), 265–6
Norfolk, duke of, 194–5
north Africa, 33–4, 38, 39, 40, 41, 44, 52, 61, 245
    France in, 140
    Germany requests territories, 46
    US troops in, 49
    wartime, 45, 50
North Atlantic Treaty Organisation (NATO), 94, 131, 154, 241, 244, 253
    and Algeria, 245
    Atlantic Assembly, 226, 227–8
    and Cyprus, 237–8, 239
    disarmament sub-committee, 236
    and EDC collapse, 179, 180, 181–2
    extension of, 152, 153
    and Ireland, 114, 185, 186, 253, 255, 256
    nuclear power, 246
    and partition, 124–8
    and post-war Germany, 155, 158, 169, 170, 173–4, 243
    rearmament, 159
    Ridgeway commands, 138

and USSR, 172, 247–8
    West Germany admitted, 183–4
    and WEU, 140, 152
Northern Ireland, 123, 124, 185, 190–1, 192–3, 251, 270, 271, 273
    Anglo-Irish relations, 251–64
    D'Alton proposals, 253–7
    defence of, 125–6
    IRA campaign, 252–3
    risk of Vatican recognition, 192–8
    Vatican recognition of, 192–8
Norton, William, 251, 257
Norway, 16, 247
Nuclear Energy Act 1954, 232
nuclear power, 241–4, 245–6
Nunan, Seán, 133–4
Nuremberg War Crimes Trials, 212

O

O'Brien, Art, 10–13, 14
O'Brien, Dr Conor Cruise, 38, 112, 114, 251
O'Brien, J., 121
O'Brien, Máire Cruise, 83
O'Brien, Miriam Hederman, 185
Observer, 97, 254
O'Byrne, P.J., 62, 92
O'Callaghan (INU), 265–6
O'Connell, Daniel, 131
O'Connor, Kevin, 267
O'Donnell, Blanca, Duquesa de Tetuan, 11
O'Duffy, Eoin, 11
O'Farrell, Fr, 24
O'Grady, Fr, 22, 24
O'Halpin, Eunan, 64
O'Hara, Mgr, 193–4
O'Kelly, Count Gerald, 14, 17, 18, 23, 25, 26
    and Beckett, 27
    reports, 39
O'Mahony, Patricia. *see* Cremin, Patricia

O'Malley, Sir Owen, 100
Operation Barbarossa, 45
Operation Catapult, 21
Operation Green, 115
Operation Harvest, 252–3
Operation Margarenthe, 67–8
Operation Market Garden, 72
Organisation for European Economic
      Co-operation (OEEC), 117,
      123, 126, 129, 131, 155, 226
Orsenigo, Mgr Cesare, 87–8
Osservatore Romano, 203, 204, 211,
      216
Ottaviani, Cardinal, 201
Ottawa, 129, 189
Oxford University, 8

p

Pakenham, Lord, 251, 255, 256,
      263–4
   partition proposal, 261–2
Palmerston, Lord, 132
Paraguay, 30
Paris, 32, 66, 68, 78, 215. *see also* Irish
      embassy, Paris; Irish legation,
      Paris
   allied bombing, 47
   Cremin in, 9–17
   Germans in, 20, 24
   Irish colony, 22
Paris Protocol, 44
Parnell, Charles Stewart, 269, 270
partition. *see* Northern Ireland
passports, 23, 24
Paul VI, Pope, 217
Pearce and Stewart, 233
Pearl Harbour, 46–7
Persia, 153
Peru, 30
Pétain, Marshal Henri, 17, 28, 30, 38,
      45, 47
   armistice request, 20
   and Catholic Church, 45–6

Cremin award, 57
   directorate, 41
   fleet scuttled, 50–1
   Irish legation on, 42, 52, 53
   and north Africa, 50
   opposition to, 40
   powers of, 22, 35–6
   treatment of Jews, 54–5, 56
   and USA, 49
   Walshe attitude to, 30, 31–2
Philip, André, 181
Phillips, Harold A., 264
Pinay, Antoine, 162, 180
Pink, Ivon, 240, 263
Pinto, A.C., 110
Pius IX, pope, 212
Pius XII, pope, 68, 189, 191–2, 195–6,
      215
   anti-Semitism alleged, 211–12
   and communism, 202, 203
   Cremin meetings, 190–1
   health concerns, 200–2
   Mendès-France meeting, 209–10
   Truman meeting, 199
Pleven, René Jean, 144, 153, 156–9,
      158, 160, 180
   Pleven Plan, 133, 153–4, 155
Poland, 14–15, 67, 74, 76, 207, 246–7
   Warsaw uprising, 92
Porter, Professor William Holt, 8
Portugal, 32, 38, 57, 88, 89, 94, 171–2
   elections, 1945, 96–103
   and Spanish monarchy, 105–10
Potsdam conference, 96, 164, 178
Poujade, Pierre, 176
Pravda, 203

Q

Quaroni, Pietro, 130, 208
Queuille, Henri, 157, 162
Quotidiano, 205

R

Raby, D.L., 101
Radcliffe, Lord, 237
Radio Luxembourg, 82
Ramadier, Paul, 119
Rassemblement du Peuple Français
    (RPF), 134–7, 144, 159
    and EDC, 161–2, 163, 173
Rassemblement National Populaire
    (RNP), 41
Reynaud, Paul, 20, 143–4
Reynolds, David, 273
Ribbentrop, Joachim von, 66, 78, 89
Ridgeway, General, 138, 162
Rioux, Jean Pierre, 152, 154, 162, 172,
    176, 177
Romania, 30, 98
Rome, 68, 95, 190. *see also* Holy See
    Treaty of, 227
Roncalli, Cardinal Angelo (Pope John
    XXIII), 131, 189, 215, 217
Roosevelt, P.D., 47–8
Roux, Charles, 39
Royal Ulster Constabulary (RUC), 252
Ruane, Kevin, 133, 160, 170, 185, 208
Russell, Seán, 78, 82
Ryan, Frank, 78–80, 81, 82

S

Saar question, 161–2, 173, 175, 183,
    184
St Brendan's College, 7, 190
St Jean de Luz, 18, 20
St Patrick's College, Maynooth, 7–8,
    190
St Patrick's day, 131, 263
Salazar, António de Oliveira, 94–5
    Cremin audience with, 103–5
    elections, 1945, 96–103
    and Spanish restoration, 106,
        108–10
Salisbury, Lord, 165, 251
Sandys, Duncan, 224, 225

Sarraut, Albert, 10
Saudi Arabia, 235
Save the German Children Society,
    115, 128
Schonebeck, Herr von, 85
Schuman, Maurice, 179
Schuman, Robert, 143, 151–2, 153,
    154, 156, 180
    and EDC, 158, 161, 167, 173, 175,
        176, 181, 185
Schuman Plan, 133–4, 139, 153, 155
Scotsman, 255
Second World War, 18–58, 68, 94,
    126–7, 204, 261, 265, 269,
    271
    aftermath, 114
    Arnhem battle, 72
    Battle of the Bulge, 72–3, 77
    build-up to, 13–17
    end of, 87–93, 96
    France, 18–58
        blitzkrieg, 16–17
        fleet scuttled, 50–1
        hostage executions, 46
        invasion of, 13
        Jewish question, 54–7, 76
        Mendès-France solution,
            147–51
        Normandy front, 68–9
        workers to Germany, 49–50, 53
    in France
        Normandy front, 68–9
    Germany losing, 59
    global conflict, 45
    Hungary invaded, 67–8
    neutralities, 15–16, 110–11
    Pius XII and Jews, 211–12
    post-war aid, 116–23
Sethe, Dr Geheimrat, 84–5
Seydoux, François, 142, 158, 159, 167,
    174, 181
Sforza, Count, 228
SHAPE, 167, 186

Sicily, 53

Sinn Féin, 124

Smith, Bedell, 148

Society of Swiss Writers, 26

'Southern Redoubt,' 71–2

Spaak, Paul-Henry, 181, 209, 215, 238, 241

Spain, 38, 88, 112, 116, 117, 125, 271
monarchy restoration plan, 105–10

Spanish Civil War, 9, 11, 14, 78, 80

Speer, Albert, 50

Spellman, Cardinal, 110, 198

Sputnik, 241, 243, 246, 269

Stalin, V.I., 92, 163, 164, 202, 209

Stauffenberg, Baron Claus von, 70

Steengracht, German foreign office, 65

Stikker, Dr Dirk, 221, 222, 231–2

Stopford-Green family, 249

Stritch, Cardinal, 199

Stuart, Francis, 60, 78–9, 80–3

Sudetenland crisis, 14

Suez crisis, 218, 219–25, 237
aftermath, 232–5
effects of, 225–6, 228–9, 230, 231, 244, 269–70

Sunday Times, The, 263

Sweden, 119, 125

Switzerland, 38, 54, 55, 69, 83, 85, 119, 147
Cremin ordered to, 87, 88–93
Jewish question, 76, 77
Stuart, 81–2

Syria, 43, 44, 45, 233–5, 234

T

Tablet, 256–7

Taiwan, 203, 204

Taoiseach, department of the, 33, 119

Tardini, Mgr, 191–2, 197
on communism, 204–5
Costello meeting, 192–3

Taylor, A.J.P., 16

Teitgen, Pierre-Henri, 145, 174, 175

Thadden, Eberhard von, 76–7

Three Power meeting, 167–9

Times, 97, 216, 233, 239–40, 263

Tisserant, Cardinal, 210–11, 215

Tovar, Count, 89, 171–2

Travers, Fr, 18, 19–20, 24

Truman, Harry, 100, 108, 151, 198

Tunisia, 144, 244

Turkey, 39, 105, 152, 156, 157
and Cyprus, 236–9
and NATO, 152, 153

U

UNEF, 223, 235

Union of Soviet Socialist Republics (USSR), 61, 67, 71, 73, 80, 98, 125, 159, 185, 232
appeasement, 163
and China, 146, 202–3
economy, 155, 206–7
and EDC, 178–9
Four Power conference, 155–8, 160–1, 163–4, 167, 168, 171–2
and German reunification, 173–4
Hungary invasion, 218, 221–2, 223, 229–30, 235–6
and Indo-China, 149
and Japan, 142
and Korea, 145
Malenkov dismissal, 205–6
and NATO, 153, 154, 172
nuclear missiles, 243–4
and Portugal, 102
post-war, 96, 162
relations with Britain, 246–9
Russo-Franco pact, 72
Sputnik, 241, 243, 246, 269
Stalin death, 163, 164–6
and Suez crisis, 219–25
threat to Europe, 151
and UN, 113

wartime, 39, 45
> invades Germany, 88–92
Unità, 207
United Nations (UN), 14, 95, 110,
> 113, 116, 135, 231
> charter reform, 234
> Cremin appointed to, 270–1
> Cyprus, 238, 239
> Ireland in, 192
> partition, 251
> Suez crisis, 221, 223–4, 235
> Taiwan, 203
United States of America (USA), 12,
> 13, 16, 17, 18, 32, 35, 73, 116,
> 130, 163, 194, 269
> Anglo-American relations, 227,
> > 240–1
> Bermuda conference, 232–3
> and communist China, 203
> de Valera in, 124
> and EDC collapse, 180
> Four Power conference, 156–8,
> > 160–1, 163–4, 168, 171–2
> and France, 37–8, 47–9, 50, 53
> and German rearmament, 151–6
> and Indo-China, 143, 145, 147,
> > 150
> and Ireland, 117, 122, 126–7, 256
> and Italy, 68
> and Korean War, 151
> Marshall Aid, 116–23
> and middle east, 233–4, 235
> and NATO, 124–8, 181
> Nine Power conference, 183–4
> Pearl Harbour, 46–7
> and Portugal, 94–5, 98, 100, 102,
> > 105, 110
> rearmament, 158–9
> San Francisco conference, 142, 158
> Southern Redoubt, 71–2
> and Spain, 106, 108
> and Suez crisis, 219–25, 226,
> > 228–9, 230–1

Three Power meeting, 167–9
troops in Europe, 168–70
and USSR, 208, 229–30, 236
Vatican representative, 195–6,
> 198–9
wartime, 43, 92
> Berlin bombings, 66
> and West Germany, 166–7, 177–8
University College Cork (UCC), 8, 12
Uruguay, 30

V

Valeri, Valerio, papal nuncio, 17, 23,
> 32, 34, 36, 40, 189
Vallat, Xavier, 55
Vatican. *see* Holy See; Irish embassy,
> Vatican
Veesenmayer, Dr, 68, 78
Venezuela, 30
Vernon, Robert, 83–4, 85–7
Victor Emmanual, King, 53
Vietnam, 141, 144, 145, 146–7, 205
> Catholics in, 210
> partition, 149–50
Vittel internment camp, 76
Völkischer Beobachter, 67
Volksmann, Klaus, 246–7

W

Walsh, Eileen, 61, 62, 80
Walsh, Liam D., 115
Walshe, Joseph, 9, 10, 54, 59, 86, 204
> and British nuncio plan, 193, 194,
> > 195
> and Cremin, 93, 216
> end of war, 87–8, 92
> health of pope, 200
> and Jewish question, 57, 74, 76
> and neutrality, 15
> reports from, 187
> retirement, 188–90
> on Ryan, 79–80
> on Stuart, 81

in Vatican, 112, 131–2, 163–4, 191
and Vichy, 24–5, 27, 30–9
and Warnock, 60, 61
Wapler, Dominique, 154, 155, 157, 159
Warnock, William, 8–9, 25, 26–7, 59, 70, 74, 80
  and Cummins trial, 84
  post-war, 113–14
  succeeded by Cremin, 60–5
  and Vernon trial, 86
Washington, 188, 189
Weber, Dr, 79–80, 86
West Germany, 158, 208
  acceptance of, 177–8
  Adenauer win, 166–7
  British troops in, 232–3
  post-war economy, 178
  rearmament, 163, 169, 176–8
    settlement, 180–5
  reunification, 173–4, 208, 230, 239–40, 246
  Saar question, 161–2, 173, 175, 183, 184
  and USSR, 243
Western European Union (WEU), 183–5, 226, 228
Weygand, General, 50
Whelan, Bernadette, 117, 119–20, 121
Whitaker, Dr T.K., 270
Whitney, John Hay, 248–9
Williams, T. Desmond, 16, 59, 123
Winter War, 67
Wodehouse, P.G., 65–6
Wylie, Paula, 116
Wysynski, Cardinal, 207

Y

Yalta papers, 209
Young, Hugo, 151, 153–4, 227
Yugoslavia, 39, 208

Z

Zehnder, Dr, 77
Zhukov, G.K., 206, 236
Zubok, V. and Pleshakov, P., 222